TRAVELER'S
COSTA RICA
COMPANION

The 2001–2002 Traveler's Companions
ARGENTINA • AUSTRALIA • BALI • CALIFORNIA • CANADA • CHILE • CHINA •
COSTA RICA • CUBA • EASTERN CANADA • ECUADOR • FLORIDA • HAWAII •
HONG KONG • INDIA • INDONESIA • IRELAND • JAPAN • KENYA •
MALAYSIA & SINGAPORE • MEDITERRANEAN FRANCE • MEXICO • NEPAL •
NEW ENGLAND • NEW ZEALAND • NORTHERN ITALY • PERU • PHILIPPINES •
PORTUGAL • RUSSIA • SOUTH AFRICA • SOUTHERN ENGLAND • SPAIN • THAILAND •
TURKEY • VENEZUELA • VIETNAM, LAOS AND CAMBODIA • WESTERN CANADA

Traveler's COSTA RICA Companion

First published 2001
The Globe Pequot Press
246 Goose Lane, PO Box 480
Guilford, CT 06437 USA
www.globe-pequot.com

© 2001 by The Globe Pequot Press, Guilford CT, USA

ISBN: 0-7627-0896-4

Distributed in the European Union by
World Leisure Marketing Ltd, Unit 11
Newmarket Court, Newmarket Drive,
Derby, DE24 8NW, United Kingdom
www.map-guides.com

Created, edited and produced by
Allan Amsel Publishing, 53, rue Beaudouin
27700 Les Andelys, France.
E-mail: Allan.Amsel@wanadoo.fr
Editor in Chief: Allan Amsel
Editor: Anne Trager
Original design concept: Hon Bing-wah
Picture editor and designer: David Henry

ACKNOWLEDGMENTS
The author wishes to thank Joe Yogerst, John Aspinall, Eldon and Lori Cooke,
Ginny Craven, Michael Kaye, Gary Grimaud, Rafael Robles, Rudy Zamora,
Marco Motoya, Amy Bonanata, Debbie Dachner, William Thomas Douglas,
Mauricio Dada and all the *ticos* who made this book such a
pleasure to research and write.

Printed by Samhwa Printing Co. Ltd., Seoul, South Korea

TRAVELER'S
COSTA RICA
COMPANION

by Maribeth Mellin

Photographed by Nik Wheeler and Buddy Mays

The
Globe
Pequot
Press

GUILFORD
CONNECTICUT

Contents

TRAVELER'S
COSTA RICA
COMPANION

NICARAGUA

Barra del
Colorado

Tortuguero

HEREDIA

apulco

Terrón Colorado

San Carlos
Vuelta de Kopper
Florencia
Aguas Zarcas
Venecia
esada
los)
San José
de la Montaña
Cariblanco
Santa Clara
Zarcero
Poasito
Llano Bonito
Naranjo
Sarchí
Grecia
Garita Alajuela
Atenas
Heredia
Guacima
Pavas
Guayabo
Santiago
de Puriscal
Tabarcia

Chilamate
Puerto Viejo
de Sarapiquí
Las Horquetas
San Miguel

Canta Gallo

Cariari
Rita
Guápiles
Jiménez

LIMÓN

Parismina

Guácimo

Santa Cruz
Santo Domingo
San Pedro
SAN JOSÉ
Escazú
Cartago
Páraiso
San Ignacio Acosta
San Juan
de Chicuá
Turrialba
Pavones
La Suiza
Orosi
Cachí
Empalme
Platanillo

Siquirres

Guayacán
Linea B
Corina

Hacienda
Grano de Oro
Chirripó Abajo

**CARIBBEAN
SEA**

Puerto
Limón
Moín
Westfalia

Cahuita

Puerto
Viejo
Manzanillo

Bibrí

Sixaola

SAN JOSÉ

Túfares
Concepcion
San Vincente
Santa María de Dota
Copey

Villa Mills

División
San Gerardo de Rivas
San Isidro de el General

CARTAGO

Parque
Internacional
La Amistad

Cordillera Talamanca

PANAMA

Esterillos
Este
Paritta
Quepos
Manuel Antonio

Palmares

Dominical
Juntas
Uvita
San
Pablo
Pelibaye

Angel Arriba
Cacao
Buenos
Aires
Cabagra
Florida
Mosca
Naranjal

Punta
Uvita
Piñuela
Tortuga Abajo

Paso
Real
Boruca
Guácimo
Coto Brus
Santa Cecilia

Alturas

San Vito

*Bahai
de
Coronado*

Cortés
Palmar
Norte
Palmar Sur
Sierpe
Villa Colón
Venecia

Curre

PUNTARENAS

Chacarita
Briceño
Río Claro
Golfito
Neilly

Isla del Coco
*Isla
Manuelita*
CABO
BARRETO
Parque
Nacional
Isla del Coco
CABO
ATREVIDA
CABO DAMPIER

Aguajitas

Isla de Caño

San Pedrillo

Parque
Nacional
Corcovado
Barrgonés
Sirena
Península de Osa

Madrigal
Cárate

Finca Ojo
de Aguaal

*Golfo
Dulce*

Puerto Jiménez

Sábalos

Corite
Nicaragua

Canoas

Bella Luz

Resbalosa

TOP SPOTS

Venture into the Past

HIGHWAYS, DAMS, HOTELS AND MARINAS ARE THE SYMBOLS OF THE NEW COSTA RICA. Bulldozers rumble through valleys and forests, shaping the land for the future. Along the way, they unearth the past.

Costa Rica has precious few archaeological sites, and the government has demonstrated little interest in preserving the country's history. But tombs and bones are popping up at construction sites all over the country, and Costa Ricans are becoming more interested in protecting their heritage. One of the most exciting recent discoveries occurred when workers constructing a new hotel near the Meseta Central uncovered some unusual rock formations and pottery shards. Their find has since become the centerpiece of the Parque Arqueológico Alma Ata in La Virgen de Sarapiquí.

The park is part of the Centro Neotrópico SarapiquíS, an ambitious tourism development that has become Costa Rica's

most exciting new cultural attraction and a model of responsible development. Owned by the Landscape Foundation Belgium, the center is part hotel, part museum, part nature preserve. Designers spent years perfecting their plans for this innovative project and garnered the support of the Costa Rican government and the Arias Foundation for Peace and Progress before construction began. Architects, naturalists, historians, and engineers used a fifteenth-century indigenous village as their model, incorporating solar energy and a biological wastewater treatment plant. The existence of an archeological site enhances the overall scheme.

Archaeologists from the Museo Nacional have thus far uncovered 12 tombs, and the site has become a living museum where onlookers watch history unfold. Visitors enter the park through an orange grove and stroll along paths through the reconstruction of a fifteenth-century cluster of houses and a market. Pathways designed to resemble *calzadas* (streets) pass by copies of pre-Columbian statues and petroglyphs. At the tomb area, archaeologists painstakingly remove dirt with paintbrushes to uncover artifacts. Anayensy Herrera, the architect overseeing the dig, says the tombs are about 600 years old and were constructed by the Votos peoples of the Vertiente Atlantico Zone. Workers are still uncovering bits of pottery with scenes of turtles, jaguars and birds, and visitors have the opportunity to view an active archeological laboratory.

The center's archaeological park is a welcome addition to Costa Rica's sparse collection of pre-Columbian attractions. The Monumento Nacional Guayabo, located near

OPPOSITE: Visitors observe ongoing archaeological excavations at the Centro Neotrópico SarapiquíS.
ABOVE: Stone *metates* have been used for grinding corn since pre-Hispanic times.

Turrialba in the Meseta Central, has long been the country's largest reconstructed site. Archaeologists have determined that the region's roads, water tanks and other structures were built between AD 300 and 700 by an agricultural society which found sustenance in the fertile valley. It is believed that no more than 500 people lived at the site at any one time, as was typical of Costa Rica's early civilizations.

The future is sure to bring an increased interest in Costa Rica's cultural history. The largest archaeological find in recent times took place not far from Guayabo as engineers were plotting the construction of the much-maligned Angostura dam and lake in Turrialba in the mid-1990s. Early surveys uncovered over 40 distinct clusters of prehistoric structures in the area. Plans were altered to preserve the tombs and ruins, which are now protected. Several sites have also been unearthed along a planned highway between San José and the central Pacific coast. Archaeologists are working at the scene, collecting artifacts that date back to 300 BC. Currently closed to the public, these sites promise to be fascinating cultural landmarks.

Tour companies in San José and at hotels in Turrialba offer day trips to Guayabo. History buffs should consider spending at least one night at the Centro Neotrópico SarapiquíS, where artistically designed guest rooms are housed under circular palm *palenques*. The center abuts the Tirimbina Rainforest Reserve and the Río Sarapiquí, allowing guests to immerse themselves in both culture and nature. Overnight guests may enter the archeological zone for free. Day visitors are charged a fee, and tours are available from San José.

Cruise the Coast

EXPLORERS HAVE BEEN APPROACHING COSTA RICA BY SEA SINCE WELL BEFORE SPANISH GALLEONS ARRIVED IN 1502. Ecuadorian Indians may have paddled their dugout canoes to the Península de Nicoya 1,000 years earlier; pirates and pioneers have been arriving at its ports ever since.

Cruise ships passing through the Panama Canal often use Puerto Caldera on the Pacific as their Central American port of call. But passengers see little of the country. Better by far is a week-long cruise on the *Temptress,* an adventure-oriented line with two ships cruising the Pacific coast. National parks and private reserves form a natural greenbelt along this coastline between the borders with Nicaragua and Panama. It would take several weeks to cover this vast, wild region by car, and months to hike into the best regions of the parks. The *Temptress* ships have enviable access to blissful, secluded spots where roads and trails have yet to carve their way through rainforests, around rivers and over canals.

The cruise begins at Los Sueños, Marriott's lavish resort near Jacó, less than a two-hour drive from San José. Each morning the ship docks in a quiet bay, and passengers assemble for hikes while animals and birds are foraging for breakfast. Birders head off with their scopes and life lists, pursuing motmots, trogons and macaws. Botanists lather up with insect repellent and debate the names of trees and leaves. Amateur naturalists learn to walk slowly and silently while peering upward for crashing branches and fluttering vines — the signs of monkeys and sloths in the trees. Afternoons are devoted to kayaking, swimming, body surfing, snorkeling and snoozing.

Itineraries differ, but most include an initial stop at the Refugio de Fauna Silvestre Curu off the southern tip of the Península de Nicoya. The coastal forests in the 84-ha (207-acre) private reserve offer some unusual wildlife sightings, along with the more common howler monkeys and sloths. Hikers spot rare white-tailed deer and anteaters during early morning jaunts; birders are rewarded with glimpses of lineated woodpeckers and laughing hawks. After lunch on the beach, passengers snorkel in crystalline coves or sunbathe on white-sand beaches where Olive Ridley and hawksbill turtles lay their eggs on summer nights.

The ship travels south as passengers settle in at the bar for sunset cocktails. At dawn, they awaken to the incomparable sight of scarlet macaws streaking above the forests of the Península de Osa and the Parque Nacional Corcovado on the southern coast. The *Temptress* ships sail into the Golfo Dulce between the peninsula and the mainland. Stops here include a visit to Casa Orquideas, a private botanical garden filled with orchids and other tropical plants that attract swarms of hummingbirds. The last stop on the Costa Rica itinerary is Parque Nacional Manuel Antonio, the most popular park in the country. While landlubbers slog through streams and muddy trails to reach the park's more secluded areas, *Temptress* passengers simply climb aboard a dinghy and ride to the southern edge, where monkeys usually outnumber humans.

Highlights? Golden dawns, lightning-streaked night skies, walks through remote villages. A constant stream of information couched in *tico* humor and myths. The opportunity to visit several national parks while unpacking just once, and having the crew dry the mud off your shoes. The chance to meet guides from Tortuguero, waiters from Puntarenas, and crew from all parts of the country. The *Temptress* is *tico*-owned and

staffed, and passengers gather innumerable insights into the country and its people while sipping *guaro* (the local firewater) at the bar. Talented, informative guides offer lectures each evening, reviewing the day's wildlife sightings and forecasting the next day's possibilities. The guides quickly learn the interests and peccadilloes of the passengers, and gear their talks to please their audiences. It takes little more than a day for everyone to become acquainted, and the cruises usually take on a familial camaraderie.

Temptress devotees are a mixed lot of alumni and naturalist groups, seniors on tour, curious independent travelers and entire families. The cruise line offers specialized family sailing, but children seem to enjoy the ride no matter what age their playmates. The *Explorer* carries only 100 passengers when fully loaded; the *Voyager* sleeps just 63. The company offers several itineraries, some combining Costa Rica with the Panama Canal and Belize. Other cruise lines have followed the wake of the *Temptress* (see TAKING A TOUR, page 47 in YOUR CHOICE). Windstar offers luxury cruises along the Pacific Coast on their sailing ships, while Lindblad Expeditions uses the *Temptress Voyager* for its winter cruises. If you haven't the budget or time for an extended cruise don't be discouraged. Calypso Cruises offers a day trip from San José to Isla de Tortuga off the Península de Nicoya on its catamaran. The idyllic island has little wildlife, but its white-sand beaches are among the most beautiful in the country. Even one day at sea is better than nothing.

OPPOSITE: The *Temptress* anchors off Parque Nacional Corcovado. ABOVE: Spectacular sunsets are just one of the rewards awaiting passengers cruising the Pacific coastline.

Spot the Elusive Quetzal

BIRD WATCHERS CAN'T RESIST THE QUEST FOR THE RESPLENDENT QUETZAL, SACRED BIRD OF THE ANCIENT MAYA. This tiny trogon with iridescent emerald and sapphire tail feathers is the ultimate quarry for diehard *pajareros* (bird watchers) who consider Costa Rica an avian paradise. Over 850 bird species have been spotted in the country; several are endangered or rare. Serious ornithologists are known to wax poetic about motmots and macaws, bellbirds and curassows. Yet even the most jaded and well-traveled endure endless hikes in chilly damp cloud forests for a glimpse of the elusive quetzal. Alexander Skutch, birder extraordinaire and author of A *Guide to the Birds of Costa Rica*, calls the quetzal "the most magnificent of all the trogons… both lovely and irreproachably peaceful."

I listened to its cackling and sometimes melodious call numerous times before catching a glimpse of its precious plumes. I searched for the bird in the land of the Maya, who used its feathers to adorn the headdresses of only the most powerful chieftains. I scanned treetops in Guatemala (where the national currency is named for the quetzal) without luck. Finally, my efforts were rewarded with an awesome display of the quetzal's flirtatious mating dance beside a trail in Monteverde.

As is typical in the avian world, male quetzals wear the more alluring feathers and use them in elaborate swooping performances to attract mating females. No shrinking violets themselves, the females puff up their ruby-red bellies while inspecting nests made by the males in deep holes high up in laurel trees. The male can swirl his tail all he wants, but the female won't settle her wings in his nest unless it's fit for her two blue eggs. Once she lays her eggs, the male babysits during the day, covering the nest with his belly as his tail feathers stream down the tree.

The quetzal's mating ritual takes place from March through June; the best place to witness the action is in the cloud forest reserves at Monteverde, Los Angeles Cloud Forest near San Ramón, and the Cerro de la Muerte area. The Chacón and Serrano families, who run lodges near San Gerardo de Dota in the Zona Sur, are legendary quetzal spotters. They say quetzals hang around the laurel trees near their lodges year round.

The quetzal may be Costa Rica's most famous bird, but it's only one of dozens that draw *pajareros* to the country. Huge flocks of scarlet macaws feed on wild almonds along the southern Pacific coast and are protected in Parque Nacional Corcovado. Guests at Lapa Ríos, the Corcovado Lodge Tent Camp, and Aguila de Osa in Bahía Drake awaken to the squawks of macaws zooming toward their feeding grounds and the sight of keel-billed toucans with their candy-colored beaks perching on balconies. Hikers at Reserva Biológica Carara on the central Pacific coast usually spot the regal red birds as well, since the reserve contains one of the world's most successful macaw breeding projects. A few great green macaws hang out around the Parque Nacional Tortuguero on the northern Caribbean coast, though they are difficult to spot.

Bird lovers are drawn to the Sarapiquí and Caribbean regions, where Amazon parrots, three species of toucans, and oropendolas find refuge in numerous reserves. Shorebirds flock to the fertile swamps and estuaries around Aviarios del Caribe near Cahuita on the Caribbean coast. Clouds of white egrets soar over the pink-hued lagoon at dawn, while herons doze in their perches in the trees.

The northwest is also known for its abundance of water birds. Refugio Nacional de Caño Negro is home to a large population of neotropic olivaceous cormorants, along with tall jabiru storks, roseate spoonbills and kingfishers. Laughing falcons, ospreys, aracaris and parrots are all visible during rafting trips on the Río Corobicí. Crested caracaras, violaceous trogons and the bizarre three-wattled bellbird nestle in the Parque Nacional Rincón de la Vieja.

ABOVE: Birders search the thick rainforest canopy for a glimpse of the elusive quetzal. RIGHT: Waterfalls fed by constant rain cascade down the sides of mountains and volcanoes.

Serious bird watchers join specialized tours (see SPECIAL INTERESTS, page 45 in YOUR CHOICE) and gravitate toward specific bird-friendly regions. Neophytes should think twice before joining a specialized birding tour, unless they are committed to learning more about the hobby. Bird watchers are an odd breed, given to lengthy arguments over the identity of scarlet rumped tanagers and buff rumped warblers. Their conversations can become a bit tiresome for non-birders. Most guides have sufficient birding knowledge to satisfy curious minds, and those with only a mild interest in ornithology can find satisfaction spotting birds on general nature tours.

Ride the Rivers

WHITEWATER FOAMS OVER BOULDERS AND FALLEN TREES IN MIGHTY RIVERS RUSHING DOWN MOUNTAIN PEAKS AND VOLCANIC SLOPES. Dark, murky rivers slither past remote settlements on both shores. It's nearly impossible to visit Costa Rica without having a river adventure.

River rafting was one of the country's first adventure tourism attractions, and it continues to draw in more participants than any other sport. Many travelers begin or end their trips with day-long excursions to the Reventazón, Sarapiquí, or Pacuare, all within a few hours' drive from San José. Most return with excited tales of thrills and spills, and say rafting was the high point of their vacation.

Diehard, death-defying river rafters may not count the country's rapids among the world's best, but there are still plenty of high points on the major rivers. All three are under assault by the Costa Rican Electricity Institute (ICE) and have been dammed for hydroelectric power. Plans for more dams are always in the works, much to the horror of rafting outfitters and environmentalists. But rapids and waterfalls abound, thanks to abundant rainfall. San José and the Meseta Central receive an average of 188 cm (74 in) of rain annually. Tortuguero on the Caribbean wallows under 523 cm (206 in) per year. There's plenty of water to keep boaters afloat.

The Pacuare is considered the most exciting river in the country, with class III to V rapids. The Reventazón has both calm and wild sections, with rapids named Horrendito and Indigestion. The Sarapiquí is a gorgeous tropical rainforest river with class I to III rapids. Rafting can be as tranquil or terrifying as your heart can handle. For me, the ultimate challenge is the Reventazón, where fully helmeted and swaddled in a life jacket I fell three times into crashing freshwater waves,

bouncing off rocks and branches. Braver (and more experienced) rafters get their thrills during the rainy season in the highest reaches of the river.

River rafting has also come under scrutiny for its inherent dangers, and demands for regulation increase each time a tourist is seriously injured on a rafting trip. There are no safety regulations for rafting companies, but the Costa Rican Tourism Institute (ICT) is considering standards for licensing. The companies listed in SPORTING SPREE (see page 28 in YOUR CHOICE) have good track records, and are considered leaders in the industry. All offer one-day excursions that include transportation, gear (durable helmets and top-notch lifejackets are a must), clear safety instructions, and a good balance of excitement and fun. Costa Rica White Water, Ríos Tropicales, and Aventuras Naturales offer multi-day trips utilizing lodges on the Pacuare, a great option for those who enjoy the combination of adventure, gorgeous scenery, and a bit of slow-paced bird watching.

Smaller companies abound, and you may be tempted to sign up for their less-expensive trips. If so, ask about their safety record and personally check out the gear before you head out. Make sure you have a good lifejacket and helmet, and don't encourage the guides to take unnecessary risks. Many rafting companies are hesitant to cancel trips during bad weather, and don't pay their guides when trips are suddenly aborted. Speak up if conditions look dangerous.

You needn't brave fierce rapids to enjoy the rivers, however. Waterways were the original roadways throughout the country, and remain the main thoroughfares to settlements in the northern Caribbean and the south Pacific. The ride through dark canals reminiscent of scenes in the *African Queen* is a rush for birders and naturalists, and entire sections of the coast lie between rivers, mangrove swamps and lagoons. Many forms of watercrafts glide under 30-m-tall (100-ft) ajillo trees, used by local inhabitants for constructing canoes. Egrets, ibises, herons, jacunas and kingfishers alight from palo verde trees, cattails and water hyacinths; lizards slither through fallen tree trunks. The best river rides for scenery include the Moín-to-Tortuguero route (a standard route for travelers staying at lodges in Tortuguero), the trip down the Río Sierpe to Bahía Drake, and the long, lazy journeys on the Río Corobicí offered by Safaris Corobicí. Most companies above offer gentler float trips in calmer sections of the rivers near the most popular tourism destinations. These casual cruises are especially suited to nature lovers more intent on the thrills of spotting tiger herons and snowy egrets than bouncing over boulders and waterfalls.

Tiptoe Round the Turtles

LIGHTNING FLASHED AND CRACKLED IN THE MIDNIGHT SKY AS WE CREPT ALONG TORTUGUERO'S BEACH, SCANNING THE SAND FOR TURTLE TRACKS. "Hush," my guide hissed suddenly, dropping into a crouch. "There's one back there hiding her nest," he whispered, nodding toward the tree line. "And another down by the surf." We huddled on the damp sand like stealth warriors, trapped by the slow, steady march of pregnant reptiles skittishly seeking a safe place to lay their eggs.

After the turtles had all settled in their chosen spots, we crept toward a 140-kg (300-lb) mama flinging sand with her leathery flippers. Once her carefully constructed trench was completed, she squatted over the hole, exhaled a shuddering sigh, and pushed several dozen squishy white eggs onto the sand in an amorphous blob. Breathing audibly, she pushed again and again, tears streaming down her sand-encrusted face. An hour later her pain was palpable, her effort exhausting, and her task only halfway complete. She lay atop the eggs as if mortally drained, then slowly edged forward.

"Watch out!" the guide snapped as the weary turtle took another deep breath, dug in her flippers, and swept a cloud of sand over the eggs (and into my eyes). She rested, regrouped, and shoveled sand until her nest blended into the landscape, then slowly turned and lumbered toward the sea. Head raised, flippers extended, she settled her bulk on the surf line and rode a gentle wave into the soothing, weight-bearing water. She'd done all she could to protect her babies.

Similar scenes are played out on beaches from Africa to South America as conservationists engage tourists in the battle to protect endangered loggerhead, hawksbill, Olive Ridley and green turtles. Turtle-nesting tours are offered all over the world in the continued race to popularize their protection. Fossils prove that sea turtles roamed the planet's ocean 100 million years ago, yet in the past century many species have been driven to near extinction. Pollution, overpopulation, the destruction of turtle nesting habitats, commercial fishing, and the demand for turtle meat, eggs, and shells have all contributed to their demise. Fortunately, sea turtles are among the world's most endearing endangered creatures, and Costa Rica is one of the best places in the world to experience their wonders firsthand.

OPPOSITE: Personable nature guides enhance wilderness experiences all over the country.
ABOVE: Nesting sea turtles leave tracks in the sands of Tortuguero's beaches.

Archie Carr, a pioneer and hero among turtle preservationists, began studying the green turtle migration to Tortuguero's beaches in 1954. Since then, this tiny outpost on Costa Rica's northern Caribbean coast has become home to the longest continuing sea turtle research program in the world. Residents of the remote backwater region are directly involved in protecting the turtles, despite a traditional fondness for turtle meat and eggs (which are credited with aphrodisiac properties). Not long ago, poachers would wait in the dark for mother turtles to come ashore, then cup their hands in the nest to capture the eggs as the turtle expelled them into the sand. Today, their descendants work as guides leading strictly regulated tours during the green turtles' nesting season from June through September.

Tortuguero now has the largest nesting population of green turtles in the Atlantic, a considerable feat in itself. Most sea turtles return to the beach where they were born to lay their eggs, drawn by some unfathomable instinct. Perhaps they recall their struggle to survive the first moments of life. After a two-month gestation period, the babies emerge from their eggs, battle their way through their sand nest, and race for the shelter of the sea while dodging attacks by voracious birds. Precious few hatchlings survive. Although it takes 20 years or more for them to reach reproductive maturity, they almost always go back to their birthplace.

In recent times, innumerable turtle nesting sites have been destroyed as modern resorts have replaced ancient natural habitats. With the help of foreign conservation organizations, Costa Rica's environmental activists have been able to convince local and national governments and business leaders to regulate development in the area and protect the beaches.

All of Tortuguero's hotels and lodges are involved in turtle conservation, and their turtle-watching tours are closely monitored. Only a specific number of guides and tourists are allowed on the beaches at night during nesting season, and each group is restricted to watching one turtle in action. Travelers determined to see the turtles should arrange their tours in advance through their hotel or lodge or a tour operator (see TAKING A TOUR, page 46).

The Caribbean Conservation Corporation ((352) 373-6441 WEB SITE www.cccturtle.org, 4424 NW 13th Street, Suite A1, Gainesville, Florida 32609, operates an exciting volunteer program. Volunteers and researchers patrol the beaches during nesting season, tag and measure turtles, locate nests and count the eggs, and otherwise assist in the effort to protect both green turtles (from June to September) and loggerheads, which nest on Tortuguero's southern beaches from March to May. Consider the words of Archie Carr: "Everyone ought to see a turtle nesting. It is an impressive thing to see, the pilgrimage of a sea creature back to the land its ancestors left a hundred million years ago."

A Mountain with Attitude

COSTA RICA'S MOST SPECTACULAR NATURE SHOW IS THE INCESSANT ERUPTION OF VOLCÁN ARENAL. The cone-shaped mountain spews forth volcanic ash, rocks, lava and poisonous gas almost every day of the year. The pyrotechnics are especially dramatic at night when the red-hot magma gleams like liquid neon flowing down the mountainside.

Arenal isn't visible every night; it's often obscured by clouds and fog. But when it performs, red and gold sparks shoot straight out of the crater and the hillsides glow with streaks of fresh lava. Geologists list three distinct types of Arenal eruptions based on their sound: "chug" is a series of rhythmic gas emissions from lava fountains; "whoosh" is a minor blast of ash and lava that sounds like a jet plane; and "kaboom" is a short but powerful discharge that feels like an earthquake and sounds like a bomb. On a good night onlookers see and hear all of the above, an experience that ranks high on lists of vacation memories.

Arenal has historically announced its fury in sudden bursts of violence. The volcano was formed a mere 3,700 years ago, about the same time as the Egyptians were building their great pyramids and the Olmec civilization was thriving in Mexico. Scientists have determined that a major eruption took place some time between AD 1200 and 1530, possibly destroying a pre-Columbian village. Archaeologists have discovered ceramic shards in the volcanic soil that prove humans were living by the crater before the Spanish invasion.

The volcano lay dormant for hundreds of years, a jungle-shrouded peak called Cerro Arenal with a tranquil crater that was popular with campers. The surrounding countryside was home to sugarcane plantations, cattle pastures and peaceful villages. Then, on July 29, 1968, Arenal erupted with all the fury of a nuclear explosion. The geological chaos lasted for three days, demolishing Pueblo Nuevo and Tabacón villages and killing 77 people, mostly from toxic gases that inundated the slopes. Later, people who lived in the area recalled warning signs — steam drifting from vents in the rock, water so hot it nearly boiled in springs and streams, rumbling tremors underground. The changes were subtle, almost imperceptible, as they have been for every eruption since.

Activity in the early 1990s created a second cone at the summit and a massive lava field on the mountain's western flank. A sudden eruption in 1998 caused officials to evacuate the area. Yet the valley along the volcano's western slope became an important tourist destination. Officials looked the other way as hotels and attractions opened in high-risk zones near the base of the volcano, providing guests with front-row seats for the nightly fireworks display.

Volcán Arenal may well be the single most popular attraction in Costa Rica. It's also the most dangerous. A few people inadvertently give their lives to the fiery demon each year. At 10 AM on August 23, 2000, Arenal belched forth a cloud of ash and gas that traveled at 80 km/h (50 mph) down the mountain straight toward hiking trails and hotels. A guide and two tourists walking along a path beneath the eruption couldn't run fast enough to escape the scorching heat and lung-burning gas — the guide and an eight-year-old child died. A swath of the mountainside turned from green to gray; ash covered trees, houses, cars and roads for miles. Nearby hotels were evacuated as the police and national guard set up roadblocks between the town of La Fortuna and Laguna de Arenal, northwest of the volcano. Residents herded their cows onto flatbeds, piled their families into pickup trucks and raced east and south toward San Carlos and San José.

An eerie stillness settled over Arenal the next morning, as residents and tourists cautiously returned to homes and hotels. The mountain looked green and inviting — except for the smoldering river of boulders, tree trunks and ash on its northwest slope. Tourism to the volcano boomed in the following days.

The fallout from the 2000 eruption was dramatic. One travel agency canceled all tours to the volcano for a few months. Others cautioned their clients against hiking on the volcano or visiting Tabacón Hot Springs, a popular resort on the volcano's slope. Yet the volcano and hot springs are still on most traveler's must-see itineraries. They're nearly irresistible, but smart travelers keep a few safety precautions in mind. The basic tenets involve place and time. Several hotels are located close to the volcano; some precariously close to the lava flows. If you decide to stay at one of the hotels facing the volcano, keep a copy of your passport and some money with you at all times. Tourists who were off rafting, hiking, or sightseeing during the 2000 evacuation were stranded for several hours before receiving their belongings. Don't wander off to isolated areas — it

Volcán Arenal spews ash and fire hourly, though the pyrotechnics often must compete with low-lying clouds and fog.

takes a while for word to spread when an eruption begins. Stick with trails recommended by nature guides, national park rangers, or responsible tour operators. You can always drive or take a cab to the lava flows and watch the show for a while, or join a night tour from San José. Just remember to keep your wits about you when facing Mother Nature's fury.

Hang Out in the Treetops

"ARE YOU READY TO FLY?" the guide asked as I quaked at the edge of a wooden platform high above the forest canopy. "Not in the least," I thought wryly, studying the tangle of harnesses and crampons attaching my leaden body to a steel cable stretched between two trees.

I stepped into a void, felt my stomach lurch, and gripped the cable with the strength of sheer fear. "Loosen your fingers," my fellow travelers yelled from their safe perches on the platform. "Not a chance," I replied between clenched teeth. After what seemed like an interminable therapy session designed to cure my fears, the guide hooked his harness to mine and dragged me from one platform to the next — four times — before I happily rappelled down a rope to the ground.

Forest canopy tours are all the rage in Costa Rica these days, thanks in large part to Donald Perry. A biologist driven to devise a risk-free way for amateurs to study the treetops, Perry created Costa Rica's ingenious Rainforest Aerial Tram in the late 1980s, opening a whole new perspective on nature for the average traveler. Over 70% of the rainforest's creatures live at least nine meters (30 ft) above ground, where orchids and bromeliads thrive in the perfect mix of shade and sun. The tram's cable-cars slowly glide horizontally just beneath the forest canopy in the Braulio Carrillo rainforest, where green parrot snakes lounge on tree limbs and fuzzy spiders the size of field mice lay their eggs.

Perry's book *Life Above the Jungle Floor* begins with a quote from William Beebe's *Tropical Wild Life*, written in 1917: "Yet another continent of life remains to be discovered, not upon the earth, but one to two hundred feet above it… There awaits a rich harvest for the naturalist who overcomes the obstacles — gravitation, ants, thorns, rotten trunks — and mounts to the summits of jungle trees."

Similar sentiments have driven a whole new industry, one that far exceeds Perry's tame tram. The most exciting and terrifying canopy tours now involve transporting

tourists several stories above the ground, then dangling them from cables in midair. Eager participants strap on harnesses and helmets, hike uphill until they reach a platform in a tall tree above a canyon or valley, hook their harnesses onto a cable, and step into space. Guiding their speed by lightly running their leather-gloved hands along the cable, they glide from platform to platform — unless they simply clench the cable and refuse to budge.

Quite a few potential flyers chicken out when they reach the first platform, and are often surprised at the gut level of their fear. Tears and screams are not uncommon. Some folks take to the trees like wannabe Tarzans; others belong on the ground. The ride itself is said to be exhilarating. You don't get much time to observe the minutiae of nature when you're swinging through the trees, however. The best tours provide long pauses on the platforms for bird watching.

The Aerial Rainforest Tram is the perfect introduction to the forest canopy. Tours buses carrying day-trippers from San José, the Meseta Central and the Caribbean region fill the attraction's parking lot most days of the year. A tour of the tram's private reserve includes educational films on the forest and the construction of the tram, and a guided ride through the trees.

Original Canopy Tours, the first company to build Tarzan-style tours for the public, has canopy rigs in several locations, including Monteverde and Iguana Park near Jacó. During the company's Kazm Canyon tour at Hacienda Guachipelín in Guanacaste, tourists glide through a narrow river gorge above foaming rapids. At Rain Maker near Manuel Antonio, hikers gradually climb well-maintained trails to platforms above a river gorge, then walk along a suspended bridge above the water. A similar bridge, said to be the longest in the country, spans the Río Sarapiquí at Tirimbina Reserve in La Virgen de Sarapiquí.

Canopy tours are popping up all over the country these days, and it's hard to tell which ones are safe. Thus far, there are no regulations regarding the construction and operation of these operations — anyone can string up a few cables and call it a tour. All involve some risks, best handled with a bit of common sense. Make sure your guide provides a safety briefing, and pay close attention. Ask if there's a backup system for tours involving cables and harnesses, and request to see the company's written safety protocols. Wear a helmet whether you're in the air or on the ground (articles flying down from above can damage faces and skulls). Most of all, follow your instincts. If you don't feel safe, feel free to resist the urge to fly.

Awaken in the Ultimate Wilderness

NATURE'S WAKE-UP CALL BEGINS WITH THE MOURNFUL GROANS OF HOWLER MONKEYS STRETCHING THEIR HAIRY LIMBS IN THE FOREST CANOPY. Branches shuffle as spider monkeys swing through the trees. Toucans croak, parrots shriek, motmots chatter, and even slumbering sloths have a hard time staying asleep.

The essence of Costa Rica seeps into your dreams in early morning, and it's nearly impossible to stay in bed past 5 AM. Most wilderness lodges provide mosquito nets, screens, strong coffee and comfortable settings for observing nature's awakening. Comfort is a matter of personal preference, of course, and tents on the sand might not fit your dream of the perfect wilderness retreat. But the most gorgeous dawn I ever experienced in Costa Rica

OPPOSITE: Guests rise above the treetops at Corcovado Lodge Tent Camp. BELOW: Reserva Biológica Carara near Jacó is immensely popular with day-trippers from San José and cruise-ship passengers from Puntarenas.

appeared outside my tent flaps at the Corcovado Lodge Tent Camp on the Península de Osa.

My cot faced the Pacific, calm as a lake on a summer morning. A soft pink glow tinged the sky and water; light glistened on damp sand. Suddenly, a flock of scarlet macaws flew through the camp, flashing red, blue and gold feathers in their extended wings. Their squawks were downright deafening. I reached for my binoculars, scrambled out of the tent, and swung in a hammock while watching these gregarious endangered birds feed on wild almond trees edging the shore. An hour later I was hiking a trail in the Parque Nacional Corcovado, literally surrounded by monkeys.

Many consider Corcovado to be Costa Rica's most spectacular national park — it's certainly one of the most remote. Located along the southern Pacific coast, the park encompasses one of the largest tracts of primary forest in Central America. Rain and cloud forests harbor four types of monkeys — howlers, white-faced capuchin, spider and squirrel — and more than 400 species of birds. Eagles and hawks soar overhead, jaguars and pumas stalk their prey along secluded rivers and lagoons. Sperm whales spout just offshore in the park's marine reserve. Sea turtles lay their eggs on protected beaches.

All the nature guides I've ever met say Corcovado is their favorite destination for wildlife sightings (always best in early morning). Fortunately, there are many ways to greet the day in or near the park and hit the trails while wild creatures forage. Backpackers who struggle with heat, humidity, high tides and snapping insects to reach the park's remote campgrounds are rewarded with nature's full bounty. But you needn't suffer great hardships to sleep in the rough. The Corcovado Lodge Tent Camp offers all the trappings of a wilderness adventure without sacrificing hot showers and gourmet meals. The lodge also offers the ultimate overnight perch, an enclosed 30-m-high (100-ft) platform overlooking the forest canopy.

More comfortable sky-high lodgings are available at the Luna Lodge, where hawks silently whoosh through the air beneath a dining room deck dangling in space far beyond the treetops. Actually, the lodge is built into a steep hill above a river valley where interlopers once panned for gold. The miners destroyed some of the primary forest along the river, leaving a swath of cleared land with unobstructed

views of the sea. The lodge's comfy cabins are surrounded by forest, however, and gangs of baby spider monkeys tumble through the woods behind the rooms. Keel-billed toucans favor the private decks at Lapa Ríos at the southern tip of the peninsula. Guests lie on soft mattresses under gauzy white nets and watch these comical characters strut along wooden railings, flash their candy-colored beaks, and squabble around prime feeding grounds in the limbs of fruit trees. Travelers reach Corcovado and the Península de Osa via flights on small planes or long, arduous drives over rough rutted roads. The lodges in this area are among the most expensive in the country, since all supplies must be flown in. Most of the adventure cruise ships that tour the Pacific coast spend at least one night by the park. Early risers with binoculars can easily spot the feeding macaws while waiting to board dinghies for a quick ride to the park's most spectacular trails.

OPPOSITE: The picturesque hills of Laguna de Arenal. ABOVE: White-faced capuchin monkeys stop off at local eateries for snacks in Manuel Antonio. RIGHT: Mud baths revive weary travelers at Buena Vista Lodge, Parque Nacional Rincón de la Vieja.

YOUR CHOICE

The Great Outdoors

Earthquakes, fire-spitting volcanoes, exorbitant rainfall and hurricanes — Costa Rica has them all. Trails and back roads etch the topography up mountains, down rivers, through cloud forests and along the sands of two seas. Visiting the country without getting involved in nature is virtually impossible. Parakeets, hummingbirds, butterflies and moths invade the most urban quarters, right down to the city park. Every type of adventurer finds challenges worth pursuing, from climbing through cloud forest to the peak of Cerro Chirripó to diving with whale sharks off Isla del Coco. Every level of skill is accommodated as well. First-time river rafters find suitable rapids for moderate thrills; amateur bird watchers get easily hooked.

Squished between the Caribbean Sea and the Pacific Ocean in the narrow land bridge between North and South America, Costa Rica is the second smallest country in Central America. Bordered on the north by Nicaragua and the south by Panama, this tiny nation of only 50,895 sq km (31,604 sq miles) lies within the tropical zone between 8 degrees and 11 degrees north of the equator. The Andean–Sierra chain of mountain ranges runs through the center, and is broken into distinct ranges by volcanic activity. Running north to south, the cordilleras de Guanacaste, de Tilarán, Central and Talamanca grow ever more rugged and indomitable as they reach Costa Rica's highest peak, Cerro Chirripó, at 3,819 m (12,529 ft) high. Cerro Chirripó is the best site for **mountain climbing**, with trails leading through lowlands and forests to the peak. Chirripó can be climbed in a day in clement weather; rustic accommodations are available near the summit. **Spelunking** is best at Parque Nacional Barra Honda, where a few operators provide gear and guides.

Lying within the Pacific Rim of Fire, Costa Rica has at least 67 major **volcanoes**, nine of which are active. Some estimate that there are some 120 volcanoes in all, some just small hills hidden by forest. Much of the country's wild beauty can be attributed to these classic cones rising above fertile valleys. Volcán Arenal, the most famous and dramatic of all the country's volcanoes, rises 1,633 m (5,356 ft) above Laguna de Arenal and spurts fiery lava into the air with disconcerting regularity. The volcano's first modern-day eruption occurred in 1968, when it blew its top and destroyed a six-square-kilometer (four-square-mile) radius of forest and homes. The most recent major eruption occurred in August 2000, and Arenal continues to burst forth with red-hot lava and rocks tumbling down its western slope. The volcano is part of Parque Nacional Volcán Arenal — a must-see on all Costa Rica itineraries.

Several of Costa Rica's most dramatic volcanoes are located close to San José. Volcán Irazú, a 55-km (34-mile) drive east of San José, enveloped the city in sooty ash when it exploded in 1963, and now occasionally rumbles and fumes as if reminding nearby residents of its potential fury. The most recent eruption at Volcán Poás, just 37 km (23 miles) from San José, occurred in 1994 and caused the Parque Nacional Volcán Poás to be closed for some time. Volcán Rincón de la Vieja in the national park of the same name in the northern part of the country continues to bubble, as do geysers and hot pools throughout the park. There's no guarantee any of these fiery giants will perform on the day of your visit, though most provide enough drama with bubbling craters and mist-shrouded cones.

Volcán Arenal explodes over a rainforest waterfall.

Costa Rica also lies in a zone of considerable seismic activity, and earthquakes are a constant consideration. The most destructive quake hit the country on Earth Day, April 22, 1991. Registering 7.4 on the Richter scale, the quake originated on the Caribbean side of Costa Rica, but was felt in San José. Limón Province was hit the worst, with 27 people killed and thousands of buildings destroyed. Mudslides closed the roads, bridges collapsed and floods destroyed villages and homes. It took several years for the region to recover, and the quake remains an indelible horror in the minds of Costa Ricans. Earthquake tremors are common in most parts of the country, but there hasn't been a serious quake since 1991. If you feel tremors, stand under a doorway or duck under a solid table — don't run outside. Chances are good the tremors will end before you even realize what's happening.

The presence of mountains, volcanoes, shifting tectonic plates and an abundance of rivers and lakes contributes to Costa Rica's immense diversity; the country has a dozen different ecosystems or life-zones, each with distinct characteristics. Rare tropical dry forests are protected in a few small reserves in Guanacaste. Tropical rainforests on the Península de Osa and southern Pacific and Caribbean coasts shelter an extraordinary number of mammal, bird, and plant species. Cloud forests such as those at Monteverde nurture epiphytes and rare birds; in the highest elevations, elfin forests and páramos resemble those in the high Andes.

About one-third of Costa Rica's terrain is protected in an impressive system of national parks, conservation areas and private reserves. But deforestation is a constant threat, as is tourism. Some areas of Costa Rica are literally being loved to death, and authorities have responded by limiting access to the more popular areas. Dozens of national, international, and private organizations are involved in protecting the country's precious biodiversity. See SPECIAL INTERESTS, page 45, for information on ways you can help through volunteering.

Twenty-five national parks and eleven conservation areas in Costa Rica are operated under the Environment Ministry (Ministerio del Ambiente y Energia — MINAE) and the National System of Conservation Areas (Sistema Nacional de Areas de Conservación — SINAC). The main information office for both agencies is at Calle 27 between Avenidas 10 and 12, San José (283-8004 or 283-8094 FAX 283-7343 HOTLINE IN COSTA RICA (192. The agencies publish a booklet listing the

parks' facilities. The Instituto Nacional de Bioversiodad (INBio) (244-4730 FAX 244-4790 WEB SITE www.inbio.ac.cr, Apdo 22-3100 Santo Domingo, Heredia, also distributes information on the parks and operates INBioparque in Heredia (see HEREDIA, page 92 in THE MESETA CENTRAL). Most ranger stations, called *puestos*, have trail maps and printed information.

Given the great biodiversity, hiking is inevitable and completely rewarding. Some of the shortest walks bring white-faced monkeys, toucans, giant iguanas and scarlet macaws into easy view. **Wildlife-spotting** can be as easy as staring for hours at sweet-faced sloths hanging beside your cabin, or as difficult as slogging through pounding rain and slipping down red clay hills for a view of the elusive quetzal. Costa Rica's many national parks, along with a slew of private reserves, offer a range of hiking options you won't find anywhere else outside Africa or the Amazon.

I find it invaluable to hike with **naturalist guides** well versed in the local wildlife scene. Many of the best guides work for top-notch adventure companies such as Costa Rica Expeditions, Horizontes and Sun Tours (see TAKING A TOUR, page 46). Web sites have become immensely valuable as a way to learn about the background and training of individual guides (see WEB SITES, page 254 in TRAVELERS' TIPS).

Bird-watching goes hand in hand with hiking; both activities will find you spending much of your time with neck craned, searching for streaks of color. *Pajareros,* as bird watchers are called, are easily spotted with their gangly tripods, scopes, binoculars, and weighty copies of A *Guide to the Birds of Costa Rica,* by Stiles and Skutch, which lists some 70 prime birding spots. Monteverde, Cerro de la Muerte, Tortuguero, Corcovado and Palo Verde are among the favorites, as is Skutch's home base in the San Isidro area. Companies specializing in bird-watching tours are listed in SPECIAL INTERESTS, page 45.

Turtle-watching is exceptional in Tortuguero and much of the Caribbean coast, along with Playa Grande on the Pacific. Green, Ridley and leatherback turtles visit these beaches during certain months to lay their eggs, sometimes arriving by the thousands in *arribadas* (mass arrivals). See TIPTOE ROUND THE TURTLES, page 17 in TOP SPOTS.

Despite this abundance of wildlife and biodiversity, some travelers complain that they don't see enough animals during their

A suspension bridge swings above a fern-filled ravine in the rainforest reserve, Parque Nacional Braulio Carrillo.

Sporting Spree

Sports are a way of life in Costa Rica, where households are stocked with soccer balls, bicycles and rafts. Serious athletes are absolutely passionate about the country, which offers an ever-increasing bounty of challenges. Costa Rica claims some of the world's most thrilling rivers, challenging surf and exciting scuba diving, and outfitters specialize in nearly every imaginable outdoor activity. Even the most sedentary visitor eventually hikes a mountain trail or paddles through a few mild rapids. Sports are an integral part of any visit to Costa Rica.

Narrow, shoulderless roads make **bicycling** in Costa Rica difficult, although *ticos* (Costa Ricans) in the countryside bike frequently between home and work. You're likely to come across local bike races while traveling back roads on weekends, but only the hardiest traveler would attempt to tour the country on a road bike. Mountain bicycling, however, is becoming more popular with adventure tour companies and local lodges, some of which now rent equipment. Laguna de Arenal and the Volcán Arenal are among the best spots for cruising past waterfalls, forests, and birds, and rentals are available. Dirt roads etch the foothills of Cerro de la Muerte and into the rainforest behind Bahía Drake. If you're serious about bicycling, check into the availability of good bikes, helmets and trail maps before your travels. Most beach resorts have bicycle rentals for cruising from cafés to surfing spots. Local bike tour operators are listed in the relevant regional chapters. **Coast to Coast Adventures** (280-8054 FAX 225-6055 or 225-7806 E-MAIL info@ctocadventures.com WEB SITE www.ctocadventures.com, Apdo 2135-1002, Lourdes de Montes de Oca, 1000 San José, operates mountain biking tours around the country, as does **Bi.Costa Rica** (/FAX 446-7585 E-MAIL bicostarica@yellowweb.co.cr WEB SITE www.yellowweb.co.cr/bicostarica.html, SSJO 611, PO Box 025216, Miami, Florida 33102-5216. Both offer tours that traverse the country from one coast to the other.

With all the rivers, lakes, lagoons and two seas beckoning boaters, it's difficult to stay off the water. **Rafting** was one of the first major attractions for travelers to Costa Rica, and it continues to draw in more participants than any other sport.

Rafting experts abound, and most of the hotels and lodges near the rivers can arrange trips. **Costa Rica Expeditions** (257-0766

adventures. Advertisements and promotional materials distributed by the Costa Rican Tourism Institute (ICT) and tour companies make it seem as though monkeys, macaws, and jaguars are hanging about the hotels posing for photographers. Tourists' expectations are high, and disappointment is inevitable. In reality, it takes some effort to see animals in the wild — most guides I've spoken with have never encountered a jaguar or puma except after spending long hours or days in remote areas. Soft adventure tours involving a bit of rafting, a few hikes and a couple of visits to natural parks rarely result in exciting encounters with mammals and birds. You'll probably see a few monkeys who know they'll find food close to certain hotels and restaurants. Sloths move so slowly that guides can count on seeing the same one in the same tree for weeks. Hummingbirds and butterflies abound, thanks to the proliferation of gardens designed to encourage their presence. But you're not going to get the rush of discovery at the side of the road.

If animal sightings are high on your list of expectations, schedule your itinerary accordingly. Allow yourself several days in one place, preferably at the edge of a remote reserve such as Tortuguero or Corcovado. Start hiking at dawn, if not earlier. Move slowly and quietly; save your jokes and conversations for later in the day. Listen for the faint rustling of leaves, then stop moving. With any luck, you'll soon spot a shy capuchin monkey crawling along a faraway tree limb, headed in your direction, followed by another, and yet another. Gradually, a whole troop will emerge, clambering right overhead, claiming the forest as their home. Humans who treat the wilderness with quiet respect reap the greatest rewards.

FAX 257-1665 E-MAIL costaric@expeditions.co.cr WEB SITE www.expeditions.co.cr, Apdo 6941, 1000 San José, Calle Central at Avenida 3, is often credited with starting the rafting craze in the country, and now operates **Costa Rica White Water**. The company uses custom-made rafts, runs trips on the Pacuare, Reventazón, and Sarapiquí rivers, and emphasizes safety. Unlike many other companies, White Water pays their staff when trips are canceled because of weather or high water conditions, thus further ensuring the safety of their clients.

A good source for general information and one of the country's leading rafting companies is **Ríos Tropicales** (233-6455 FAX 255-4354 E-MAIL reserve@riostropicales.com WEB SITE www.riostropicales.com, Calle 38 between Avenida Central and Avenida 2. The company offers one-day trips from San José along with multiple-day itineraries, and operates a lodge on the Pacuare. The Fundación Ríos Tropicales is spearheading the effort to protect the Pacuare, and is also seeking volunteer assistance. **Aventuras Naturales** (225-3939 TOLL-FREE IN THE US (800) 514-0411 FAX 253-6934 E-MAIL avenat@sol.racsa.co.cr WEB SITE www.toenjoynature.com, Avenida Central between Calles 33 and 35, San José, operates trips on all the major rivers and has a riverside lodge on the Pacuare.

Aguas Bravas (292-2072 FAX 229-4837 E-MAIL info@aguas-bravas.co.cr WEB SITE www.aguas-bravas.co.cr, in the green building 250 m (270 yards) north of the Formula 1 building in Ipis de Guadalupe, San José, and on the main road between La Fortuna and Laguna de Arenal, offer rafting on the Sarapiquí, Peñas Blancas and Toro rivers and has a lodge on the Sarapiquí. They also offer horseback riding and mountain bike tours.

You needn't brave fierce rapids to enjoy the rivers, however. The Río Corobicí in Guanacaste is one that is particularly well suited to birders. **Safaris Corobicí** (/FAX 669-1091 E-MAIL safaris@sol.racsa.co.cr WEB SITE www.nicoya.com, four kilometers (two and a half miles) west of Cañas on the Carretera Interamericana, is the largest operation in the area, and offers guided tours on the river.

Waterways are the main roads in some parts of the country. **Motorboats, canoes and kayaks** glide through the canals in the northern Caribbean and southern Pacific regions, ferrying guests to remote lodgings and carrying wildlife watchers past herons, egrets, monkeys, turtles and innumerable other creatures and plants. Canoe and kayak rental agencies are not as prevalent as you might hope. The best availability is in

Tortuguero, Bahía Drake, Manuel Antonio, the Río Sarapiquí region and Laguna de Arenal. Most of the river-rafting companies listed above offer kayaking.

Marlin, sailfish, dorado, tarpon, snook, trout and other estimable catches have long attracted serious anglers to great **sport fishing** spots on both coasts and in the interior. Deep-sea anglers get most excited about the big ones around Playa del Coco, Tamarindo, and Flamingo on the northern Pacific coast and Manuel Antonio, Dominical, and Golfito to the south. Tarpon and snook are the quarry in the northern Caribbean, where remote lodges exist strictly for their pursuers. Operators for each area are listed under the appropriate destination chapters. Some charter boat companies will take their boats to the area you wish to fish. **Flamingo Bay Fishing Charters** (253-6713 TOLL-FREE IN THE US (800) 836-7133 FAX 234-0906 E-MAIL billfish@sol.racsa.co.cr is based in Flamingo but offers fishing along the Pacific coast. **Marina Flamingo** (654-4203 FAX 654-4536 E-MAIL marflam@marflam.com WEB SITE www.marflam.com works with several charter boats. **JJ Sportfishing Tours** (257-8503 TOLL-FREE IN THE US (800) 308-3394 E-MAIL jpfishin@sol.racsa.co.cr operates on the Pacific as well. **VIP Sportfishing Charters** (654-4049 TOLL-FREE IN THE US (800) 346-2629 FAX 654-4968 E-MAIL twocan@racsa.co.cr WEB SITE www.vipsportfishing.com has a 28-m (90-ft) live-aboard boat perfect for diehard anglers and divers and a 12-m (38-ft) custom

OPPOSITE: When they are not dammed to provide electricity, the waters of the Río Corobicí provide more tranquil rafting than the Reventazón or Pacuare rapids. ABOVE: Divers exploring the waters of Isla de Caño discover their camera has a new attachment.

sport-fishing boat. They'll take either vessel to your preferred destination. Most of the fishing on the Caribbean is handled through specialized lodges. Up-to-date fish reports are published in the magazine *Costa Rica Outdoors* (282-6514 FAX 282-7241 WEB SITE www.costaricaoutdoors.com.

Surfing is legendary as well. Australian and American surfers with sun-bleached hair and bronzed bodies follow the wave action to Jacó, Dominical and secluded beaches in the southern Pacific coast, Tamarindo and Playa Grande in the north, and Cahuita and Puerto Viejo on the Caribbean coast. The mother of all surf spots is Playa Pavones, home to one of the longest waves in the world. There is also a good break at the mouth of the river between Playa Grande and Tamarindo. There are waves most of the year off the Pacific coast. The Caribbean coast is best from November to April. **Tico Travel** TOLL-FREE IN THE US (800) 493-8426 E-MAIL tico@gate.net WEB SITE www.ticotravel.com, 161 E. Commercial Boulevard, Fort Lauderdale, Florida 33334, can arrange surfing tours and provide information on surf areas. **Alacrón Surf Tours** (/FAX 777-1721 E-MAIL info@alacransurf.com WEB SITE www.alacransurf.com arranges customized surf trips.

Windsurfing is best at Laguna de Arenal, considered one of the best spots in the world for high winds. The best winds blow through between December and March. The winds are also good at Bolaños Bay in Santa Cruz, Guanacaste. Windsurfing companies are listed in the destination chapters. **Scuba diving** and **snorkeling** off Islas Murciélago, Santa Catalina and Caño in the Pacific can be sublimely rewarding when whale sharks, manta rays and other pelagics make a showing; playas Coco and Flamingo have the best dive shops in the north, while Manuel Antonio and Bahía Drake are good bases in the south. Diving and snorkeling can also be good in the Caribbean, but your chances for finding clear water are dicey. The coral reefs off Cahuita are your best bet. But the best spot by far is Isla del Coco, 480 km (300 miles) off the southern tip of Costa Rica, where hammerhead, white-tipped and whale sharks are common. **Aggressor Fleet** ((504) 385-2628 TOLL-FREE IN THE US (800) 348-2628 FAX (504) 384-0817 WEB SITE www.aggressor.com, based in the United States, operates the live-aboard *Okeanos Aggressor* and offers trips to the island. **Undersea Hunter** TOLL-FREE IN THE US (800) 203-2120 E-MAIL cocos@underseahunter.com WEB SITE www.underseahunter.com has two live-aboards traveling to Coco. Operators along both coasts offer scuba

diving and snorkeling trips to a variety of other destinations.

Guanacaste is the province of *sabaneros*, true cowboys who work the cattle ranches on typical *criollo* horses. **Horseback riding** is available throughout the northwest region; the best places to ride are at the lodges in family ranches haciendas such as Los Inocentes, Buena Vista, and Borinquen. Other great rides include those around Laguna de Arenal and Monteverde cloud forest, as well as Turrialba in the Meseta Central. Horses are also available at many beach areas, where sturdy mounts carry riders past waterfalls, through rainforests and down steep trails to gallop along secluded beaches.

Golf is beginning to take hold around the resort areas, and future plans include a number of golf resorts. San José has long had its 18-hole Cariari course at the Meliá Cariari

hotel outside the city (see HEREDIA, page 93 in THE MESETA CENTRAL), and the Meliá Playa Conchal in the Pacific northwest opened an 18-hole course designed by Robert Trent Jones in 1997 (see PLAYA CONCHAL, page 155 in THE NORTH PACIFIC). The **Los Sueños Resort and Marina** (see JACÓ AND ENVIRONS, page 178 in THE CENTRAL PACIFIC COAST) opened an 18-hole Ted Robinson-designed course in 1999. **Golf Costa Rica Adventures** ((970) 356-1028 TOLL-FREE IN THE US (800) 477-8971 FAX (970) 352-6324 E-MAIL golf@centralamerica.com WEB SITE www.crsite.com/golf, Interlink 854, PO Box 02-5635, Miami, Florida 33102, arranges golf tours in Costa Rica.

Ballooning over the Volcán Arenal provides an extreme, nearly mystical rush. **Serendipity Adventures** (556-2592 TOLL-FREE FROM THE US (877) 507-1358 FAX 556-2593 E-MAIL costarica@serendipityadventures.com

WEB SITE www.serendipityadventures.com can take you over the crater or over the region of Turrialba.

Soccer is the leading spectator sport, and it is of nearly religious importance in Costa Rica. Every small town has its soccer field, and games between major teams practically shut down the country on Sunday afternoons. Flags billowing outside rural homes are hung in honor of winning provincial teams; the best players go on to contribute to the national team which fares well in international competitions. **Bullfighting** is enormously popular at local fiestas. In line with the peaceful nature of the country, the bulls are never slaughtered or even hurt to any bloodletting degree.

Poles, paddles and motors power ferries along Playa de Coco, Nicoya Peninsula.

The Open Road

Driving can be the most thrilling way to see Costa Rica, and often the most dangerous. Road conditions are abysmal, but the scenery is utterly spectacular and worth every pothole and rut (see DRIVING TIPS, page 241 in TRAVELERS' TIPS, for detailed information on the delights and drawbacks inherent in driving around the country). If the thought of conquering the roads becomes intimidating, consider hiring a car and driver through a tour or rental-car company. Having a driver eliminates most of the hassles of seeing the country from the road and enhances the experience, since guide-drivers are familiar with local restaurants and sights and offer a running commentary on Costa Rican culture. Some tour companies offer self-drive itineraries with detailed directions — a delightful touch in a country where road signs are considered redundant. If you do drive around on your own, ask for directions before you set out and confirm your route along the way. I've yet to spot many signs indicating a highway number; the best you can hope for is a twisted bit of metal indicating the possible turnoff to a small town along your route.

You needn't range far and wide to enjoy the pleasures of a scenic drive. Standard sedans can handle some of the prettiest routes in the Meseta Central; though I've wandered afar and found every road a worthwhile

experience, some of the best drives have been close to San José. *Josefinos* are masters of the Sunday drive. At times it seems the entire city empties onto roads in every cardinal direction.

Nearly every road that provides an exit from San José offers an entry to spectacular scenery. City dwellers eagerly drive west towards **Orotina**, where roadside stands display homegrown cashews, dried papaya, homemade *cajeta* candies and local coffee. Continuing west, the road leads to the central Pacific coast. The southern route along **Cerro de la Muerte** is equally rewarding with its ascent of the Cordillera Talamanca foothills and descent into the agricultural valley of San Isidro de El General. I'd gladly do this drive just for lunch at Mirador Vista del Valle.

Highly memorable is a long afternoon's ramble around the **Orosí Valley**, considered by many to be the most beautiful valley in the country. Every twist in the road presents a view: bougainvillea entwined with pines, rivers splashing building-sized boulders, the Casa el Soñador (the Dreamer's House) covered in woodcarvings, a young girl shaded under broad coffee leaves. The valley is located just an hour outside the city (provided you don't get lost). Drive southeast from the city to Cartago, then to Paraíso and Orosí. Once you're in Orosí follow the mostly paved road to Cachí, over the dam, and back to Paraíso.

Favorite day trips are the spooky, surreal climbs through fog and mist to **Volcán Poás** and **Volcán Irazú**. Be on the road by 7 AM,

Potholes, sandy roads and terrifying one-lane bridges greet those meandering along the **Pacific coast** from the Nicoya to Osa peninsulas. All these drives require patience, fortitude and flexibility and are best approached as adventures unto themselves rather than simply a means for getting from point A to point B.

Backpacking

Costa Rica has a higher standard of living than its bordering countries, and is a far more expensive vacation destination overall. Yet there are ways to curb expenses, as budget travelers hanging on for months here can attest.

The first rule for saving money is to avoid travel in peak seasons and on holidays. Travelers on extended stays typically hole up in low-cost regions and wait out the hordes at more popular spots. The best time of year for all travelers is just before or after the dry season, which typically lasts from November to April. The rainy season, called the "green season" in Costa Rica, has definite drawbacks the longer the rains last. But you may experience dry days and even weeks in May, June and October and be able to take advantage of lower room rates.

Certain areas, especially along the beaches, are established budget destinations with a fervent following. Cahuita and Puerto Viejo on the Caribbean coast are the epitome of backpacker havens, offering space in cheap *cabinas* and private homes. Montezuma and Brasilito are the magnets in the North Pacific, while Jacó and small towns south of Dominical draw their share of hangers-on. Surfers and beach dwellers with plenty of time head far south to playas Zancudo and Pavones, close to the Panama border. There is a remarkable abundance of inexpensive hostelries in La Fortuna near Volcán Arenal. All of these areas have upscale accommodations as well, but specialize in inexpensive and moderate options. For lodging slightly above the rock-bottom range you can get cold-water showers, sturdy window screens and mosquito netting, dependable locks and clean sheets. Youth hostels are not as common here as in Europe or the United States (see YOUTH HOSTELS AND CAMPING, page 243 in TRAVELERS' TIPS).

rapidly leaving the city behind and cruising past small towns and settlements. The roads to both volcanoes begin with a gradual ascent past cattle ranches and farms, twisting and turning past staggering vistas of checkerboard valleys and wisps of smoke from distant chimneys. The temperature drops and wisps of cloud and fog descend toward the treetops. Near the end of the ascent the landscape grows ever more eerie, stripped of greenery by lava flows and ash. If the timing is right, the parking lots at the edge of the volcanoes will be empty, and you can walk in solitude toward smoldering craters. With luck, you can beat the fog that descends with unpredictable frequency upon the volcanoes and can clearly see the vast expanses of barren landscape while shuffling through fields of ash. The road to Irazú begins in Cartago, southeast of San José; the road to Poás juts off Highway 9 north of Heredia. Allot a full day for either trip to allow for stops at scenic lookouts and mountainside restaurants.

Longer road trips are even more rewarding, but a four-wheel drive is essential for true road warriors. With sturdy tires and high suspension to support your wanderings, drivers can master rutted dirt and mud, slippery bridges and shallow river crossings leading into the wilderness. Among the best long drives are the route through the **Parque Nacional Braulio Carrillo to** the Caribbean coast, and the Pan-American Highway north through the vast cattle ranges in **Guanacaste**.

A San José-bound bus bumps and jiggles its way along a country road. ABOVE: Drivers reach remote regions of the Zona Sur by crossing rivers on rustic ferries.

At many budget destinations, food is half the price of what you find in Manuel Antonio, San José or the resort towns. But your choices can be severely limited. Stick with rice, beans, chicken and fish on the coast and you'll stretch your dining dollars farthest.

Despite the prevalence of parks and reserves, camping isn't as easy as you might think. Inclement weather is a serious drawback, and tents are a must for any length of stay. Many of the national parks have at least rustic facilities and welcome a certain number of campers; for easiest access, arrange permits in advance through the main information office for the parks (283-8004 FAX 283-7343 HOTLINE IN COSTA RICA (192, Calle 27 between Avenidas 10 and 12, Apdo 10104, 1000 San José, or through each individual park. You may also be able to sleep and eat at the park ranger stations, especially during low season. The parks and reserves of Monteverde, Rincón de la Vieja and Corcovado are particularly popular with experienced backpackers.

Getting around by bus is cheap and not terribly difficult, at least between major destinations. It is, however, time consuming. Just as those with the colónes to rent cars must deal with horrid road conditions, bus passengers must adjust to flat tires, breakdowns and accidents. As a rule the first-class buses are comfortable, relatively clean and safe. Travel off the beaten path, however, and you deal with old rattletrap contraptions of the ancient school bus genre. The beds of pickup trucks serve as local transport in some rural areas, and hitching a ride from passersby is common in these areas. When hitching, remember that drivers are more likely to stop for travelers who look sane and pleasant. Costa Ricans despise confrontation and avoid potentially unpleasant situations. Practice your Spanish manners liberally, thanking drivers and showing consideration to fellow passengers.

Air transport to remote regions is worth considering even if you're on a slim budget, especially if your time is limited. Small planes commute between the cities and wildly remote areas, and the fares are quite reasonable. You may end up on a puddle jumper landing by beaches, lagoons and even cemeteries en route to your final destination, but it's great fun to see civilization yield to wilderness from above.

Boats of all sorts ferry passengers to bays, towns and settlements along rivers and lagoons. Most travelers reach Tortuguero via river ferry from Moín, spotting herons, cayman and Jesus Christ lizards along the route. For the lowest fares and best cultural immersion, choose a local boat rather than one carrying tourists. It may take a few hours to reach your destination, but along the way you'll get a glimpse of the river lifestyle as passengers loaded with purchases disembark at basic riverside shacks they call home.

Budget travelers should consult the busy experts at **Ecole Travel** (223-2240 FAX 392-7275 E-MAIL ecolecr@racsa.co.cr WEB SITE www.travelcostarica.net, Calle 7 between Avenidas Central and 1, inside 7th Street Books. Ecole is the most comprehensive source for budget travelers, and publishes a list of all the departure points, times, and prices for the major bus routes throughout the country. They also offer several tours utilizing public transportation to reach out-of-the-way destinations.

Living It Up

EXCEPTIONAL HOTELS

Big, lavish resorts are not Costa Rica's style, though they are starting to shape the future of pristine bays along the Pacific coast. The Spanish Meliá chain was the first to open a full-scale resort on the coast; its success has spurred similar development. The **Meliá Playa Conchal** in Guanacaste is an elaborate affair, with an 18-hole golf course, white-sand beach, an enormous free-form swimming pool, several restaurants and a casino. Marriott followed suit in late 1999 with the ostentatious **Los Sueños Marriott** at Playa Herradura on the central Pacific coast. An isolated bay and beach have been completely transformed into a large-scale resort with a marina, 18-hole golf course, health club and casino. The Marriott is popular with small meeting groups and independent travelers seeking familiar comforts in a foreign setting. The **Costa Rica Marriott Hotel** near San José and the international airport is equally comfortable and elegant, with its golden arches and towers set against a mountain backdrop.

Costa Rica's best gems are the small, one-of-a-kind hotels designed to blend into their surroundings and accentuate the country's best attributes. In San José, a tropical Victorian mansion houses the incomparable **Grano de Oro**, the standard bearer for design detail, amiable service and fantastic food. Several hoteliers operate deluxe inns in the Meseta Central, offering luxurious surroundings with convenient access to the airport and countryside. In Escazú, **Tara** poses atop a hill like a pure white antebellum mansion ready to comfort weary travelers with mimosa and massage, while **Chalet Tirol** brings a bit of Austria to Volcán Barva. **Finca Rosa Blanca** in Heredia is an artistic hideaway with a drop-dead gorgeous tower suite. Similarly artistic, **Xandari**'s white villas rise amid a landscape of forest, waterfalls and coffee plantations in Alajuela. The most perfect climate in the world (along with an excellent gym and spa) draws guests to **Hotel Club Martino** in La Garita. **Casa Turire** near Turrialba is Costa Rica's loveliest country inn, with suites overlooking the Río Reventazón.

The tendency toward intimate elegance is reflected throughout the Pacific coast. Most guests arrive at **Punta Islita** on the Nicoya coast on private planes and hide away in luxurious suites far from reality. Guests at **Capitán Suizo** in Tamarindo are lulled to sleep by the sounds of crashing waves and chirping frogs. Those at **Sí Como No** in Manuel Antonio awaken to spider monkeys crashing through trees just off their balconies. Manuel Antonio's natural beauty has inspired many an architect, and the neighborhood is home to a series of exceptional inns. Lovers on holiday are enamored with the deluxe villas at **Makanda by the Sea**, but the ultimate lover's hideaway is located a few miles north near Jacó at **Villa Caletas**, an extraordinary cluster of villas surrounding an elegant mansion atop a cliff overlooking the Pacific.

The remote Península de Osa seems an unlikely setting for luxury. Yet it is home to **Lapa Ríos**, an extraordinarily civilized outpost boasting toucans on the decks of spacious bungalows, sloths in cecropia trees above the pool, and sublime fruit salads and fresh veggies under ceiling fans in the towering thatched restaurant. Those who traverse the rivers and ruts up the steep mountainside road/path to **Luna Lodge** find absolute privacy in handsome bungalows above the forest canopy.

EXCEPTIONAL RESTAURANTS

Until recently, fine dining in Costa Rica was an oxymoron, a foreign concept in the land of rice and beans. But the presence of an enormous expatriate community, along with an influx of European and North American chefs, has completely altered the restaurant scene. In fact, traditional Costa Rican dishes are practically nonexistent in popular tourist destinations, and pizza and pasta prevail everywhere. A distinct nouveau Costa Rican cuisine has yet to emerge, though imaginative Costa Rican and foreign chefs are beginning to combine techniques and ingredients with unusual results. The future is promising.

Many of the country's finest and most innovative restaurants are located in the smaller hotels. Nearly every establishment mentioned above has an exceptional restaurant. The **Grano de Oro**'s classy dining room and courtyard are almost always packed with locals and travelers — don't miss the creamy hot

cheese and hearts of palm appetizer, the filet mignon with gorgonzola, and the killer chocolate cake. **Chalet Tirol** and **Villa Caletas** both have excellent French restaurants.

San José and the Meseta Central have the most vibrant (and erratic) restaurant scenes. **Ambrosia** in the San Pedro barrio of San José stands out for its *corvina* (sea bass) preparations, soups, wholegrain breads and vegetarian selections. **Café Mundo** in Barrio Amón draws an eclectic, enthusiastic following with its gourmet pizzas, bountiful fresh salads and seafood pastas. **Machu Picchu**, a tiny neighborhood café, is the enduring favorite for Peruvian *ceviche* and *anticuchos* (beef hearts), though the upstart **La Palma** is providing some competition with its open-air balconies and gardens and Peruvian-style with seafood and beef.

European chefs have created a culinary enclave in Tamarindo on the Guanacaste coast, preparing tender veal and seafood pastas at **La Meridiana**, weiner schnitzel at **Stella's**, crêpes at **El Vaquero, and** beef with *roesti* at **Capitán Suizo**. Manuel Antonio has the greatest variety of restaurants outside San José and the Meseta Central. Thai curries and Hungarian goulash share the menu at **Plinio's**, and the setting in the ultra-private **Sunspot** at Makanda by the Sea is sure to inspire romance.

A muse floats above the windowside tables at the Café Ruiseñor at the Teatro Nacional.

Family Fun

Costa Rica is an ideal destination for children, and several tour companies offer family-oriented itineraries. Adventures are endless, and any imaginative child will feel like he or she has landed in *Jurassic Park*. Costa Rica inspired Michael Crichton to write his dinosaur-theme book and screenplay; some scenes in the movie were filmed at Isla del Coco and on Costa Rica's Pacific coast.

Even San José is a relatively kid-friendly city, though the noise, crowds and smog can rattle even the most intrepid child. The **Serpentarium** in San José offers a great introduction to poisonous snakes, scorpions, and other creepy creatures, and the city's **Museo del Niño** has interactive exhibits that allow visiting children to mingle with their *tico* counterparts. Try to visit San José's **Parque Zoológico Simón Bolívar** on a Sunday afternoon, when *tico* families fill the pathways and picnic areas.

Even kids who hate museums are delighted to explore the exhibits at **INBioparque** in Heredia. The educational center and museum focus on Costa Rica's biodiversity, and there are enough interactive computerized exhibits and preserved insects (or look for the octopus in a jar) to keep active imaginations stimulated.

Animal refuges give everybody a chance to get close to boas, sloths, toucans and even jaguars. **Zoo Ave** in La Garita (see page 87 in THE MESETA CENTRAL) has an impressive collection of tropical birds. **La Marina Zoo** in Ciudad Quesada cares for wounded and abandoned jaguars, eagles and toucans.

Depending on age and ability, kids have a great time on nature hikes; most guides will adjust the pace and difficulty to accommodate little legs. Children may get impatient waiting for the monkeys to show up, but a good guide will keep them fascinated by finding frogs, millipedes, spiders and leaf-cutter ants close to ground. The best place for kids to spot monkeys up close is in **Parque Nacional Manuel Antonio**, where the squirrel monkeys are so intrepid they might make a grab for your kids' lunches.

Forest canopy tours are the biggest attraction in Costa Rica at the moment, and daredevil teenagers are thrilled by the rush that comes from swooshing along a cable strung high in the treetops. Parents may feel justifiably anxious about this adventure, and should be selective when choosing a tour (see HANG OUT IN THE TREETOPS, page 20 in TOP SPOTS). I suggest you include a session at one of the **Original Canopy Tour** sites in your overall itinerary so the kids don't get antsy every time they see a canopy sign on the road. The little ones (who probably won't mind being excluded from this adventure) can experience the canopy by taking a ride on the **Rainforest Aerial Tram** in Braulio Carrillo or the **Skytrek** in Monteverde. Children must be seven years old to hike **Rain Maker** at Manuel Antonio — anyone over that age will be suitably challenged by long suspension bridges strung over rushing rivers.

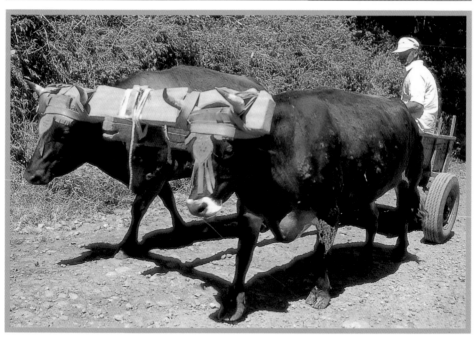

River rafting is another activity that might make parents a bit queasy; again, it all depends on where you choose to sink your paddle. All the rafting companies listed under SPORTING SPREE, above, have trips that involve low-key rapids or float trips than combine a bit of paddling with swimming under cool waterfalls. Pint-sized **surfers** can learn to hang ten in the waves off Jacó, Tamarindo and Manuel Antonio. Stronger teens can take windsurfing lessons at Laguna de Arenal. Most of the Pacific coast beach destinations (except those with just one or two romantic hotels) are excellent headquarters for extended vacations; Tamarindo and Manuel Antonio have the most diversions.

Certain hotels and lodges are particularly well suited to families. If you're looking for a laid-back beach vacation, consider **Capitán Suizo** in Tamarindo, **Costa Verde** (which has a separate pool and block of rooms for families) in Manuel Antonio, the **Flamingo Marina Resort** at Playa Flamingo, and the **Meliá Playa Conchal** at Playa Conchal. If you're looking for animals, birds, and natural adventures, the number-one family-friendly experience is the **Corcovado Lodge Tent Camp** on the Península de Osa, run by Costa Rica Expeditions, which offers several family itineraries in its repertoire. Kids of all ages can't help but enjoy camping on the sand beside the pounding surf and awakening to the sound of screeching scarlet macaws. The camp's canopy platform is the safest such experience I've encountered, and the rainforest reverberates with the sounds of monkeys crashing through the trees. Kids won't mind talking cold showers if they can watch baby spider monkeys from the outdoor bathrooms at **Tiskita Lodge** on Punta Banco.

The lodges in Tortuguero are also family friendly. Kids love hunting for bright green tree frogs in the palm trees around the pools at **Mawamba Lodge** and **Laguna Lodge**, or searching for howler monkeys in the trees behind **Tortuga Lodge**. If you visit Costa Rica during summer school vacations Tortuguero is a must-see on your itinerary, so the kids can watch sea turtles nest on the beach late at night.

There are major drawbacks to trying to see too much in one trip to Costa Rica. Children, and most adults, grow weary of riding in a Jeep over bumpy roads for hours on end to reach the next hotel on a crowded itinerary. If you're determined to pack all of Costa Rica's highlights into one trip, be sure to spend at least two nights at each destination. Plan some nighttime activities, since few lodges have televisions. **Arenal Volcano's** natural fireworks beat any sitcom your kids might be missing, and shooting stars are far more entrancing than boy bands on MTV.

Several tour companies offer special itineraries for families, particularly from June

OPPOSITE: The aerial tramway at Parque Nacional Braulio Carrillo gives day-trippers an overview of the rainforest. ABOVE: A team of oxen pulls a workaday *carreta*.

knives, vases are artfully displayed in minimalist exhibits that highlight the pieces' fragility. The **Museo de Oro** beneath the city's Plaza de la Cultura is the most modern cultural center, displaying shimmering gold treasures from the country's few archaeological sites. Gold figurines representing frogs, eagles and serpents are elegantly displayed in glass cases; other exhibits include necklaces and earrings worn by tribal leaders. Rotating art and photography exhibits fill the vast halls at the **Museo de Arte y Diseño** in the **Centro Nacional de la Cultura**, a rambling complex that once housed the National Liquor Factory. The **Museo de Arte Costarricense** is housed in San José's original airport terminal in Parque la Sábana, and offers the best overview of traditional murals, religious paintings and contemporary art.

San José's frothy **Teatro Nacional** is the country's most endearing architectural landmark and the home of the national symphony. The symphony season runs from April to November. The theater also hosts an international music festival in July, and a dance festival in December. I try to stop in for whatever performance is taking place when I'm in San José. A night at the theater sheds a whole different, classier, light on the city.

Small regional museums are beginning to appear throughout the countryside, though most are poorly staffed and have erratic hours. A must for history buffs is the **La Casona Hacienda** at Parque Nacional Santa Rosa in Guanacaste. The restored nineteenth-century hacienda houses a museum explaining Costa Rica's most important war, the battle against American intruder William Walker and his band of mercenaries. A monument behind the museum commemorates the battle against Walker and the skirmish against the Somoza regime from Nicaragua.

The most significant archeological site in the country is **Guayabo** near Turrialba in the Meseta Central. Sprawling *calzadas* (roads), well-engineered aqueducts, stone carvings and a few small structures are the visible remains of a city archeologists believe was begun around 1400 BC. Archeological buffs are pleased with the new museum and small archeological site at the **Centro Neotrópico SarapiquíS** in Sarapiquí, which will likely become an important educational center.

Travelers who visit Costa Rica in August may stumble upon an **international music festival** hosted by several small hotels. Performance have been held at Chalet Tirol in the Meseta Central, Villa Caletas near Jacó, and Villa Alegre in Tamarindo.

through August. *Tico* children are in school at the time (their holidays coincide with the coffee-picking season from October to February), and tours are geared toward foreign families. **Costa Rica Expeditions** offers considerable discounts for children sharing rooms with parents at this time; **Temptress Cruises** offers family-oriented trips (see TAKING A TOUR, page 46).

Parents: bring plenty of film and quick-dry shorts and socks, encourage both caution and curiosity, and carry sunscreen and insect repellent everywhere.

Cultural Kicks

Culture plays second fiddle to nature in Costa Rica, where the great outdoors is worshipped like some pantheistic god. In fact, recent letters in the local newspapers bemoaned the lack of enthusiastic support for the national symphony, and museums are treated as rainy day diversions in most tourist itineraries.

San José is certainly the cultural capital of the country, though it has no world-class museums, theaters or galleries. The **Museo Nacional** presents a good overview of Costa Rica's history and indigenous peoples, and should definitely top the first-time visitor's itinerary. The museum recently acquired the world's largest collection of American jade from the now defunct Marco Fidel Tristan Museo de Jade; the translucent pendants,

Shop till You Drop

Costa Rica is not a haven for folk art collectors, unless they zone in on the Guatemalan textiles sold in most souvenir shops. There is no strong artistic tradition here. Instead, hand-painted miniature *carretas* (oxcarts) are Costa Rica's souvenir cliché, followed by **mountain-grown coffee and tropical wood boxes**, **plates**, **bowls**, **picture frames and furniture**. Artists are reacting to the demand for high-quality pieces that evoke fond memories for travelers. The finer shops (many in hotels) are beginning to display paintings of typical village scenes and familiar landmarks. Birds, monkeys and frogs decorate everything from T-shirts to tin coffee mugs. Pads of paper made from banana fibers make nice small gifts.

San José has the best selection of shops and galleries, including Atmósfera and the art and wood sculpture galleries near Parque Morazán. Some of the best quality can be found at hotel gift shops: Annemarie's in the Hotel Don Carlos is a traditional favorite for bits of everything; the Grano de Oro displays unusual paintings, enamel ware, banana-paper stationery and a few masks; the Meliá Cariari has a modest array of sleek wooden boxes and puzzles by master craftsmen.

Sarchí in the Meseta Central is the crafts hub of the country, with rows of warehouse-sized shops selling miniature oxcarts, wood

and leather furniture, and all sorts of souvenirs. You can quickly slip into overload here and discover that everything looks alike. Bring along a gift list and pick up purple-heart wood bowls, plates and jewelry boxes. Some of these shops also stock purses and hats from Guatemala.

Woodcrafts in general are the best buy in Costa Rica. Artists including Barry Biesanz (who has a workshop in Escazú and a shop in San José) and Jay Morris have perfected woodcraft and turned it into an art form; their rounded, beveled and highly polished boxes are gorgeous. The hardwoods themselves are so lovely that some shops sell charts of wood samples, with small, slick squares of rosewood, mahogany, teak, and purple-heart wood. Given the endangered status of many precious tropical forest trees, much of the woodcraft is done from trees felled by nature or wood salvaged from old buildings.

Regional crafts and traditional folk arts are also gaining attention. The Chorotega peoples of the Guanacaste region produce terracotta pottery with fascinating animal and human motifs. The water jars, pots and figurines are fired in outdoor ovens and burnished with river stones which give a gleam unlike any glazed finish. Guaitíl, a

OPPOSITE: A monument marks a battleground at Parque Nacional Santa Rosa. ABOVE: *Carretas*, oxcarts, are displayed in parades and exhibitions in provinces throughout the country.

small village near Santa Cruz on the Península de Nicoya, is the center for this pottery. You'll see stands set up along the highway between Santa Cruz and Liberia, where hammocks hang in front of the pottery displays. The Boruca peoples of the Zona Sur make fanciful and sometimes frightening balsa-wood masks, which are used during the Fiesta de los Diablitos in December. They are also noted weavers, creating textiles from cotton dyed with plants, mud and mollusk shells. Their work can be found at Drake Bay Wilderness Camp, Tiskita and the Mirador Vista del Valle restaurant near San Isidro. Caribbean Bribrí and Kéköldi groups weave baskets and mats from natural fibers; women from the groups visit Cahuita and Puerto Viejo to sell their wares at local shops and street stands.

Savvy shoppers keep an eye out for exceptional folk art collections displayed in various lodges and restaurants. Among the best are those at Toad Hall by Laguna de Arenal, Casem Gallery in Monteverde, and Buena Nota in Manuel Antonio.

Jewelers are using gold to create reproductions of pre-Columbian **jewelry** and **figurines** reminiscent of the gold designs found in Oaxaca, Mexico. Some shops are importing high-quality silver jewelry from Mexico and Guatemala; some even have pieces from Bali. In fact, Balinese items are showing up all over the place as they are in gift shops around the world.

Food items fulfill the need for souvenirs nicely. Most travelers stuff a few bags of coffee into their suitcases, giving their clothes an unusual scent. Café Britt is the leading purveyor of souvenir coffee; their distinctive shiny green and red bags appear and shelves everywhere. Anyone who has sipped a chilled mocha at Café Milagro in Manuel Antonio is quickly addicted to these gourmet beans. Several small shops in Monteverde sell beans grown in the cloud forest. I used to carry a few bottles of Lizano sauce onboard after every trip, until I found a shop that imports the tangy salsa near home. Salsas made from mango and papaya juice are also tasty, and the bottles usually have imaginative labeling.

Short Breaks

San José and the Meseta Central are perfect bases for short trips to several of Costa Rica's biggest attractions. Tour companies in the city list enough day-trip options to keep you busy for a week or more, combining the Britt Coffee Tour with the Butterfly Farm in Guácima, or Volcán Poás with Sarchí.

You can adjust these jaunts to suit your interests by using a little imagination. If rafting is your thing, head for Turrialba, the site of Costa Rica's newest water attraction, Lake Angostura. You can shoot the rapids on the Pacuare or Reventazón, then have lunch by the lake. Or head over to Laguna de

Arenal for windsurfing followed by Volcán Arenal's fireworks at night. Garden enthusiasts should definitely see the heliconias and orchids at La Paz Waterfall near Volcán Poás and Jardín Botánico Lankaster near Volcán Irazú. The eerie lack of flora at the volcanoes creates a greater appreciation for the flowers.

For a complete change of scenery, join a full-day excursion on the Calypso catamaran to Isla de Tortuga in the Golfo de Nicoya. The road to the coast passes through fruit orchards and vegetable farms atop hills with views to the sea. Once you reach the 30-m (100-ft) *Manta Raya*, specially designed for these tours, cares drift away in the breeze. The boat passes by several islands on its short trip to the white sand, crystal blue water and sky-high palms of Tortuga. A hot lunch with white wine enhances the mellow mood, and coffee is served after the boat lands in Puntarenas at the end of the day.

San José and the Meseta Central are both excellent bases for touring the rest of the country on weekend or holiday excursions. Regional airlines have flights to the most popular areas at least once daily. Costa Rica Expeditions offers a tour that flies you to Tortuguero and back in one day. **Pitts Aviation** (296-3600 FAX 296-1429 (which handles the flights for the Tortuguero expedition) offers a Rain Dance Sky Tour that's the ultimate day trip, accompanied by a bit of Beethoven.

A couple of nights in a new place certainly helps to shift your consciousness. If you have just a small bit of time, it helps to make the contrast so extreme you completely forget about everyday responsibilities. If money's no problem, catch a plane to Puerto Jiménez and stay at one of the wilderness outposts near Parque Nacional Corcovado. Tortuguero is also good for instant immersion. Begin with the drive through the moist envelope of green surrounding the Braulio Carrillo Highway, then take a boat through dark, steamy canals to a riverside lodge. By nightfall you'll be surrounded by chirping tree frogs.

The beach resorts are the best choice if you have just two or three days and prefer a more civilized escape. For an idyllic, secluded romantic holiday, head to Villa Caletas near Jacó and spend one morning hiking at Carara. Or go for complete isolation at Punta Islita on the Península de Nicoya. Manuel Antonio and Tamarindo have the greatest variety of international restaurants, hotels, and residents if you need a bit of human stimulation with your monkey sightings.

Festive Flings

Costa Rica is not known for its elaborate processions and parades marking saints' days or political holidays. Instead, sports and nature are celebrated with near religious fervor. The country rollicks with riotous celebrations during the World Cup soccer games, and Sunday afternoons are devoted to *fútbol* in every hamlet in the land. In fact, one of the best ways I've found to feel like I'm part of a town is to follow the crowd to the field. The manicured green rectangles take the place of central plazas in the social scene. Boys cluster at one end of the field with their bikes and balls. Girls huddle nearby. Grandparents supervise toddlers, neighbors catch up on their gossip, and everyone cheers a goal.

Horseback riding is a part of most celebrations in Guanacaste, one of the largest provinces in the land. *Guanacastecos* who reside in the vast dry forest regions of northwest Costa Rica are typically ranchers and cowboys (*sabaneros*) who work vast herds of cattle from their mounts. *Sabaneros* are part of every celebration in Guanacaste, as are folkloric dances, regional songs, bloodless bullfights and rodeos. The musical instruments and dances of the region's

OPPOSITE: Local artists incorporate jungle themes in their work. RIGHT: An Easter procession leads to more boisterous celebrations in Nicoya.

Chorotega indigenous groups are giving way to more Spanish-oriented guitars and swirling flourishes. The entire country celebrates the **Annexation of Guanacaste** on July 25. The biggest province won independence from Nicaragua in 1824; its leaders choose to become a part of Costa Rica instead. Guanacaste played an important role in Costa Rica's history, and is the site of the country's only skirmish with armed battle. It also has a strong regional identity. July 25 is celebrated with proud intensity in Liberia.

Around January 15, the indigenous Chorotegas of Santa Cruz on the Península de Nicoya celebrate the **Fiesta de Cristo Negro de Esquipulas** honoring a statue of Christ that is considered to hold miraculous powers.

Even those who shun Limón the rest of the year can't resist **Carnaval**, which takes place (strangely enough) in mid-October. Scheduled around the October 12 national holiday of Día de las Culturas, celebrating the country's cultures and Columbus Day, Carnaval attracts some 200,000 people to the port city. This week-long debacle shuts down businesses and all civic functions and brings everyone into the street, dressed in spangles, glitter, beads and glow-in-the-dark colors. The festivities culminate in an hours-long riotous parade. Gorgeous teenage girls in ruffled yellow miniskirts and skimpy tops carry giant plastic bananas with the Chiquita label. Men glistening with sweat wear ruffles as well, on their pants, on their shirt sleeves, even crowning their heads. The music is downright cacophonous with an underlying steel-drum beat luring everyone to shimmy, shake, shuffle and swing. Calypso, reggae, rap, merengue, cumbia — all forms of tropical music fill the air for the entire week, when sleep is abandoned for revelry. Hotels are booked months in advance, and buses are added to carry passengers from the interior to the coast.

Puntarenas also celebrates Carnaval; it's usually scheduled in November while the schoolchildren are on holiday. The port town's largest celebration takes place on July 16 to celebrate the **Fiesta de la Virgen del Mar** (Feast of the Virgin of the Sea), the patron saint of Puntarenas.

Though Costa Ricans are not, as a rule, fervently religious, they make great use of Catholic holidays and saint's feast days for celebrations. **Christmas**, the highlight of the year, starts early. Decorations fill San José's shops by early November, while ornament and gift salesmen trod door to door in rural areas with their glittering temptations. December 15 marks the beginning of **Las Posadas**, recreating the search for a birthplace

for the Baby Jesus. Candlelit processions, fireworks and partying surround the Christmas season, which culminates in San José's Festival of Lights parade and an enormous regional fair in the suburban town of Zapote the week after Christmas. A big bash and dance take place in the Parque Central on **New Year's Day**.

In February, the Boruca Indians of the Buenos Aires region in the Zona Sur don garish devil masks for the **Fiesta de los Diablitos**, which commemorates the Spanish conquest of central America. **Ash Wednesday** and **Semana Santa** (the week before Easter) are celebrated throughout the country, though in many cases religion plays a minor role. Instead, *ticos* celebrate Easter as the first major holiday of the year and flock to vacation homes at the beach. Religious processions do take place in some towns. The most important religious event of the year is the **Fiesta de la Virgen de los Angeles** at the basilica in Cartago on August 2. Pilgrims arrive from throughout the country, walking on their knees down the long cement plaza in front of the church to honor the country's patron saint.

In the Meseta Central, **Día del Boyero** (Oxcart Drivers' Day) is celebrated on the second Sunday of March in Escazú, where the streets are filled with brightly painted carts with designs representing the various provinces of the country. **Día de la Independencia** on September 15 is the most important national holiday, with **Día de los Trabajadores** (Labor Day) on May 1 running a close second. There are 17 official holidays, or *días feriados* in Costa Rica when banks, shops and businesses shut down and everyone takes to the countryside or beach. **Juan Santamaría**, Costa Rica's national hero, is honored with a parade in Alajuela on April 11.

Galloping Gourmet

Costa Rica is not known for brilliant cuisine; it takes some time to get acquainted with the most flavorful selections and find the best cooks. *Gallo pinto* (black beans and rice) is the ubiquitous national dish, served with eggs or cheese at breakfast. The next step up is the one-dish mix of beans, rice and meat, fish or vegetables called *el casado* (the married one). Tropical fruits abound, and restaurants are serving more export-quality seafood and beef. Seasonings are used sparsely; you won't find fiery hot *jalapeño* or *habanero* chilies here. Instead, the daily diet is rather bland — and healthy, except for the fondness for frying nearly everything. One of the most popular herbs is *culantro*, which is the same as the cilantro used in Mexico and Thailand.

APPETIZERS OR *BOCAS*
Some of the best treats are the snacks and side dishes served in neighborhood restaurants and bars. *Patacones*, refried plantain patties, are great when cooked fresh, salted and topped with sour cream, which also garnishes corn pancakes called *chorreadas*. Deep-fried pork skins, or *chicharrones*, inspire thirst (and raise cholesterol), as do salty banana chips. Sandwiches are called *arreglados; empanadas*, turnovers filled with beans, potatoes, cheese or meat are a better choice.

VEGETABLES
Fresh, crisp salads and vegetables have finally earned their rightful place on tables throughout Costa Rica. Most hotels, lodges, and tourist-oriented restaurants offer several salads on their menus, though typical *tico* sodas still rely on shredded cabbage and pale tomatoes for salads served with *casados*. The ubiquitous *platoons* (plantains), related to the banana, are actually a vegetable but they become sweet as they ripen and cook. Chayote, another fruit, is also often served as a vegetable, as is cassava root, called yucca.

Salads are often garnished with *palmitos* or hearts of palm, each of which comes from the trunk of a small tree. *Palmitos* are peeled and cooked, then served chilled. Try a salad of sliced avocado and *palmitos* — you'll most likely order it again and again. Canned and bottled *palmitos* make good souvenirs.

Don't get excited if you see pasta primavera or steamed veggies on a soda menu — they're usually made with carrots, cabbage and perhaps a bit of cauliflower. Some restaurants have their own vegetable and herb gardens or buy from small organic farms — if you find such a place eat all you can handle.

SEAFOOD
Though Costa Rica has two coasts, seafood is surprisingly scarce and often unimaginatively prepared. Highland restaurants tend to favor *corvina* (sea bass) served with *casados*. Far better is *ceviche*, fresh fish marinated with lime juice and spices. Since the fish is essentially raw, be careful where you eat it — stick to places on the coast or exceptional San José restaurants. Sport fishing is big on the Pacific coast; if you're staying in a fishing lodge you're sure to sample dorado, wahoo, marlin and the occasional swordfish. Whole fried fish is common on both coasts. Shrimp and lobster are available but cost dearly — most are exported.

MEAT
Much of Costa Rica's rainforest was destroyed for cattle grazing in the early 1900s, and Costa Rican beef is excellent if you can get the export-quality cuts served in more expensive hotels and restaurants. Here you'll find thick, tender fillets cooked to order. In Costa Rica, meat ordered *rojo,* or rare, is barely cooked; though I prefer rare meat, I usually order mine *medio* (medium) and get what I want. The beef served in *sodas* is usually tough, thin and not worth eating. My favorite beef dish is *bisteck* or *lomito encebollado*, a tender beefsteak marinated with Lizano sauce (see SAUCES, below) and grilled or sautéed with sliced onions.

In Costa Rican homes and typical restaurants, meat is usually used as an ingredient in stews, including the satisfying *olla de carne* (simmered beef and vegetables) and *chiprio*, a mix of *chicharrones*, onions and beans.

Chicken roasted over a wood fire (*pollo de la leña) is* fragrant and filled with juices; *arroz con pollo* is a filling mix of rice, carrots, celery, onion and chicken slivers.

SAUCES
The key to typical daily Costa Rican dishes is Lizano sauce, a bottled marinade of spices and vegetables. Ask for it as you would salsa or soy sauce and sprinkle it liberally on nearly everything. Pepper sauce is also common; for a spicy kick ask for *chilero,* a marinade of onions, peppers and vinegar. There are also some wonderful bottled sauces made from papaya, mango and lime, though most restaurants shun them. The tomato, onion and chili salsa common in other Latin American countries is nonexistent here, except in Mexican restaurants.

Pineapple plantations are common in the warm, dry Guanacaste climate.

The local ice creams are exceptional, especially those made with tropical fruits. Don't miss the *guanábana, coco,* or *mango* blends.

FRUITS

Tropical fruits are varied, abundant and delicious: pineapple, watermelon, bananas and papayas frequently appear on *platos de frutas* (fresh fruit plates), which you can order any time of day. Costa Ricans mark the seasons by what's ripe at the time — mangoes in March, *jocotes* (also called mombins or hogfruit) in September, apples imported from Washington State at Christmas. Fruits are used in *frescas and batidos,* fruit drinks with water and sugar, ice creams, and sauces for fish and meat.

BEER, WINE AND LIQUOR

Imperial and Bavaria beer (*cerveza*) seem to be the national drinks, though more hardcore imbibers prefer *guaro,* the local firewater made from fermented sugarcane. Café Rica, a coffee liqueur similar to Kahlua is served alone or with milk. Local wines are to be avoided; stick with the more inspired Chilean and Argentinian wines.

JUICES AND DRINKS

Costa Rica's abundant tropical fruits make extraordinary fresh juices. Try guava, mora or pineapple, or ask to have a tropical flavor blended with fresh orange juice. *Refrescos, or* simply *frescos,* are made of fruit blended with water or milk — nothing tastes better after a hot hike. Carbonated sodas are called *gaseosas.*

COFFEE

The *grano de oro,* coffee, is Costa Rica's great pride and a major export crop. Few travelers leave the country without several kilos packed in their bags. The coffee served in hotels and restaurants may not be the best, however. Export coffee fetches a much higher price than that made from rejected beans. *Café con leche* is served with hot milk; ask for *sin leche or negro* if you want it black. Some places serve coffee ground with sugar; when purchasing bags to take home make sure they don't say *con azúcar* unless you like sweet coffee.

Café Britt is the leading label and has become so synonymous with vacationing shoppers that the company even runs daily tours of its plantations and processing plants. Café Britt coffeehouses are springing up around San José and serve cappuccino, espresso and flavored coffee. Though I typically carry a few bags of Britt home (it's the only good decaffeinated brand), I like to experiment with the numerous labels now

RICE AND BREAD

Rice is to Costa Rica what pasta is to Italy — an absolute essential for any meal and the base for regional dishes. Most menus list rice with chicken, palm hearts, pork or fish, called *arroz con pollo, arroz con palmito, arroz con cancho or arroz con pescado.* Beans are usually served on the side rather than blended with the rice mix as they would be in *gallo pinto.* Rice is also used in *arroz con piña,* a refreshing drink of blended rice and pineapple.

Tortillas are not the staple item you might expect, but small corn tortillas are served with some dishes. Sliced white bread is used for sandwiches and toast; cross your fingers when you ask for *pan integral* if you want whole wheat.

CHEESES

With so much cattle grazing about the countryside, it's no surprise that Costa Rica has great cheese. Many of the best cheddars and *queso blanco,* a low-fat white cheese with the consistency of tofu, come from the Monteverde Quakers and the Italian communities in San Vito. *Natilla* is sour cream of a thin consistency.

DESSERTS, SWEETS AND PASTRIES

Costa Ricans love their sweets, and every town has at least one *panaderia* or bakery selling cookies, Danish-like sweet rolls (called *pan dulce*) and fancy cakes (called *queques*). *Tres leches,* or three-milk cake, *is* rich, moist and sweet. Though coconut is the typical ingredient in *flans* (custards), some places also serve wonderful *flans* made with mangoes, papaya or blackberries.

Candies shaped like Christmas trees, hearts, dolls and animals are made of *cajeta,* a sticky sweet paste of condensed milk and sugar. Nougat bars with almonds or macadamias are great treats and travel well.

appearing on grocery store shelves. Sunburst, though far more expensive than the others, is truly wonderful; Café Zeus, one of the least expensive, is among my favorites and comes in small bags that make great gifts.

Special Interests

Travelers typically have some form of education on their minds when visiting Costa Rica. Birders are intent on expanding their life lists, and surfers count on mastering a north break. Botanists go wild over rare orchids, biologists over butterflies. At least one-quarter of Costa Rica's guests attend universities or language schools. There is no shortage of special interests to pursue.

LANGUAGE CLASSES
Spanish language schools abound in San José and around the country, especially at Monteverde, the cultural center of the northwest. The quality of education varies; it helps to talk with other students before committing to a course. Most offer the opportunity for students to live with Costa Rican families for full immersion, and most tailor their classes to your level of ability.

Academia Tica (229-0013 FAX 292-7136 E-MAIL toyopan@intercentro.net, Apdo 1294, Guadalupe, San José 2100, offers language and culture courses that can be extended indefinitely, and is popular with German-speaking visitors.

Central American Institute for International Affairs (233-8571 FAX 221-5238 E-MAIL icai@expreso.co.cr WEB SITE www.educaturs.com, % Educators, Apdo 10302, San José 1000, mixes culture, including dance lessons, with language study. Dance and cooking classes are interspersed with language study at the **Costa Rican Language Academy and Latin Dance School** (233-8938 TOLL-FREE IN THE US (800) 854-6057 FAX 233-8670 E-MAIL criang@solracsa.co.cr, Apdo 3362070, San José 2070, Avenida Central between Calles 25 and 27.

Centro Panamericano de Idiomas (265-6866 IN THE US (409) 693-8950 TOLL-FREE (800) 347-8087 FAX 265-6213 E-MAIL cpi@huracan.cr, Apdo 161, San Joaquin de Flores, Heredia 3007, has group and private classes and a one-day "survival course" for tourists at schools in Heredia and Monteverde.

If you want to enjoy the beach while pursuing your studies, consider signing up for classes at **La Escuela de Idiomas D'Amore** (777-1143 E-MAIL damore@racsa.co.cr WEB SITE www.escualadamore.com, in Manuel Antonio.

BIRDING
Scarlet macaws, quetzals, trogons and toucans lure bird watchers to Costa Rica's rainforests and isolated beaches. At least 850 species of birds have been spotted within the country's borders, and birders gripping their life lists and binoculars are common sights on most hikes. Serious bird watchers are best off having a tour company prepare an individual itinerary with a driver and a specialist guide through Horizontes, Costa Rica Expeditions, or Costa Rica Sun Tours (see GETTING TO COSTA RICA, page 236 in TRAVELERS' TIPS for details on tour operators and travel agencies). Birding is included on most nature tours, but not all address the subject with a high level of expertise. Ask in advance about the availability of specialist guides when signing up for a tour. There is usually a birding guide on board the *Temptress* cruise ship, and lodges in prime birding spots such as Monteverde, Cerro de la Muerte and the Parque Nacional Corcovado can arrange guided hikes. **Field Guides** ((512) 327-4953 TOLL-FREE (800) 728-4953 E-MAIL fgileader@aol.com, PO Box 160723, Austin, Texas 78716, offers bird-watching tours in both popular and remote areas of the country.

BUTTERFLIES
The dazzling blue morpho is but one of about 3,000 species of butterflies found in Costa Rica. Net-covered butterfly gardens and farms filled with flowering tropical plants are beginning to appear alongside hotels and parks throughout the country. The best gardens include educational displays on the emergence of butterflies from their larvae and chrysalis, and plenty of varieties of fluttering adults. Several Jardines de Mariposas (butterfly gardens) are located close enough to San José to be included on day trips; check out the **Spirogyra** butterfly farm near the Villa Tournon Hotel or the **Butterfly Farm** in La Guácima de Alajuela. The netted enclosure at **La Paz Waterfall Gardens** near Volcán Poás is said to be the largest in the country. Among the best butterfly exhibits in outlying areas are **Selva Verde and La Quinta de Sarapiquí** in the Sarapiquí region, the **Butterfly Garden** in Monteverde and the garden at **Villa Lapas** near Jacó on the Pacific coast.

MOTORCYCLING
Diehard bikers eye Costa Rica's roads longingly, imagining the thrills involved in guiding a motorcycle along tortuous paths. **Rent-a-Harley** (289-5552 FAX 289-5551,

Colorful and friendly toucans appear in the most unlikely spots — such as right outside your shower.

Centro Comercial Trejos Montealegre in Escazú, offers motorcycle rentals and guided Harley tours to outlying areas.

GARDEN VISITS

Orchids, heliconia, bromeliads and an abundance of tropical plants thrive in Costa Rica's climate. The most famous of all the nation's gardens is the **Wilson Botanical Gardens** at the **Las Cruces Biological Station** south of San Vito (see SAN VITO, page 199 in THE ZONA SUR). The 10-ha (25-acre) gardens were created by Robert and Catherine Wilson with the help of Brazilian landscape designer Roberto Burle-Marx. Over 7,000 species of tropical plants, including 700 species of palms, attract hummingbirds, tanagers, toucans, trogons and a bounty of butterflies. **Jardín Botánico Lankaster** near San José has 10.5 ha (26 acres) of landscaped gardens including a miniature bamboo forest, a cactus and succulent garden, several palm groves and vivid clusters of heliconia. Over 800 species of orchids are showcased in greenhouses and along paths through the gardens; the best time to see them in bloom is from February to May. Many of the hotels, lodges, restaurants and private reserves throughout the country are landscaped with impressive gardens. Of particular interest are the acres of tropical fruit tree orchards at **Tiskita Lodge** in the Zona Sur: the heliconia collections at **Tortuga Lodge** and **Laguna Lodge** in Tortuguero; orchids at **Casa Orquideas** near Golfito; and the medicinal plants at **Centro Neotrópico de SarapiquíS**. Plant lovers won't want to miss the fanciful topiaries in **Zarcero and** the overview of the forest canopy from the **Teleférico del Bosque Lluvioso** (Rainforest Aerial Tram).

VOLUNTEERING

Nearly every worldwide conservation agency is active in Costa Rica. Many rely on volunteers to keep projects running. Some count migrating sea turtles in Tortuguero; others keep an eye on scarlet macaws above the Península de Osa. Students from all over the world pursue volunteering opportunities in marine biology, botany and dozens of fields related to nature. Many programs are affiliated with colleges and universities. Agencies that work with volunteers include:

The **Organization for Tropical Studies** (OTS) (240-6696 FAX 240-6783 IN THE US (919) 684-5774 FAX (919) 684-5661 E-MAIL cro@ots.ac.cr WEB SITE www.ots.ac.cr, Apdo 676-2050, San Pedro, San José 2050, is a nonprofit consortium of more than 50 universities and research institutes. OTS oversees three prime biological stations

with research facilities: La Selva in the Sarapiquí region; Palo Verde in Guanacaste; and Las Cruces, which includes the Wilson Botanical Gardens, in the Zona Sur.

The **Caribbean Conservation Corporation** (CCC) ((352) 373-6441 TOLL-FREE (800) 678-7853 E-MAIL ccc@cccturtle.org WEB SITE www .cccturtle.org, PO Box 2866, Gainesville, Florida 32602, enlists paying volunteers, students and researchers to assist with conservation efforts, such as tagging sea turtles.

Earthwatch TOLL-FREE (800) 776-0188 FAX (978) 461-2332 E-MAIL info@earthwatch.org, WEB SITE www.earthwatch.org has several ongoing projects in the country.

Taking a Tour

Guided tours abound, and there are several excellent international and Costa Rican companies covering a broad variety interests. The majority of companies have set itineraries that run the full gamut of activities; most will also arrange independent trips. See also GETTING TO COSTA RICA, page 236 in TRAVELERS' TIPS for a list of tour operators and travel agencies specializing in Costa Rica.

NATURE & ADVENTURE

Total immersion in the natural habitats, wildlife and topography of Costa Rica is available on specially designed tours that incorporate visits to several nature reserves, volcanoes, rivers and beaches. Most include opportunities for rafting, climbing, and other adventures. If you wish to arrange your vacation around a particular sport or nature activity, see SPORTING SPREE and SPECIAL INTERESTS, above.

Several companies offer enough options to satisfy most interests. Safety is the paramount concern of the agents at **Costa Rica Expeditions** (257-0766 or 222-0333 FAX 257-1665 WEB SITE www.costaricaexeditions.com. Their adventure itineraries highlight climbing at Mount Chirripó, bird watching from a canopy platform at Corcovado, and whitewater rafting on the Pacuare. The company has excellent naturalist guides on staff and will shape an itinerary to fit your needs. **Costa Rica Connection** ((805) 543-8823 TOLL-FREE (800) 345-7422 FAX (805) 543-3626 WEB SITE www.crconnect.com in the United States and its counterpart in Costa Rica **Costa Rica Sun Tours** (296-7757 FAX 296-4307 WEB SITE www.crsuntours.com represent excellent nature lodges in Arenal and the Zona Sur. They have a wide range of tours with a *tico* slant. Known for its superb multilingual

guides and individualized itineraries,
Horizontes Nature Adventures (222-2022
FAX 255-4513 E-MAIL horizont@sol.racsa.co.cr
WEB SITE www.horizontes.com, is at Apdo
1780-1002, San José, Paseo Colón 150.
Grupo Mawamba (223-2421 FAX 222-5463
E-MAIL mawamba@racsa.co.cr WEB SITE
www.grupomawamba.com operates nature
lodges in Tortuguero and San Gerardo de
Dota and works with well-trained
knowledgeable guides.

Camino Travel (257-0107 or 234-2530
FAX 257-0243, Calle 1 at Avenida Central, is
conveniently located in downtown San José;
its agents are quite adept at arranging on-the-
spot itineraries for any budget, and they
work well with undecided travelers. Your
options are greater if you contact them well
in advance.

Rafting, biking, and yoga retreats are all
handled by **Remarkable Journeys** ((713) 721-
2517 TOLL-FREE (800) 856-1993 FAX (713) 728-
8334 E-MAIL cooltrips@remjourneys.com WEB
SITE www.remjourneys.com, PO Box 31855,
Houston, Texas 77231. **Wilderness Travel**
((510) 558-2488 TOLL-FREE (800) 368-2794
WEB SITE www.wildernesstravel.com, also in
the United States, has long been one of my
favorite adventure companies; they always
find something new to check out.

INDEPENDENT TRAVEL

Many visitors to Costa Rica, especially those
on their second or third trip, prefer to rent a
car and follow their interests. With the help
of the Internet, these independent travelers
have seemingly unlimited choices. Arranging
such an expedition can be time consuming
and costly, however, and it often pays to
work with an agency adept at juggling all
the details. Using an agency also gives you
some reassurance as to the quality and
safety of your chosen adventures. All the
agencies listed above can arrange
independent itineraries.

BUDGET TRAVEL

Ecole Travel (223-2240 FAX 392-7275 E-MAIL
ecolecr@racsa.co.cr WEB SITE www.travel
costarica.net, Calle 7 between Avenidas
Central and 1, inside 7th Street Books, is
a good source for the budget traveler.
Otec International (256-0633 FAX 257-7849
E-MAIL otec@gotec.com WEB SITE www.gotec
.sol.racsa.com, 275 m (300 yards) north of
the Teatro Nacional, San José, specializes in
student and budget travel and uses a travel
voucher system to allow its clients to pick
and choose their transportation and
accommodations.

CRUISES

Several major cruise lines include Costa Rica in
their ports of call on Panama Canal itineraries,
but passengers see little of the country. More
satisfying are the week-long cruises to national
parks along the Pacific on the *Temptress*
((954) 983-2989 TOLL-FREE ((800) 336-8423
FAX (954) 983-0646 WEB SITE www.temptress
cruises.com. **Lindblad Expeditions** ((212) 765-
7740 TOLL-FREE IN THE US (800) 397-3348 FAX (212)
265-3770 E-MAIL travel@expeditions.com WEB
SITE www.expeditions.com uses the *Temptress*
vessels for its winter Pacific Coast cruises.
Another American company, **Windstar** TOLL-
FREE (800) 258-7245 WEB SITE www.windstar
cruises.com offers upscale nature-oriented
cruises of the Pacific coast of Costa Rica and
Nicaragua. **Clipper Cruises** ((314) 727-2929
TOLL-FREE (800) 325-0010 FAX (314) 727-6576
WEB SITE www.clippercruise.com begins its
Panama Canal cruise with three stops in
Costa Rica.

An enduringly popular day trip from
San José is a cruise on the *Calypso* (256-2727
FAX 256-6767 WEB SITE www.calypsotours.com
to Tortuga Island in the Golfo de Nicoya.
The trip includes transportation to and from
Puntarenas and a cruise past isolated islands
and beaches with time for feasting, drinking,
sunbathing and swimming.

WOMEN'S TRIPS

Mariah Wilderness Expeditions ((510) 233-
2303 TOLL-FREE (800) 462-7424 FAX (510) 233-
0956 WEB SITE www.mariahwe.com arranges
women-only rafting, cruising, and
adventure trips.

Cowboys herd cattle, compete in rodeos and follow
a lifestyle pioneered by European settlers and
indigenous peoples in the Guanacaste range lands.

Welcome to Costa Rica

OVERWHELMINGLY GREEN AND MOIST, smelling of river mud and the salty sea, Costa Rica is Earth's national park. Cupping the Mar Caribe, the skinny country curves snake-like from Lago Nicaragua to the Isthmus of Panama in the tropical belt. Nearly impassable mountains, *cordilleras*, bisect rainforests, cloud forests, lowland forests and savannas, trapping valleys and settlements against Pacific and Caribbean coasts. Mammals, birds, reptiles and insects fare far better than humans in this country, which is comparable in size to Nova Scotia, Holland or West Virginia. Passion flowers twine, orchids flourish between ajillo trees, ferns wave beside sky-high cecropia hiding monkeys and sloths.

Nearly one third of Costa Rica's land mass is protected by international, national or private preserves. Environmental organizations from the Nature Conservancy to the World Wildlife Fund have stakes in the land and sea. I sometimes envision howler monkeys, jaguars, quetzals and whale sharks swarming across invisible borders to this gentler wilderness.

Costa Rican poet Yolanda Oreamundi describes her homeland in El Espíritu de Mi Tierra:

"I have seen sunny afternoons on the high plains of my land.

"But if I had seen only trees moored eternally by their umbilical cord to the land's womb, if I had seen only carts writing songs on the road, if I had seen only roofs of the little houses and the campesinos in their Sunday best wandering idly in the ditches along the road, I would not have seen the meaning of my land.

"If I had seen only that, I would have seen nothing."

Perhaps what Oreamundi was getting at is the country's *costarricense*, which makes it such an unusual presence in Central America. Costa Rica sits below Guatemala, Honduras, Belize, El Salvador and Nicaragua, and above Panama and the Colombian coast of South America. Surrounded by revolutions, spies, internal intervention and human cruelties, the country of some three million residents has been internally peaceful since 1949. Costa Ricans call themselves *ticos*, a diminutive endearment that camouflages their power. The *costarricense* approach to conflict is based on negotiation and a certain finesse in conversation. Ex-president Oscar Arias used his native skill with utmost advantage to win the Nobel Peace Prize in 1987 when he brokered a signed accord between the chaotic governments of Central America.

Nature conspires to protect Costa Rica from outside intervention. *Ticos* tend toward isolationism and fierce national pride. Mountains, rivers, volcanoes, and endless forests separate communities within the country as well, and regional blood runs strong. *Ticos* can typically identify the

region other Costa Ricans are from, and are intensely proud of the cities, villages and provinces of their youth. Guanacaste residents boast of broad savannas, cattle ranges, skillful *sabaneros*, and a pioneer spirit. *Alajueans* are proud to have raised the country's only national military hero. Flags hanging outside rural homes support provincial soccer teams, and *boyeros* (oxcart drivers) claim that the wheels of a cart sing differently in Heredia than they do in Escazú.

In a prescient and practical approach to husbanding natural resources, Costa Rican governments have long protected critical watersheds in the mountains, creating informal refuges for hawks, marguays, anteaters and sloths. The

official national park movement began in the 1960s, and by the mid-1980s foreigners were trampling through rainforests and forcing wildlife to respond to human intrusion. In only three decades Costa Rica has created at least 15 national parks and a dozen natural reserves supervised by the national government. Countless other private reserves, ranches, farms and indigenous settlements protect lands around the parks, creating corridors of forest canopy.

Visitors tend to get caught up in the environmental spirit when hiking across rivers, up volcanoes, and deep in primary rainforest — an ever-shrinking resource. Like most *ticos* and many travelers, I think of Costa Rica as a place to be protected and cherished as a living natural history exhibit to be explored for centuries. But all those who are attuned to the country's marvelous natural attributes sense damage in the air. Too many

PRECEEDING PAGES: Horseback riders LEFT have endless landscapes to explore, from the fires of Volcán Arenal to the coffee and sugarcane plantations of Turrialba and the beaches of Dominical. RIGHT *Cocos helados* (cold coconuts) provide refreshing sweet milk straight from the source. OPPOSITE: Manuel Antonio may be the most popular beach in Costa Rica, but you can still find solitary hideaways. ABOVE: Imperial beer and Derby cigarettes are staples in neighborhood bars from Nicoya to Tortuguero.

endangered animals must be rescued from poachers, loggers and car accidents. Too many raging rivers have been dammed for hydroelectric power. The latest environmental controversy involves oil, the bane of all Third World countries. A Louisiana-based company was awarded to the right to drill for oil in a vast region that spreads south of Tortuguero to the Panamanian border, including parts of several nature reserves in the Talamanca region. Drilling was halted in mid-2000, though not permanently. Environmental groups have been extremely vociferous in protesting this latest threat to their country's valuable natural resources; it remains to be seen if their protests will have any long-range effects.

of rainforest and jungle, adding to the protected land mass.

At the same time, foreign investors are eyeing the beaches of the Nicoya and Osa peninsulas and the central Pacific coast, envisioning marinas, golf courses and massive hotels. All indicators lean toward the need for these large developments to ensure Costa Rica's standing in the demanding tourism market. The coast's largest resorts have been hugely successful, while some small hotels are struggling to survive. Still, studies by the ICT (Costa Rican Tourism Institute) show that the majority of tourists are drawn to Costa Rica because of its rainforests, volcanoes, rivers and parks.

The country struggles with a major balancing act, weighing the short-term payoffs of tourism and industry against the long-term benefits of preservation. The whole world is cheering for nature to come out the winner. The World Bank and the United Nations have contributed large chunks of cash to establishing a Mesoamerican Biological Corridor, a swath of protected land from Mexico to Panama. Costa Rica is considered the leader in this movement, with the largest proportion of land devoted to reserves. Environmental groups from Austria, Canada and Wisconsin are buying up chunks

Today's tourists have the good fortune of seeing Costa Rica in its prime. The country's infrastructure, so maligned by First World developers, is perfectly adequate for the average traveler. Lodges and hotels offer the ideal mix of comfort and isolation, and tour operators are constantly finding new ways to keep their clients amused. Best of all, adventurers can still feel the thrill of discovery in untrammeled wilderness.

There are no guarantees that Costa Rica will remain one of the planet's most precious natural resources. When giant tour buses clog park entrances and spider monkeys swing by happy-hour haunts for treats, the country feels more like an amusement park than a natural sanctuary. Progress is inevitable. All one can hope is that it travels in accord with the natural realm. My best advice? Get there soon.

ABOVE LEFT: Bright awnings decorate jungle boats on the Río Tempisque in Palo Verde.
RIGHT: Chunks of hardened lava tumble down the sides of Volcán Arenal. OPPOSITE: A pleasure boat finds snug harbor along Playa Espadilla, Parque Nacional Manuel Antonio.

The Country and Its People

COSTA RICA IS CENTRAL AMERICA'S ANOMALY. It lacks the conflict, culture and controversy of Panama, Nicaragua, El Salvador or Guatemala, and seems most akin to former British Honduras (now called Belize) in terms of European influences. It's the third smallest nation in a cluster of countries as inter- and independent as Scandinavia or the British Isles, squeezed between the massive powers of North and South America.

PRE-COLUMBIAN YEARS

Unlike its neighbors north and south, Costa Rica lacks evidence of huge pre-Columbian cities or civilizations. Its earliest inhabitants appear to have lived in several isolated and distinct groups. Little is known about the residents of Guayabo, the country's largest archaeological site, near the modern city of Turrialba. The ancient city, with burial mounds, sophisticated irrigation systems, stone monoliths, petroglyphs, and cobblestone streets called *calzadas*, is believed to have been inhabited as early as 1000–1400 BC, and deserted by AD 1400. Archaeologists call the residents of this city — which at its height may have held about 500 people, with thousands living in the surrounding region — the Guayabo peoples, and have little knowledge of their daily lives or connection to the other early peoples of Costa Rica.

The Península de Nicoya on the Pacific coast is believed to have been a port of call for early marine traders, perhaps from Ecuador. They carried precious metals and stones, jewelry and pottery between Mexico and South America, and traded with the people of the Nicoya region who were known as the Chorotega, or "fleeing people." Perhaps the most advanced of the groups in this region, the Chorotega seem to have been influenced by the Olmec and other groups from the north and developed towns and agricultural systems. They produced highly detailed pottery, which today is still produced by their descendants in this region.

The names now used for the various groups spread sparsely throughout the country were created by the Spaniards, who used the region or name of the chief in power at the time to distinguish the groups. The Caribes, Bribrí and Kékóldi were located on the Caribbean, while the Borucas and Diquis were located in the southwest. They were all semi-nomadic hunters and fishermen who raised yucca, squash, *pejibaye* (bright orange palm fruits) and tubers.

Intricate jade and gold figurines and jewelry, along with painted pottery, indicating sophisticated artistry, have been found at several archaeological sites in the country. The jade, in particular, is puzzling, since it is not native to this region. The figurines may have been used for trading.

Gold, on the other hand, was mined in isolated regions of the country, and hundreds of pieces have been found and displayed at San José's Museo de Oro.

The most arresting archaeological presence is that of lithic spheres — huge, nearly perfectly round stone balls that weigh several tons. The spheres have been found in the south and northwest, often grouped in formations that appear to relate to the constellations. Whether the rocks were made by nature or man is still under dispute, but their perfection is indeed astounding.

THE CONQUEST

On September 8, 1502, Christopher Columbus arrived on the east coast of Costa Rica, anchoring between Isla Uvita and today's Puerto Limón. It was his fourth journey to the New World, and yet another attempt to find a passage to the Pacific Ocean. His vessels damaged by storms, Columbus held anchor in the area for 18 days, and was much impressed with the amount of gold worn by the people who met his ships. His soldiers made excursions into the country with the Indians and reported an abundance of wildlife, fertile countryside and more gold. He later named the place La Huerta, "the Garden." Columbus reported his findings, believing he had indeed found a treasure land that would greatly add to Spain's holdings in Nueva España.

In 1506, King Ferdinand of Spain dispatched Governor Diego de Nicuesa and a group of settlers to establish a colony in La Huerta. The group ran aground in Panama, and were nearly decimated by tropical diseases, Indian resistance and lack of food on their trek north into Costa Rica. By 1513, Vasco Nuñez de Balboa had discovered the Pacific Ocean, and future expeditions concentrated on the Pacific coast, which was believed to have more gold and better ports for further explorations. In 1522, Captain Gil González led an expedition to the Pacific. Soldiers hiked much of the Costa Rican Pacific coast into Nicaragua, baptizing Indians along the way and collecting as much gold as they could carry. The Indians, while curious about the Spaniards and their horses, were not interested in being conquered and assimilated, and they rebelled in short spurts of battle; they were quickly repelled. The Spaniards left the region once again in search of riches elsewhere on the continent, leaving behind the seeds of destruction — smallpox and other diseases that rapidly decreased the Indian population.

PRECEEDING PAGES: Work and play continue into evening hours on Playa Hermosa LEFT, Nicoya Peninsula. Vivid angels RIGHT adorn an Easter procession. OPPOSITE: A lone fisherman explores the waters of Barra del Colorado near the Nicaraguan border.

Subsequent expeditions proved frustrating and futile. The Spaniards, always intent on finding the source of the gold that adorned the Indians, were directed south to the rivers of the Península de Osa, where all they found was placer gold (found on stream beds and not in mines) and not the vast amounts they were seeking. They never found the legendary gold mines of southern Costa Rica, and had to be content with what they could loot from the Indians, a paltry amount by the greedy standards of those seeking the wealth of the New World.

Attempts to conquer Costa Rica continued, though there was little to be conquered. This section of Central America held none of the mighty

cities and thousands of potential slaves that existed in Mexico or Guatemala. The indigenous groups were small, nomadic and little impressed with the attempts of their conquerors, who were thwarted by endless mountain ranges, impenetrable jungle, tropical heat, diseases and a resistant populace. Having better luck in Panama and Nicaragua, the Spaniards established settlements there and in 1539 deemed the area between the two countries to be called Costa Rica.

Phillip II of Spain insisted that Costa Rica be colonized, and in 1561 a well-equipped expedition led by Juan de Cavallón achieved what Columbus had started decades earlier. Leading his troops inland, Cavallón established the settlement of Garcimuñoz, named after his place of birth. Juan Vásquez de Coronado arrived the following year, moved Garcimuñoz to what is now Cartago and renamed it El Guarco.

Coronado was Costa Rica's first true leader. He traveled throughout the country, visiting Spanish settlers barely eking out an existence and Indian leaders resistant to being conquered. The indigenous groups had their own battles going, which Coronado helped mediate and resolve, all the while approaching the Indians in a peaceful, friendly manner. Battles still took place between the indigenous residents and the settlers, but there

was little of the overwhelming bloodshed so common in other conquered lands.

Still, the Spanish settlers found Costa Rica to be nearly uninhabitable. Without slaves they were unable to build colonial cities and churches or establish vast agricultural fields. They continued moving inland to the more fertile volcanic lands, cultivating their own property with the few Indians they could press into service. In 1569, the struggling settlers demanded that Coronado's successor allow enslavement, but few Indians were left to be conquered. Those who hadn't fled to the hills or jungles had been killed by disease, and Costa Rica became the province of the Spanish settlers willing to shape a new country.

THE COLONIAL PERIOD

By 1573 Cartago (El Guarco) contained about 50 families and smaller settlements that had grown within the Meseta Central and the Península de Nicoya. Lacking gold or other precious metals for trade, these settlers used what they could raise on the land: corn, cacao, tobacco — and lived at marginal, subsistence levels. Feuds between landowners were few, since there were no real class distinctions and little to fight over. The Catholic Church, so influential in New Spain, was of little importance here. The bishop was located in Nicaragua and rarely made the trip of several months to reach his flock in Costa Rica. The country grew slowly over the next century, largely uninfluenced by events taking place in the outside world, developing its own system of peaceful negotiation, democracy and independence.

As Spanish settlements took hold in the interior during the 1700s, a few of the more established *criollos* (Spaniards born outside their country) began planting cacao on the Caribbean coast and importing African slaves to tend the crops. But British pirates allied with the Moskitos, a band of African slaves who had intermarried with the Indians in Nicaragua and Honduras. They found the plantations easy conquests and plundered the coast. The *criollos* built Fort San Fernando in Matina, north of Limón, to protect their plantations. But they were easily outnumbered and overwhelmed by the British. At the same time, the Spaniards and *criollos* continued attempting to enslave the Indians who had fled to the Caribbean Talamanca mountain range, where dense vegetation and the harsh tropical climate discouraged Spanish settlement.

The Meseta Central continued to grow with the establishment of Cubujugui (now called Heredia), Villa Nueva de la Boca del Monte (now San José) and Villa Hermosa, now Alajuela. Still seeking manpower, the Spanish government instituted the Indian Resettlement Policies of 1747 and hundreds of Indians were forcibly relocated

58

to the Meseta Central to provide a labor force. In 1779, Costa Ricans began paying tributes (or bribes as they might more accurately be called) to the pirates to protect their plantations, a practice that continued into the mid-1800s.

INDEPENDENCE

Isolated from the turmoil in Mexico and Central America, Costa Rica was little involved in its neighbors' fight for independence from Spain. As the story goes, a letter from officials in Guatemala arrived on October 13, 1821 in Cartago, informing Costa Rica that Guatemala, head of the Federation of Central American States, had declared its inde-

Fernández led the country for nine years, overseeing its first printing presses and newspapers and the beginning of the coffee plantations that would shape Costa Rica's future. As *cafeteros* (coffee growers) around San José began attaining some wealth and prestige, the need for a strong leader became evident. In 1835, lawyer Braulio Carrillo was named president; he later declared himself the benevolent dictator of Costa Rica and moved the capital to San José. Coffee continued to take hold as the leading crop in the countryside, and the infant government grew evermore factious. Francisco Morazán, a Honduran and leading power in the attempt to create a united Central America, was enlisted by the coffee

pendence—and that of its neighbors—from Spain. The leaders of the small country's main settlements —Cartago, Alajuela, Heredia and San José—were at a loss. They had felt Spain's influence only minimally, but were not united with their Central American neighbors by a common identity.

On December 1, 1821 the local leaders drafted their first constitution, the *Pacto de Concordia.* Some felt the country was too small and sparsely populated to stand independently, and favored unification with Guatemala or the Mexican Empire. Others opted for independence. On April 5, 1823, the debate ended with a short battle in which 20 men were killed. The *independencistas* won, taking control of Cartago. The *Ley de Ambulancia* (Law of Mobility) was established, rotating the capital between the major towns. In 1824, teacher Juan Morn Fernández was named the first head of the sovereign state of Costa Rica.

The Country and Its People

barons to overthrow Carrillo in 1842; a year later, Morazán was overthrown and executed. A series of shaky governments ensued as Costa Rica abolished its military and all ties to a Central American federation.

A strange historical quirk fueled the national identity of Costa Rica in the mid-1850s. William Walker, an American character of bizarre influence in much of Mexico and Central America, had failed in his attempts to create a slave state in Mexico. With the backing of wealthy United States capitalists who hoped to open tradeways through Central America, Walker landed in Nicaragua in June, 1855. Walker's intentions were even more grandiose than those of his backers. He aimed to

OPPOSITE: Rainforest villagers cruise in their wooden skiff off the Burica Peninsula near the border with Panama. ABOVE: This venerable Josefina claims to be 101 years old.

establish a union of the five Central American countries and rule the union as emperor. He was able to win over and conquer Nicaragua's leaders and became their president, but was less successful with Costa Rica. When Walker attempted to invade Costa Rica's northern border at Guanacaste, he met an army of some 9,000 peasants who routed the potential potentate and his band in a battle that lasted less than 15 minutes. The site of the battle, La Casona in Parque Nacional Santa Rosa, is now a museum. Juan Santamaría, a youth from Alajuela, became Costa Rica's sole military hero when he followed Walker back to Nicaragua and lost his life while setting fire to the invader's fort.

The coffee barons continued to accumulate money and power through the 1800s, cultivating huge swaths of land in the Central Meseta with the *grano de oro*, grain of gold. They began building mansions around San José and fought amongst themselves for control of the country. By the end of the century Costa Rica had an established constitution, a controlled military and mandatory primary education for both sexes. A railroad to Puerto Limón was under construction for transporting exported coffee, and Costa Ricans began looking towards Europe for their sense of style and grandeur. In 1897 a coffee tax financed construction of the elegant Teatro Nacional in San José.

In 1889, those who were not female, Indian or black were allowed to vote in free elections.

THE TWENTIETH CENTURY

Although it is known today as a peaceful country, Costa Rica marked the first five decades of the twentieth century with a series of military takeovers, political and social reforms and a civil war. A series of political parties — conservative, reformist, Communist, Christian — took control while debating taxes, social justice and the country's future. Unable to remain isolated, Costa Rica was financially affected by World War I and the Great

Depression, both of which reduced the international coffee market. Politics proved risky business: over its first 100 years Costa Rica saw presidents and ex-presidents executed or assassinated. In 1842 Francisco Morazán was executed in San José; Braulio Carrillo was assassinated in El Salvador in 1844. Army chief Joaquín Tinico, brother of military dictator Federico Tinico, was gunned down in 1919.

As other Latin nations were struggling to define their political character, Costa Rica underwent a social revolution, of sorts, led by ex-Catholic priest Jorge Volio. Head of the Reformist Party, Volio served as vice-president during the 1920s, often rattling the elite power brokers with his demands for social justice. In 1931, Manuel Moras — an intellectual concerned with the growing influence of not just the coffee barons but also the United Fruit Company and its vast banana plantations on the Caribbean coast — formed Costa Rica's Communist Party.

From the first isolated indigenous groups, the country of Costa Rica grew into a collection of individualistic and relatively independent provinces, ultimately ruled by the coffee barons of the Meseta Central. By the 1930s, the United Fruit Company had become a measurable political and financial force, with its vast landholdings and banana plantations on the Caribbean coast. Social and financial inequities were more visible than ever, and the educated populace resisted control by the elite. Moras and the Communist Party led a strike in the banana plantations in 1934; eventually, the largely black workforce was granted wage guarantees and the right to unionize.

In 1939 Rafael Angel Calderón Guardia was elected president. Though supported by the coffee elite, Calderón proved himself to be a liberal leader, instituting the social security system, the right of workers to strike, and other reforms. He also used his declaration of war against Nazi Germany during World War II as an excuse to confiscate the lands of powerful German coffee barons, which decreased his constituency considerably. Calderón gradually became allied with the Communist Party and the Catholic Church in an odd triumvirate that led to long-term partnerships. Calderón lost the 1944 election to his supporter, Teodoro Picado, in an election some said was filled with fraud. He lost again to Otillio Ulate Blanco in 1948, but both Calderón and Picado called the election a fraud. A brief, bloody civil war ensued on the streets of San José, with skirmishes throughout the country. Over 2,000 Costa Ricans are believed to have died during the 44-day war.

José Figueres, known as Pepe and eventually Don Pepe to his fellow countrymen, led the opposition forces in what he called "The War of National Liberation." Apparently backed by the United States and supplied with soldiers and arms from other Central American countries, Figueres won the war and leadership of Costa Rica for the next year. In that brief span of time he ensured passage of the Constitution of 1949, which abolished the military, gave citizenship to everyone born in Costa Rica, including the Afro-Caribeños of the Caribbean coast, and granted women the right to vote. Over the following two decades Figueres served nine years in intermittent presidential terms under the banner of the National Liberation Party (PLN).

The transfer of power has remained fairly orderly since Figueres moved in with his guerrilla band in 1948. Subsequent presidential elections have favored the Liberation Party, and power has been concentrated within a few politically elite families. The wave of revolutions in surrounding countries has tested, but not defeated, Costa Rica's desire for peace. In the country's greatest moment of international recognition, Costa Rican President Oscar Arias was granted the Nobel Peace Prize in 1987 for engineering peace in Central America.

TODAY'S COSTA RICA

The years since the Civil War of 1948 have been remarkably peaceful and largely prosperous for Central America's most stable country. The economy and living standards are among the highest in the region, and citizens enjoy the benefits of free education and health care (paid for with taxes that some find exorbitant), generally sanitary and comfortable living conditions and an absence of armed conflict. Costa Rica has maintained a peaceful attitude towards its warring neighbors, managing to stay away from conflicts in El Salvador, Guatemala, Nicaragua and Panama through the past few decades of revolution, military intrigue and strife.

Granted, the tiny country of peace amidst revolution has not been allowed to be completely free of involvement. The United States, a longtime ally of Costa Rica, unofficially installed military bases and training camps along Costa Rica's border with Nicaragua as part of its campaign to destabilize the Sandinista government during the Contra insurgency. In the 1980s the United States poured money into Costa Rica, constructing a massive embassy with over 200 employees and a second huge edifice to house the Agency for International Development (AID). Both buildings, set amidst the nouveau riche suburbs of San José, provide visible evidence of the United States' presence and Costa Rica's growing dependence on United States investments. Between 1983 and 1990, Costa Rica received over $1.1 billion from AID, creating what some *ticos* called a "parallel state" intent on promoting the country's private sector economy.

Despite United States involvement, the Costa Rican government, led by President Oscar Arias, refused militarily involvement in its neighbor's conflicts. Reports of military training camps on the borders still occasionally surface, and the country was certainly a center of intrigue during the 10 years that the United States supported the Nicaraguan Contras. But Arias remained firm in his commitment to peaceful negotiations over armed conflict, bringing the wrath of some United States politicians and the support of others. Arias is largely credited with introducing peace to the region by bringing the five presidents of the Central American nations into a mutual accord.

Dependence on United States funds created a false economy in Costa Rica during the 1980s; with the end of armed conflict in Nicaragua and Panama, United States aid began drying up. Costa Rica was considered to be financially stable and able to control its future finances without such mighty intervention. The transition was less than comfortable.

The 1990s were hard on Costa Rica's economy. Immigrants from all over Central America put a heavy strain on the country's social services. Though the population increase within the country has been stabilized through successful birth-control programs, the influx of new poverty-stricken residents is difficult to stem. Drug trafficking has become a serious concern, particularly on the Caribbean coast. In a concession to the United States, the Costa Rican government has allowed the DEA to maintain an active presence as part of its war against drugs within Costa Rica's borders, policing the waterways, roadways, and airways for traffickers. Cocaine and crack are now abundantly available, especially on the Caribbean coast, a sad development that mars that area's attempt to gain respectability. In a new twist, gun running has also become a major concern, as customs officers uncover large caches of weapons in vehicles traveling through Costa Rica to Panama and Colombia.

Petty crime has increased at an alarming rate, and though Costa Rica is far safer than its neighbors (and many developed countries), *ticos* are reluctantly locking their doors, putting bars over the windows, and generally becoming much more fearful, particularly when in San José. Costa Rican law demands that criminals who cannot pay their fines be released from prison; the fight is on to change that law to prevent captured thieves from immediately returning to the streets.

At the same time, however, Costa Rica has become extraordinarily attractive to international investors and retirees. Real estate prices in suburban and coastal areas have risen dramatically as expatriate communities have grown in clusters of villas, condominiums and entire neighborhoods of United States-style ranch houses. The popula-

Coffee beans, called the *grano de oro*, grain of gold, are among the country's leading exports.

tion of North Americans and Europeans living in Costa Rica has reached over 30,000, in a country of three million people. *Pensionados*, as these gringo retirees are called, must prove they have an independent monthly income, which the retirees find goes a lot farther in a Third World country. English is as common as Spanish in many parts of the country, where it seems all the landowners are expatriates.

International electronics companies are also attracted by the country's stability and its educated work force. Large factories, called *maquiladoras*, have risen in the Meseta Central, and more and more *campesinos* are leaving the countryside for the city, hoping to improve their status in the

Miguel Angel Rodríguez, the current president, is accused by some of literally selling the country off to the highest bidder. Foreign investors encounter an extremely friendly welcome, as Rodríguez has removed many of the barriers to foreign investment. Huge international companies are rapidly changing the coastal landscape, building marinas, golf courses, and fancy resorts on pristine bays. The president is credited for his attempts at improving the country's infrastructure, particularly its roads. But some fear his largesse toward outsiders.

As Costa Rica enters the twenty-first century, it appears far better prepared for the future than its neighbors. Democracy seems to be firmly en-

industrial sector. Clusters of makeshift shacks cover hillsides outside San José as the poor struggle to eke out a living in the factories. Poverty is more immediately apparent than ever, and slums have overtaken the scenic outskirts of the city.

Politically, Costa Rica remains stable, though the citizenry is highly vocal and critical of the government. The country's infrastructure is in need of a comprehensive overhaul — one need only drive the roads to perceive that — and middle-class workers are expressing their resentment over high taxes that hardly improve their daily lives. After Oscar Arias brokered peace among his neighbors, Costa Ricans elected the son of ex-president Rafael Angel Calderón to the presidency; in 1994 the son of Don Pepe Figueres, José María Figueres became president. Figueres was much maligned by his countrymen, who witnessed an unprecedented rise in corruption and crime in Costa Rica.

trenched, and international companies look to this peaceful nation for expansion of high-tech industries. Outside the cities and burgeoning coastal resorts, Costa Rica remains the same as it was in decades past, when *campesinos* tended their sugarcane, coffee, and cows in relative tranquillity.

THE PEOPLE

Often overlooked in the turmoil that besets most Central American countries, Costa Rica is a relatively peaceful enclave boasting more teachers than policemen, more nature preserves than cities, and an enviable absence of confrontation. Its character is subtle yet enduringly strong, able to resist the political influences of mightier governments and interference from its neighbors.

Europeans conquered Costa Rica in a far different manner than in more valuable lands such as Guatemala or Mexico. They settled in haciendas, stripped the land for cattle ranches, and relied on their wits and skills to survive. The society that emerged during the region's next century emphasized independence from outside influences and interdependence within small communities. Geographically isolated between mountains, rivers, volcanoes and rainforests, Costa Rica's early communities developed distinctive characters based on nature's influences and the immigrant families shaping a new world.

Costa Rica's indigenous peoples — the Bribrí, Boruca, Kékóldi and Chorotega groups living in coastal outposts and verdant valleys when the Spaniards arrived — were gradually displaced during the seventeenth and eighteenth centuries. Today, their influence is nearly invisible to the casual eye, which makes this Central American nation rather disconcerting for fans of Guatemala, Mexico or Peru. Some tourists are shocked to discover the absence of important archaeological sites, indigenous communities, folk art and colorful clothing amidst the country's natural beauty. Less than three percent of Costa Rica's current population is made up of indigenous peoples. And these small indigenous communities live primarily in remote reserves.

The people of Costa Rica's major settlements reflect a polyglot heritage. Waves of immigrants from Europe and North and South America have been settling in the country's fertile agricultural valleys and ranch lands ever since Columbus and his men first arrived in 1502. In some places Italian is spoken as readily as Spanish; in others, German prevails. In the northern Caribbean region, you hear the lisping, melodic Spanish of Honduras; along the Pacific, you learn Nicaraguan slang. English is pervasive in the capital, but in the countryside Spanish prevails, filled with the clever *tiquismos* that make it worth learning the local accent.

Costa Ricans have avoided military action since the Civil War of 1948 — no mean feat when one thinks of the Nicaraguan Contras, Manuel Noriega and other characters fomenting turmoil in neighboring countries. The *costarricense* approach to conflict is based on negotiation. The *costarricense* manner is to use humor, charm or disappearing acts to avoid offending anyone. *Ticos* and *ticas* are among the most pleasant people you'll ever meet, filled with sincere courtesies.

Yet racial and ethnic equality among the country's citizens is a fairly recent phenomenon. Afro-Caribeños first began settling on the Caribbean coast and working at cacao and banana plantations in the mid-1800s, but were denied citizenship until 1949. Indigenous peoples of the Bribrí, Boruca, Kékóldi and Chorotega groups were given citizenship in 1992, and allowed to vote for the first time in the 1994 elections.

More than 30,000 out of the country's three million residents have *pensionado* status. In other words, they've proven their economic viability and emigrated from Canada, the United States, Germany, Switzerland and Italy. Entire communities of North American and European *pensionados* have sprung up on the edges of towns throughout the country, escalating land values to the peak of any found in a Latin Third World country. Many of the finest hotels, restaurants, private nature preserves and beach resorts are owned by non-citizens.

These outside entrepreneurs are attracted by Costa Rica's independence from Central America's woes and its relatively stable financial and political climate. The military was abolished in 1949, and democracy bordering on nepotism has been the government of choice ever since. Nearly 90% of the registered citizens vote in national elections. Public education is mandatory through sixth grade, though many children are too busy working on family farms and coffee plantations to attend school.

Though Costa Rica is far more peaceful than its neighbors, crime is on the rise and people are learning to fear their neighbors. Private security officers patrol banks, public parks, homes, and ecolodges, and guns are now part of the standard uniform. In a bold move forward, President Rodríguez has declared that all police officers should have at least a sixth-grade education (many current officers can barely read or write). The public health system, free to all taxpayers, is decent but inefficient; the public education system is burdened by an onslaught of illegal resident students. Though still in the Third World, Costa Rica is relatively advanced technologically, financially and socially, and has many of the modern problems of a First World nation.

But out in the provinces, beyond the city smog, Costa Rica remains a landscape of small towns and villages, each with a unique identity — from Guanacaste with its skillful *sabaneros* and cowboy spirit to Alajuela where the national hero Juan Santamaría was raised. Flags billow outside rural homes in support of provincial soccer teams and *boyeros* (oxcart drivers) know they're nearing home when the wheels of their *carretas* sing a familiar tune.

Costa Rica feels like a country in transition, yet much tradition remains. Costa Ricans have juggled environmental, social and financial issues in a temporizing manner ever since declaring themselves independent of any Central American federation in 1823. In enduring *costarricense* style they remain subtle, amiable and tenaciously proud of their homeland.

Mares and their colts are herded along a Nicoya Peninsula road.

San José

THOUGH ITS CHARMS ARE OFTEN HIDDEN behind a façade of traffic congestion and big-city noise, San José is an important destination for those who want to understand the country. Ringed by mountain peaks and volcanoes, the city attracts culture-oriented travelers along with humming-birds, parrots, and flocks of dull-brown hilgueros, the country's national bird. The markets, parks, neighborhoods and business district pulse with a frenzy utterly absent in other parts of the country. *Josefinos*, as San José's residents are called, are as amiable and helpful as *ticos* in the country-side, but they face an ever-increasing array of disturbing challenges.

San José's potholed streets are jammed with bumper-to-bumper traffic, and pedestrians clutch their parcels and purses with obvious caution. Purse snatching, muggings and other crimes have become far too common, and *ticos* are calling for more police protection. Security guards have become a common sight at banks, shops, and hotels. Pollution often obliterates the beauty of the countryside encircling the city, which sprawls over the Meseta Central 1,220 m (4,000 ft) above sea level. One-third of Costa Rica's citizens live in the greater San José region, along with an unknown number of foreign entrepreneurs who own and manage many of the city's tourism services. The constant influx of newcomers has severely impacted the city's fragile infrastructure, and city leaders are hard put to keep up with the strain on public services.

San José is far from scenic, but it does have its attributes. I enjoy strolling along the side streets of the city's older neighborhoods on a clear Sunday afternoon. Couples nuzzle on benches in a half-dozen green and fertile parks. Men in berets study the news under violet halos of jacaranda blossoms in the Parque España, while sidewalk vendors display feathers covered with delicate paintings at the Plaza de la Democracia. Cars cruise the streets around the Parque Central, where political dissidents are likely to be lecturing the crowd.

On weekdays, downtown San José is something of a battleground, a challenge to travelers seeking tour guides, rental cars, and supplies. At such times you're inclined to agree with *josefinos* who dread trips to (or through) the city center. Most are embarrassed by what they face — handsome buildings crumbling in disrepair backed by bureaucratic towers of gray cement, and masses of buses, taxis, cars and pedestrians. Despite the country's ecological stance, its capital city is polluted and overpopulated. Buses belch noxious fumes night and day, and the heart of the city looks like it's been hit by a disastrous earthquake. Prostitution (a traditional tourist attraction) has expanded from the tolerated Red Light District into much of downtown, leading city leaders to fear San José's emergence as a leading destination for

sex. The police began seriously clamping down on prostitution in 2000, arresting customers as well as prostitutes. Several agencies have begun a campaign to get underage girls and boys out of the sex trade, and officials no longer look the other way when faced with the realities endured by children on the street.

All in all, San José is growing into a typical Latin American metropolis, though it will never be as imposing as many South American or Mexican cities. Although over 300,000 residents live in the city, slums are still the exception rather than the rule. Costa Ricans are too proud to let their capital, with its museums, historical mansions and seats of government, disintegrate much farther.

San José is famous for one of the best climates in the world, with daily temperatures averaging above 20°C (70°F). Rain falls in sudden showers from May through October, cleaning the air and streets. But even then the air is crisp rather than chilly, an invigorating change from the sweltering heat at the beach.

First-time visitors to San José tend to find lodging downtown; returning travelers opt for the quieter urban or suburban neighborhoods. Tourists on tight schedules stick to the modern resorts by the airport, zipping away as soon as possible. Sooner or later everyone wanders down Avenida Central to the pedestrian zone by the Plaza de la Cultura, sampling San José's shops, churches, museums and landmark sidewalk cafés. It's a good idea to get to know San José if you think you'll be back to Costa Rica. You just might find neighborhoods, hotels, restaurants and shops that you wouldn't dream of leaving the country without visiting the next time around.

BACKGROUND

When the Spaniards first settled in Costa Rica in the sixteenth century, they chose Cartago, 20 km (12.4 miles) south of San José, as their capital. Until 1737, Villa Nueva de la Boca del Monte del Valle de Abra (as San José was then awkwardly named) was nothing more than a few muddy streets and ramshackle buildings. Then the Catholic Church and the Spanish government declared it to be the focal point for villages and farms scattered through the valley. When much of Central America gained independence from Spain in 1821, various factions in Costa Rica fought for power. In 1823 a short civil war gave control of

PRECEEDING PAGES: A night or two at the Gran Hotel LEFT acclimates travelers to the noise and bustle of downtown. RIGHT: Statues of European conquerors and national heroes overlook most plazas in San José. OPPOSITE: The Teatro Nacional, built in the late 1800s with funds from coffee taxes, has become Costa Rica's enduring architectural and cultural landmark.

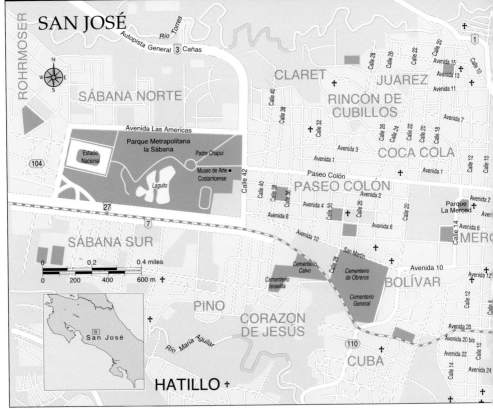

the country to the *independencistas* of Alajuela and San José, who favored the country's independence over control by a larger nation such as Mexico or Guatemala. The winning faction conquered Cartago and made San José the capital city.

San José was attacked by opposing forces in 1837, but stood strong and has remained the tiny country's capital ever since. Traveling in 1841, the explorer John Lloyd Stephens described the burgeoning city:

"San José is, I believe, the only city that has grown up or even improved since the independence of Central America... The buildings in San José are all Republican; not one is of any grandeur or architectural beauty, and the churches are inferior to many erected by the Spaniards in the smallest villages. Nevertheless, it exhibited a development of resources and an appearance of business unusual in this lethargic country."

Little did Stephens know how much the city would change in the next few decades. By the mid-1800s San José was attracting tobacco and coffee barons and an intelligentsia seeking a cultural center. Civic leaders looked to both France and Italy for their monuments and mansions.

The Teatro Nacional, which was built in 1897, firmly emphasized the European influences of im-

ported artists, designers and craftsmen. Public electric lighting brightened the streets and electric trolleys ran through downtown around the turn of the century. In the early 1900s San José was a cosmopolitan city with a strong cultural and financial base, often compared to New Orleans.

An influx of foreign money in the 1960s and 1970s caused the city to boom. Several foreign governments established embassies and consulates in Barrio Amón, Escazú and Rohrmoser, which created a demand for high-class housing, services and cuisine. Tourism to the city increased, and émigrés from the United States, Canada and Europe settled in various neighborhoods. The 1991 earthquake, which devastated areas around Limón on the Caribbean coast, was felt as far inland as the capital. The tremors severely damaged the Teatro Nacional and left cracks and fissures in walls and streets.

But Chepe, as *ticos* call their capital, is slowly revitalizing. Several parks have been manicured, the Catedral Metropolitano has undergone a facelift and the Plaza de la Cultura, long the hub of tourists, vendors and thieves, has been remodeled. Government plans to reduce traffic congestion and air pollution are regular fare in the daily news. It will take considerable effort to turn San

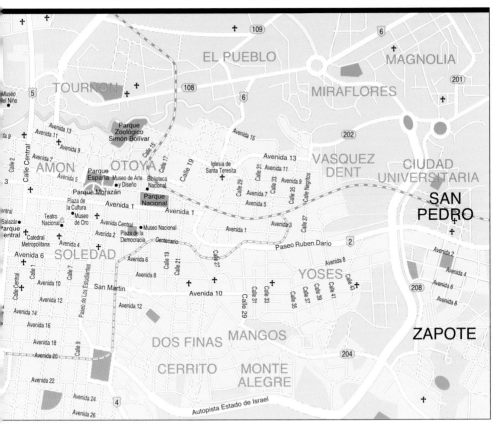

José into an attractive city, however. It seems the government will never have enough funds to give San José the attention it needs.

GENERAL INFORMATION

The **Costa Rican Tourism Institute (ICT)** (223-1733 FAX 223-5452 WEB SITE www.tourism-costarica .com, Edificio Genaro Valverde, on Avenida 4 between Calles 5 and 7, is woefully understaffed and unreliable. It does operate a **Tourist Information Office** (223-1733, extension 2777, Calle 5 between Avenidas Central and 2 beside the Museo de Oro in the Plaza de la Cultura. The quality of assistance offered varies considerably, but the office does distribute maps, some brochures, and general information. They also have fairly up-to-date information on the location of bus terminals (which change frequently). The office is open Monday to Friday from 8 AM to 4 PM.

The offices of the **Sistema Nacional de Areas de Conservación (SINAC)** and **Ministerio del Ambiente y Energia (MINAE)** (283-8004 or 283-8094 FAX 283-7343 operate a hotline (192 for questions and information about Costa Rica's biological reserves, national parks and protected areas.

The main information office for both agencies is at Calle 27 between Avenidas 10 and 12, Apdo 10104, 1000 San José.

The least expensive place to make international phone calls and send and receive faxes is **Radiográfica Costarricense** (287-0087, Avenida 5 at Calle 1. Surf the Internet at **Cyber Café Las Arcadas** (233-5449 Avenida 2 in the Edificio las Arcadas. Like a full-service tourist refuge, the café has several computers available, along with a tour desk, book exchange, bulletin board loaded with information, and self-service laundry facilities. **Internet Café** (224-7295, Avenida Central in San Pedro is open 24 hours daily and has dozens of computers.

Black-market money exchangers wander the streets of downtown soliciting clients, but there is a problem with counterfeit currency so you're best off changing money at banks or hotels. The **Banco de San José** (257-0155, Calle Central between Avenidas 3 and 5, operates a foreign exchange office and allows you to draw cash on your credit cards. It's open Monday through Friday 8:30 AM to 3 PM. The bank's ATM is open 24 hours. There are several other banks around the intersection of Avenida Central and Calle Central. Most have ATM machines, and there are machines in most shopping centers and at the Plaza de la Cultura.

Travel agencies abound in the San José area, and they are the best source for up-to-date information. Most hotel and street-side agencies distribute maps and make tour, car-rental and hotel reservations. Several of the country's major adventure travel companies (with day trips to San José's outlying areas) are also headquartered inside the city (see TOUR OPERATORS, page 236 in TRAVELERS' TIPS, and TAKING A TOUR, page 46 in YOUR CHOICE).

For fire, police, health or other emergencies in San José dial (911. The recommended hospital for English-speakers is **Hospital Clínica Bíblica** (257-5252 EMERGENCIES (257-0466, Calle 1 at Avenida 14.

The pharmacists at **Farmacia Italiana** (222-2349, Avenida Central at Calle 3, are accustomed to dealing with travelers' maladies and can recommend treatments for common complaints.

GETTING AROUND

Walking is by far the easiest way to see downtown San José, as long as you keep your eyes on your feet when in motion. The sidewalks in many areas are in dreadful condition, with crumbled pavement and potholes nearly as large as those in the streets.

Crossing most streets is another challenge. Pedestrians appear to be considered fair game by drivers, who edge forward at red lights as if their lives depended on a quick getaway. Crossing lights are hung so high that they're difficult to see. Watch the locals instead, and cross with a group.

Despite these drawbacks, you can often reach your destination far more quickly by walking than by riding in a bus or cab. Most of downtown's sights are within a 20-block radius, and walkers can ignore the baffling one-way street design that makes driving an utter nightmare.

A few important tips: *avenidas* (avenues) run east and west; *calles* (streets) run north and south. Odd-numbered avenues are north of Avenida Central; even-numbered avenues are south. Odd-numbered streets are found east of Calle Central; even-numbered streets are located to the west.

Even when walking, directions can be downright baffling. I've had police officers, knowledgeable pedestrians, and cab drivers scold me for knowing only the street address of my destination. Landmarks are preferred, usually with some reference to meters. For example, *ticos* refer to a city block as being *cien metros,* 100 meters, long. Many buses to outlying areas depart from the Coca-Cola terminal, roughly bordered by Calles 16 and 20 and Avenidas 1 and 3. Mind you, there is no actual terminal building, and the Coca-Cola bottling plant for which the area is named was torn down years ago. But the address is imbedded in the collective memory.

Taxis are cheap and abundant and use meters (called *marías*). If the driver says his meter doesn't work, confirm the fare before he starts driving. You can travel from one end of town to another for under US$5; the fare is about 20% more after 10 PM. Taxis congregate at the Plaza Central and the Plaza de la Cultura.

Buses are equally omnipresent and run the full gamut from dilapidated, smoke-belching contraptions to clean Mercedes Benz machines. The route is written on the windshield. The Cementerio–Sábana route runs east–west from downtown to Parque la Sábana.

I've driven many times through downtown San José, despite strong admonitions to avoid it. Some people love the rush and challenge; I tend to crawl between lanes of cars more dented than my own. It may take a full hour to cross the city in any direction, especially if you stick to the obvious routes. Locals are savvy about alternate routes; ask about shortcuts at your hotel or car rental company. Nervous, cautious drivers are best off renting their cars at the airport or an outlying hotel on the edge of town, although depending on your destination, you still might have to drive through San José.

WHAT TO SEE AND DO

Downtown San José attractions are within easy walking distance of each other and most sit at the edge of a plaza or park with benches for resting and regrouping. The best place to start exploring is the **Museo Nacional** (257-1433, Avenida Central between Calles 15 and 17, housed in the imposing, bullet-ridden Bellavista Fortress, built in 1870. The bullet holes on the south side of the gray-brown fortress were left during the civil war of 1948. The museum's exhibits are labeled in English and Spanish and offer a worthwhile historical overview. New in 2000 was an exhibit of jade jewelry and figurines formerly housed in Marco Fidel Tristan Museo de Jade, which is now closed. The Museo Nacional is closed on Monday; admission is charged.

The stark, imposing concrete **Parque de la Democracia** slants down a slight hill on Avenida Central in front of the fortress. The park's design shows none of the warmth it represented when built in 1989 to commemorate President Oscar Arias's key role in establishing peace in Central America; instead, it consists of a series of cement stairways and terraces. But it's a popular gathering spot for impromptu concerts and speeches. Folk art and souvenir vendors are relegated to a permanent open-air structure at the foot of the plaza; treasures lie waiting amidst Guatemalan textiles and manufactured trinkets.

The **Palacio Nacional**, which houses the national legislature, is across Avenida Central from the museum on Calle 15. Demonstrations blocking the surrounding streets are common, especially around election time. About 85% of the population votes in local and national elections, and *ticos* are both philosophically and physically involved in their local governments.

One block north, at Calle 15 and Avenida 1, the **Parque Nacional** provides a peaceful green belt with bamboo and palm groves and the **Monumento Nacional**. This frothy white marble sculpture depicts four women who represent the spirits of the Central American nations; potential conqueror William Walker is shown fleeing from the powerful woman representing Costa Rica. A statue of Juan Santamaría, the country's national hero, stands at the park's southwest corner. The **Biblioteca Nacional** opposite the park is the country's largest library. Visitors can browse through the stacks. Also in the neighborhood at the far end of Avenida 3 between Calles 21 and 23 is the **Estación Ferrocarril**, once the terminus for the Jungle Train from Limón to San José. The long brick building, constructed in 1907, now holds a collection of photographs of the old train line, which ceased operation after the April 1991 earthquake. The building is used for large fairs and concerts and is not open on a regular basis. If you do find it open, take note of the tiled floor and wood carvings on the walls and ceiling.

A vast expanse of cement with park benches designed to prevent loiterers from stretching out for a nap, the **Plaza de la Cultura**, bordered by Avenida Central and Avenida 2 and Calles 3 and 5, is the heart of downtown. A few palms and patches of flowers break up the monotony, but the plaza is far from inviting. Still, it's packed with families on weekends, when city dwellers descend upon downtown to shop and socialize. The plaza is in the center of a five-block-long pedestrian zone that has been somewhat spruced up with plants and refurbished storefronts. Under the Plaza de la Cultura at basement level is the **Museo de Oro** (243-4202, Calle 5 at Avenida Central, housing more than 2,000 pre-Columbian gold artifacts. Given the country's paucity of archaeological sites the collection is impressive, with items dating from AD 500 to 1500. The museum is run by the state-owned Central Bank and is protected by gun-toting guards. The building also houses a shop and the Tourist Information Office. The museum is closed Mondays and admission is charged.

The **Teatro Nacional** (221-1329 or 221-5341 (ticket information), at the south side of the plaza, is San José's most striking architectural sight, a tribute to the will and power of nineteenth-century coffee barons. Embarrassed at not having an appropriate venue for traveling artists, the barons put a tax on every bag of coffee they exported to finance a European-style opera house. Ships laden with marble and glass from Italy and France unloaded their precious wares at Limón; from there the valuable materials were brought by train to San José. The official history of the theater states it was built between 1890 and 1897 in an eclectic neoclassic German style; the stone façade underwent changes in 1921. The theater opened on October 10, 1897, with a performance of *Faust* by the Paris Opera and Ballet. Legend has it the 1,040 wrought-iron and carved wood seats weren't ready in time for the show; instead, volunteers hustled up folding chairs from all over town to accommodate the sold-out house.

The best way to view the theater is by purchasing an inexpensive ticket for a show. I saw a performance of the university's guitar orchestra for US$5 one night and brought home a compact disc of Latin American guitar classics as a treasured souvenir. The theater has a rotunda ceiling mural of naked cherubs with trumpets and harps painted by Italian artist Arturo Fontana in 1897. The national symphony and touring groups appear frequently, and the theater hosts a music festival in July. Visitors are allowed to tour the theater for a fee Monday through Saturday; the building is closed on Sundays. Guided tours are no longer available. Check out the native cedar, mahogany and rosewood doors, floors and ornaments, and the mural of the coffee-harvesting scene depicted on the old five-colon note. If you stop for a coffee or dessert at the theater's **Café Ruiseñor** (221-3262, ask for a token to use the grand restrooms.

A standard stop-off for nearly anyone in this busy area is the **Café Parisienne** in front of the golden-yellow **Gran Hotel**, designed by architect Juan Joaquín Jiménez in 1930. The sidewalk tables topped with white umbrellas are the province of travelers and a few regulars who lay claim to their seats for long hours of coffee and conversation.

A child delights in chasing pigeons in the square adjacent to the Teatro Nacional.

Though I prefer the Ruiseñor, nothing gets you in the touring mood better than a morning coffee or evening beer at the Café Parisienne.

The pedestrian walkway runs east to west along Avenida Central behind the Gran Hotel. Attempts have been made to beautify the strip and a few trees seem to be thriving. Walk this route to cut through downtown's madness without dodging cars. There are a few good department stores, takeout eateries and a bank of public phones along the walkway.

A hangout for downtown denizens, **Parque Central** at Calle Central and Avenida 2 is an elevated square framed by royal palms. It's a good place to review your maps, sample some sliced

spring, pineapples and bananas year round. Inside, narrow claustrophobia-inducing aisles lead past fishmongers, butchers, spice and herb stands and trinket salespeople, all competing for your attention. Though it's not as colorfully indigenous as markets in Guatemala or Mexico, the *mercado* displays accouterments from every Costa Rican lifestyle. Authentic *sabaneros* (cowboys) study leather saddles and boots; homemakers haggle over the price of chayote, tomatoes and plastic housewares; believers stock up on herbal remedies and religious trinkets; and tourists stick out like plucked ducks. You may be tempted to snap photos while in this hellacious maze. If you do, make sure your valuables are safely tucked out of sight.

papaya or mango from a corner stand, and get your hiking boots shined. The plaza is landscaped with Guanacaste trees, and bands play at the center *kiosko* bandstand. The hulking gray **Catedral Metropolitano** faces the square. The cathedral has little of the dazzling gilt common in major Latin American churches, and its popularity as a religious center is overshadowed by the basilica in Cartago.

The neoclassic **Teatro Melico Salazar** (221-4952 or (257-6005 (ticket office), at Calle Central and Avenida 2, hosts live performances, some presented by gringo theater groups. The theater presents a folkloric dance performance twice monthly. Three blocks west on Avenida Central at Calle 8, the **Mercado Central** bustles even on Sunday, when most downtown shops are closed. A traditional commercial center since 1880, the market displays the season's delicacies — imported apples for Christmas, ripe mangoes in

URBAN NEIGHBORHOODS

Downtown San José's prettiest small parks and neighborhoods lie northeast of the Plaza de la Cultura, beginning at the **Parque Morazán** at Calle 7 and Avenida 3. The continuous activity of the Red Light District ends at the southeast corner of the park. Several bus lines converge on Avenida 3, and streams of commuters flow through the park's pathways during the rush hours. One of my favorite spots for resting and people-watching, the park was landscaped in 1992 with lawns and benches laid out around the white-domed Temple of Music. The 17-story nondescript Aurola Holiday Inn faces the park's north side; although I would not recommend staying there, you might want to visit the top-floor casino and lounge for a view of the city at night.

If creepy, crawly creatures are of interest (or you want to bone up on possible sightings in the wild), take a detour to the **Serpentarium** (255-4210, Avenida 1 between Calles 9 and 11. Don't be deterred by the nondescript entrance — just keep climbing the narrow dark stairway until you reach the main room. Its spooky collection of live tropical reptiles and amphibians will inspire a healthy respect for the outback. It's open daily; admission is charged.

A block east of Parque Morazán, the **Parque España** is a more peaceful and densely landscaped refuge with statues of Juan Vásquez de Coronado (a Spanish settler) and Simón Bolívar, the great liberator who attempted to unite the nations of

Latin America. Bamboo groves, heliconia and ginger blossoms, and intermittent flocks of parakeets make a walk though the park feel like an unexpected commune with nature. On the east edge of the park facing Avenida 5 is the **Edificio Metálica**, a metal building that is said to have come from the Eiffel company in France. The building, now painted light yellow, is an elementary school. The **Casa Amarilla**, a yellow colonial-style mansion housing the State Department, stands guarded on the northeast side of the park.

Facing the east side of Parque España is the **Museo de Arte y Diseño** (257-7202, at Calle 13 between Avenidas 5 and 7, housed in the **Centro Nacional de la Cultura**, a block-square complex of buildings that once housed the National Liquor Factory. *Evelia con Batan*, by world-renowned Costa Rican sculptor Zuñiga stands at the entryway. Art exhibits, live performances, and lectures are held

in the many yellow buildings which surround an unadorned courtyard; the museum's main exhibits are usually cutting edge and fascinating. The museum is closed on Sunday and Monday; admission is charged.

Take time to wander the side streets in this area through **Barrio Amón** and **Barrio Otoya** (roughly bordered by Avenidas 3 to 11 and Calles Central to 17). The coffee boom of the late 1800s brought several wealthy growers to the city; a few purchased large tracts of land and turned them into genteel neighborhoods. Barrio Amón, named for French businessman Amón Fasileau Duplantier y Roussand, is one of the loveliest parts of the city, with an abundance of Victorian and neocolonial mansions. North of Parque España, steep sidewalks (some covered in handcrafted tiles) lead past several of the mansions which have been protected and restored as small hotels. If you're interested in architecture, get to know these neighborhoods. Don't miss the **Castillo el Moro** at the north end of Calle 3. Built in 1925 as a private residence, the Moorish-style white castle is ostentatiously decorated with rows of keyhole windows and plaster crenellations. Strips of hand-painted tiles border the castle's dome, which towers beside the main road to Siquirres.

Barrio Escalante, directly east of the Parque Nacional, was one of the city's wealthiest neighborhoods at the end of the nineteenth century, filled with small farms, gardens, and the mansions of coffee barons. Many of the houses, some covered with ornate mahogany carvings, have been lovingly restored by wealthy *ticos*. Carefully tended ginger, coffee, coconut, and pineapple plants thrive behind wrought iron gates. Wander the side streets of Avenidas 5 and 7, 9 and 11 for the best sights, including the **Iglesia de Santa Teresita**, the small **Parque de Francia**, and the **Museo Doctor Rafael Angel Calderón Guardia** (255-1213, Avenida 11 between Calles 25 and 27. Calderón was one of Costa Rica's most liberal-minded presidents, who instituted the national university, the social security system and other measures that seemed too socialist-minded for the elite. His presidency ended in 1948 at the culmination of Costa Rica's civil war. The big yellow mansion is open to the public daily except Monday, and portrays (in a rather self-aggrandizing style) the ex-president's lifestyle and efforts to help the poor. Calderón's wife, Gloria, was instrumental in creating the **Museo del Niño** (227-7485, Avenida 9 at Calle 4. Bizarrely housed in the former city prison, the museum is heavy on interactive exhibits, including several focusing on environmental issues. It's closed Monday; admission is charged.

Parque Zoológico Simón Bolívar provides a greenbelt at the edge of these neighborhoods.

Signs in English often overwhelm their Spanish competitors along San José streets.

The zoo is only worth visiting on Sunday afternoons, when *josefino* families picnic and party on its lawns. Some of the park buildings have been refurbished, and the animals are a bit better off than they were in the past. The zoo attracts hordes of city residents and school kids and is a great place to soak in the local culture. I prefer to slip in for a quick go-round, then wander the hilly *callejones* (alleyways) bordering the park's canyon walls. Butterflies and hummingbirds flutter about the **Spirogyra Jardín de Mariposas** (222-2937 on Avenida 13 past Calle 3. It's open daily, and there is an admission fee.

San Pedro and the University of Costa Rica lie east of downtown en route to the Carretera Interamericana. Home to students, faculty, artists, musicians and suburban dwellers, San Pedro is at first glance a nightmare of through-traffic exiting the city on residential streets. Once out of your car, however, you'll find it a fascinating place. Several small budget bed and breakfasts are located in the area along with the ultramodern San Pedro Mall. The University of Costa Rica was established in 1940. Its campus covers several blocks of trees and lawns off Calle José María Muñoz. Considered prestigious, conservative and elite, the university attracts students from around the world and has the feel of an Ivy League campus. A botanical garden on the campus contains labeled specimens.

At the west side of downtown, Avenida Central becomes **Paseo Colón**, a broad thoroughfare and one of the main routes in and out of town. Hotels, auto dealerships, rental car companies and a few nice restaurants and shops line the *paseo*, though you must look past a lot of commercial clutter to find the gems. It's about a 20-minute walk from downtown to the best hotels in this neighborhood, sometimes called **El Bosco**. Tour groups and solo travelers with a bit of cash prefer this area for their base. It's close to the regional and international airports and the *autopista* to Escazú, Heredia and points northwest. El Bosco is a good walking neighborhood, with side streets leading past small parks, arty bars, and international restaurants. Work out the travel kinks by taking a brisk walk five blocks south of the *paseo* to Avenida 10 and the **Cementerio de Obreros**, the deep, wooded municipal cemetery. If you're really into tombstones and floral arrangements check out the nearby Cementerio Calvo and Cementerio Israelita. Both Avenida 10 and Paseo Colón run west to **Parque la Sábana**, the largest urban park in San José and the center of the La Sábana neighborhood. Once the region's international airport, the park now includes some cement jogging trails along eucalyptus groves, the national stadium and the national gymnasium. The **Museo de Arte Costarricense** (222-7155, housed in the old airfield terminal, contains the works of twentieth-

century Costa Rican artists, along with murals and dioramas of the country's history. It is open Tuesday to Sunday from 10 AM to 4 PM; admission is charged.

Escazú, southwest of Parque la Sábana, feels like a country town within sight of the city lights. Those who can afford to be *josefinos* without actually living within the city limits have driven real estate values to the sky in this woodsy enclave. Bus and cab service to downtown San José is inexpensive and accessible (except for those in private residences tucked in a maze of side roads in the hills). Several good inns and restaurants attract residents and visitors who want the pleasure of country living without having to depend on a car.

SPORTS

Fútbol (aka soccer) is a national passion so fervently followed that, as one local said, "During a game you could run through the streets of downtown naked and no one would know." Costa Rica won second place in the 1990 World Cup, and has made a decent showing in tournaments ever since. The national league has 12 teams with enthusiastic fans, and games are held year round on Sundays and Wednesday evenings. Want to watch a game? Call the Fútbol Association at (222-1544. Keep an eye out for local games as you travel about the country. Even the smallest village has some sort of soccer field; in many places the playing field is in far better condition than most homes. Should you have the nerve to ignore this national passion, you'll find streets, shopping centers and museums virtually empty during Sunday games.

SHOPPING

When I first began visiting Costa Rica, it was difficult to find souvenirs other than the ubiquitous wooden bowls made from local hardwoods and miniature painted oxcarts from Sarchí. But the art scene has expanded considerably with the growth of tourism, and San José now has several fine shops and galleries. The largest and best of the lot is **Atmósfera** (222-4322, housed in a block-wide, colonial-style building at Calle 5 between Avenidas 1 and 3. Several galleries within the shop feature one-of-a-kind ceramic ware, paintings, masks, sculpture and woodcrafts; all purchases come with a certificate of authenticity and background information on the artist. The prices are staggering and the quality unsurpassed. Closed Sundays in low season. **Suriska Gallery** (222-0129 at Calle 5 and Avenida 3, showcases expert woodcrafters Barry Biesanz and Jay Morrison. Morrison also shows his work at **Magia** (233-2630, at Calle 5 between Avenidas 1 and 3. **Annemarie's Boutique** in the Hotel Don Carlos grows larger each year, with several rooms devoted to wooden bowls, plates and boxes, masks (including a few balsa masks from the Boruca Indians), books and a comprehensive sampling of the country's souvenirs. Go there before you begin your travels, and stop back for last-minute purchases.

A jumble of shops packed with standard crafts from Costa Rica, Guatemala and Panama fills the arcade at **La Casona**, Avenida Central and Calle Central. Artisans display their wares by the Plaza de la Cultura and the Plaza de la Democracia; good buys include hammocks, woodcarvings and amazingly detailed village scenes painted on the feathers of tropical birds. The **Mercado Central** is always worth some browsing time, but be watchful of your belongings. The **Mercado Nacional de Artesanía** (221-5012, Avenida 4 at Calle 11, is packed with crafts, coffee and souvenirs; there's a branch at the Museo Nacional.

The biggest grocery store chain is **MásXMenos**, where you'll find export-quality coffee, local and imported liquor, wine and beer, cheeses from San Antonio de Belén and Monteverde, and most essentials. There are several locations throughout the city and suburbs. **Supermercado Periférico** on Avenida Central at Calle 1 is ideally located and well stocked with everyday essentials. **Café Trebol** in the market area on Calle 8 between Avenida Central and Avenida 1 sells excellent coffee beans by the kilo.

Travelers in the know gravitate to **7th Street Books** (formerly called Chispas) (256-8251 E-MAIL marroca@sol.racsa.co.cr, on Calle 7 between Avenidas Central and 1, which specializes in books on science, nature and Costa Rican lore, and also has a fine selection of new and used novels at reasonable prices. The back of the shop is devoted to **Ecole Travel** (223-2240, which specializes in budget travel. The **Librería Francesa** (223-7979, Avenida 1 between Calles 5 and 7, has a good selection of guide books and novels in French.

Most shops are open Monday to Saturday from 9 AM to 5 PM; some close for lunch and all are closed on Sunday except when tourism is particularly high.

WHERE TO STAY

San José has an overabundance of hotels — a situation which encourages competition. Luxurious chain hotels have popped up near the airport, and are best for those wishing to get out of the city as quickly as possible. Refurbished residences, with a dozen or more rooms, are the norm in the downtown neighborhoods. Those closest to the museums and tourist sights are often burdened with horrendous street noise; small inns in nearby neighborhoods are quieter. Light sleepers are best off in outlying neighborhoods with good bus service to downtown. Most hotels will store your luggage while you travel around the country.

Consider your overall itinerary when choosing a hotel in San José, especially if you'll be driving. Those around La Sábana and the *autopista* are close to the roads to the north and west, while Barrio Amón and Barrio Otoya are right by the main road leading to the east and the Caribbean coast. The southern route is best accessed from San Pedro. You can certainly stay anywhere and still get to your next destination, but you'll save yourself the hassle of driving through downtown if you begin your trip near the road that will quickly lead you into the countryside.

Most of San José's most luxurious hotels are located well outside the city, in Heredia and Alajuela (see pages 87 and 92 in THE MESETA

CENTRAL), close to the international airport. The Marriott, Meliá and Sheraton hotels in this area (about a US$15 cab ride from downtown) are full-scale modern resorts with several restaurants, casinos, tour and car-rental desks, fitness and business centers and rooms with direct-dial phones, satellite television, air-conditioning and room service. Business travelers hover in this area, along with explorers who want to begin and end their adventures in total comfort.

Reserve a room far in advance for the high season — some of the most popular spots are booked solid three months ahead. Don't panic, however. All sorts of circumstances can upset the best-laid plans, and rooms sometimes become available in places you would least expect. Rates decrease and availability increases in the green (rainy) season.

VERY EXPENSIVE

Utterly unique and somewhat bizarre is **Tara** (228-6992 FAX 228-9651 E-MAIL taraspa@sol.racsa.co.cr, sitting atop a steep hill in Escazú. The white plantation mansion reminiscent of *Gone with the Wind* is almost too much for liberal sensibilities. The

Downtown San José's streets are a nightmare even for local drivers.

lily-white pillars, manicured gardens, fine white linens and almost campy southern-belle style suit those with fantastic imaginations, who luxuriate in the full-scale spa, order rum poolside, and dress formally for dinner.

EXPENSIVE

San José's older resort-style hotels are located just north of Parque la Sábana on the *autopista* to the airport. Their casinos and restaurants cater to business travelers and city dwellers as well as to tourists, and are often populated with tour groups getting acquainted. The **Meliá Confort Corobicí** (232-8122 TOLL-FREE (800) 336-3542 FAX 231-5834 E-MAIL corobici@sol.racsa.co.cr WEB SITE www .solmelia.es, on the Autopista General Cañas next to Parque la Sábana, is well suited to travelers adjusting to a new country. Cable television, room service, restaurants serving international cuisine,

and courteous staff members satisfy the needs of tour groups and business travelers.

Parque la Sábana provides a green belt on the western edge of the city, and a few of San José's best small hotels are located within walking distance of both the park and downtown. My favorite by far is the 35-room **Hotel Grano de Oro** (255-3322 FAX 221-2782 E-MAIL granoro@sol.racsa.co.cr, Calle 30 between Avenidas 2 and 4. Canadian owners Eldon and Lori Cooke have transformed a turn-of-the-twentieth-century wooden house into a charmer, with indoor gardens and fountains, a rooftop sundeck with hot tub, and one of the city's best international restaurants. The rooms of various sizes and styles are all decorated with cheery florals and comfy furnishings; room 22 sits beside a fountain and has a private garden. The Vista de Oro suite, with hardwood ceilings and wainscoting, and handsome furnishings, has a private Jacuzzi and mountain view. All rooms are

good *sodas* (coffee shops) and international restaurants. The **Hotel Occidental Torremolinos** (222-5266 FAX 255-3167 E-MAIL occhcr@sol.racsa .co.cr WEBSITE www.occidentaltorremolinos.com, Avenida 5 at Calle 40, has 80 similarly equipped rooms plus a pool. Go for an upstairs room, unless you want to eavesdrop on the conversations of those passing by the street level windows.

On the north side of the city proper in Barrio Tournon, the **Hotel Villa Tournon** (233-6622 FAX 222-5211 E-MAIL hvillas@sol.racsa.co.cr is just two blocks from El Pueblo's restaurants and clubs. Sloping wood ceilings, brick walls, and gardens give the 80-room hotel the feeling of a country hideaway, yet downtown's museums and sights are within walking distance.

In Barrio Amón, one of the finest renovated mansions houses the bright pink **Britannia Hotel** (223-6667 TOLL-FREE IN THE US (800) 263-2628 FAX 223-6411 E-MAIL britania@sol.racsa.co.cr, Calle 3 at Avenida 11. The 24 large rooms and suites are tastefully decorated with antiques, and the downstairs restaurant aptly named The Cellar is an intimate refuge. The fanciest hotel in the neighborhood is the modern pink **Barceló Amón Plaza** (257-0191 FAX 257-0284 E-MAIL amonpark @sol.racsa.co.cr, Avenida 11 at Calle 3. All of its 91 rooms have air-conditioning, coffee makers, hairdryers, and bathtubs; handicapped-access and nonsmoking rooms are available. The hotel has a gym, restaurant, room service, casino and business center, and a quiet location next to the zoo. Though it doesn't have the charm of the neighborhood's restored mansions, the Barceló dominates a quiet residential street and offers enough pampering to soothe those tired of roughing it in the wilderness.

MODERATE

A number of interesting small hotels are scattered through downtown's barrios. Behind the to-be-avoided Holiday Inn in Barrio Amón is the classy **Hotel Santo Tomás** (255-0448 FAX 222-3950 E-MAIL info@hotelsantotomas.com, Avenida 7 between Calles 3 and 5, a converted century-old mansion filled with the burnished glow of rare hardwood floors and Louis XV furnishings. The 20 rooms vary in size and style. The best are on the second floor and have balconies with views over the city. Useful and interesting maps of Costa Rica decorate the walls, there's a good selection of guidebooks available for perusal at the front desk, and guests have free Internet access. Breakfast (included in the rate) is served in an interior courtyard. Smoking is prohibited in the guest rooms but allowed in the dining area and front sitting room.

nonsmoking; smokers can request rooms with outdoor patios or confine their smoking to the courtyards and sun deck. The hotel's professional and amiable staff, excellent restaurant and accommodating layout are often imitated by envious hoteliers, but not many places achieve the Grano de Oro's comfortable efficiency.

Some tour groups use hotels in the neighborhood of Parque la Sábana as their city base. The 39-room **Parque del Lago** (257-8787 FAX 223-1617 E-MAIL parklago@sol.racsa.co.cr, Avenida 2 between Calles 40 and 42, is well located across from the park, though pedestrians risk their lives when crossing Calle 42; they should use the pedestrian overpass. The decor incorporates carpeting throughout the hotel, mirrored elevators, bathtubs, air-conditioning, and good-sized desks next to the windows, which open only at the very top. Other draws are guarded parking and the hotel's proximity to the *autopista*, several bus lines, and

The bandstand, kiosko, in San José's Parque Central.

Even if you're not staying amidst the ferns and fountains at the venerable **Hotel Don Carlos (** 221-6707 FAX 255-0828 E-MAIL hotel@doncarlos.co.cr WEB SITE www.doncarlos.co.cr, Calle 9 between Avenidas 7 and 9, be sure to check out its excellent gift shop and courtyard café complete with gurgling fountain and rock walls covered with reproductions of pre-Columbian masks. The hotel was founded by Carlos Balser, an art collector and major contributor to the jade collection now housed in the Museo Nacional. The 36 rooms are spacious and comfortable (though some are subject to street noise), and the hotel offers some great perks including an airport shuttle, free e-mail service, guarded parking, and free local phone calls for guests.

In Barrio Otoya, guests gather in the covered courtyard to breakfast on wonderful breads and fresh fruit at **Edelweiss (** 221-9702 FAX 222-1241, E-MAIL edelweis@sol.racsa.co.cr WEB SITE www.edelweisshotel.com, Avenida 9 between Calles 13 and 15. The Austrian and American owners have taken three adjoining houses and divided the space into 27 rooms with floral wallpapers and stencils, exotic wood floors, private bathrooms (some with tubs) and handmade furniture including desks. **La Casa Verde de Amón (** 223-0969 FAX 257-1054, Avenida 9 and Calle 7, is well situated in Barrio Amón, and each of the large, airy, comfortable rooms and suites is distinctly decorated. The green Victorian house is itself quite beautiful, with several covered patios and indoor salons, one with a grand piano.

Set back from the traffic madness on a side street in San Pedro, the **Hotel Milvia (** 225-4543 FAX 225-7801 E-MAIL hmilvia@sol.racsa.co.cr WEB SITE www.novanet.co.cr/milvia, 50 m (55 yards) north and 200 m (220 yards) east of Muñoz y Nanne Centro Comercial on Avenida Central, is housed in one of the city's loveliest mansions. Built in the 1930s for engineer Ricardo Fernández Peralta, the house has been lovingly restored and furnished with antiques. Two wings downstairs face a garden, while a terrace is the perfect place to write postcards and sip coffee. Most of the rooms are surprisingly large and have televisions, fans, and air-conditioning. Guests gather in the dining rooms for breakfast. The front desk clerks go beyond all expectations to help confused travelers. Upon hearing of my frustration over the lack of road signs, the clerk Greiven drew the most detailed map (complete with mountains and shining sun) to get me to my next destination. Touches like that make the Milvia feel even better than home.

Moving on to downtown, the choices grow staggering both in variety and drawbacks. Among the larger properties is the 105-room **Gran Hotel Costa Rica (** 221-4000 FAX 221-3501, Calle 3 between Avenidas Central and 2. This Plaza de la Cultura landmark has a promising setting, but the noise factor outweighs the charm. Having spent my requisite night here, I much prefer hanging out at the hotel's Café Parisienne and finding accommodation elsewhere.

Architect Juan Joaquín, who designed the Gran in 1930, also designed the refurbished 104-room **Hotel del Rey (** 221-7272 FAX 221-0096 E-MAIL info @hoteldelrey.com WEB SITE www.hoteldelrey.com, Avenida 1 at Calle 9. The pink, neoclassic building is just next to Parque Morazán, in the heart of hooker heaven. Services include a good travel agency, an American-style deli, and a raucous bar and casino. Choose your room carefully here. Those that face the street can be unbearable; this is the first hotel I've stayed in where the noise level increases as the night wears on and peaks at about 2 AM. Located on the pedestrian zone, the **Hotel Presidente (** 222-3022 FAX 221-1205 E-MAIL info @hotel-presidente.com WEB SITE www.hotel-presidente.com, Avenida Central at Calle 7, is somewhat quieter. The rooms are designed to please demanding travelers, and have safe-deposit boxes, direct-dial phones, and cable television. The in-house travel agency is excellent, and the guarded parking lot a plus.

Several inns and hotels in Escazú offer comfortable, pleasing accommodations in close proximity to the city. The **Costa Verde Inn (** 228-4080 FAX 289-8591, sprawls along a slope overlooking Escazú's neighborhoods. Returning guests settle in for months in the fully-equipped apartments; short-term visitors grab the more modest rooms in several buildings surrounding a garden and tennis court. Some rooms have balconies and gorgeous views; meals are available on request. The inn has a sister property in Manuel Antonio with transportation between the two.

Located near bus stops and shops on the side highway through San Rafael de Escazú is the **Hotel Sangildar (** 289-8843 FAX 228-6454 E-MAIL pentacor @sol.racsa.co.cr. Modern in terms of creature comforts and services, the hotel has a full-service restaurant, a pool and large air-conditioned rooms, and is popular with small tour groups.

INEXPENSIVE

The room rates just barely squeak into the inexpensive range, yet the **Hemingway Inn (**/FAX 221-1804, Avenida 9 at Calle 9, is a great bargain. Guests feel right at home in the 17 rooms, each with distinct attributes. Some have balconies with park views, other have canopy beds and antique armoires, guests are free to use the kitchen and are served homemade *tamales* and fresh tropical fruits at the complimentary breakfast. There's a hot tub in the courtyard, original paintings on the walls, and a feeling of camaraderie among the guests and staff. The **Hotel Vesuvio (**/FAX 221-7586

E-MAIL info@hotelvesuvio.com WEB SITE www
.hotelvesuvio.com, 1333 Avenida 11 between
Calles 13 and 15, also ranks at the high end of the
inexpensive scale. The owners manage the property (always a good sign) and the large, clean rooms
are carpeted and quiet. The on-site restaurant
serves good Costa Rican and international dishes
at reasonable prices. Fanciful and gay, the **Hotel
Kékoldi** (223-3244 FAX 257-5476 E-MAIL kekoldi@
sol.racsa.co.cr WEB SITE www.kekoldi.com, Avenida 9 at Calle 3, is decorated with a melange of
pastel murals with a Caribbean flair. Each step to
the second-floor rooms is painted pink, green,
yellow or blue; each wall is a different color. The
effect is surprisingly soothing, as if guests are swept

up in a heavenly fantasy. The 14 rooms attract a
mixed international crowd who mingle in the
downstairs lounge and breakfast room.

German owned and operated **La Amistad Inn**
(258-0021 FAX 221-1409 E-MAIL wolfgang@sol
.racsa.co.cr, Avenida 11 at Calle 15 in Barrio Otoya,
attracts a European clientele to its 22 economically-
priced rooms, all with ceiling fans and private bath.
Breakfast is included in the rate. Rooms with a
shared bath at the **Joluva Guesthouse** (223-7961
WEB SITE www.joluva.com, Calle 3 between Avenidas 9 and 11, fall into the low inexpensive range,
allowing budget travelers to enjoy the Barrio Amón
neighborhood and the pleasures of staying in a
handsome restored mansion.

Those on a bottom-line budget who plan ahead
will be lucky to grab one of the 80 beds or two
private rooms at the **Toruma Hostel** (/FAX 224-
4085, Avenida Central between Calles 29 and 31.

San José

WHERE TO EAT

San José's dining scene has changed dramatically
in the past few years, becoming more varied, sophisticated, and expensive. The most exciting
restaurants are clustered in fashionable and hip
neighborhoods including barrios Amón, Otoya,
la Sábana, and San Pedro, while downtowners rely
on old favorites. Familiar chain burger and pizza
restaurants are scattered all over the city, and
are wildly popular with tourists and locals alike.
Some of the country's finest restaurants are located
just a few miles outside the city center in the urban
neighborhoods of the Meseta Central (see the
next chapter) and city dwellers think nothing of
driving 30 minutes or more for a good meal. But
if you're staying within the city limits, you'll pay
dearly for a cab to Alajuela or Escazú. Wander the
neighborhoods of downtown, instead. You're sure
to find new and exciting restaurants as *ticos* and
foreign residents cash in on the growing interest
in fine dining. Many restaurants in the city have
nonsmoking areas, and many are closed on Sunday, especially during the low season. Most hotel
front desk clerks have information on hours and
will check for opening times and make reservations for their guests.

EXPENSIVE

The majority of San José's finest restaurants
straddle the moderate-to-expensive price range,
and diners on a budget can sample the fare without breaking the bank. You can easily turn dinner
at any of these restaurants into a major splurge by
ordering several courses along with imported
wines. Or you can sip a glass of house wine, order
appetizers and salads, and still have enough cash
for desserts.

My first choice for a quiet, romantic dinner (or
any meal) is the restaurant at the **Grano de Oro**
(255-3322, Calle 30 between Avenidas 2 and 4.
The recently renovated interior rooms feel serene
and spacious, glowing with candlelight and abuzz
with conversation. The courtyard tables are set
amid palms and an impressive collection of bromeliads. Try to dine with a small group so you
can sample more offerings from the inventive
menu. Surefire palate pleasers include the corn
chowder, warm palm and cheese dip, salad with
asparagus and hearts of palm, filet mignon with
gorgonzola, sea bass with a macadamia nut crust,
and the sinfully satisfying *tres leches* and chocolate cakes. If you're on a strict budget, stop by for
breakfast and order the *tico* plate, an excellent
rendition of the traditional plate of *gallo pinto*, eggs,
cheese, and plantains.

Office workers, tourists and street vendors congregate
under the umbrellas at the Café Parisienne.

Suits, ties and fancy dresses are in order for an evening at **Le Chandelier** (225-3980, 100 m (110 yards) east and the same distance south of the ICE building in San Pedro. The most elegant restaurant in town features the creations of Swiss chef Claude Dubuis and has 10 elegant dining rooms in a restored mansion. The chef imports many of his ingredients for both classic French dishes and nouvelle Costa Rican cuisine.

Il Ponte Vecchio (283-1810, 75 m (82 yards) east and 10 m (11 yards) north of Salón de Patines in San Pedro, is considered to be the best Italian restaurant in the city. Chef Antonio D'Alaimo, a transplanted New Yorker, makes his own pastas and offers an extensive list of imported wines. **La Piazzetta** (222-7896, Paseo Colón at Calle 40, offers some serious competition, however. Despite the name, there's nary a pizza on the menu. Instead, the chef focuses on homemade pastas and traditional veal, beef, and seafood recipes.

Though often packed with tourists, **La Cocina de la Leña** (223-3704, at El Pueblo Center in Barrio Tournon, is a festive place to sample Costa Rican cuisine. The menu (listed on a brown paper bag) features far more than rice and beans. Try the *olla de carne* (boiled beef and vegetable soup), the *tamales*, and the *chilaquiles* (tortillas stuffed with spiced beef). Though large and sometimes deafeningly loud, the restaurant resembles a warm, rustic farmhouse and offers live music on most nights. You might want to come by more than once to get a full education in *tico* tastes. **El Fogón de la Leña** (223-5416, at El Pueblo Center in Barrio Tournon, next door is a bit more subdued and expensive. Make a night of it by visiting El Pueblo's shops before a late dinner followed by dancing at one of the center's clubs.

MODERATE

Barrios Amón and Otoya are home to several trendy, crowd-pleasing restaurants, including the wildly popular **Café Mundo** (222-6190, Avenida 9 at Calle 15. A small sign points the way up a nearly hidden stairway to a rambling old house with several dining areas. The tables on the front porch are pleasant and quiet, while the interior rooms bustle with lively chatter. Vegetarians delight in the roasted vegetables, which show up in salads and entrees, atop gourmet pizzas, and the crisp tempura veggies. The fettuccini and shrimp, thick steaks and snapper with lime and tequila are all excellent, and the lemon pound cake is the perfect dessert. The café is closed Sundays. The aroma of roasted coffee is enough to draw you through the doors into the papaya-colored warmth of **La Esquina del Café** (257-9868, Avenida 9 at Calle 3, in Barrio Amón. Originally a small coffeehouse and shop, La Esquina

has expanded into a plant-filled café serving enormous salads, savory curried chicken, great brownies, and fruit shakes (called *batidas*). The *sopa negra* (black bean soup with rice, eggs, fried plantains and corn tortillas) is one of the least expensive and most nourishing items on the menu, and the daily specials include full meals with beverages at budget prices. The shop's shelves are stocked with fresh-roasted coffees from various regions of the country, fanciful coffee accoutrements, and *chorreaduras*, the simple sock-like contraption inside a wooden frame that's used to brew coffee in Costa Rican homes and restaurants. One of the city's best restaurants is tucked into a bland strip mall in San Pedro. **Ambrosia** (253-8012, Centro Commercial de la Calle Real, Avenida Central, San Pedro, soothes diners with a fresh, no-frills decor featuring soft watercolors, plants, and candlelight along with an innovative, health-oriented menu. The warm, wholegrain rolls that quickly appear on your table are a good harbinger of what's to come — cream cheese and veggie sandwiches, bountiful Greek salads, spinach crêpes, and several savory sea bass preparations. Ask about daily specials, which feature homemade cheeses, pastas, and locally grown chilies and herbs.

Machu Picchu (222-1384, Calle 32 No. 124, between Avenidas 1 and 3 near Kentucky Fried Chicken in La Sábana has long been San José's best Peruvian restaurant. The setting is simple — a few fishnets and posters on the walls, bare tables (sans cloths) crowded together in three dining rooms, busy waitresses rushing about. But pisco sours, made of Peruvian firewater, pack quite a punch, and the seafood soups, tangy *ceviches* and *anticuchos* (beef hearts) taste as good as any you'll find in Cusco. More upscale, with upstairs balcony tables overlooking a lush courtyard, **La Palma** (258-4541, Avenida 9 at Calle 9, is reminiscent of Lima's best seafood restaurants. Start with *pulpo al oliva* with black olive sauce or the *causa limeña*, cold mashed potato shaped around a shrimp and avocado filling. The *corvina en salsa andina* (sea bass with a smoked salmon and ricotta sauce) and the sirloin with *chimichurri* sauce are both excellent, as is the spicy *chupe de camarones*, a seafood soup with potatoes and poached egg. Paella, octopus, squid and game are the specialties at the Spanish **La Masía de Triquel** (296-3524, Avenida 2 at Calle 40, and the wine list has an impressive selection of Italian and French imports. **Tin-Jo** (221-7605, Calle 11 between Avenidas 6 and 8, is consistently named the city's best Asian restaurant, serving Sichuan, Cantonese, Thai and Indian dishes in an elegantly restored mansion. **Ariang** (223-2838, in the Edificio Colón on Paseo Colón between Avenidas 38 and 40, is popular with both locals and the foreign community. This small, comfortable restaurant near Parque la Sábana serves good Korean food and Japanese dishes for lunch and dinner, including tempura, sashimi, sushi and meats barbecued at your table. It's closed on Sunday.

Redolent of gorgonzola, prosciutto and garlic, **El Balcón de Europa** (221-4841, Calle 9 at Avenida Central, is one of the oldest mainstays on the downtown dining scene. The 15 tables fill quickly with tourists in early evening and locals later, all feasting on antipasto, pasta and risotto. It's closed on Saturday.

INEXPENSIVE

The most inexpensive, filling meals can be found at *sodas*, small diner-like cafés where a full meal of chicken, beef or fish, rice, beans, fried plantains, cabbage salad and coffee costs less than US$5. You'll find *sodas* in nearly every neighborhood. **Soda y Restaurant Vegetariano Vishnu** (256-6023, Avenida 1 between Calles 1 and 3, serves vegetarian dishes including steamed veggies and rice, cheese sandwiches and meat-substitute burgers; granola, honey and whole-wheat breads are sold at the cash register. A smaller café and shop across the street handles the overflow.

Patrons dine on sandwiches and *casados* at sidewalk tables facing an endless stream of traffic at **Soda Tapia**, on Calle 42 across from Parque la Sábana; it's noisy but it's one of the more affordable places in the neighborhood. **RostiPollos** (256-2626, Calle 5 at Avenida 1, serves fast-food *tico* style, including rotisserie-cooked chicken, beans, rice and *patacones*. There are outlets all over town.

My favorite escape from downtown's madness is in the Teatro Nacional's **Café Ruiseñor** (221-3262. Ideally, I claim a table by the few narrow windows looking out to the Gran Hotel and linger over a strong *café con leche* and flaky apple pie. The cherubic ceiling mural, marble-paneled walls, heavy green drapes and courtly waiters are a relief from the bustle outside. Sandwiches and salads are served along with a variety of coffee drinks from 10 AM to 6 PM and before and after scheduled performances. The café is closed on Sunday. There's a second Café Ruiseñor in the Museo de Arte Costarricense at Parque la Sábana. Across from the theater is downtown's most popular sidewalk hangout, the **Café Parisienne** in the Gran Hotel. The best people-watching spot in San José serves decent, inexpensive meals and good coffee. Vendors wander through, selling newspapers and souvenirs or offering to shine your shoes.

The three dining areas and 24-hour service at **Manolo's** (221-2041, Avenida Central at Calle 2, make it a standby for nearly everyone in San José. Sightseers meet up over *churros* (fried strips of dough coated in sugar) at the sidewalk tables,

while regulars chow down on inexpensive chicken and rice inside the Formica tabletops. Upstairs, lucky diners claim tables by the window, where they pay a bit more than downstairs for formal ambiance, plates of *fajitas, lomito* and *arroz de la casa* (a pile of rice topped with sautéed celery, onions and meat), and a pigeon's-eye view of the pedestrian walkway.

ENTERTAINMENT AND NIGHTLIFE

The **Teatro Nacional** (see above) is home to both the national symphony and the national theater company, which stages hit dramas and musicals. Check the *Tico Times or* stop by the box office for

the current listings. Several small theaters present comedies and experimental plays. Check out the schedule for the **Teatro Melico Salazar** (see above), which stages English-language shows. If your Spanish is advanced enough to grasp the subtleties of humor, you'll likely enjoy the goings on at the **Teatro La Comedia** (255-3255, Avenida Central between Calles 13 and 15. **Sala Garbo** (222-1034, Avenida 2 at Calle 28, screens art films in a coffeehouse setting, and movie theaters in downtown and San Pedro feature current hits, often in English with Spanish subtitles.

Downtown's more traditional nightlife scene centers around **La Esmeralda** (233-7386 on Avenida 2 between Calles 5 and 7, home of the local mariachi union. Action doesn't begin until midnight, when dozens of mariachi bands take

Folk art galleries present the works of the country's best artists.

requests from patrons stimulated by bountiful *bocas* (appetizers), beer and amiability. **El Cuartel de la Boca del Monte** (221-0327, on Avenida 1 between Calles 21 and 23, is far more hip and trendy, attracting a young, well-heeled crowd mixed with travelers and neighborhood residents, especially on Wednesday, Thursday and Friday nights, when bands play to a packed house. Some locals put **Chelles** (221-1369, on Calle 9 between Avenidas Central and 2, at the top of their cheap-eats-and-good-drinks lists, but women going there unaccompanied may find it off-putting. The staff can be unfriendly to single women, perhaps because the *taberna* is located in the Red Light District. The **Jazz Café** (283-5047 in San Pedro attracts upscale university students with its eclectic selection of recorded music and performances by live bands.

Centro Commercial el Pueblo is a tourist trap that's been around long enough to become an institution even among locals. It's on the north side of the Río Torres, across from Barrio Amón, Parque Simón Bolívar and the zoo. The walk between downtown and El Pueblo is notoriously dangerous at night and hardly scenic in the daytime. Evening visits are best. Dine early at El Fogón de la Leña, wander through the shops, then dance at **Cocolocos or La Plaza**. Like most Latins, *ticos* tend to party late and long, and these discos are best after midnight.

HOW TO GET THERE

All cars, buses, planes and trucks make their way to San José at some point. All international flights into the country arrive at Aeropuerto Internacional Juan Santamaría; buses from Panama, Honduras and Nicaragua end up at or near the Coca-Cola bus station.

Once you've passed the immigration desk in the lower level of the San José airport, you must haul your bags up escalators or elevators to street level. The transportation situation has become a bit less frenetic with the new terminal, but it still can be confusing. Licensed taxis line up just outside the doors; unofficial taxi drivers rush forth to take your bags and rush you off to their cars — possession being half the sale. Ignore them until you've got your bearings. Some hotels and tour companies offer airport transfers, which must be arranged in advance. **Gray Line** ((800) 326-8279 (in Costa Rica and the Unites States) is now offering an airport shuttle at nearly half the price of a cab.

The Meseta Central offers a peaceful green landscape within minutes of San José.

San José

San José

The Meseta Central

SAN JOSÉ SITS ROUGHLY AT THE CENTER OF THE MESETA CENTRAL, a lush region of valleys, rivers, pastures and rolling hills surrounded by bold green volcanoes. The country's other main cities, all founded in colonial times, lie within a few kilometers of each other around the outskirts of the capital. Cartago, Costa Rica's first capital and the site of its most important basilica, acts as an outpost of resources for travelers headed east to Turrialba and the Volcán Irazú, and south to the fertile Orosí Valley. Alajuela and Heredia, just north of San José, are home to the country's original coffee plantations, rising in swaths of emerald leaves against rich red soil in the foothills of the Barva and Poás volcanoes. Many of the country's finest hotels are located in this region, offering sensible base camps for travelers headed in various directions. Many travelers, in fact, choose to begin and end their trips in the Meseta Central rather than the capital, and visit San José on day trips from their hotels.

Once forested and nearly impassable, the Meseta Central has now become Costa Rica's most populous region. Nearly one-third of all Costa Ricans, along with retired expatriates and impoverished immigrants, live in its cities and rural neighborhoods bordered by mountain ranges and national parks. The landscape is disciplined here, meticulously planted with tropical plants imported from throughout the world. Lavender jacaranda, yellow palo verde and pink palo blanco blossoms litter the asphalt highways running past white wooden houses framed with bougainvillea, calla lilies and roof-high poinsettia branches. Homeowners look after their lawns with obsessive care, cutting the grass level with machetes and sweeping away leaves with plastic brooms. Waist-high fields of shiny green coffee shrubs are set against forests of macadamia trees and billowing fields of sugarcane.

Fed by the ash and mud left from volcanic eruptions and watered with predictable rainfall and the tributaries of mighty rivers, the lands of the Meseta Central are a farmer's paradise. Cattle range in wheat fields and wander across main roads while daring drivers with haughty stares and indifferent "moos." Horses clomp along roadside trails; oxcart wheels sing their discordant rhythms on gravel paths. And just over the next rise, bridge or patch of rock-strewn mud lie the rainforests of Braulio Carrillo, the cloud forests of Monteverde, the fiery lava of Arenal.

It's hard to stop driving once you begin following winding side roads through this verdant countryside; more than once I've found myself happily lost. I've made visits to Costa Rica and never left these outskirts of San José, escaping the city for day trips of river rafting, mountain climbing, horseback riding and general wandering in the always-intriguing Meseta Central.

ALAJUELA AND WESTERN MESETA CENTRAL

The city of San José sprawls out into the southern regions of Alajuela province; in fact, Aeropuerto Internacional Juan Santamaría is actually in Alajuela rather than San José, as are the main offices for many car rental companies. This province is one of the largest in the country, spreading north to the Nicaraguan border, east to the cowboy ranges of Guanacaste and the shores of Laguna de Arenal, and west to the Río Sarapiquí, Parque Nacional Braulio Carrillo and Heredia. Densely populated near the capital, Alajuela quickly becomes remote and unexplored — only one road runs through the province to Nicaragua. Beyond Alajuela city are several major attractions: the crafts center at Sarchí, the gardens of Zarcero, Volcán Poás and the Sarapiquí region. Travelers headed to Monteverde, Arenal and both coasts will have a wide range of choices for day and overnight visits in Alajuela.

ALAJUELA

The city of Alajuela has little to offer the traveler, other than a few hotels near the airport and a maze of bus-clogged streets. The country's national hero, Juan Santamaría, was born here; a statue and the **Museo Juan Santamaría** (441-4775, Avenida 3 at Calle Central, are dedicated to his short life. Several interesting attractions are located in smaller towns clustered around the city.

The **Butterfly Farm** (/FAX 438-0400 WEB SITE www.butterflyfarm.co.cr, in La Guácima de Alajuela, is one of the best in the country. Over 75 native plant species in a tropical garden serve as breeding grounds for hundreds of butterflies; guests on the two-hour tour learn about butterfly exportation, an increasingly popular environmentally friendly business. Tours to the farm, located near the airport, are available from hotels in San José, Heredia and Alajuela.

A far superior alternative to visiting the Parque Zoológico Simón Bolívar in San José is **Zoo Ave** (433-8989, in La Garita de Alajuela, about 15 minutes from Alajuela city. The former coffee plantation is now home to more than 1,000 birds and mammals, many recovered from accidents, poachers nets and other precarious situations. The collection includes all the species of monkeys found in Costa Rica, both green and scarlet macaws and many of the rainforest birds. The cages are labeled

PRECEEDING PAGES: A sulfurous lake of emerald green LEFT has formed in one of Irazú's craters. RIGHT: Coatamundis become acclimated to nature guides along popular trails in Parque Nacional Braulio Carrillo. ABOVE: A typical ox cart on the side of the Monteverde–Arenal road.

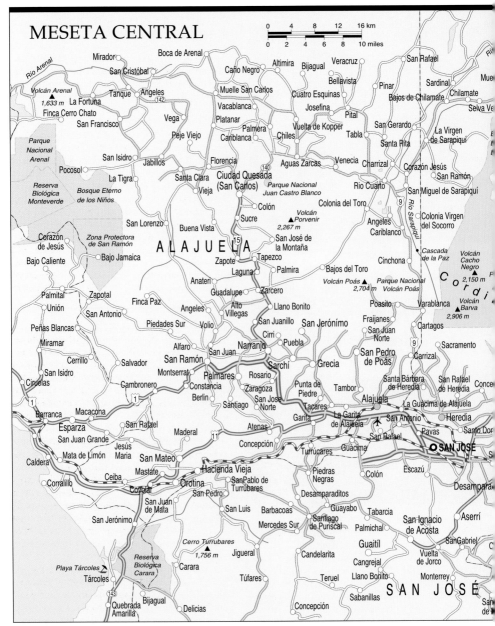

so you can bone up on your bird facts before heading into the wilderness. Tours including transportation from San José are available. La Garita is said to have the most pleasant climate in the country, perhaps in the world. Nearby Atenas is equally delightful, and both towns boast excellent inns.

Where to Stay

Hotels near the airport but well outside Alajuela city are a good choice for those with rental cars or transportation arranged in advance with a tour company. Many inns in the area also offer transportation to and from the airport and tours to nearby attractions. Alajuela is convenient for those headed on to the Sarapiquí region, Poás, or the Pacific coast.

VERY EXPENSIVE

Italian hotelier Alfonso Martinez first read about La Garita in *National Geographic* and thought it sounded like a fine spot for a Mediterranean-style spa. His **Club Martino Hotel and Spa** (433-8382

service spa. Some guests check in for cosmetic surgery procedures offered in conjunction with Derma Clinic USA, and recovery in the lap of luxury. The excellent restaurant overlooks the grounds and features southern Italian cuisine.

Beware of beginning your vacation at **Xandari** (443-2020 TOLL-FREE IN THE US (800) 686-7879 FAX 442-4847 E-MAIL hotel@xandari.com WEB SITE www.xandari.com, in Alajuela. You might not get any farther than the trails surrounding your private terrace. Architect Sherrill Broudy and artist Charlene Broudy poured considerable talent into this picturesque paradise, where sleek white villas rise amid fruit orchards overlooking the central valley. Each piece of furniture is a work of art, and the blend of modernistic paintings, stained-glass windows, and cool blue fabrics make the rooms feel like cozy wombs. The restaurant menu emphasizes healthy, fresh foods — vegetarians find plenty of choices. With two lap pools for the 16 villas you never feel crowded while lounging in the sun, and the 16-ha (40-acre) property incorporates heliconia gardens, a bamboo grove and waterfalls.

MODERATE
Just 20 minutes west of the airport near Atenas, **El Cafetal Inn** (446-5785 FAX 446-7082 feels like a country estate that happens to have a few rooms available for friends. Like many small business owners in Costa Rica, Romy and Lee Rodriguéz invested everything they had in their coffee plantation and gorgeous inn with views of the Río Colorado Valley and the Poás, Barva and Irazú volcanoes. The two-story inn is an architectural wonder with a waterfall in the downstairs lounge and curved glass walls in some upstairs rooms. The 10 rooms have private baths — the best is the huge tower room with a 180-degree panoramic view of the countryside. The grounds are equally beautiful, with fountains, waterfalls and bougainvillea-lined paths leading to the large shamrock-shaped pool. Papaya, citrus and yucca trees ring the pool area, where a large tiled bar and dining area are used for weddings and parties. Romy whips up extraordinary breakfasts (included in the room rate) and elegant gourmet dinners are available if you make reservations in advance. Tours to the volcanoes, orchid and butterfly farms, waterfalls, and other nearby sights are available.

Orquideas Inn (433-9346 FAX 433-9740 E-MAIL orchid@sol.racsa.co.cr WEB SITE www.hotels.co .cr/orquideas.html, Cruce de Poás/Cacao, about 10 minutes north of Alajuela on the way to Poás, is a delightful, friendly escape set in the midst of orchid gardens. Many of the guests are regulars who make themselves at home in the 18 large rooms in the main building or the geodesic dome suite. The owners are quick to provide all sorts of worthwhile information (they even put a map to

FAX 433-9052 E-MAIL martino@sol.racsa.co.cr WEB SITE www.hotelmartino.com, on the main road through La Garita, might well be on the Isle of Capri, yet it fits right into the Costa Rican landscape. Parrots screech in an aviary near the manicured lawns and long pool guarded by marble statues. The 34 junior suites are enormous, with private porches or balconies complete with comfy chairs and closets the size of small studios. A separate building houses the enormous gym filled with state-of-the-art exercise equipment and a full-the inn on their web site), and you're sure to pick up a few helpful hints from the folks hanging out by the pool.

Architecturally bland yet convenient, the motel-like **Hampton Inn** (443-0043 TOLL-FREE (800) 426-7866 FAX 442-9532 E-MAIL hampton@sol .racsa.co.cr WEB SITE www.hamptonhotel.co.cr, Autopista General Cañas, is a wildly successful, tourist-oriented hotel across the highway from the airport. It's a good choice for quick getaways and is the headquarters for many tour groups. Several other hotels close to the airport are located in Heredia (see below).

How to Get There

Alajuela is 16 km (10 miles) from downtown San José; the city of Alajuela is three kilometers (two miles) from the airport. Buses run from San José throughout the day and night. Taxi fares to the hotels above are about the same as those to hotels in San José.

SARCHÍ

Traveling northwest from Alajuela city, follow the signs for Sarchí, the most popular crafts town in the country. Just 30 km (19 miles) from the town of Alajuela and 47 km (29 miles) from San José, Sarchí is almost overwhelming in its quaintness — even the trash cans and trucks are decorated with fanciful designs that resemble Pennsylvania Dutch plaques combined with Moorish tiles. The designs have appeared on wooden oxcarts since at least the early 1900s, and at one time each region in the country had its own typical design.

Oxcarts were the main means of transport throughout Costa Rica's countryside until the mid-1900s, and can still be seen nearly everywhere, from the market streets in San José to the sandy beach paths in the Península de Burica. The artisans of Sarchí have transformed the traditional oxcart into every sort of souvenir cliché imaginable. In store after store and roadside stand after roadside stand, tourists comb through miniature oxcart business-card or napkin holders, liquor cabinets, trays and toys. Full-sized oxcarts can also be purchased and shipped in case you need a garden ornament. More practical, perhaps, are the handsome wooden rocking chairs with leather seats and backs which fold for easy shipping. The shops also display a mesmerizing array of tropical wood bowls, plates, cups, platters — you name it, they've got it. As I've learned more about Costa Rica's woodcrafters, I'm less attracted to these manufactured goods, though the mahogany, cedar and purple-heart wood bowls make great inexpensive gifts. **Plaza de Artesanía** (454-4755 at the south end of town is a full-scale shopping center with restaurants and information center, restrooms, and, conveniently enough, ATM

machines. **Coopearsa** (454-4050, at the north end of town, is a more modest effort displaying the creations of a woodworkers' cooperative. The oxcart factory **Fábrica de Carretas Joaquín Chaverri** (454-4412 is a family operation run by Don Carlos Chaverri; the workers are accustomed to chatting with visitors and showing off their oxcarts. **Restaurant las Carretas** (454-4411 next to the factory serves regional dishes including *picadillo de papaya*, a patty of ground papaya stalk mixed with vegetables and meat.

Buses run from San José and Alajuela to Sarchí throughout the day, and the town is on every tour company's list of day trips from San José.

ZARCERO

In the competition for the most picturesque colonial town in the country, Zarcero wins hands down. An absolutely charming blue and white church dominates the plaza, where topiary artist Evangelisto Blanco wields his pruning shears on cypress bushes. Precious elephants, matadors, bulls and rabbits, or whatever strikes his fancy, pose against green lawns like hallucinations, begging to be photographed if only to assure the onlooker that they really exist. I've been told Don Evangelisto was offered a job by the Disney company but he turned them down, saying he didn't want to work anywhere where he couldn't leave his shears overnight next to his current project.

Zarcero is in the center of rich, scenic agricultural lands where fields in every shade of green check the foothills. Roads in this region twist and turn dizzyingly, and turnoffs are few. If you're tired, stop by a roadside stand to sample *cajeta* (candy of caramelized goat milk), *palmito* (the local soft white cheese, not to be confused with hearts of palm) and whatever fruits may be in season.

VOLCÁN POÁS

Directly north of Alajuela (although by an indirect route) is the simmering Volcán Poás, looming 2,704 m (8,871 ft) over the Meseta Central. The road weaves up the mountains during the 90-minute ride from Alajuela to the crater, passing vistas of regimented rows of coffee plants, swirls of smoke rising from cattle ranches and rivers flowing in deep green valleys. The air feels moist and chilly as you climb, and a gray-white mist streaks the sky. For blue skies and shimmering vistas, see Poás early in the morning before fog shrouds the peaks, though visiting in a shroud of drizzle and mist is enjoyably eerie as well.

Poás is by no means inactive; its first recorded eruption was in 1747, its biggest on January 25, 1910. Poás spewed ash, stones and steam again in the 1950s, and the area was temporarily closed in 1989 when gases and ash belched from the crater.

The unmistakable smell of sulfur draws visitors to the edge of the volcano's main crater, a short walk from the ash-covered parking lot at the entrance to Parque Nacional Volcán Poás. On clear days you may spot the milky-green lake cupped in the barren crater and see plumes of muddy water spewing in the air. Trails lead from the main crater to Laguna Botos, a lake formed from rain collecting in an inactive crater. Poás has five craters in all, and several trails lead through stunted forest to misty groves filled with bromeliads, epiphytes and a variety of bird species.

Many visitors arrive at Volcán Poás on bus tours from San José, spend an hour or so taking snapshots of the moon-like terrain, then depart for other attractions. I prefer to visit the volcano (and the rest of the area) in a rental car or to ride with a hired guide.

My favorite part of the trip may be the steaming cup of Café Britt coffee served at the park's restaurant after a chilly hike. And I've always thought it would be wonderful to spend the night at the **Poás Volcano Lodge** (/FAX 482-2194 (moderate), 16 km (10 miles) southeast of the crater. The lodge, resembling an English country manor, is set high in the cool mountain air, over 1,829 m (6,000 ft) above sea level. The lodge offers rooms in the main house and in several outlying cottages, and breakfast is included in the room rate.

How to Get There

Poás is 37 km (23 miles) north of Alajuela and 53 km (33 miles) north of San José. The most direct route is on Highway 9 toward Varablanca. You may be able to catch sight of Volcán Barva in a protected area of Parque Nacional Braulio Carrillo to the east. Turn left at the signs for the volcano at Poasito; the road is paved all the way to the park

Steam billows from a Volcán Poás crater surrounded by layers of ash from recent eruptions.

entrance. Public buses don't go all the way to the volcano. If you don't have access to a car either hire a car and driver at your hotel or join an organized tour that arrives at the crater by 9 AM (the park is open from 7 AM to 4 PM). Allow at least one full hour at the main crater.

HEREDIA AND NORTHEASTERN MESETA CENTRAL

Like Alajuela, the province of Heredia borders San José and extends north to Nicaragua. The city of Heredia, about eight kilometers (five miles) north of San José, is the capital of the province and home to the Universidad Nacional de Costa Rica. Several of the finest hotels near the airport are located in Heredia's small communities south of the city, while the spectacular rainforests of Parque Nacional Braulio Carrillo are spread out between Heredia and the province of Limón.

HEREDIA

Heredia is one of the country's few colonial-era cities. Its manicured **Parque Central** faces the **Basílica de Inmaculada Concepción**, a rather dumpy edifice that has withstood several earthquakes since its construction in 1797. The population of the city fluctuates with the schedule at the university, which attracts hundreds of international students. The city's youthful ambiance encourages the survival of small inexpensive *sodas*, coffeehouses and vegetarian restaurants, and the market is one of the cleanest and most pleasant in the country. Exhibits on the colonial era in Costa Rica are featured at the small **Museum of Popular Culture** (260-1619 in Barva de Heredia.

Scientists, students and amateur naturalists are delighted with the educational resources at **INBioparque** (224-4730 FAX 244-4790 E-MAIL inbioparque@inbio.ac.cr WEB SITE www.inbio.as

.cr/inbioparque, in Santo Domingo de Heredia. New in 2000, this museum of nature immerses visitors in the biological wonders of Costa Rica through interactive exhibits and interpretative trails. Run by the Instituto Nacional de Biodiversidad, the park is a valuable preparation for anyone traveling into the wilderness. One entire building is devoted to the national parks, with wall-sized maps, photos, and descriptions of the individual parks; another exhibit focuses on the uses of many uses of plants; and another includes a gorgeous array of butterflies. Several trails run through the eight-hectare (20-acre) park to waterfalls and butterfly gardens. The park's shop is packed with books, crafts by Costa Rica's indigenous tribes and other souvenirs, and the restaurant serves excellent Costa Rican dishes. Transportation is available from hotels in San José, Alajuela and Heredia. The admission fee is a bit steep, but the complete immersion in Costa Rica's natural side is worth the price. The park is open daily.

Coffee plantations cover the countryside in Heredia province. One of the most popular and well organized tours from San José is a visit to the coffee plantations and roasting plants of **Café Britt** (260-2748 FAX 238-1848, three kilometers (two miles) north of Heredia city. Britt is Costa Rica's largest coffee exporter, and their distinctive green and red foil packets of beans or ground coffee are sold in nearly every market and souvenir shop in the country. Their multimedia presentation covers every aspect of coffee growing, roasting, harvesting and shipping; naturally, their coffee and logo-imprinted gift items are sold in the shop. The plantation tour can be arranged through any hotel or travel agency in the area.

Moravia, less than 10 km (six miles) northeast of San José, is a good alternative to Sarchí for folk art shopping. Several small shops frame the pretty **Parque Central**. Though much of the merchandise is the same as you find elsewhere in the country, some shops here carry work by the indigenous Bribrí; others sell local leather crafts.

Where to Stay and Eat

Though the international airport is in Alajuela, many of the hotels closest to the airport lie in Heredia. Several smaller communities dot the countryside farther north and are home to fine country inns and resort hotels. Since most are located less than a half-hour drive from the international airport, they make a fine base for tourists and business travelers who don't care to stay in San José. Many travelers start and finish their wilderness jaunts in these elegant surroundings. Some have incorporated tours to nearby nature preserves, horseback riding, and rafting trips, encouraging guests to stay put for a while. Advance reservations are advised year round.

VERY EXPENSIVE

Dramatic and strangely isolated, the **Costa Rica Marriott Hotel** (298-0000 TOLL-FREE IN THE US (800) 228-9290 FAX 298-0011 E-MAIL costaric@marriott .co.cr, in San Antonio de Belén, Heredia, sits against the mountains just 10 minutes from the airport. The handsome hacienda-style estate with golden stucco walls, red-tiled roofs, arches, cupolas, and towers is filled with folk art and colonial touches — domed brick ceilings, heavy hardwood beams, hand-painted tiles and a swimming pool set amid lawns and palms. The rooms have all the latest gadgetry, including satellite televisions, mini-bars, in-room safes and hair dryers; three good restaurants offer guests a range of dining options within the resort grounds. Business and tour groups and individual travelers seeking familiar comforts are all happy here, as are those who've been roughing it for a while and yearn for bathtubs, room service and overall pampering.

One of the original luxury hotels near the airport is the 220-room **Meliá Cariari** (239-0022 TOLL-FREE (800) 336-3542 FAX 239-2803 E-MAIL cariari@ sol.racsa.co.cr WEB SITE www.solmelia.es, on Autopista General Cañas at the San Antonio de Belén intersection, Heredia, refurbished to meet the competition of the 1990s. It's right off the airport highway. Public buses to downtown San José stop in front of the hotel; coming back from town by bus you're faced with the challenge of vaulting the highway median to get to the other side or riding to the next stop and taking the inbound bus back to the hotel. The Meliá feels remote because it's set on 54 ha (134 acres). Amenities include a large free-form swimming pool, fitness equipment, an 18-hole golf course, excellent Costa Rican beef served in the **Los Vitrales** restaurant, a nice selection of high-quality folk art in the gift shop, and the inevitable casino.

In the same neighborhood, and with similar prices, the **Herradura Resort** (239-0033 FAX 239-2292 E-MAIL hheradu@sol.racsa.co.cr WEB SITE www.costasol.co.cr, on Autopista General Cañas at the San Antonio de Belén intersection, Heredia, sits beside San José's largest conference center. As a result, the hotel is often booked solid for meetings and conventions. Thanks to its concentration of international guests, the hotel's staff are multilingual and efficient, and the facilities are up-to-par with international-standard business hotels.

Impressively original, **Finca Rosa Blanca** (269-9392 FAX 269-9555 E-MAIL rblanca@sol.racsa.co.cr WEB SITE www.finca-rblanca.co.cr, in Santa Bárbara de Heredia, may well be the most artistic small inn in the country. Set amidst the shiny green leaves of coffee plants, the stark white inn with its windowed dome appears from afar as an apparition rising 1,300 m (4,264 ft) above sea level. The nine

El Fortín stands guard over Heredia.

rooms are constructed from salvaged tropical woods and white plaster; each is decorated individually with wall murals, antiques and contemporary furnishings. Light streams from the dome into the atrium-style lounge, where overstuffed couches encircle the fireplace. Breakfast is included in the rate.

EXPENSIVE

Architecture befitting the mountainous setting (and Costa Rica's enduring reputation as the Switzerland of Central America) defines the **Hotel Chalet Tirol** (267-6222 FAX 267-6229 E-MAIL info @chalet-tirol.com WEB SITE www.chalet-tirol.com, near San Rafael de Heredia. Individual chalets and a gourmet French restaurant are nestled in pine-scented forest 1,800 m (5,900 ft) above sea level. The hotel is surrounded by cloud forest, an ideal spot for horseback riding and hiking. Its services are always expanding as the owners attempt to offer their guests enough diversions to keep them put for a while. The most exciting development is the presence of the Whitten Etymological Collection, said to be the largest collection (with over one million specimens) of tropical forest insects and other anthropoids in the world. The exhibit is part of the BIOPLANET biodiversity institute housed on the 15-ha (38 acre) property. The hotel is near the Barva entrance to Parque Nacional Braulio Carrillo (see below).

MODERATE

The modern exterior belies the charm of the **Hotel Bougainvillea** (244-1414 FAX 244-1313 E-MAIL bougainvillea@centralamerica.com WEB SITE www.bougainvillea.co.cr, in Santo Domingo between San José and Heredia town. The interior design is reminiscent of a ranch manor with stone walls, wood-beam ceilings, original Costa Rican art and fireplaces. The 44 carpeted rooms are comfortable, well-lit and tastefully furnished. The gardens are not to be believed: Every imaginable shade of bougainvillea grows in hedges along paths to the large swimming pool, tennis court, condominiums and forested jogging trails. The dining room is also exceptional. There seems little reason to leave the grounds.

PARQUE NACIONAL BRAULIO CARRILLO

Heredia is the launching point for Highway 32, also called the Guápiles Highway, to Limón and the Caribbean coast. The highway runs right through Parque Nacional Braulio Carrillo, a spectacular moist, green, and muddy wonderland of waterfalls and virgin rainforest just 20 km (12 miles) northeast of San José. The park and highway were jointly conceived from the need for an efficient road between San José and Limón and the desire to protect 45,899 ha (113,415 acres) of

mountainous forest and the Meseta Central's most critical watershed. The park was established in 1978 and the highway, an extraordinary feat of engineering versus nature with the country's only mountain tunnel, opened in 1987.

Despite its proximity to the paved road, Braulio Carrillo is not an easy park to visit — don't expect picnic tables and toilets beside the road. There are, however, several view points where you can pull off the highway and appreciate the extraordinary lush, green landscape. There are short paths formed by adventurous walkers by most of the turnoffs, but don't wander too far on your own. Curiosity has led to a number of lost hikers, accidents and even deaths within the park's embrace.

Two official park entrances with ranger stations are located at Zurquí, and Quebrada Gonzáles (also called Carrillo). Both have short hiking trails. Reports of car break-ins at both entrances and other parking areas along the highway are common. Although it's tempting to undertake a hike while en route to your next destination, you may return to find your possessions (and even your car) gone. Braulio Carrillo's interior is more easily accessed from the Volcán Barva ranger station 29 km (18 miles) north of San José. Barva is the highest point in the park at 2,906 m (9,535 ft) and contains 12 eruption points and several crater lakes. Trails lead from the station to the lakes, which can be visited on day hikes. Overnight camping is allowed near the ranger station; permits must be arranged in advance through the San José office (283-8004 FAX 283-7343 HOTLINE IN COSTA RICA (192. Be sure to check in at the ranger station wherever you enter the park, and wear mud boots and a rain poncho.

Several private reserves and lodges extend the park's natural habitat at the north in the Sarapiquí region (see SARAPIQUÍ REGION, page 96). This area is technically within Heredia province and can be reached from Highway 32 on the road to Las Horquetas or from Alajuela via the route to the Volcán Poás and Varablanca.

What to See and Do

Near, if not at, the top of most travelers' lists for day trips from San José is a ride above the forest canopy on the **Teleférico del Bosque Lluvioso**, the Rainforest Aerial Tram (257-5961 FAX IN SAN JOSÉ 257-6053 WEB SITE www.rainforest.co.cr, at the eastern edge of the park. The brainchild of American naturalist Donald Perry, the Arial Tram is an engineering wonder. Perry, a devoted rainforest fanatic, refused to use tractors to erect the poles and attach the cables for the skyway; instead, he enlisted the help of Nicaragua's Sandinistas and their combat helicopters in the

Rain ponchos, binoculars, tripods and cameras all come in handy on hikes through Parque Nacional Braulio Carrillo.

construction. A film on Perry's work begins the tram tour. For more information you can purchase his fascinating book, *Life Above the Jungle Floor,* at the gift shop. The tram ride itself is a thing of wonder. Twenty cable cars whoosh almost silently into and above the forest canopy, offering a bird's-eye view of epiphytes, orchids, mosses and ferns. Don't expect to see a lot of animal or bird life unless you arrive when the tram opens at 6 AM; Perry himself warns that the ride is not a zoo, but rather a hanging garden. His fascination, which might well become yours, is with the vegetation: the tree ferns that reach higher than the treetops, the vines twisting like acrobat's wire.

The parking lot outside the 450-ha (1,000-acre) reserve is filled with tour buses whose drivers typically stay with their vehicles, so your car is relatively safe here. The entire tour of the rainforest trails, classrooms, film and tram ride takes about three hours. Be sure to bring a rain poncho and binoculars.

Sustainable agricultural methods are the focus of **EARTH** (Escuela de Agricultura de la Región Tropical Humeda) (255-2000 FAX 255-2540 E-MAIL relext@ns.earth.co.cr, east of Guápiles. The university's grounds include a banana plantation and forest reserve, and students work on research projects with medicinal plants and pesticide-free banana cultivation. Visitors are allowed to stay in the dorm-type facility with advance reservations. Several farmers in the region have developed tropical flower farms and are exporting plants. **Costa Flores** (716-6457 FAX 716-6439 east of Guápiles provides tours of their heliconia farm.

Where to Stay

There are no hotels within the park's boundaries, and few along Highway 32 until you reach Guápiles. The best places to experience a similar climate and topography to the park are located in Sarapiquí (see below) and near the Volcán Barva.

Wounded parrots, toucans and tanagers along with weary travelers find refuge at the moderately-priced **Casa Río Blanco** (/FAX 382-0957 E-MAIL crblanco@sol.racsa.co.cr in Guápiles. This small lodge with cabins and rooms for 12 people is as much an educational center as it is a hostelry. Owners Thea and Ron are experts in sustainable tourism and the concept that lodgings can be nature-friendly. They take in wounded animals and provide a gorgeous setting above the Río Blanco in the rainforest. Several not-to-be-missed attractions are within a half-hour's drive, and you could easily spend three or four nights here resting in hammocks after day trips to the aerial tram, Braulio Carrillo, Sarapiquí, the Río Sarapiquí, and Limón or San José.

While driving the highway to Limón I was pleased to discover the inexpensive **Río Palmas** (760-0330 or 760-0305 FAX 760-0296, in Guácima.

The location, nearly midway between San José and Limón, it is ideal for those who want to explore the park and byways. And the setting right next to the highway and above the river is astounding. A swimming pool is fed from a natural waterfall and trails lead along the river banks through luxuriant tropical gardens into the rainforest. A one-story building framing a central courtyard has 15 guest rooms, some with television and hot water. The large restaurant under a thatched roof is the perfect spot for a break from driving.

How to Get There

Highway 32 runs northeast from San José to the park and on to Limón. Despite its modern appearance, it is one of the most terrifying roads in the country. North of Heredia the slick asphalt lanes climb quickly to 2,000 m (6,560 ft) and almost certain mist, fog or rainfall. Temperatures drop, visibility decreases and trucks barrel down hills. Mud and rock slides (*derrumbes*) are common, and the highway is frequently closed as workers use bulldozers to clear natural debris or vehicular accidents. Road closures can last from a few hours to days; traffic is directed to lengthy alternate byways through Turrialba or Sarapiquí. Don't even think of driving this road after dark; always start out as early in the day as possible.

There is a ranger station at Zurquí just outside the highway tunnel with a few short trails that take you far enough into the forest for some good bird watching. Take extreme care on the trails — robberies have occurred here. Check in at the ranger station before and after your hike. Buses from San José to Guápiles will drop you off and pick you up at the ranger station.

The Volcán Barva ranger station is 29 km (18 miles) north of San José at the end of the road to Sacramento and San José de la Montaña. A precarious but passable dirt and mud road runs four kilometers (two and a half miles) from Sacramento to the Barva station; four-wheel drive is essential year round, but the road may be completely impassable in the rainy season.

SARAPIQUÍ REGION

Located north of the Meseta Central in Heredia province, the Sarapiquí region is one of Costa Rica's newest destinations. Conservationists have long treasured the area as a natural extension of Parque Nacional Braulio Carrillo, and several private enterprises have established large natural reserves to protect the flora and fauna of the region. There are no paved roads north of Puerto Viejo de Sarapiquí; instead, boats traverse the Río Sarapiquí, which flows south from Nicaragua's Río San Juan. These two rivers connect Sarapiquí with Barra del Colorado and Tortuguero on the northern Caribbean coast. Tour companies now offer circuits that combine the two areas, but the trip takes several hours by boat and has yet to catch on in a major way. For the moment, Sarapiquí remains a delightful off-the-beaten-track destination for rafters, bird watchers and wanderers.

What to See and Do

The drive to Sarapiquí is part of the adventure. There are several ways to reach this region. I prefer the mystically scenic route on the winding, climbing stretch of Highway 9 north of Alajuela or Heredia towards Volcán Poás. Just to the north of Poasito, the highway cuts through dense forest to the entrance of the amazing **La Paz Waterfall Gardens** (482-2720 WEB SITE www.waterfall

Río la Paz. It takes about four hours to explore the trails, then you're ready for lunch in the enormous restaurant with balcony seating overlooking the gardens. The whole setup is a bit disconcerting to those who prefer the real wilderness. But even the most diehard naturalist can't help but experience a shiver of excitement when faced with the extraordinary heliconia, bromeliad, and orchid collections or the 15-m-tall (50-ft) butterfly garden (said to be the largest in the world). The designers considered every detail, from the quality of the food at the buffet lunch to the hammocks on the restaurant balcony and the hairdryers in the bathrooms. Even the gift shop has an amazing collection of souvenirs. The entry fee

gardens.com, near Varablanca. The Cascada de la Paz (La Paz Waterfall) tumbling down a hillside has long been a popular stop off along the road, but this new project (which opened in 2000) has utterly transformed the area.

Owner Lee Banks has created what might best be called a natural theme park that is the envy of every gardener and landscape architect who walks through the front doors of the visitor's center. Four manicured trails lead through the property, past a hummingbird garden, an enormous enclosed butterfly garden, orchid houses, and fern gardens. As you hike along, you begin hearing the sounds of rushing water; before long you approach the first of four spectacular waterfalls. At one point the trail detours to a viewing platform under the Magia Blanca waterfall; at another, platforms overlook the gorge created by the confluence of the Río la Paz Grande and the

is quite high, so you should plan on spending at least a half day here, perhaps in combination with a trip to Poás.

The road continues on past La Catarata San Fernando, through the rural towns of San Miguel de Sarapiquí, La Virgen de Sarapiquí, and Chilamate en route to Puerto Viejo de Sarapiquí. A few special lodges provide comfortable accommodations for those wanting to explore this area further. Puerto Viejo de Sarapiquí, the largest town in the region with some 7,000 residents, sits at the crossroads to further wilderness explorations or the road south to Las Horquetas, Parque Nacional Braulio Carrillo and the Guápiles Highway between San José and Limón.

Estación Biológica la Selva (766-6565 FAX 766-6535 E-MAIL laselva@ns.ots.ac.cr, near Puerto Viejo,

Clouds nestle in forested hills in Parque Nacional Braulio Carrillo.

is essentially an outdoor laboratory for researchers from all over the world. Now operated by the Organization of Tropical Studies (OTS), Apdo 676-2050, San José, La Selva began as an experimental farm owned by Leslie R. Hodridge, who began planting *pejibaye*, cacao and laurel trees amidst primary and secondary forest in the 1950s. Today La Selva is a living research center for visiting scientists. The reserve covers more than 1,215 ha (3,000 acres) and has some 56 km (35 miles) of trails. Day visitors must be accompanied by a guide; tours are offered twice daily. The hike begins at the Stone Bridge, a long suspension bridge over the Río Puerto Viejo that leads to a compound of cabins, classrooms and greenhouses where researchers study everything imaginable, from arthropods (over 200,000 species have been identified in la Selva) to poisonous frogs. In the space of two hours we saw a bat falcon eating a pigeon, several violaceous trogons, a chestnut-mandible toucan that posed for photographers for at least 10 minutes, and a full grown red poisonous dart frog no bigger than a baby's fingernail. La Selva has rooms for overnight guests, but they must be reserved far in advance and are usually set aside to accommodate visiting scientists. Reservations for day visits must also be made in advance, since only 10 guests are allowed on the trails at any time. To reach la Selva turn south at Puerto Viejo towards Las Horquetas.

Selva Verde (not to be confused with La Selva) is a private reserve and lodge in Chilamate. Trails lead through 214 ha (529 acres) of tropical lowland forest by the Río Sarapiquí. Guided hikes and self-guided trail maps are both available; unless you're an expert it's always best to walk with a guide who can spot oropendolas, toucans, river otters and monkeys. The **Botanical and Butterfly Garden** is a delightful resting spot after a long hike. Wear a bright shirt and the butterflies might mistake you for a flower. The reserve has a wonderful lodge for overnight guests (see WHERE TO STAY, below) and the trails and gardens are open to the public for a fee.

Jean Pierre Knockaert, president of the Landscape Foundation Belgium and director of the **Centro Neotrópico SarapiquíS** (see WHERE TO STAY, below) relied on drawings of pre-Columbian villages when designing the foundation's ecolodge. Little did he know that part of the property would become an archeological site. As workers were digging in a field near the Río Sarapiquí, they uncovered several curious rock structures. Archeologists from the Museo Nacional subsequently supervised further digs, revealing four shallow tombs dating from AD 800 to 1550. Hailed as the first archeological discovery in the region, the tombs may be part of a larger pre-Columbian site. Work on the site was just beginning in mid-2000, and speculation about the site's significance was

running high. Archaeologist Anayensy Herrera, who is supervising the dig, says the tombs may have been constructed by the Votos peoples who inhabited the region before the fifteenth century. The site is an unexpected supplement to the center's museum of rainforest ecology and pre-Columbian culture, scheduled to open in late 2001. Botanical gardens and fruit orchards round out the center's attractions; all are open to the public for a fee.

The center abuts the private 300-ha (750-acre) **Tirimbina Rainforest Reserve** (761-1418 FAX 761-1415 E-MAIL tirimbin@racsa.co.cr. A long suspension bridge spans the Río Sarapiquí at the entrance to the reserve's well-maintained trails, and a stairway leads down from the bridge to a small island where rare white tent bats curl themselves into little balls in the folds of palm fronds. Advance reservations are necessary for admission to the reserve.

River rafting on the Sarapiquí is another big attraction in the area, though the river has lost some of its power due to the construction hydroelectric dams, but it still has sufficient rapids to thrill casual rafters. Several operators in San José offer trips on the Sarapiquí. The locally based **Oasis Nature Tours** (/FAX 766-6108 E-MAIL oasis@arweb.com offers boat trips up the river. **Costa Rica Paddle Sports** (766-6768 FAX 230-0814 E-MAIL rodolfo@underseahunter.com is a local rafting company. Trips can be booked through lodges in the area.

Where to Stay and Eat

Lodges in the Sarapiquí region are beginning to attract small tour groups, and they fill quickly in the high season. Reserve a room in advance by fax, and confirm your reservation when you enter the country. Most lodges serve meals for an additional fee (with little choice for outside dining). There are small *sodas* in the towns of La Virgen, Chilamate, Puerto Viejo de Sarapiquí and San Miguel.

EXPENSIVE

The ecolodge concept reaches new heights at **Centro Neotrópico SarapiquíS** (761-1004 FAX 761-1415 E-MAIL magistra@sol.racsa.co.cr WEB SITE www.sarapiquis.org, in La Virgen de Sarapiquí. Guest rooms are covered by 18-m-tall (59-ft) *palenques*, peak-roofed palm-frond structures similar to those used by the indigenous peoples of the region. The earth-toned rooms are far from rustic, however, and are comfortably equipped with ceiling fans, large bathrooms, and telephones with Internet connections. The 24 guest rooms are just part of the overall center, which includes a museum, archeological site, rainforest reserve, and botanical gardens beside the Río Sarapiquí. An even larger *palenque* serves as the restaurant, bar, and lobby, all decorated with historic photos and drawings. There are enough diversions on the property to keep guests busy for several days. The center aims to be a model of ecologically sustainable tourism, and uses solar energy and has its own natural wastewater treatment plant. Smoking is allowed only in the restaurant and bar, and is not allowed in the rooms or on the grounds.

Guests sleep in 40 rooms built of tropical hardwoods linked together by palm-covered walkways at **Selva Verde Lodge (** 766-6800 TOLL-FREE IN THE US (800) 451-7111 FAX 766-6011 E-MAIL selvaver@sol .racsa.co.cr WEB SITE www.selvaverde.com, just off the main road in Chilamate. The 214-ha (529-acre) lowland rainforest reserve around the lodge gives

guests a feeling of true escape, which explains its popularity with bird-watching groups. All meals, taxes, and service charges are included in the rates; guided hikes and river trips cost extra. Meals are served cafeteria style in the large dining hall with its river-view deck; those not staying here are welcome to walk the trails, visit the butterfly garden and join the meals, with advance reservations. Canoeing, river rafting, horseback rides and nature hikes are available.

MODERATE

Simple and comfortable, **La Quinta de Sarapiquí (**/FAX 761-1052 E-MAIL laquinta@costarica.net WEB SITE www.laquintasarapiqui.com is located down a dirt road in La Virgen. Take care when you drive over the slippery bridge that crosses the Río Sardinal as you come in to the compound. Part nature reserve, part lodge, La Quinta has 23 rooms

in several buildings hidden behind blooming ginger and heliconia bushes. The large rooms — with ceiling fans, good screens and powerful hot showers — have terraces facing flower beds where hummingbirds feed. Meals are served family style in the central lodge beside the river; hammocks hang on the large river deck for lounging to the sound of splashing water. A small swimming pool, a butterfly garden, and a frog garden offer distractions within the property. Guests can also schedule rafting trips and tours to Estación Biológica la Selva and Selva Verde, go horseback riding on riverside trails, travel by boat up the river to Tortuguero, photograph monarch butterflies in a netted garden, or simply lounge through the frequent rain showers in swinging chairs. Owners Beatriz and Leonardo Jenkins are great promoters of the region and do everything possible to make their guests feel at home. The rates do not include meals.

Its name means "rare bird," and **Rara Avis (**/FAX 253-0844, near Las Horquetas, is indeed a rare gem—as is its owner Amos Bien. Unlike most sensible hoteliers, Bien built his beautiful Waterfall Lodge before slashing a good road through the rainforest to reach it. At first guests endured an infamous three-hour tractor-drawn cart ride through mud and rivers, or hiked for nearly a day to reach the reserve. Such adventures only make Rara Avis more desirable for those who feel Costa Rica has gotten too soft. But even Amos Bien has begun to relent, and gravel and bridges now make the trip just a bit easier. Once inside the reserve, guests are enfolded in the atmosphere of a true rainforest, where the annual rainfall is over six meters (20 ft) and a dry season doesn't exist. Patient hikers slogging through the mud can spot howler, spider and capuchin monkeys. Near the Waterfall Lodge, hummingbirds glitter in the spray given off by a 55-m (180-ft) double cascade. Rooms are available in several settings. The least expensive are housed in **La Casita**, a newer lodge with shared baths, and in **El Plástico**, a former prison barracks turned hostel with several rooms containing 30 beds with shared baths and hot showers. The impressive **Waterfall Lodge** has eight rooms with private baths and hammocks on the balconies that look out on the forest; the **River Edge Cabins** have a similar setup. Rates for both are based on a per-person system, which puts doubles into the expensive range. The **Treetop Cabin** is the most expensive room and the most exciting, since it's nestled in a tree like a modern tree house 30 m (98 ft) above ground. Meals are served family style in a separate dining room, and are included in the room rates.

ABOVE: School vacations coincide with the coffee harvest so children can help pick the ripe beans and earn colones. OVERLEAF: A cenizero tree spreads its leafy umbrella.

How to Get There

It takes about two hours to drive to the Sarapiquí region from San José via the route to Volcán Poás, two hours from La Fortuna and Volcán Arenal, or 90 minutes from the Rainforest Aerial Tram in Braulio Carrillo. Road signs lead the way to Puerto Viejo de Sarapiquí, not to be confused with Puerto Viejo on the Caribbean coast. The lodges will arrange transportation for a fee. Public buses access the region from San José, Limón and La Fortuna. You can also get to Sarapiquí by boat from Tortuguero; the trip takes about four hours.

CARTAGO AND THE SOUTHEAST REGION

The colonial capital of Costa Rica until 1823, Cartago is now the capital of the province of the same name and the gateway to the south-central region of the country. Travelers rarely spend the night here; instead, they stop to view the town's colonial structures before heading on to Turrialba, Orosí or the Volcán Irazú.

CARTAGO

A bustling, populous city of 13,500 inhabitants, Cartago retains bits of colonial charm left from the days when it was first founded by Juan Vásquez de Coronado in 1563. Its greatest attraction is the **Basilica de Nuestra Señora de los Angeles**, the most important Catholic church in the country.

If possible, visit the church on a Sunday when you'll see Costa Ricans from surrounding towns dressed in their finest spending the day at the church and nearby park. I was fortunate to arrive on a Sunday when there was a big soccer game on television (thus clearing the streets of traffic) and First Communion was being held at several churches in the area. It seemed everyone in town had brought their daughters and sons — dressed in frilly white dresses and stern suits — to be photographed in front of the church: the children, regardless of their fine attire, were soon chasing pigeons around the dull gray cement plaza that faces the basilica. The church itself is the most imposing in the country, a massive gray hulk with white domes. An earthquake nearly destroyed the church in 1926; it was quickly rebuilt with Byzantine touches.

Crowds pack the interior on Sundays, lined up against the wood-paneled walls under stained glass windows. Equally popular is the shrine behind the church devoted to La Negrita, the country's patron saint. La Negrita, also called the Virgin of Los Angeles, is said to have appeared to a small girl on a rock below where the church is built; some say the virgin was a doll made of black stone. Her statue is above the main altar. The shrine behind the church is built around a spring whose waters are said to have curative powers. Believers wait their turn to touch the spring's water, splashing it over their heads and faces, drinking it and filling bottles of every size and shape imaginable with water to take home.

Across the street behind the church is **El Sancturario Exvotos y Articulosos Religiosas**, a shop packed with T-shirts depicting the virgin, holy cards, prayer books and glass counters filled with *milagros*, tiny metal arms, hearts, spines and other body parts used by the faithful to deposit at religious statues for help with whatever ails them.

Some picnic tables, a basketball court and ice cream vendors surround the shop.

Five blocks from the church are the ruins of **La Iglesia de la Parroquí**, first built in 1575. The church was destroyed by earthquakes and volcanoes several times and was rebuilt each time until it completely crumbled in the earthquake of 1910. The stone walls draped in scarlet bougainvillea remain, and a garden fills the interior courtyard which is very occasionally open to the public.

How to Get There

The Bernardo Soto Highway (for the most part unlabeled) travels southeast from San José 18 km (11 miles) to Cartago. A large parking lot is across from the basilica; there is a small charge for parking but the lot is guarded and it has clean restrooms. Public buses from San José stop directly opposite the church.

VOLCÁN IRAZÚ

Usually visited on a day trip from San José, the Volcán Irazú looms 3,432 m (11,260 ft) high above Cartago province's agricultural valleys. The road from Cartago quickly climbs past ranches and farms to a nearly barren, veritable moonscape of rock and ash in the Parque Nacional Volcán Irazú. Bring a jacket and umbrella or poncho; the annual rainfall is more than two meters (more than seven feet), and the average temperature is 11°C (52°F). The volcano's name comes from the word *istarú*, which means "Thunder and Earthquake Mountain," an apt description, for Irazú has been

tion, below us at a distance of perhaps two thousand feet, the whole country was covered with clouds and the city at the foot of the volcano invisible.

"By degrees the more distant clouds were lifted, and over the immense bed we saw at the same moment the Atlantic and Pacific Oceans. The points at which they were visible were the Gulf of Nicoya and the harbor of San Juan, which were not directly opposite but nearly at right angles to each other, so that we could see both oceans without turning the body."

Accommodations are sparse near the park, but you must stop at the wonderful **Restaurante Linda Vista** (380-8090, a mountain cabin with wooden

active and highly destructive since colonial times at least. The first recorded eruption took place in 1563, the latest in 1963, when United States President John F. Kennedy was visiting the country. This volcano has been dormant since 1965, though occasional bursts of steam, gas and ash and underground tremors inspire respect. A trail leads from the parking lot to the main crater, one of five. Stubby trees and scrub grasses attempt to thrive in the ash, but little life can exist near the craters. It's said that you can see both coasts from the craters on a clear morning, though a cold mist and fog will likely obscure the view. John Lloyd Stephens, who climbed the volcano in the 1840s, witnessed the clouds lifting from under the volcano's peak:

"The lofty point on which we stood was perfectly clear, the atmosphere was of transparent purity, and, looking beyond the region of desola-

walls covered with business cards, passport photos and friendly notes from visitors who have traveled here from all over the world. When I last stopped by on a freezing, rainy morning I was the only guest except for two dripping-wet motorcycle cops. The three of us sat in front of a roaring fire, drying our clothes and sipping strong coffee as the rain pounded outside. There are two simple, inexpensive cabins behind the restaurant available for overnight guests.

How to Get There

Irazú is 32 km (20 miles) north of Cartago on a good paved road. Most visitors arrive on tours from San José. Make sure your tour arrives at the park early in the day. Those driving on their own

OPPOSITE: First communion in Cartago.
ABOVE: The Basilica in Cartago is the country's most important church.

can combine a visit to the volcano (about two hours from San José) with stops in Cartago and the Orosí Valley. The only bus to the park travels on weekends, departing from San José's Gran Hotel. Check at the hotel for information and schedules.

OROSÍ VALLEY

One of the most beautiful drives in the entire country begins in Cartago and heads south through Paraíso and the Orosí Valley over the Río Reventazón and the Cachí Dam. The first stop is at the **Jardín Botánico Lankaster** (552-3247, just outside Paraíso, a paradise for orchid enthu-

siasts. British naturalist Charles H. Lankaster began the garden in the 1950s; it now belongs to the University of Costa Rica. Plant lovers are enamored with the 10.7-ha (26-acre) botanical gardens, and they can spend hours wandering the paths, viewing more than 40 species of bamboo surrounding a Japanese temple, a startling cactus and succulent garden that seems out of place in the humid setting, several palm groves and vivid clusters of heliconia. Lankaster was particularly interested in epiphytes (plants that live on other plants), and you can see this phenomenon of interdependence in the brilliant pink, red, and yellow bromeliads hanging from tree trunks and branches. Greenhouses and the orchid trail contain approximately 800 species of these delicate, showy flowers; the best time to see them in bloom is from February to May. The road to the garden is just west of Paraíso; look for the sign and sky-high electricity transformers on your right. Buses from Cartago to Paraíso will let you off at the entrance.

The road south from Paraíso cuts through a jumble of bougainvillea, ferns and coffee plants to the village of Orosí tucked in a small valley. Stop off at the **Mirador Orosí**, a park and lookout point run by the ICT (Costa Rican Tourism Institute). Landscaped paths and stairways lead up a

steep hill to platforms overlooking the valley; the panorama of rivers, lakes, coffee plantations, and flowering trees is breathtaking. The park has public restrooms and picnic areas. The red-tiled roof of the **Iglesia de San José de Orosí**, a simple adobe church built in 1735, peaks over a cluster of small neat houses. The small museum next to the church contains a fascinating collection of religious icons and paintings.

The road (part pavement, part dirt) continues on to the Río Palomo and **Parque Nacional Tapantí**, one of the wettest spots in the country. Scores of rivers and streams run through the park, making it an important watershed. The Costa Rican Electric Institute (ICE) has constructed a hydroelectric dam here on the Río Macho. Birders and hikers revel in the park's dense vegetation and, bundled up in jackets and rain gear, slog along trails through the forest; the **Sendero la Pava** leads from the **Sendero Oropendola** to a powerful waterfall over the Río Grande de Orosí. There are restrooms and picnic shelters near the ranger station, but lodging is not available in the vicinity. Most visitors arrive on day trips from San José. The road into the park is nearly impassable in rainy season. The **Tapantí Ranger Station** (551-2970 at the park entrance has a few rooms for rent.

Back at Río Macho another road curves east and north to the village of Cachí and the lake of the same name, formed by a dam built by ICE through the Río Reventazón. At the side of the lake is the astonishing **Casa el Soñador**, the House of the Dreamer (533-3297. Covered in woodcarvings, the house is home to the Quesada family, who will give you a tour of the interior and offer woodcrafts for sale. The road continues on through coffee plantations to a lookout point with views of Ujarrás, one of the most picturesque colonial villages in Costa Rica. Follow a narrow, winding road down to the village to see the ruins of the **Iglesia de Nuestra Señora de la Limpia Concepción**, built in 1693. The main road continues back to Paraíso and Cartago; the entire circuit takes about three hours.

Where to Stay and Eat

Stop for lunch at **La Casona del Cafetal** (533-3280 in Ujarrás overlooking the Cachí reservoir. Set in a family-owned coffee plantation, the brick restaurant has inside and terrace dining; the menu features trout and other river fish along with traditional Costa Rican *casados*. Horseback riding tours of the plantation are available. New in 2000, the **Orosí Lodge** (/FAX 533-3578 E-MAIL ccneck@ sol.racsa.co.cr WEB SITE sites.netscape.net/ timeveit/orosilodge, in Orosí village, is a charming inn with six spotless rooms, all with white tiled wet bars with sinks, coffeemakers, and small refrigerators. Breakfast is served in the lodge's café, complete with a jukebox stocked with Latin tunes from the 1960s and 1970s. Rates are inexpensive, and guests have use of the Balneario Martínez thermal hot springs next door. Though Orosí has not yet made it onto the main tourist circuit, it's a perfect small town where farmers gather around the plaza on weekends to sell their wares. Spending a night or two here is a great way to learn about traditional small-town life.

TURRIALBA

An agricultural town adjacent to the two rivers Reventazón and Pacuare, Turrialba is becoming an increasingly popular destination for travelers. Sugarcane fields and coffee and macadamia nut

settlements outside Turrialba, and turns from pavement to rock and dirt intermittently. After climbing through forest and clouds you'll spot a turnoff to the ruins on the left; from here to the ruins is a slow four-kilometer (two-and-a-half-mile) drive, which took me more than a half-hour to traverse in a rented sedan.

The archaeological site is in far better condition than the road and covers about 20 ha (50 acres), though only a portion has been excavated. The **Sendero de los Montículos** through the site is marked with signs describing the archaeological and natural importance of each section. The site contains the only primary forest left in Cartago province, along with secondary forest. At least

plantations surround the crowded town, headquarters for workers constructing yet another hydroelectric dam nearby on the Río Pacuare. The dam was completed in 2000 (much to the horror of environmentalists and river-rafting operators), flooding the valley. Several rafting companies use Turrialba as their launching point for trips down both rivers, and Costa Rica's largest archaeological site, Guayabo, is nearby.

What to See and Do

The town of Turrialba is worth a quick go-round if you're in need of groceries or other supplies. From town, one road leads southeast to the Turrialba Valley and the best accommodations in the area, while another runs north to **Monumento Nacional Guayabo**, a site well worth visiting if you are interested in Costa Rica's pre-Columbian history. The road to Guayabo runs through small

173 species of birds, 14 species of mammals and 15 species of snakes have been spotted here — the snakes include the deadly terciopelo or fer-de-lance, much feared and respected throughout Central America. Wear sturdy hiking boots when walking these trails.

Archaeologists believe Guayabo may have been inhabited as early as 1400 BC, and had about 500 residents (their origins are unknown) at its peak. Most of the structures uncovered thus far were built between AD 300 and 700. Construction seems to have halted and the site to have been abandoned by 1400. Important structures that have been excavated include three tombs, where bodies were buried on top of each other with pottery and food, and several rock monoliths with

OPPOSITE: A turkey buzzard scans the horizon for its next meal. ABOVE: The Casa el Soñador, House of the Dreamer, in Orosí Valley.

paintings and carvings. The **Monolito Jaguar y Largarto**, with carvings of the gods of water and earth, sits by the path, and workers have unearthed tools and materials believed to have been used in creating sculptures and petroglyphs. You can see most of the excavated site from atop **El Mirador Encuentro con Nuestros Origenes** ("The Encounter with Our Origins Lookout Point"), before climbing downhill to the main aqueduct and *tanque de captacion* (water tank) that shows the Guayabo people used advanced methods of agriculture. Wide cobbled *calzadas*, or roads, connect various parts of the site. Guayabo is closed on Mondays, and open from 8 AM to 3:30 PM the rest of the week. It's best to visit the site with a guide, since few of

the structures are labeled. Local guides are available at the site, or you can visit the ruins with a guide from a tour company.

Enormous **Lake Angostura**, product of the new hydroelectric dam, covers 265 ha (655 acres) at the southeast end of the Turrialba valley. The lake was just beginning to flood the valley when I last visited; it will take some time to see if it becomes a recreational attractions. Archeologists believe the valley was a center for indigenous groups some 2,000 years past. The ICE (Electricity Institute) undertook an extensive archeological survey of the valley before building the dam, and found several distinct sites, many with tombs. Now called the **Angostura** archaeological area, the site is currently closed to the public.

A giant rainforest locust ABOVE and a howler monkey RIGHT find their lunches in trees.

River rafting is the main activity in the Turrialba area, and several rafting companies in San José offer day and overnight trips on the Pacuare and Reventazón (see SPORTING SPREE, page 28 in YOUR CHOICE). **Ríos Tropicales** (233-6455 FAX 255-4354 E-MAIL reserve@riostropicales.com WEB SITE www .riostropicales.com operates a lodge on the Pacuare for their clients, as does **Aventuras Naturales** (225-3939 TOLL-FREE FROM THE US (800) 514-0411 FAX 253-6934 E-MAIL avenat@sol.racsa.co.cr WEB SITE www .toenjoynature.com. **Serendipity Adventures** (556-2592 FAX 556-2593 TOLL-FREE FROM THE US (877) 507-1358 E-MAIL costarica@serendipity adventures.com WEB SITE www.serendipity adventures.com operates hot air balloon trips over Turrialba and river rafting trips.

Where to Stay

Several small hotels are available right in Turrialba town, but traffic noise and the blare of a siren every morning at 6 AM are major deterrents to staying here. Far preferable are the lodgings near the Río Reventazón southeast of town.

Spend a lazy afternoon sipping coffee on your terrace as the rain feeds the Reventazón and you may decide to extend your stay at **Casa Turire** (531-1111 FAX 531-1075 E-MAIL turire@ticonet.co.cr, Turrialba (very expensive). Designed as a country estate in the midst of sugarcane, coffee and macadamia fields, this 16-room inn is indeed exquisite and serene. Formal gardens and lawns line the driveway to the peak-roofed, golden-colored Casa. A two-story atrium in the lobby leads to a wood-paneled library, a cozy bar that opens to a verandah and the dining room with French doors leading to the patio and pool. The 12 standard rooms are spacious, decorated with antiques and filled with light from glass doors leading to balconies; the large bathrooms have showers and bathtubs (a true luxury) and hairdryers. Each of the four suites has a separate seating area. Casa Turire is now a lakefront property; it's the only business that sits at the edge of Lake Angostura at the moment. Horseback rides through the Hacienda Atirro property of the Rojas family (who own the hotel) lead through cane fields and up steep mountain trails. Rafting, mountain biking, hiking, kayaking and tours to Guayabo are available.

A rough road leads up the mountainside 11 km (seven miles) from Turrialba to the inexpensive **Pochotel** (556-0111 FAX 556-6222, E-MAIL pochotel @hotmail.com Turrialba. This six-cabin rustic hostelry sits atop a mountain with fabulous night views of the lights of Turrialba (from below, the hotel's illuminated Coca-Cola sign looks like a red beacon in the sky). The restaurant, serving basic rice, beans, chicken and beef, is a favorite of river rafters who drip their way in at lunch. The rooms have private baths and hot water.

The Northwest

GUANACASTE PROVINCE DOESN'T START UNTIL YOU CROSS THE RÍO LAGARTO, but political boundaries can't disguise the fact that Costa Rica's cowboy country has little regard for provincial boundaries. Cattle ranches sprawl on both sides of the Carretera Interamericana, populated with sturdy zebu stock with big floppy ears and immense humps, imported from India (via Brazil) more than a hundred years ago because their temperament is ideal for the region's hot, dry climate.

Although 75% of the province is flat, a chain of towering volcanoes snakes up its eastern flank, a primeval landscape of smoldering cinder cones and cloud forest that harbors more plant and animal species per hectare than any other part of the Americas. The Río Tempisque meanders through central Guanacaste, carving out a massive flood plain that harbors crocodiles and profuse bird life before it empties into the Golfo de Nicoya. Guanacaste encompasses a huge portion of northwest Costa Rica, including Laguna de Arenal, much of the Península de Nicoya's Pacific coastline and several national parks. The fiery Volcán Arenal and the cloud forests of Monteverde lie beside Guanacaste's eastern borders.

BACKGROUND

The *sabaneros* (cowboys) of Guanacaste have always considered themselves different from their countrymen. And for good reason. Their ancestors were among the earliest European settlers in Central America, settling the region in the late sixteenth century. When the region broke away from Spanish rule in the 1820s, Guanacaste nearly became a small independent nation wedged between Nicaragua and Costa Rica. Locals voted to become part of Costa Rica, but the province remained nominally independent for another 30 years.

There is still a great deal of local pride, reflected in the fact that *guanacastecos* continue to cherish their cultural heritage — music, dance and cowboy skills demonstrated at scores of local fiestas and rodeos during the dry season (November to April). Bullfights and equestrian parades are also popular, especially on July 25, a provincial holiday that commemorates Guanacaste's "independence" from Nicaragua. The province's trademark — and Costa Rica's national tree — is the huge, leafy guanacaste (also called the "ear tree" because its dark-gray seed pods resemble a pair of ears).

Although ranching still dominates the local economy, Guanacaste also supports a thriving sugarcane industry. Tourism has become increasingly important in recent years thanks to the area's many national parks, reserves and beaches. The Carretera Interamericana allows quick access from San José, with most of the major sights within a three- or four-hour drive of the capital.

MONTEVERDE

One of the most popular tourist areas in Costa Rica, Monteverde (Green Mountain) is a lush plateau that hovers at a breezy 1,400 m (4,592 ft) above the Guanacaste plains. The mist-shrouded Cordillera de Tilarán and its fabulous cloud forest tower behind, is an ever-present reminder that Monteverde lies at the edge of Costa Rica's greatest wilderness. Santa Elena is the area's only village, but Monteverde's built-up area stretches for six kilometers (nearly four miles) along the plateau, alternating between pastureland and pine groves.

The road to Monteverde is one of the worst in the country, but that doesn't keep thousands of tourists from visiting each year. The region's cloud forest is its main attraction, and visitors thrive on the cool, moist air and the mystical aura of the mist-shrouded trees. Birdwatchers are in their element here, especially during April and May when the famed resplendent quetzals perform their elaborate mating dance (see SPOT THE ELUSIVE QUETZAL, page 14 in TOP SPOTS). The quetzals are elusive and shy, but Monteverde's hummingbirds flutter about everywhere. Hummingbird feeders hang from front porches, restaurant terraces, and trees all over the area. Over 30 species can be spotted, including the omnipresent purple-throated and violet-winged birds. The forest is home to about 400 species of birds, including the crowned motmot, several types of trogons, emerald toucanets, and the rare (and hard to spot) wattled bellbird. Over 500 types of butterflies flutter about, and over 100 types of mammals

PRECEEDING PAGES: In the Monteverde Cloud Forest LEFT, it rains 300 inches per year. Visitors to the Butterfly Garden RIGHT, in this damp region, get close to hundreds of species of these ephemeral creatures. OPPOSITE: Salvadorian writer Marcelino García Flamenco's grave is perched over Bahía Salinas. ABOVE: The Cordillera de Guanacaste looms over grazing lands in the northwest.

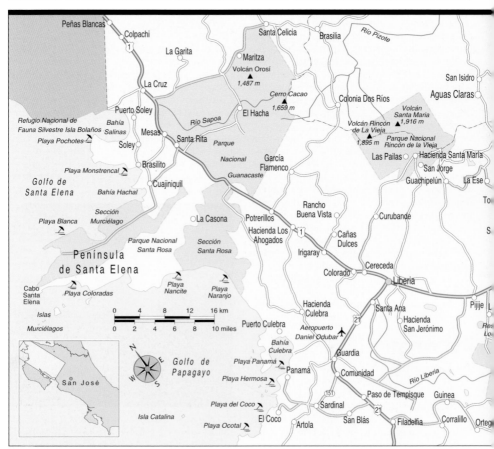

including sloths, howler monkeys, and jaguars (though your chances of seeing wild cats are nearly nonexistent) find refuge in the forests.

Monteverde's popularity has its drawbacks. Visitors frequently complain that they didn't see nearly as much wildlife as they expected. A few brazen monkeys hang out near trails where hundreds of humans clamber about noisily. But most self-respecting mammals and birds hide deep in the forest. Serious bird watchers and naturalists must be willing to hike long distances, often on muddy trails in the rain, to reach these more remote areas; their effort is almost always rewarded.

BACKGROUND

The human history of Monteverde is almost as fascinating as its natural heritage. Once upon a time (1951) a dozen Quaker families fled the United States in search of a country without an army or military service. They found exactly what they were looking for in Costa Rica, which had abolished its army several years earlier. The Quakers purchased a large tract of virgin land in the Tilarán mountains and went to work building

a new community. Dairy farming seemed natural here because of the verdant local pastures and the alpine climate, and this evolved into a cheese-making business that still thrives today. Although Quakers are now a minority in Monteverde, their presence is still strong. Their cheese factory is the area's largest single employer, they own many of the hotels and shops on the mountain, and the Friends Meeting House doubles as an active community center.

In the early 1950s, the Quakers decided to preserve a large section of woodland as a watershed for their power plant and various rural enterprises. But they were also conscious that the local rainforest would eventually disappear if land clearance wasn't stopped. The Quakers opened the area to scientific study and eventually set aside part of the watershed as a small conservation zone. In 1975, the Reserva Biológica Monteverde came into being.

Now managed by a private trust called the Centro Científico Tropical (Tropical Science Center of Costa Rica), the preserve encompasses 10,500 ha (26,000 acres) of unspoiled rainforest on the upper reaches of the Río Peñas Blancas.

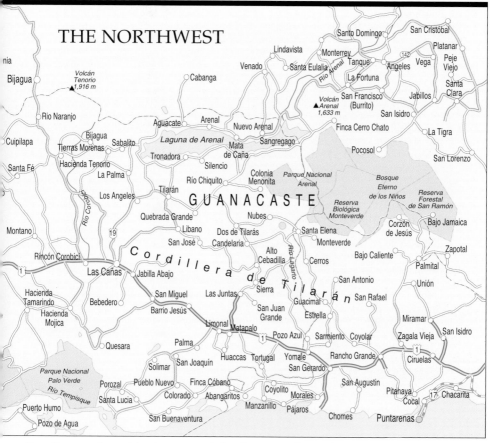

THE NORTHWEST

Over the years the park has been expanded and augmented with grants from a number of international organizations including the Nature Conservancy, the World Wildlife Fund, the Rare Animal Relief Effort and the governments of Canada, Denmark and the United States.

WHAT TO SEE AND DO

Monteverde's **Reserva Bosque Nuboso** (Cloud Forest Reserve) (645-5122 FAX 645-5034 WEB SITE www.cct.or.cr is extraordinary — a lush mountain habitat formed by a combination of high humidity and low cloud cover from trade winds that blow across the *cordillera*. The area receives between three and five meters (10 and 16 ft) of rain each year, water which provokes incredibly lush plant growth: ferns and moss, orchids and magnolia and huge zapote trees with their buttress roots. Animal life is also abundant. Jaguars and puma are known to exist in the park, but sightings are rare because they live deep in the forest. Nearly everyone sees at least one semi-tame monkey. Most people come for the bird watching, especially a chance to spot the resplendent

quetzal, sacred bird of the Maya, which is found in greater number at Monteverde than most other places in Costa Rica.

All told, there are about 120 km (74 miles) of hiking trails. The most popular walks are in the western corner, an area called **The Triangle** that fans out from the entrance gate and visitor center.

Sendero Bosque Nuboso (Cloud Forest Trail) is a self-guided nature walk with numbers that correspond to a booklet that can be purchased at the entrance. The **Sendero Pantanoso** (Swamp Trail) crosses over a marshy region on wooden boardwalks. **Sendero Río** (River Trail) hugs the banks of Quebrada Cuecha, with an observation deck that looks over a double waterfall.

Most people walk the park unescorted, but you can join a guided tour if you like. Bird-watching tours and night tours are also available. The preserve is open daily 7 AM to 4 PM, and reopens at night for hikers with advance reservations.

The **Santa Elena Forest Reserve** (645-5014, another private rainforest park, is six kilometers (nearly four miles) north of town, off the Tilarán Road. In many respects Santa Elena is a carbon copy of the large Monteverde preserve. Entrance fees support reserve operations and local high school education.

Although it is still largely off-limits to the general public, another important wilderness area is the **Bosque Eterno de los Niños**, the Children's Eternal Forest, which wraps around three sides of the Reserva Bosque Nuboso. This reserve traces its origins to nine-year-old Roland Tiensuu, a Swedish schoolboy who penned a letter to the Monteverde Conservation League in 1987 asking what children could do to save the rainforest. Roland and his classmates later raised enough money to purchase six hectares (15 acres) of Costa Rican forest. Soon kids from 21 countries were raising funds to buy more forest. Today the Bosque Eterno de los Niños covers more than 13,000 ha (32,000 acres), with plans for expanding further along the cordillera. **Bajo del Tigre**, or Jaguar Canyon, a small section of the Bosque de los Niños, is open to the public. It has a children's nature center, a small arboretum and self-guided trails. The Bosque de los Niños and its efforts to protect additional lands are managed by the **Monteverde Conservation League** (645-5003 FAX 645-5104 E-MAIL acmmcl@sol.racsa.co.cr.

Tropical butterflies thrive within the enclosed gardens at the **Jardín Mariposa** (645-5512 (the entrance fee includes guided tour); several species of snakes are on view at the **Serpentario** (645-5772. The **Finca Ecológico** (645-5363, 650 m (just over 700 yards) south of the Cerro Plano School, is a family-run private reserve with coffee and banana plantations, forest, waterfalls, and an abundance of wildlife including coatimundi, sloths, and porcupines.

Monteverde was one of the first places where entrepreneurs introduced forest canopy tours (see HANG OUT IN THE TREETOPS, page 20 in TOP SPOTS), and there are several versions to choose from. The **Original Canopy Tour** (645-5243 or 257-5149 (in San José) FAX 256-7626 E-MAIL canopy@sol .racsa.co.cr WEB SITE www.canopytour.com company built their first set of platforms and cables at the Cloud Forest Lodge in 1993. **Skytrek** (645-5238 FAX 645-5769 WEB SITE www.skywalk.co.cr operates a canopy tour and suspended bridge in the forest near Santa Elena. **Aerial Adventures** (645-5960 FAX 645-5315 uses a series of tracks and electrically propelled cars to span the forest canopy near the Finca Ecológico. Keep in mind that none of these experiences provide great wildlife viewing. They're more like amusement rides, though you'll get a better understanding of the forest canopy. Horseback riding is big here, and **Meg's Stables** (645-5029 has horses for every level of rider.

Monteverde's business center is a bustling little village area that surrounds a grassy square about halfway between Santa Elena Reserve and the Monteverde Reserva Bosque Nuboso entrance. The artistic side of Monteverde's eclectic assort-

ment of residents shines through in downtown's shops. **Casem Gallery** (645-5190 is a handicrafts shop run by a cooperative of local artists who create wooden bowls and carvings, jewelry, embroidered wall hangings and clothing. **Café Monteverde** is a pint-sized coffee factory where you can watch the roasting process and buy beans for home consumption. **Stella's Café** (see below) doubles as a bakery and art gallery for original works by sisters Stella and Meg Wallace. There's a small grocery store, too. Up the road is **La Lechería** (945-5029, the cheese factory, which sells 16 varieties. The aptly named **Hummingbird Gallery** (645-5030 on the road to the reserve features T-shirts, photographs, and hats featuring its namesake, as well as other nature-oriented themes. If you happen to visit between January and March, catch the **Monteverde Music Festival** featuring artists from around the globe. Proceeds support music programs in the local schools.

WHERE TO STAY

Monteverde offers a wider range of accommodations than any other nature area in Costa Rica except Manuel Antonio. Lodges fill quickly in the dry season; make reservations far in advance by fax or e-mail.

Expensive

The top of the line is the **Monteverde Lodge** (645-5057 FAX 645-5126 E-MAIL costaric@expeditions .co.cr. What do you say about a place that has a huge Jacuzzi inside a glass-walled atrium at one side of the lobby? You can soak in the pool, sip a margarita and watch the sunset over the Golfo de Nicoya — something you can't do anywhere else on the mountain. The gourmet restaurant is equally renowned. And the rooms are of rare quality: comfortable furnishings, wood and glass decor and modern, American-style bathrooms. Hummingbirds and butterflies buzz about the extensive gardens.

Moderate

It might well be difficult to find a more romantic abode than **El Sapo Dorado** (645-5010 FAX 645-5180 E-MAIL elsapo@sol.racsa.co.cr. The creation of local rancher Geovanny Arguedas and his Quaker partner Hannah Lowther, the "Golden Toad" sprawls across a wooded hillside with lavish views in all directions. The chalets include 20 rooms with private baths, fireplaces and terraces or balconies. El Sapo Dorado also offers five kilometers (more than three miles) of trails through the neighboring woodland.

Hotel Fonda Vela (645-5125 FAX 645-5119 E-MAIL fondavel@sol.racsa.co.cr occupies a 14-ha (35-acre) farm on the edges of the cloud forest. Hardwoods and native stone abound in the

A-frame chalets. Views from some of the guest rooms and restaurant look across emerald-green pastures and ranch land to the Golfo de Nicoya. The reserve is two kilometers (less than one and a quarter miles) up the road, and the hotel will organize backcountry trips to Peñas Blancas and San Gerardo. This is a great place to stay if you're relying on public transportation. Even closer to the Monteverde Reserva Bosque Nuboso is the **Villa Verde** (645-5025 FAX 645-5115, about one kilometer (a little over half a mile) from the park entrance. Run by Costa Rican nature-lover Irene Villalobos and her two affable sons, the Villa Verde is a rustic lodge built of wood, stone and glass. The rooms are tidy, the bathrooms are large and

a model of sustainable tropical ecotourism. All of the usual Monteverde activities are available to guests, and the lodge offers a unique opportunity to meet local farmers, participate in research programs and get your hands dirty on various farm chores such as picking coffee and delivering it by horseback to the processing plant. Accommodations are in spacious *cabinas* with private baths, or at the bunkhouse.

Inexpensive

Guests rave about the amiable ambiance at the **Arco Iris Ecolodge** (645-5067 FAX 645-5022 E-MAIL arcoiris@sol.racsa.co.cr in Santa Elena. Set amid six hectares (15 acres) of forest with trails, the lodge

have hot water; suites have kitchenettes and fireplaces. The food is excellent, from hearty breakfasts to superb *tico* cuisine at night. In the evenings guests gather around the stone fireplace.

Originally built by Quakers and Costa Ricans to serve biologists visiting the cloud forest, the **Hotel de Montaña Monteverde** (645-5046 or 224-3050 (in San José) FAX 645-5320 or 222-6184 (in San José) E-MAIL monteverde@ticonet.co.cr sits amid a 15-ha (37-acre) private reserve. Slide shows are held nightly in the conference center, and the 26 rooms (including a suite with Jacuzzi overlooking the forest), all have private baths and hot water.

For an escape from the crowds at Monteverde spend a few nights at the **Ecolodge San Luis** (/FAX 380-3255 E-MAIL smithdp@ctrvax.vander bilt.edu. Situated 40 minutes southeast of Santa Elena, the ecolodge is part of a 66-ha (162-acre) coffee plantation and fruit farm that bills itself as

has simple rooms with twin or bunk beds and private bath; the restaurant serves great salads made with produce from their organic garden, along with typical Costa Rican dishes. **Mirador Lodge San Gerardo** (645-5254 FAX 645-6087 E-MAIL miradorq@sol.racsa.co.cr, eight kilometers (five miles) north of Santa Elena, is removed from the action — a blessing for those seeking solitude. The lodge's 200-ha (500-acre) preserve overlooks Volcán Arenal, and the rustic cabins and dorms have hot-water showers. The restaurant serves above-average lodge-type meals. **Hotel el Bosque** (645-5221 FAX 645-5129 E-MAIL elbosque@sol .racsa.co.cr features 21 *cabinas* that sprawl across the forested hillside in helter-skelter fashion. Each has a private bath and hot water. The wood-paneled restaurant is one of the best in Monteverde;

Roses bushes frame tame green lawns behind the Monteverde Lodge.

you can pitch a tent in the small campground for a small fee.

Santa Elena has half a dozen pensions and small hotels within a block of the bus station. One of the best of these is **Hotel el Tucán (** 645-5017 FAX 645-5462, a modest but pleasant, small hotel that is run by Rosa Jiménez and her family. The wood-paneled rooms come with private or shared bath with hot water. El Tucán can organize horseback riding trips. **Pensión Manakín (** 645-5080 FAX 645-5517, named after a local bird, is farther up the road towards Monteverde reserve. Nothing fancy here, but the price is right and the owners will treat you like part of the family.

WHERE TO EAT

Moderate

Many of the hotels at Monteverde offer excellent meals. Locals say **El Sapo Dorado** has the best food and probably the most romantic atmosphere — a hilltop location overlooking the forest. The menu specializes in vegetarian fare (for example, grilled tofu), but there's plenty on offer for omnivores, including steamed shrimp and clams, white sea bass and beef tongue with asparagus. There's also a good wine selection. Another gourmet choice is the **Monteverde Lodge**. The glass-enclosed dining area seems to hover over the mountainside and is a magical place at sunset. The menu ranges from filet mignon and grilled chicken with palm hearts to dorado and pasta alfredo. The wine cellar includes labels from France, Spain, Chile and California.

The influx of tourists in recent years has lead to the establishment of a number of Italian restaurants. **Da Lucia (** 645-5337 (on the same road as the Jardín Mariposa) has fairly good Italian cuisine, but you may have to wait for a table because this place is very popular. **La Pizzeria (** 645-5066 on the Santa Elena road offers basic Italian fare (pizza, pasta, garlic bread) with bright decor and a friendly staff.

Inexpensive

For local food, both the **Villa Verde** and **El Bosque** hotels offer wholesome *tico* cuisine in large quantities. **Stella's Café (** 645-5560 on the road between Santa Elena and the cloud forest reserve is without a doubt the best place in Monteverde to forget about your diet. Offerings range from fruit milk shakes (avocado, papaya, banana, blackberry), hot chocolate and fresh coffee to chocolate brownies, mango pie and fresh-baked bread. Stella's also serves breakfast and light lunches. **Chunches Café (** 645-5147 in Santa Elena offers espresso along with its selection of used books and foreign newspapers, and the café doubles as a laundromat.

If you're in the mood for nightlife, try **Taberna Valverdes** in Santa Elena, with music and cold beer that attracts a young crowd of locals and tourists. If the tunes are too loud for you, sit beneath the pine trees in the garden.

HOW TO GET THERE

The turnoff point for Monteverde is a tiny place called Lagarto, on the Carretera Interamericana, about two hours from San José. The junction is marked by a large sign and two roadside cafés with cold drinks and toilets. The 35-km (22-mile) route up the mountain is almost as legendary as the place itself — one of the worst roads in a country which is known for horrible highways. A four-wheel-drive vehicle isn't necessary, but it

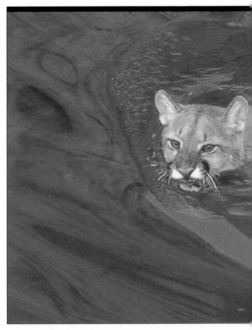

would help in negotiating the countless potholes, ruts and protruding rocks.

Monteverde can also be reached via a 40-km (25-mile) back-road from Tilarán. Despite rumors to the contrary, this route is no worse than the road from Lagarto to Monteverde and it's much more scenic, through rolling ranch country where you're sure to come across cowboys and oxcarts.

An alternative when leaving Monteverde is combined horse and water travel. **Leonel Quesada (** 645-5087 or 645-5354 provides horseback trips through the San Gerardo Valley to Laguna de Arenal, where a boat takes you across to the north shore. From there, take a taxi to La Fortuna or any of the Arenal hotels.

Express buses run twice daily between San José and Monteverde (four hours). Buy your return ticket as early as possible because buses back to San José are often full.

CIUDAD QUESADA

The commercial capital of the northern agricultural zone, Quesada (also called San Carlos) is the largest city on the route between San José and Volcán and Laguna de Arenal. Fuel up your car, do your marketing and take care of any other business here. Though not on the typical tourist circuit, the Quesada region is very popular with Costa Ricans and those who've already conquered Monteverde and Arenal. It's also a good base for exploring the outer reaches if the Meseta Central, and is a good resting point when traveling between Volcán Poás and Sarapiquí and the western region.

WHERE TO STAY

Two fine resorts attract locals and independent travelers seeking a change from the normal tourist hotels. The **Hotel Occidental el Tucano Resort and Spa** (460-6000 FAX 460-1692 WEB SITE www.occidentaltucano.com is eight kilometers (five miles) north of Ciudad Quesada on the road to Aguas Zarcas (expensive). One of the oldest resorts in the country, El Tucano has endured through several changes in management and remains a classic *tico* hideaway. Thermal waters feed the pools, steam rooms and whirlpool tubs; mud baths, tennis, fitness equipment and a natural

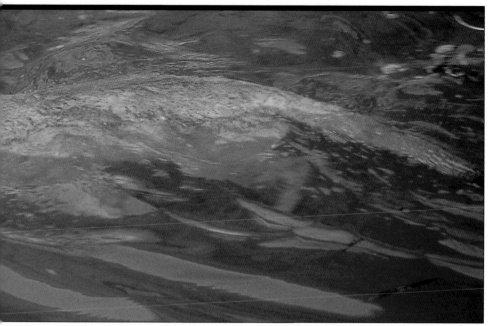

WHAT TO SEE AND DO

The **Original Canopy Tour** (257-5149 FAX 256-7626 E-MAIL canopy@sol.racsa.co.cr WEB SITE www.canopytour.com operates an exciting tour at Termales del Bosque (see below), 10 km east of Quesada. The ride through the treetops is just part of the journey, which also includes a horseback ride and a chance to soak your sore muscles in the thermal waters of the Río las Palmas. Animal lovers may want to stop by **La Marina Zoo** (460-0946 on the road to Aguas Zarcas, a reserve for wounded and abandoned jaguars, toucans and eagles. **Parque Nacional Juan Castro Blanco**, one of the country's newest national parks, covers 142 sq km (55 sq miles) east of Quesada. The park protects one of the last swaths of virgin forest in the region and the headwaters of several rivers. There are no facilities at this time.

health clinic are also available. El Tucano has grown considerably since I first visited in the early 1990s; it is now a full-fledged country inn with 90 rooms, often filled with small tour groups using the resort as their base for exploring Arenal.

The grounds around the moderately-priced **Tilajari Resort Hotel** (469-9091 FAX 469-9095 E-MAIL tilajari@tilajari.com WEB SITE www.tilajari.com, north of Quesada in Muelle, are sufficient reason to spend a few nights. Owners Ricardo Araya (a passionate amateur botanist) and James Hamilton first began developing their property in 1987; over the years it has emerged as one of the most tranquil resorts in Costa Rica. The resort spreads over 14 ha (35 acres) along the banks of the Río San Carlos, with plenty of space between the pool, hot tubs, racquetball courts,

Pumas are rare, but still inhabit many forests in Costa Rica.

tennis courts, soccer field, restaurant, and rooms. The 76 rooms have air-conditioning and ceiling fans, comfy beds, low-key decorations (including some original paintings) and terraces; a few have handicap access. Families are pleased with the seemingly endless diversions, while solitary travelers can choose a quiet room and simply relax in peace. There's an extensive selection of tours to choose from. The adjacent private Tilajari Rainforest Reserve helps give the resort a feeling of isolation; it also improves the bird-watching possibilities.

Best known for its hot springs and canopy tour, **Termales del Bosque** (/FAX 460-1356, 10 km (six miles) east of Quesada, has a few inexpensive cabins with private bath and a good restaurant.

HOW TO GET THERE

Ciudad Quesada is 115 km (71 miles) northwest of San José on Highway 15. It can be reached by taking the Sarchí turnoff from the Carretera Interamericana from San José or via Highways 9 and 140 from Sarapiquí. Public buses run frequently from San José.

REFUGIO NACIONAL DE CAÑO NEGRO

Rivers run through the largely deforested Refugio Nacional de Caño Negro (661-8464 FAX 460-0640, near the Nicaraguan border. The Río Frío is the major waterway through this remote area, and boat trips along the river travel through marshes and swamps harboring flocks of waterfowl. The region is most interesting (and most easily traversed) during the rainy season, when rivers, streams, and lakes fill with water. Crocodiles slink along muddy riverbanks, snook and tarpon feed in the lakes, and turtles slumber in the sun on shore. Migrating birds swarm through Caño Negro from November through January, with bird-watching groups in their wake. Roseate spoonbills fill the sky with their flapping bright pink wings, egrets, storks, and anhinga dip their bills into the water, feeding on bugs. Mosquitoes buzz about the birds and boats; bring plenty of repellant. Tour companies at Quesada and the Arenal region offer boat trips through the reserve.

VOLCÁN ARENAL AND LA FORTUNA

Many visitors feel that Volcán Arenal is the most spectacular sight in all of Costa Rica, and for good reason. This behemoth erupts several times daily, spewing molten lava and noxious gases, hurling house-sized stones and clouds of ash into the deep blue sky, and rumbling with the ferocity of an angry giant. Unfortunately, low lying clouds and fog often obscure the volcano, and there's no guarantee you'll see sparks flying from the crater and lava flowing like red rivers down the mountain side. If you're really determined to see the volcano in action, try to stay here more than one night. Better yet, take your chances, watch the weather reports, and rush from wherever you're staying to the volcano when the skies are clear. Arenal is mesmerizing at any time of day, but it's especially magical on clear nights, when a river of red-hot magma flows down its northern slopes.

The nearest major town to Arenal is La Fortuna, a busy agricultural center packed with restaurants, budget hotels, tour operators and other services. La Fortuna is the best place in the area to stock up on groceries and take care of any car repairs you might need.

BACKGROUND

Formed roughly 4,000 years ago, 1,633-m-tall (5,356-ft) Arenal was sacred to the pre-Columbian Indians who inhabited this area. It was dormant in modern times and covered in thick rainforest — until July 1968, when the mountain trembled and suddenly blew its top. The eruption destroyed the villages of Pueblo Nuevo and Tabacón, killing 77 people. Magma flowed freely for nearly five years, creating massive lava fields around the mountain's base. Another large eruption occurred in the late 1970s, creating a second cinder cone at the summit. Another major explosion occurred in 1993, and a stronger eruption in 1998 caused the evacuation of hotels and homes in the area.

The worst eruption since the destruction of 1968 occurred on August 23, 2000. A sudden pyroclastic avalanche of hot gases, rocks and ash raced down the volcano's northeast slope at approximately 80 km/h (50 mph), surprising naturalist guide Ignacio Protti and his clients, a mother and daughter from Boston. Nearly overcome by gases and ash, Protti grabbed his clients and raced from the scene. He died 12 hours later from respiratory failure. The volcano continued to erupt in violent bursts, settled down for a few hours, then burst forth again, creating a monstrous cloud of ash. As gas fumes reached onlookers on the road at the base of the volcano, hotel and homes were evacuated.

I was at Arenal on that day, and unwittingly drove through the cloud of ash from the first eruption. Watching subsequent blasts from a relatively safe vantage point along with rescue workers and the police, I learned firsthand how frightening and destructive Arenal can be. Boulders and fallen trees tumbled down the mountain with incredible speed, and the fumes were nearly overpowering. Protti and his clients were walking on a popular

Waterfalls cascade down the sides of the steaming Volcán Arenal.

trail far below the crater and were simply in the wrong place at the wrong time. Torrential rains deterred other hikers from following the same trail; had the weather been clear, Arenal would have claimed many more victims that day.

Climbing Arenal is a nearly irresistible challenge for some adventurers; hiking trails along its base is a common activity. Hundreds of people walk along trails around the volcano every month without incident. But Arenal is an active volcano, one of the most active in the world. Use extreme caution when hiking on the volcano, and stick to marked trails. Better yet, restrict yourself to admiring the volcano from afar. Its pyrotechnic shows are dazzling, and will continue to be one of Costa Rica's top attractions. Just remember to treat the volcano with respect.

WHAT TO SEE AND DO

The best view of the nightly lava flow is on the northern flank, from Tabacón Springs anywhere along the La Fortuna–Nuevo Arenal road. However, there are no trails into the lava fields on this side. Trails and guided tours start on the south side, primarily from the **Arenal Observatory Lodge** (see below). Even if you're sleeping somewhere else, spend at least a day exploring the lodge and its environs. There's a volcanology museum with a seismograph and a glass-enclosed restaurant-bar, where you can enjoy a meal or sip a cold beer as Volcán Arenal works its magic.

Four trails lead away from the lodge. The short **Cascade Trail** (90 minutes) leads to a small waterfall in the jungle. The **Cerro Chado Trail** (four to five hours) cuts through a macadamia plantation and up a dormant volcano shrouded in thick rainforest. Inside the crater is an aquamarine lake that can be explored by canoe. The **Old Lava Field Trail** (two hours) runs through a jungle-shrouded valley and up Arenal's south flank to the rocky remnants of the 1968 eruption. You can also walk to the **New Lava Field** (three hours) inside the national park — dark-gray stones that rushed down the western slope in 1993. Just below (buried beneath millions of tons of lava and rock) is Pueblo Nuevo.

Parque Nacional Volcán Arenal (695-5180 FAX 695-5982, created in 1994, covers the volcano area and rainforest on the southeast shore of Laguna de Arenal. The only ranger station is five kilometers (just over three miles) south of the La Fortuna–Nuevo Arenal road on the road to the Observatory Lodge. Rangers collect the US$6 entry fee here; the station has clean restrooms and a small store. Self-guided trails lead to the New Lava Field. The park is open from 8 AM to 8 PM. Under no circumstance should you attempt to scale Arenal. Hired guides (available at the Observatory Lodge and the ranger station) can take you to

about 1,000 m (3,280 ft), but that's as close as you can get to the summit without risking life and limb.

Rest your weary feet at **Tabacón Hot Springs & Spa** on the mountain's northwest flank. Probably nowhere else in the world can you lie on your back in a hot-water pool, margarita in hand, and watch bright-red lava flow from a volcano. That is what makes Tabacón so special. Most people come here for at least half a day, roaming between the hot pools, streams, water slides, mud and massage treatments, and the swim-up bar. Tabacón's steamy waters (temperatures range from 27 to 39°C or 81 to 102°F) are reputed to cure any number of maladies, including arthritis and dermatological problems. Amenities include changing rooms, towels, lockers, showers and a restaurant. It's open 10 AM to 10 PM. The entry fee to the hot springs is rather high, and doubles if you add lunch or dinner to the tab. But that doesn't discourage its many visitors. The best time to visit is in the evening, when you can sit in the bubbling hot pools and watch the red lava flows gradually appear on the mountainside as the sun sets. The spa is directly beneath the volcano, and is evacuated when Arenal starts spewing ash.

Las Fuentes Termales (460-2020, extension 800, across the road from Tabacón, is wryly called Tabacón de los Pobres (Tabacón for the poor) by its fans. The entry fee is just over half that of the fancier establishment; both are owned by Tabacón Resort. A stairway leads down from a large parking lot to the complex, where a small waterfall flows into several natural and man-made pools. A small *soda*-type restaurant is open weekends, but most visitors bring picnics and claim one of the covered tables facing the pools. The bathrooms, showers, and changing rooms are located by the entrance.

The ever-changing and expanding **Jungla y Senderos Los Lagos** (237-3198 between La Fortuna and Tabacón is part theme park, part nature reserve, and part hotel. Waterslides, pools, hot springs and a crocodile pond make up the theme park area; hiking trail lead into the reserve on the side of the volcano. Rafting on the Peñas Blancas, El Toro, and Sarapiquí rivers can be arranged through **Aguas Bravas** (479-9025, on the La Fortuna–Nuevo Arenal road just west of La Fortuna. A few tour operators in the area offer trips to the **Venado Caverns**, about an hour's drive on a rough road northwest of La Fortuna. Stalactites, stalagmites, underground streams and waterfalls await those willing to endure a dirty climb through the limestone caverns — an adventure best suited to those who don't suffer from claustrophobia. **Boboadventures** (479-9058 at Celin's restaurant in La Fortuna arranges tours to the caves and provides helmets, flashlights and rubber boots. Tours are also available through many of the area's hotels and lodges. **Sunset Tours** (479-9415 FAX 479-9009 E-MAIL info@sunset-tours.com

WEB SITE www.sunset-tours.com in La Fortuna is the largest tour operator in the area.

WHERE TO STAY

The most popular hotels in the area face the volcano's lava flows, and are evacuated during times of extreme volcanic activity. Advance reservations are essential most times of year.

Expensive

If you plan on spending a considerable amount of time soaking in the hot springs, you might as well book a room at **Tabacón Resort** (256-1500 FAX 221-3075 WEB SITE www.tabacon.com. The hotel facilities are located a short way up the road from the hot springs; a shuttle runs between the two frequently. Hotel guests have unlimited use of the hot springs facility, and can schedule spa treatments to coincide with times when the spa and hot springs area is least crowded.

Moderate

The best abode in the entire region is the **Arenal Observatory Lodge** (695-5033 or 257-9489 FAX 257-4220 E-MAIL arenalob@sol.racsa.co.cr WEB SITE www.arenal-observatory.co.cr. Owned and operated by the Aspinall brothers, who also run the adjacent macadamia plantation, the lodge was built in 1987 as a volcano observatory for the University of Costa Rica and the Smithsonian Institute. Now open to the general public, the lodge represents rustic elegance at its finest. Trails and a suspension bridge lead to several clusters of rooms, most with huge picture windows facing the steaming volcano and the rainforest below. You can literally lie in bed and watch the fireworks. Horseback riding trips and guide services are available, including marvelous night walks and a hike to the New Lava Field each morning. Self-guided trails lead through the gardens and forest around the lodge. Meals are served in a glassed-in dining room with great views of the volcano; meals are not included in the room rate, but you can arrange a package including meals — a good idea since there's nowhere else to eat on the mountaintop. The road to the lodge is rough and steep, crossing several rivers that run high in rainy season. A four-wheel-drive vehicle is best, or you can arrange transportation through the lodge in advance of your stay. Be sure you're headed to the right place when you take the turnoff from the main road to the lodge. Guests booked at the Arenal Lodge (see below) often undertake the rough drive by mistake.

A mixed bag of anglers, naturalists, hikers, bird watchers and volcano enthusiasts flock to **Arenal Lodge** (228-3189 FAX 289-6798 E-MAIL arenal@sol.racsa.co.cr WEB SITE www.arenallodge.com on the La Fortuna–Nuevo Arenal road by Arenal Dam.

The lodge is perched on a ridge near the eastern end of Laguna de Arenal, with panoramic views of both the lake and volcano. Separated from the crater by a deep river valley, the lodge is one of the safest places to stay near the volcano. The 34 rooms run the gamut for individual cabins (expensive) on hills above the lodge to basic rooms (moderate) with private baths in the main building. The enormous restaurant faces the volcano (take advantage of the bountiful breakfast buffet and you won't need to eat lunch). The library is a cozy spot with fireplace, pool table, a large selection of books and games, and a television. Mountain bikes are available for rent, and fishing trips, horseback riding, and tours can be arranged

through the front desk. The road to the lodge is steep but well maintained.

The best volcano-watching perches near La Fortuna may well be the broad glassed-in porches fronting A-frame wooden cottages at **Montaña de Fuego Inn** (460-1220 FAX 479-9579 E-MAIL monfuego@sol.racsa.co.cr WEB SITE www.montanadelfuego.com. The 42 cottages are set about the forested property and are constructed of burnished hardwoods; the larger suites have coffeemakers and air-conditioning. The pool is fed from a hot spring, and a spa opened at the end of 2000. Hot springs are but one of the attractions at **Los Lagos** (479-9126 FAX 261-3075, six kilometers (four miles) east of La Fortuna. Hotel rooms with fans, private baths, cable television and small

ABOVE: The view from the porch at the Montaña de Fuego Hotel. OVERLEAF: An arcade of saplings leads into the countryside below the mighty Volcán Arenal.

refrigerators are clustered around the pool; more rustic, inexpensive cabins are located at the end of a 45-minute hike into the reserve.

Inexpensive

One of the most impressive developments in the La Fortuna area is the **Albergue La Catarata** (479-9522 FAX 479-9168 E-MAIL cooprena@sol.racsa.co.cr WEBSITE www.agroecoturism.net, three kilometers (two miles) up the dirt road to the Catarata La Fortuna waterfalls east of town. A cooperative ecotourism project involving local *campesinos*, the small lodge has nine immaculately clean rooms with green walls, single beds, private baths with hot-water showers and floor fans (when needed). The setting is blissfully serene and the whole project a fascinating introduction into the benefits of involving the community in tourism. The men and women working at the lodge take pride in making it clear that they eschew the concept of working for a single owner or manager. Instead, each person handles a specific responsibility, maintaining the butterfly garden (filled with ethereal bright-blue morphos) or caring for endangered *tepezcuintles* (a small agouti hunted for food) in the breeding project. The workers also raise and harvest herbs, spices and medicinal plants for export. The lodge's restaurant is open to the public, and serves great regional dishes.

The town of La Fortuna is a budget traveler's haven, with several small hotels offering basic accommodations at extremely low prices. The **Hotel San Bosco** (479-9050 FAX 479-9109 E-MAIL fortuna@sol.racsa.co.cr, one block north of the main road through town, is the fanciest hotel in town with a pool, hot tub and 29 rooms with private baths and air-conditioning. Some rooms are in the inexpensive range; larger suites are a few dollars more. Small *cabina*-style hotels line the side streets; some consist of a couple of rooms added on to the owner's home. **Cabinas Sissy** (479-9256, one block south of the main road through town, is one of the best. The simple rooms have cement floors, single beds and private bathrooms with hot water. The adjacent house sleeps 10 guests and has a living room and full kitchen.

WHERE TO EAT

The best restaurants in the area are at the lodges and hotels, though there are a few good places serving *tico* dishes in La Fortuna.

Moderate

Dine with a view of red-hot lava at **Restaurant Acuarelas Steak House** (460-1220 at the Montaña de Fuego Inn. Along with several beef preparations (try the *churrasco* marinated steak served with homemade tortillas and beans), the menu features sea bass with caper sauce, fresh trout from Laguna de Arenal and a creamy peach cheesecake. **Arenal Observatory Lodge** has an excellent breakfast buffet and a good selection of beef, chicken, and seafood meals for lunch and dinner; if you drive up the mountain to visit the lodge's observatory, stay for dinner and watch the lava flows. The **Hot Springs Restaurant** inside the Tabacón hot springs, serves pricey North American and local dishes with a view of the pools and hot springs; most visitors who spend time at the springs are famished by the time they finish playing and are content to dine here. Locals congregate at **El Novillo Steak House** (479-9178, a wildly popular open-air eatery on the road between Tabacón and La Fortuna. An enormous palm frond rancho

covers **La Pradera** (479-9597. The burgers and fries are pretty good, as are the typical *casados*.

Inexpensive

Budget travelers gather at **Restaurant Celin's** (479-9058 in La Fortuna to access the Internet (for a fee) and dine on inexpensive salads, sandwiches, burgers, and seafood dishes. The offices of Boboadventures are located beside the restaurant. **La Choza de Laurel** (479-9231, near the soccer field in the center of town, is a favorite with locals feasting on grilled chicken, fish, and *casados*.

HOW TO GET THERE

Volcán Arenal can be reached from San José via either Tilarán or La Fortuna, but the latter route (which also runs through Zarcero and Ciudad Quesada) is shorter — about three hours in total.

Buses run daily from San José to La Fortuna and Nuevo Arenal; from La Fortuna you can take a taxi to the national park or hotels around Arenal's base.

LAGUNA DE ARENAL AND TILARÁN

In 1973, the Costa Rican government built a large earthen dam on the Río Arenal, creating Laguna de Arenal, a 30-km-long (19-mile) reservoir that is now the country's premier recreational lake. Arenal is surrounded by rolling hills — a picturesque landscape of cattle ranches and dairy farms reminiscent of central California and southern Spain. A highway snakes around the west and

villagers displaced by the rising waters of the dam. It's a compact little town with a school, post office, gas station and small markets and shops. **Tilarán**, five kilometers (three miles) south of the lake, crowns an emerald-green ridge. It's more of a cowboy town than a resort village, with rodeo and livestock shows in April and June. There's a small expatriate community here, with activity centering around La Carreta restaurant (see WHERE TO EAT, below). Tilarán is an important crossroads: Cañas is 23 km (14 miles) to the west via a good paved road that links up with the Carretera Interamericana; Monteverde is two hours or 42 km (26 miles) to the southeast on a rough and tumble back road that starts at Quebrada Grande.

north shores, but east of Nuevo Arenal most of the road is unpaved.

Activities in the lake area include boating, fishing, windsurfing, horseback riding, mountain biking, hiking and camping on small islands. Arenal is said to be well-stocked with game fish including *guapote* (rainbow bass), *machaca* (shad) and the tasty African tilapia. This lake is also wonderful for swimming, with water temperatures hovering at 20°C (68°F) year round. Windsurfing enthusiasts flock to Arenal from around the globe to catch the lake's strong, consistent winds — 15 to 35 knots from December to May. The "bump and jump" is excellent.

WHAT TO SEE AND DO

Two towns serve the lake region. **Nuevo Arenal** on the north shore was created in 1973 to resettle

In addition to the lake, there are several worthwhile sights in the immediate area. **Jardín Botánico Arenal (** 694-4273, five kilometers (three miles) east of Nuevo Arenal, offers a lavish assortment of tropical plants and flowers, created by American Mike LeMay. **Lago Coter** is five kilometers (three miles) northwest of Nuevo Arenal. A lodge that overlooks this tiny crater lake (see below) offers horseback riding, hiking and mountain biking on 740 ha (300 acres) of private forest. You can also kayak and fish the lake. The original owner of **Toad Hall (** 381-3662 WEB SITE www.toadhall-gallery.com had a fondness for *The Wind in the Willows*, thus the odd name for this fine gallery and restaurant beside the lake. New owners David and Jan Warner

OPPOSITE: Laguna de Arenal is a playground for boaters, anglers and windsurfers. ABOVE: The porch is an essential ingredient of a Laguna de Arenal vacation.

decided to stick with the name and expand the gallery's excellent selection of Costa Rican art and crafts. Hammocks, tiles, original paintings, typical tin mugs painted with village scenes, and gourmet coffee beans fill the shop's shelves.

The recently created **Parque Nacional Volcán Tenorio**, which embraces a 1,916-m (6,284-ft) volcano of the same name, is due east of Laguna de Arenal. The turnoff to the park is at Río Piedras. There are no visitor facilities at the present time.

Water sports occupy much of the visitor's time here. **Tilawa Viento Surf (** 695-5050 TOLL-FREE (800) 851-8929 FAX 695-5766 E-MAIL tilawa@sol.racsa .co.cr, at the edge of the lake and at Tilawa Lodge (see below), rents Hobie Cats and windsurfers. Equipment includes Nash custom and Mistral production equipment. Windsurfing classes from beginner to advanced are available. **Tico Wind (**/FAX 283-2694 E-MAIL ticowind@compuserve.com rents windsurfing equipment including Ezzy Wave and Transformer sails, and BIC and Gorge Animal custom boards. Classes from beginner to advanced levels are available. They also rent mountain bikes.

JJ's Fishing Tours (695-5825 offers half- and full-day fishing excursions including all equipment, lunch and drinks; the company also rents rooms in a small B&B. Horseback rides into the forest around Lago Coter can be arranged through **Stables Arenal (** 694-4092 FAX 695-5387.

WHERE TO STAY

Moderate

Windsurfers make themselves at home at Hotel Tilawa **(** 695-5050 FAX 695-5666 E-MAIL tilawa@ sol.racsa.co.cr, near Tilarán. The Tilawa bills itself as the Costa Rican version of the ancient palace of Knossos in Crete, a fantasy land of ochre columns, colorful hand-painted frescoes, handmade textiles and custom-made furniture. The guest rooms are modern and spacious, with air-conditioning and private bathrooms with large bathtubs. The largest rooms have kitchenettes with refrigerators, toaster ovens and coffeemakers. Amenities include swimming pool, tennis courts, a windsurfing center, car rental, horseback riding and fishing trips. A trail leads down a steep hill from the hotel to the windsurfing center on the lake; the hike back up is exhausting, especially after you've been hoisting sails for a few hours.

Don't worry — you're not hallucinating. The **Hotel los Héroes (**/FAX 384-6315 E-MAIL heroes@ sol.racsa.co.cr is for real, though it would be better situated in Zermatt or Interlaken. As cutesy as a chalet straight from *Heidi*, Los Héroes is a fantasy of red and white gingham curtains, wood shutters with heart cutouts, and front desk clerks wearing embroidered shirts. It's situated near the lake's eastern extreme, where pastureland gives

way to rainforest. The 12 rooms are Spartan but spanking clean, with private baths. The restaurant serves Swiss and Austrian specialties.

Welcoming **Chalet Nicholas (**/FAX 694-4041 E-MAIL chaletnicholas@costarica.net, near Nuevo Arenal is a family establishment, although it's difficult to tell who really runs this place — John and Cathy Nichols or their three great danes! About five minutes from Nuevo Arenal, this top-notch bed and breakfast has three unique rooms that overlook either lake or forest. Breakfast is prepared with organic fruits grown on the property (try the macadamia pancakes). Cathy tends an orchid garden, John tinkers in a woodworking shop, and either is happy to show you the ins and outs of their hobbies. Windsurfers and mountain bikers congregate at **Rock River Lodge (**/FAX 695-5644 WEBSITE www.rokriver@sol.racsa.co.cr, on the road between Tilarán and Nuevo Arenal. The main building is a rustic wooden affair with several rooms sharing a shaded front porch. Larger freestanding cabins are spread up the hillside. A main lodge houses the restaurant, lobby and room for guests to get together around the fireplace. The lodge has a windsurfing center and gear rentals; mountain bikes are also available for rent.

The **Eco Lodge Lake Coter (** 257-5075 FAX 257-7065 is almost a world unto itself. Poised on the edge of tiny Lake Coter, the lodge offers 24 rooms (most with shared bath) and 16 cabins (all with private bath) in a wilderness setting. The main building here has a restaurant, lounge with fireplace, game room with pool table, bar and library. Activities include hiking, horseback riding, boating and fishing.

Inexpensive

Perched on a hill above the lake's western shore is **Mystica Lodge (** 385-1499 FAX 695-5387 E-MAIL mystica@aol.com WEB SITE members.aol.com/ mysticacr. Barbara and Francesco, a delightful Italian couple, run the spacious, six-room lodge with a family style that includes hearty meals; their pizza is said to be the best in the Arenal region. Equestrian and aquatic activities are the main themes at **Xiloe Lodge (** 259-9806 FAX 259-9882. Like many of the hotels at the lake's western extreme, Xiloe caters to windsurfers. But it's also big on horses, arranging scenic rides into the nearby hills. The lodge has a cowboy-theme restaurant, the **Equus BBQ**, down on the lake shore. Accommodations are in bungalows with refrigerators or cabins with small kitchens. All units have private baths and hot water. The **Full Moon** disco behind the lodge is the hottest night spot in the region. **Cabinas El Sueño (** 695-5347 near the main plaza in Nuevo Arenal is a good choice for budget travelers dependent upon public transportation. The 12 small rooms face a quiet center courtyard, and the restaurant serves great seafood dishes.

WHERE TO EAT

Where you dine depends largely on which end of the lake you're staying. Centrally located **Toad Hall** (see above) is probably the lake's best restaurant, serving fresh juices, gourmet coffee drinks, herb-roasted chicken, salads, and excellent cakes and cookies. At the western end of the lake, try the great pizzas at **Mystica Lodge** (695-5387 and **Equus BBQ** (259-9806 for chicken and steaks. **Soda la Macha** (no phone) in Río Piedras village has a spectacular open-air dining room (with fireplace) which overlooks the lake. A good place for lunch is **La Rana de Arenal** (694-4031, which has

an outdoor terrace, fabulous garden and superb lake views. **Rosetta** restaurant at the Hotel Tilawa has probably the best menu on this side of the lake. Near the eastern end, try **Sabor Italiano** for pizza or **Los Héroes** restaurant for Alpine specialties such as fondue, smoked pork cutlets and wiener schnitzel.

In the center of Tilarán, **La Carreta** (695-6654 FAX 695-6593 WEB SITE aarenaltours.com is far more than just a restaurant. Owners Tom and Billie Jafek are the town's biggest promoters. Spend a few minutes chatting with them and Tom is sure to cart you off to see the biggest tree in Costa Rica, a giant ceiba measuring 10 m (30 ft) across the trunk. By the end of the tour you'll probably sign up to spend a few nights in La Carreta's new guest rooms. Even if you just stop by for a meal, you're sure to enjoy the food — lobster omelets, shrimp cocktail, fresh grilled tuna, pizzas with every

imaginable topping — the book exchange, and the display of gorgeous orchids. Two guest rooms were nearly finished when I last visited, and eight more are in the works.

HOW TO GET THERE

Laguna de Arenal can be approached from two directions: via Las Cañas and Tilarán or via La Fortuna. Either way the lake is a three- to four-hour drive from San José, along fairly good roads (by Costa Rican standards). The road between Cañas and Tilarán runs through heavy-duty cattle ranching country — deforested tracts of rolling hills that straddle the Continental Divide. There is daily bus service from San José to Nuevo Arenal and Tilarán.

LAS CAÑAS AND ENVIRONS

The sleepy cowboy town of Las Cañas (population: 21,000), at the junction of the Carretera Interamericana and the Tilarán–Arenal road, is named after the wild cane that grows in this part of Guanacaste. Las Cañas is the gateway to Guanacaste's most remote regions, an area of rivers, swamps, dry forests, and several parks and preserves. Few travelers venture far in this area, since there are precious few places to spend the night. One of the best choices, Hacienda la Pacifica, closed in 2000. With any luck new owners will reopen it soon.

WHAT TO SEE AND DO

Las Cañas sits in the middle of cattle country. The local bullfight ring (Plaza de Toros Chorotega) is located on the main road opposite the town cemetery. Bloodless bullfights are staged here during fiestas, including Palm Sunday when a street market and carnival erupts around the arena. The most important attractions in the area are along rough roads radiating from town.

Parque Nacional Palo Verde (671-1062, 30 km (19 miles) west of Las Cañas, is the closest thing that Costa Rica has to North America's Everglades or Australia's Kakadu—a massive area of swamp and forest that hugs the north banks of the ríos Tempisque and Bebedero. The park embraces 12 different life zones including mangrove swamp, marshes, savanna grasslands, lagoons and various forms of tropical forest. The park takes its name from the palo verde (green stick) tree, but the area harbors more than 150 different tree species.

Most people come to Palo Verde for the birds — the largest gathering of waterfowl in all of Central America, including storks, herons, egrets,

Out on the range a cowboy shades his eyes with the traditional wide-brimmed cotton hat.

spoonbills, ibises and ducks. Also famous are the rare scarlet macaws that nest in this park, reduced to about a thousand mating pairs throughout the country because of rampant poaching in the past. Other denizens include the howler monkey, iguana and saltwater crocodile; a known man-eater that is just about impossible to see in the other Pacific coast parks.

Palo Verde is under water for most of the rainy season, and even during dry season (December to April) the park is virtually impossible to tour without a boat. Several companies offer guided boat tours of Palo Verde, including Liberia-based **Asmiturli** (666-1606 and **CATA Tours** (669-1026 or 296-2133 (in San José). You can usually hire your

developed into the tourist hub of south-central Guanacaste. Two distinct attractions bring visitors to the region: river rafting on the Río Corobicí and the Las Pumas Wildlife Center.

Rapids in this stretch of the **Río Corobicí** are rated at class I and II, which means that rafting is more of a gentle float than a raging whitewater adventure. But it's one of the more pleasant things you can do in Guanacaste and a terrific way to see wildlife. The trip is also a great opportunity to view the Guanacaste backcountry and various forms of rural life.

Floating down the Corobicí, directly down river from the bridge, you'll see a few shanties; this is an aspect of country life that isn't always

own boat and local guide in the village of Bebedero, 14 km (nine miles) southwest of Las Cañas.

There is no lodging available inside the park, and permission to camp must be gained from national park authorities. The nearest hotels are in Las Cañas and Laguna de Arenal. The **Organization for Tropical Studies (OTS)** (240-6696 FAX 240-6783 (in San José) WEB SITE www.ots.ac.cr operates the **Estación Biológica Palo Verde** in the reserve's central sector, 38 km (24 miles) down a rough flagstone road that starts at Bagaces on the Carretera Interamericana. The biological station has rustic dormitory lodging (inexpensive) with shared bath (cold water). The facilities are most often used by scientists and researchers, but travelers can also stay here with advance reservations.

Rincón Corobicí, six kilometers (three and a quarter miles) north of Las Cañas on the Carretera Interamericana, is a riverside hamlet that has

visible from the Carretera Interamericana. The shanties eventually give way to hacienda country with grazing horses and cattle. Soon the pastures evolve into riverside jungle. It's easy to spot howler monkeys and iguanas in shoreline trees. Bird life is phenomenal: snowy egrets and blue herons flit back and forth across the water, ospreys ride the thermal updrafts, huge tiger herons hide among the reeds and various types of night herons stalk the undergrowth. Vegetation is also fantastic, with giant mahogany, guanacaste and kapok trees shading much of the river. The trip lasts about two hours. **Ríos Tropicales** (233-6455 FAX 255-4354 is the best of the raft companies, with professional guides, good equipment and a tasty riverside lunch at the end of the journey. **Safaris Corobicí** (/FAX 669-1091 E-MAIL safaris@sol.racsa.co.cr WEB SITE www.nicoya.com, just over four and a half kilometers (two and a half miles) west of Cañas on the Carretera Interamericana, is the largest operation in the area, and offers guided tours on the river.

It is difficult to see big cats in the wild because they've been hunted to extinction in most parts of Costa Rica. The **Las Pumas Wildlife Center** (no phone), located beside the Safaris Corobicí office, offers an opportunity to view indigenous felines and support a good cause at the same time. The brainchild of Lilly Bodmer de Hagnauer, a transplanted Swiss environmentalist, this animal orphanage shelters a number of rare or endangered species including jaguars, jaguarundi, marguays, ocelots and puma. It also sustains a fair number of birds and at least one white-tailed deer.

The big cats are not taken from the wild — they come to Las Pumas as orphaned babies whose parents were killed by poachers, or as exotic pets that got too big (and dangerous) for suburban houses. Lilly and her small staff nurse them back to health or into adulthood. Originally her plan was to release the animals back into the wild, and to track them by radio transponders so as to observe their range and behavior — a Costa Rican version of *Born Free*. However, she gave up on this practice as the animals were being quickly dispatched by hunters. A group of marguays, for instance, was wiped out within a couple weeks of their release.

Lilly (a spirited septuagenarian) has lived at Las Pumas for four decades. While she gets many orphaned animals that have been rescued by private citizens and public agencies, the center doesn't get a penny from the Costa Rican government.

It's supported entirely by donations from visitors. Contributions go towards the purchase of food, vitamins and medicine for the cats, as well as better homes. The big cats snooze in the daytime, but begin to wake up in the late afternoon, which is probably the best time to visit.

Also in the area, the **Reserva Biológica Lomas Barbudal** (no phone) is midway between Las Cañas and Liberia; the turnoff from the Carretera Interamericana is at a tiny hamlet called Pijije, about 10 km (six miles) from Bagaces and 16 km (10 miles) from Liberia (look for the Km. 221 marker). It's then 30 minutes down a rough flagstone road to the park headquarters.

These "bearded hills" are an island of tropical dry forest in the heart of cattle country, with thickly wooded rolling terrain that serves as a refuge for monkeys, coatis and coyotes, as well as a stopover for migratory birds such as herons and egrets. Scarlet macaws visit from nearby Palo Verde and the park is endowed with more than 230 bee species. There are also many rare trees including mahogany, rosewood, gonzalo-alvis and Central American redwood. Perhaps the best time to visit is March, when the cortéz trees are in full yellow bloom. Park headquarters on the banks of the Río Cabuyo offers information and picnic tables. There are walking trails along the river and several swimming holes. Founded in 1986, Reserva Biológica Lomas Barbudal covers about 2,270 ha (5,607 acres). There is no lodging in the park other than primitive camping near the ranger station. The nearest hotels are in Liberia.

WHERE TO STAY AND EAT

There are precious few places to stay in this area, and many travelers visit the reserves and parks on day trips from Laguna de Arenal or Liberia. The **Hotel Corral** (669-0622 in Las Cañas has 12 rooms with private baths (cold water only). **Hotel Cañas** (669-0039 has a similar setup; both are inexpensive.

Sublime seclusion and surprising luxury are the reward of driving to **La Carolina Lodge** (380-1656 E-MAIL info@lacarolinalodge.com WEB SITE www.lacarolinalodge.com, located about 50 km (31 miles) northwest of Las Cañas off Route 6 (the road to Upala) in a remote region on the slopes of Volcán Tenorio. Surrounded by 69 ha (170 acres) of rainforest and pasture, the lodge sleeps 11 guests in private and family-style rooms immaculately decorated with imported linens and artistic flair. The showers have steaming hot water (thanks to propane heaters) but no electricity. Instead, candles and oil lamps provide light once the sun sets, and a car battery keeps the stereo system running.

OPPOSITE: A round-up at Cañas Dulces.
ABOVE: The Río Corobicí flows peacefully through southern Guanacaste.

Green parrots, aracaris, and keel-billed toucans provide the wakeup calls, though they don't seem to rouse the sloths dozing in nearby trees. You can literally fish off the lodge's deck in a small lagoon (a great swimming hole) or doze in hammocks on the back porch.

The working dairy provides fresh cheese and milk, and horses are available for rides to dozens of drop-dead gorgeous trails leading to secret waterfalls, through forest, macadamia fields, along rivers to mountaintops with views stretching all the way to Lake Nicaragua. The main event is a five-hour guided hike into the Parque Nacional Volcán Tenorio to see the 21-m-tall (70-ft) Río Celeste waterfall, along with the hot springs, blue lagoon and mint-green mineral mud pits. Meals, hikes, and horseback rides are included in the moderate rate.

LIBERIA

The capital of Guanacaste province hugs the banks of the Río Liberia which flows down into Parque Nacional Palo Verde and the Río Tempisque. Dubbed the Ciudad Blanca (White City) because of chalky soil and whitewashed houses, this formerly languid outpost was founded 1769.

Liberia doesn't look that old, although some of the buildings around the central plaza still bear a colonial flavor. Huge leafy matalpo trees shade many of the streets, but can't disguise the fact that Liberia is hot and dusty for much of the year. Most tourists don't give the town more than a passing glance; they're too busy heading for the coast and the nearby national parks. But the town of 23,000 residents gets chock-a-block full of cars during holiday weekends, when it seems everyone who lives in the Meseta Central is headed to the beach. Chain restaurants and mini malls mark the main intersection, and gas stations and car repair shops abound. Take care of any business matters while you're here. Liberia is the only place in Guanacaste that makes an attractive hub for visiting the best of both beach and nature attractions.

WHAT TO SEE AND DO

La Agonía (The Agony) is a charming nineteenth-century church at the eastern end of Avenida Central. Casa de Cultura (666-4527. Three blocks south of the central plaza has a small museum with exhibits about *sabaneros* or local cowboys and a tourist information service called Asmitourli (666-1606, which offers brochures, maps, hotel reservations and guided tours to various Guanacaste attractions. Check out the display of ceramics with pre-Columbian designs made by Chorotega women.

Liberians let their hair down on July 25, a fiesta day that celebrates the province's separation from Nicaragua in 1824 as well as the Feast Day of St. James. Events include bullfights, rodeos, cattle shows, marimba bands, folk dancing, food stalls and horse parades. There's a youth parade called the Posada del Niño on Christmas Eve each year and a local cultural week (Semana Cultura) each September.

WHERE TO STAY

Moderate
Anyone with a hankering for motel life should try Hotel el Sitio (666-1211 FAX 666-2059, south of the big intersection on the road to the Aeropuerto Daniel Obudar. A popular stop for Costa Ricans

on their way to the beach, El Sitio has 52 rooms with private baths, hot water, air-conditioning, satellite television and safe-deposit box. Amenities include two swimming pools, gym, sand volleyball court, restaurant and bar, laundromat and a babysitting service. Las Espuelas (666-0144 FAX 666-2441 sits in a large grove of trees off the Carretera Interamericana and has comfortable rooms with private baths, hot water, satellite television and air-conditioning. The garden features a pool and hammocks strung between the giant shade trees.

Inexpensive
Hotel Boyeros (666-0995 FAX 666-2529 is on the Carretera Interamericana a block south of the big crossroads. The spacious rooms have private baths, hot water, air-conditioning and balconies. Expansive matalpo trees shade the open-air restaurant

and the nearby playground. Affiliated with Hostelling International, **Hotel Guanacaste** (666-0085 FAX 666-2287 E-MAIL htlguana@sol.racsa.co.cr has rock-bottom rates for shared rooms with shared baths.

WHERE TO EAT

Most of Liberia's restaurants are in the inexpensive-to-moderate range, and specialize in Costa Rican food. **El Bramadero** (666-0371 at the Carretera Interamericana junction, is popular with Costa Rican travelers, offering hearty portions of *comida tipico* and ice cold beer. **Restaurant Pókopi** (666-1036, opposite Hotel el Sitio, is the best steak-

charter and regional flights arrive. The airport is called **Aeropuerto Daniel Obudar** (668-1010, though locals usually refer to it as the Liberia airport. TravelAir and SANSA have several flights every week from San José to Liberia, with return flights on the same days. Flight availability is highest in dry season. There are car rental desks at the airport, only open when major flights arrive.

PARQUE NACIONAL RINCÓN DE LA VIEJA

One of Costa Rica's best-kept secrets, Parque Nacional Rincón de la Vieja is a sprawling area of 14,000 ha (34,580 acres) in northern Guanacaste

house in town; there are several fish choices on the menu as well. Pokópi's tiny discotheque is the only place in Liberia that swings at night. The **Hotel Boyeros** restaurant features simple but filling international and local *tico* dishes.

HOW TO GET THERE

Liberia is roughly 220 km (136 miles) from San José via the Carretera Interamericana. The journey takes three to four hours, depending on traffic conditions. There are numerous daily bus services from San José, as well as other Guanacaste destinations including Santa Cruz, La Cruz, Nicoya, Las Cañas and the major beach resorts. Most buses headed for Nicaragua will also pick up passengers in Liberia.

There is a small airport 12 km (seven and a half miles) west of Liberia where international

that harbors a wide range of natural attractions: an active volcano, mud pools and hot springs, dry coastal forest and cloud forest and myriad forms of wildlife. The park is a walker's paradise, with more than 100 km (62 miles) of well-marked trails.

Park headquarters is at Santa María, due north of Liberia. But most people enter through Las Pailas, where there's a ranger station (695-5598 (with maps) and the park's only campground. Trails spread out in three directions from Las Pailas.

WHAT TO SEE AND DO

The park's **Central Trail** leads up to Rincón de la Vieja Volcano, 1,895 m (6,217 ft) high, which last

OPPOSITE: Jaguars are protected in reserves such as Las Pumas, but are rarely sighted along nature trails. ABOVE: A boa constrictor strangles its prey, a hapless iguana, at Rincón de la Vieja.

erupted in 1984 and 1991. Unlike Arenal, which is far too dangerous to climb, you can climb up Rincón and peer down into its steaming caldera. Rincón is a composite volcano that features nine different eruptive spots or craters. The round trip from the ranger station is roughly 15 km (nine miles), but the journey usually takes all day because of the steep ascent. If the weather is clear, you will be able to see Lago de Nicaragua and the Península de Nicoya. The summit trail also passes Von Seebach, an adjacent crater that has a beautiful aquamarine lake. Be sure to take water and a windbreaker or jacket in case the weather turns nasty at the summit.

The **Sendero Las Pailas** (Eastern Trail) skirts the campground (a great place to spot iguanas) and crosses the Río Colorado on a small suspension bridge before heading into a large thermal zone called Las Pailas (The Cauldrons). You can veer right or left after the bridge; the trail is a seven-kilometer (four-and-a-third-mile) loop through the various volcanic attractions including boiling, bubbling mud pots, steaming fumaroles and hissing gas vents. At the far end of the loop is the start of another trail that leads six kilometers (just under four miles) to **Los Azufrales** (The Sulfurs) hot springs, which bubble at a blistering 42°C (108°F). One kilometer (just over a mile) beyond the springs is Santa María ranger station.

The **Sendero de Cataratas** (Western Trail) breaks off from the volcano route about half a kilometer (a third of a mile) from the ranger station. It crosses the Río Blanco on a suspension bridge and plunges deep into the dry tropical forest. There are huge trees all around, and this is a great place to spot wildlife including howler and white-faced monkeys, coatimundi, agouti, armadillo and myriad avian creatures (the park has more than 300 bird species). This trail eventually splits: The north fork runs two kilometers (one and a quarter miles) to the four **Cataratas Escondidas** (Hidden Falls). The south fork leads another two and a half kilometers (one and a half miles) to **Catarata la Cangreja**, a 40-m-tall (131-ft) waterfall that plunges into a brilliant turquoise-colored pool. This is a perfect swimming hole, so bring your suit.

A curious side note: The name Rincón de la Vieja means "corner of the old lady," but nobody seems quite sure how the mountain got that tag. There is a legend that suggests that the matriarch of the Spanish family that first settled this area in the late eighteenth century lived by herself at the base of the volcano. Another story is reminiscent of Romeo and Juliet: a young Spanish woman, spurned by her lover's family, lived out the rest of her years on the mountain, turning her back on the conservative colonial society that destroyed her romance. Either way, Rincón de la Vieja remains a haunting and beautiful place.

The imaginative designers at **Original Canopy Tour** (257-5149 FAX 256-7626 E-MAIL canopy@sol .racsa.co.cr WEB SITE www.canopytour.com operate the exciting **Kazm Canyon Tour** on the Hacienda Lodge Guachipelín (see below) property. Unlike most forest canopy tours, Kazm involves a bit of rock climbing and rappelling along with rides along cables suspended over the Río Blanco gorge. Few experiences equal the rush that comes from zipping along a cable over huge boulders and foaming river rapids. Lodges in the area will book the tour for you, or you can arrange it yourself by contacting the canopy tour offices.

WHERE TO STAY

Rincón de la Vieja is an out-of-the-way destination, and the lodges that abut are difficult to reach. A four-wheel-drive vehicle is essential, as are advance reservations.

Expensive

An amazing vision greets those who struggle up the steep rutted road to **Hotel Borinquen** (666-5098 FAX 666-2931 E-MAIL borinquen@sol .racsa.co.cr, 40 km (25 miles) north of Liberia off the Carretera Interamericana. Handsome white villas with red tiled roofs and wood balconies dot the green hills above the main building; each villa comes with a golf cart for easier access to the restaurant and spa. The villas are the loveliest rooms in the area, with red-tiled floors, white-tiled bathrooms, air-conditioning, mini bars, televisions tucked into handcrafted wood armoires, and porches with rocking chairs and astounding views. Dinner is served by candlelight in the elegant restaurant. The property's best feature is its spa, centered around several pools fed by hot springs. Thick, skin-smoothing mud bubbles in specially-designed cauldrons that cool the viscous substance just enough to keep it from burning your skin. Guests lather mud all over their bodies, let it harden in the sun, then rinse under tepid showers before leaping back into the hot pools or stepping into the sauna heated by natural steam vents. Hiking and horseback rides complete the activities, leaving plenty of time for guests to lounge around their pricey digs.

Moderate

The most convenient base is **Rincón de la Vieja Volcano Mountain Lodge** (695-5553 or 284-3023 (in San José) FAX 256-5410 E-MAIL rincon@sol .racsa.co.cr, three and a half kilometers (just over two miles) from Las Pailas ranger station off the Carretera Interamericana. The lodge offers various means to explore the park including guides, horses and mountain bikes. It also stages a forest-

Mud pools and boiling thermal waters bubble at Las Pailas, The Cauldrons, Rincón de la Vieja.

canopy tour run by Treetop Trails on private land outside the park. Accommodation is in rustic cabins or rooms with private bath (but no hot water or air-conditioning). It has a small swimming pool and an outdoor bar, frequented by a chatterbox parrot and two friendly dogs. The meals are basic but filling. The beer is always cold.

Buena Vista Lodge (/FAX 695-5147, 40 km (25 miles) north of Liberia off the Carretera Interamericana bills itself as a "mountain lodge and adventure center" but it is also a working hacienda — 648 ha (1,600 acres) of cattle pastures and forest that are crisscrossed by horse and hiking trails. The rustic lodge nestles at 800 m (2,624 ft) in the volcanic foothills of Rincón de la Vieja volcano with panoramic views of the Guanacaste plains, Península Santa Elena and the Pacific Ocean in the distance. On clear days you can see the southwest coast of Nicaragua from up here. Much of the wildlife found in the national park spills over onto the Buena Vista land: monkeys, white-tailed deer, anteaters and myriad bird species (including a pair of talkative green amazons that live in a tree outside the lodge entrance).

One of the prime reasons for coming to Buena Vista is the ranch's famous mud baths and hot spring, which are said to cure just about anything that might ail your skin. The horseback trip to the thermal area takes about one hour, traversing rolling hills punctuated by spreading guanacaste trees and gentle streams. On arrival at the spa (and changing rooms) you spread mud over every inch of your body, let it dry in the sun to the consistency of chalk and then submerge yourself in a stone hot tub. You can also dip in a nearby cold-water stream fed by mountain springs.

Buena Vista also organizes horseback and hiking tours into Parque Nacional Rincón de la Vieja, including trips to the volcano summit and the hidden waterfalls. The lodge offers inexpensive accommodation in 37 rustic rooms, most with private bath and fluorescent lights over the thin beds. Meals are not included in the room rate — since there are no other places to eat, the price of dining raises the rate to moderate range. I suggest you bring some snacks along, as the meals I had there left a lot to be desired.

Inexpensive

The turnoff for **Hacienda Lodge Guachipelín** (384-2049 FAX 442-1910 WEB SITE www.guachipelin .com, is located five kilometers (three miles) north of Liberia off the Carretera Interamericana at the signs for Las Pailas, and another 21 km (13 miles) up the mountain. The ranch house, built in the 1870s, was transformed into a cozy but rather basic bed and breakfast that feels much more like a working ranch than the Volcano Mountain

Lodge. The 25 rooms have private baths with cold water, and a bunkhouse style room has several beds at very inexpensive rates. Hikes to waterfalls, boiling mud cauldrons, natural hot springs, and forests where howler and capuchin monkeys hang out are available, along with horseback riding and mountain bikes. The park entrance is only 10 minutes from the lodge, and the Kazm tour (see above) is located on the hacienda's property.

Camping

Las Pailas campground is top-notch by Costa Rican standards, with a new toilet block, fresh running water and a picnic table area. Arrange camping in

PARQUE NACIONAL SANTA ROSA

Costa Rica's oldest national park, Santa Rosa was founded in 1971 to safeguard vast tracts of tropical dry forest and the nation's two most important battlefields. The Sección Murciélago was added in 1979, with land expropriated from former Nicaraguan dictator Anastasio Somoza. President Oscar Arias declared the land between Murciélago and Santa Rosa part of the park in the late 1980s, so Santa Rosa could cover the entire Península Santa Elena (about 50,000 ha or 123,500 acres in total).

This is an eclectic park that includes historical sights, massive tracts of wilderness, offshore coral

advance through the national **parks authorities** in San José (283-8004 FAX 283-7343 HOTLINE IN COSTA RICA (192.

HOW TO GET THERE

The Las Pailas ranger station is about 25 km (15.5 miles) from Liberia. Take the Carretera Interamericana five kilometers (just over three miles) north to Cereceda, turning right onto a very rough unpaved road which leads 12 km (seven and a half miles) to a sleepy village called Curubande, and then another eight kilometers (five miles) to the park entrance. There is no public bus service and it's doubtful that a Liberia taxi would be willing to tackle this road. However, some of the lodges will fetch you from Liberia or the Guanacaste beaches if you're staying with them.

The Northwest

reefs and miles of unspoiled beaches on the Santa Elena and Papagayo gulfs. Landscape and vegetation vary widely. Within the space of an hour you can travel from tropical dry forest to savanna-like pastureland to thorn scrub with cacti and agave to mangrove swamp. There is also a wide array of life forms: tapirs, sloths, anteaters, iguana, opossums, coatimundi, white-tailed deer, howler and spider monkeys, jaguars, ocelots and more than 300 bird species and 5,000 types of moths and butterflies. Santa Rosa's beaches provide nesting sites for three species of sea turtles,

OPPOSITE: Boiling mud pools at Las Pailas in Parque Nacional Rincón de la Vieja. LEFT: A drive along the Carretera Interamericana is filled with unexpected sights and ever-changing scenery. ABOVE: Churches in rural Costa Rica have little ornamentation and serve as village gathering places.

including the largest *arribadas* of Olive Ridley turtles in tropical America.

The park headquarters is at La Casona (666-5051, seven kilometers (four and a third miles) west of the Carretera Interamericana. This is also headquarters for the Guanacaste Conservation Area, a loose confederation of the northwestern national parks, nearly one million hectares (2,470,000 acres) of coast, mountain and forest. La Casona also has a campground and scientific research center — one of the world's most important stations for tropical dry-forest study.

WHAT TO SEE AND DO

La Casona Hacienda has been beautifully restored and is now a museum commemorating the battle in which 9,000 Central American volunteers beat back William Walker and his Yankee marauders. In front of the house is a huge guanacaste tree that shades 200-year-old stone corrals where much of the fighting took place. On the hill behind is **Los Héroes**, a monument to the brave Costa Ricans who turned back Walker's mercenary threat in 1856 and Somoza's invasion in 1955. The sunsets are fabulous from here. Nearby is an excellent nature walk called the **Sendero Indio Desnudo** (Naked Indian Trail) which loops a kilometer (two thirds of a mile) through dry tropical forest. The trail takes its name from the resident red-bark trees that are said to resemble disrobed Indians.

Longer trails include the **Sendero los Patos** (Ducks Trail), **Sendero Valle Naranjo** (Naranjo Valley Trail) and **Sendero Palo Seco** (Dry Trees Trail) which offer the park's best possibilities for wildlife spotting. The ideal times for animal watching and photography are early morning and late afternoon.

Santa Rosa also offers fabulous coastline. During dry season you can drive the 13 km (eight miles) from La Casona to the **Golfo de Papagayo**, but even then you'll need a four-wheel drive to make the journey. The road forks before hitting the beach. The southern (left) route leads to **Playa Naranjo**, one of the best surf spots in Central America, according to those who ride the waves. Also in this area are Laguna el Limbo with its resident waterfowl. Off the coast is **Peña Bruja** (Witch's Rock) which is popular with both surfers and aquatic birds. The northern (right) fork leads to the secluded **Playa Nancite** on the north side of the **Estero Real** (Royal Estuary), where as many as 100,000 Olive Ridley turtles nest during rainy season (September and October).

Sección Murciélago occupies the northern flank of the Península Santa Elena and is reached via a rough flagstone road from Cuajiniquil on Golfo de Santa Elena. Before you reach the park entrance you'll pass a national guard camp on the right which was once Somoza's hacienda and a

CIA training base for the Contras, then a grassy airstrip on the left that was used by Oliver North and company to supply the Nicaraguan rebels. Despite this sordid history, Murciélago's scenery is gorgeous — unspoiled beaches and coral reefs backed by thick forest. **Playa Blanca**, 17 km (10.5 miles) from the Murciélago ranger station, with its soft white sand is one of the most beautiful strands in Costa Rica. Five kilometers (three miles) from the Murciélago ranger station, Bahía Hachal offers a stony gray beach and turquoise water.

Those in quest of still more beach tranquillity should make for the western parts of Santa Rosa such as **Cabo Santa Elena**, **Playas Coloradas** and **Bahía Potrero Grande** (another great surfing spot), which are accessible only by boat. You'll have to hump in everything, including food and water.

WHERE TO STAY

Santa Rosa's only indoor lodging is the **Centro de Investigación Daniel Janzen** (/FAX 695-5598, Apdo 169-5000, Liberia. This research station provides inexpensive accommodation in the form of eight-person bunk rooms at La Casona, but visiting scientists and researchers get first crack at the beds. Be prepared for shared baths with cold water. Cooking facilities are available.

Camping is permitted at six different areas inside the park. There are improved campgrounds with toilets and running water at La Casona and Murciélago ranger station. Primitive camping is allowed at **Puesto Argelia** on Playa Naranjo and **Estero Real** near Playa Nancite, as well as at **Playa Blanca** and **Bahía Hachal** in the Sección Murciélago. Arrange camping in advance through the national **parks authorities** in San José (283-8004 FAX 283-7343 HOTLINE IN COSTA RICA (192.

HOW TO GET THERE

The Santa Rosa turnoff on the Carretera Interamericana is 35 km (22 miles) north of Liberia. La Casona is seven kilometers (four and a third miles) west along a good paved road. Buses will set you down near the park entrance, where it's easy to hitch a ride to La Casona. Taxi service is available from Liberia or La Cruz.

The turnoff to the Sección Murciélago is eight kilometers (five miles) further north — a paved road that curves down to Cuajiniquil on the Golfo de Santa Elena, where a rough flagstone road leads to the ranger station and Playa Blanca.

PARQUE NACIONAL GUANACASTE

The twin volcanic cones of Orosí, 1,487 m (4,877 ft), and Cerro Cacao, 1,659 m (5,441 ft), dominate Parque Nacional Guanacaste. Established in 1989, the reserve protects 85,000 ha (209,950 acres) of tropical dry forest and cloud forest on the other side of the Carretera Interamericana from Santa Rosa. The two parks form a single giant wildlife corridor stretching from the arid Pacific coast beaches to the steamy Caribbean lowlands.

A patchwork of former hacienda property, the park harbors an amazing array of flora and fauna — more than 300,000 plant and animal species — with more discovered every year by researchers who inhabit three field stations inside the park. Among the larger animals dwelling here are sloth, jaguar, puma, peccary, coyote, white-tailed deer, ocelot, marguay, anteater and coatimundi.

This is not a visitor-friendly park. The roads are horrible and the field stations are for the con-

WHERE TO STAY

Guanacaste doesn't have any overnight visitor facilities *per se*, but you can bunk down or camp at any of the research stations with prior permission from national parks authorities. Arrange camping in advance through their offices in San José (283-8004 FAX 283-7343 HOTLINE IN COSTA RICA (192.

HOW TO GET THERE

The turnoff to Cacao is 23 km (14 miles) north of Liberia on the Carretera Interamericana, at a small

venience of visiting scientists rather than tourists. Still, there are ways to explore Guanacaste. **Cacao Biological Station** in the southern part of the park is the best jumping off point for treks up Cerro Cacao. Even if you don't make the climb, a trip to Cacao offers a chance to explore the cloud forest around the field station. **Maritza Biological Station** is near the base of Volcán Orosí in the northern part of the park. You can clamber up the volcanic slopes or explore the **Llano de los Indios** (Plain of the Indians) with its ancient petroglyphs at **El Hacha** and other sites. **Pitiya Biological Station** is on the eastern side, with researchers who study the Caribbean watershed.

Before entering Parque Nacional Guanacaste, it's best to check on road conditions and accommodation availability at the administrative office of **Area de Conservación Guanacaste** (695-5598, at La Casona in Santa Rosa park.

The Northwest

hamlet called Potrerillos on the banks of the Río Tempisquito. Follow the rough dirt road through Quebrada Grande, park your vehicle on the south bank of the Río Gongora and walk the remaining distance to the field station.

The Maritza turnoff is 50 km (31 miles) north of Liberia on the Carretera Interamericana, at the same junction as the road to Cuajiniquil and Sección Murciélago. Head east along a primitive dirt road through virgin forest and savanna lands. Santa Cecilia, 28 km (17 miles) east of La Cruz by paved road, is the jumping off point for Pitiya Biological Station.

La Casona Hacienda, in Santa Rosa, houses a museum commemorating the battle between Central Americans and the American William Walker's mercenaries.

LA CRUZ

Sleepy, sultry La Cruz is the last major town before the Nicaraguan frontier. It is perched on a volcanic escarpment 250 m (820 ft) above Bahía Salinas, an imposing landscape reminiscent of East Africa's rift valley. Other than the whitewashed grave of Salvadorian writer and patriot Marcelino García Flamenco, the town doesn't have much to offer visitors.

What to See and Do

Several nice beaches are nearby including **Playa Pochotes** on Bahía Salinas, **Playa Monstrencal** at Brasilito on Bahía Junquillal, and secluded **Playa Jobo** at the tip of the unspoiled Descartes Peninsula. Boats for exploring **Bahía Salinas** can be rented at the fishing village of Puerto Soley, about six and a half kilometers (four miles) west of La Cruz. Further afield is the lovely beach at **Bahía Junquillal** or **Area Recreativo Cuajiniquil**, 27 km (17 miles) to the southwest via Cuajiniquil.

Refugio Nacional de Fauna Silvestre Isla Bolaños floats in the middle of Bahía Salinas, accessible only by boat. This 25-ha (62-acre) reserve provides a home for various bird species, including the frigate bird, brown pelican, black vulture and oystercatcher. It's forbidden to disembark on Isla Bolaños without permission from the park authorities in San José or Santa Rosa, but you can watch the avian action from boats anchored offshore.

The border post is 19 km (12 miles) north of La Cruz on the Carretera Interamericana, at **Peñas Blancas** on the banks of the Río Sapoá (which flows into Lago de Nicaragua).

Where to Stay

Moderate

A quite interesting place to bunk down is **Los Inocentes Lodge (** 679-9190 or 265-5484 FAX 265-4385. Just outside Parque Nacional Guanacaste's northern boundary, this ecolodge offers overnight accommodation as well as horseback and walking trips to the nearby forest and Volcán Orosí. Named after the family that pioneered this area, the hacienda was built in 1890 — a handsome wooden house that was remodeled into a modern lodge in 1982. Even if you don't spend the night, come here for a ride and lunch. Los Inocentes is reached by turning off the Carretera Interamericana about three kilometers (two miles) south of La Cruz (look for signs to Santa Cecilia) and driving 16 km (10 miles) along a good paved road.

Pastureland in Guanacaste where the Volcán Orosí looms.

Windsurfers are delighted to find **Three Corners Bolaños Bay (** 679-9444 FAX 679-9654 E-MAIL 3cornco@sol.racsa.co.cr WEB SITE www.three corners.com on the shores of Bolaños Bay facing Isla Bolaños, 17 km (just over 10 miles) west of La Cruz. Delightfully isolated, the Belgian-owned 72-room hotel sits right on the beach, with one-story buildings housing the air-conditioned rooms and two large ranchos covering the restaurants. The bay is perfect for swimming, and a fresh-water pool, children's pool, and hot tub satisfy those who shun salt water. Guests can swim, go horseback riding, water skiing, or kayaking, and the hotel is perfectly located for excursions to Guanacaste's parks. But the big attraction is the windsurfing. The bay has ideal wind conditions much of the year, and the hotel offers lessons and gear rental.

Inexpensive

An unexpected touch of class (and bastion of modern art) in the northwest is **Amalia's Inn (**/FAX 679-9181. There's nothing quite like it anywhere in Costa Rica — a cozy little bed and breakfast perched on the edge of the escarpment, with sweeping views across Bahía Salinas and the Península Santa Elena. The rooms are furnished with double beds, black leather sofas and Picasso-esque original artwork by Amalia herself. All rooms have private baths with hot water. There's a small pool on the terrace. Amalia will treat you like one of her own family.

Where to Eat

Ehecatl Restaurant (679-9104 in La Cruz is remarkable both for its food and location. The name means "God of the Wind" in the Chorotega Indian language, an apt description for this unique, moderately priced eatery. Poised on the brink of the escarpment with panoramic views of Bahía Salinas, this carefree, casual place serves delicious lobster, shrimp, fish, octopus, mussels, ceviche and other seafood delights. Try for a table on the second floor. Ehecatl has another location at **Potrerillos**, on the Carretera Interamericana between Liberia and Santa Rosa.

How to Get There

La Cruz is 55 km (34 miles) north of Liberia on the Carretera Interamericana. There are daily buses from Liberia and San José.

The North Pacific

CATTLE COUNTRY TUMBLES DOWN TO THE SEA along the northern Pacific coast, which features more beach resorts than any other part of Costa Rica. Hot, dry weather and a short rainy season make this region ideal for sunbathing and water sports. It's especially popular with surfers and sport fishermen, who find conditions among the best on the planet.

The northern coast incorporates part of Guanacaste province and the Península de Nicoya. The most popular beaches are within a four- or five-hour drive from San José. As a consequence, *ticos* flock to this coast on school breaks and national holidays. During Christmas and Easter it's nearly impossible to find an empty hotel room in Coco, Tamarindo, Flamingo, Brasilito, and Hermosa. At other times of year, many of the strands are empty, especially around the Golfo de Papagayo and on beaches south of Tamarindo.

The arid climate makes Guanacaste beaches far different than the Caribbean and Central Pacific strands. The dry coastal forest is more open and much browner than the rainforest found elsewhere in Costa Rica, especially during the dry season when the region takes on desert-like traits.

Rolling hills, sugarcane plantations, and cattle ranches dominate the landscape between the coast and the Río Tempisque. Although the residents are friendly, market towns such as Santa Cruz and Nicoya sustain a rough edge gleaned from several hundred years of cowboy life. It's still not unusual to see mounted riders amble up to an open-air bar or restaurant.

Farther south, the Península de Nicoya is virtually cut off from the rest of the northwest coast. The roads are dreadful, impassable for much of the year and a bone-jarring adventure even at the best of times. Isolated expatriate communities and budding beach resorts exist at Sámara and Nosara on the peninsula's west coast, as well as Tambor and Montezuma in the south. Nicoya's rugged beauty and welcome seclusion offset the area's inaccessibility.

GETTING THERE

The beaches of Guanacaste and Nicoya, located geographically side by side, can be difficult to reach. Those in the north are best accessed by air from San José or by road from Liberia. Charter planes taking tour groups to the beach resorts land at the Liberia airport.

If you are traveling to the northern Nicoya beaches from San José by car, you're best off taking the **Río Tempisque Ferry** (661-8105 that runs from Puerto Níspero to Puerto Moreno in the middle of the Península de Nicoya. The ferry departs every 45 minutes during daylight hours; the trip takes 20 minutes. Heavy rains wreak havoc on the schedule, however, and you may wait for hours for the ferry to depart. Check with your car rental agency or hotel; if it sounds like the ferry may leave you high and dry, take the Interamericana to Liberia and head to the coast from there.

A new road is nearly completed on the mainland side of the ferry, and what a stretch of road it is — wide, smooth concrete with well-marked lanes running in a virtual straight line toward Puntarenas. Naturally, the police in the area have acquired radar guns, so watch your speed. There are plans underfoot to build a bridge to replace the ferry, a development that would certainly please all the *ticos* who race to the beach on holidays.

The southern beaches are best reached by ferry from Puntarenas.

For the most part you can't drive between the beach towns. Instead, you must head back to the main paved roads, then drive to the exit for the next beach. Most of the roads to the beaches consist of rutted dirt or slippery sand.

THE GOLD COAST

PLAYA DEL COCO

Playa del Coco is the northern hub of Costa Rica's self-proclaimed Gold Coast. It's about four and a half hours from San José, on paved road, which makes Coco the most accessible beach in the area. Because of this, there's nothing remotely serene or silent here, especially during national holidays and school breaks when thousands of *ticos* flock to Coco from San José and environs.

El Coco, the only village on the bay, is not especially attractive. Fishing used to be the primary

PRECEEDING PAGES: The Río Tempisque empties into the Golfo de Nicoya. Playa Hermosa RIGHT, "Beautiful Beach," lives up to its name. OPPOSITE: Several species of parrots and parakeets thrive in the northern forests. ABOVE: An evening dip in cool river waters.

occupation (there's still a fishing pier and a few boats bobbing in the offshore swell), but tourism is now firmly entrenched as the number one money spinner. The town plaza, where buses and taxis gather, is dominated by shabby souvenir stands and the local police station.

What to See and Do

Coco is one of the best headquarters for scuba diving in the north Pacific. Shore diving and trips to offshore dive spots are easily arranged. Serious divers get excited about trips to Isla Santa Catalina, a half-hour from shore, and Islas Murciélagos, about 90 minutes by boat from Coco. Experienced divers find an abundance of sharks at Murciélagos and rays at Catalina. **Mario Vargas Expeditions** (670-0351, offers PADI instruction and scuba trips, as well as fishing charters and scenic boat trips. "Mario Vargas is generally considered to be the most experienced divemaster in Costa Rica," says *Skin Diver* magazine. **Rich Coast Diving** (/FAX 670-0176 E-MAIL scuba@divecostarica.com also offers topnotch scuba instruction and trips. Other services include sport fishing, surfing, water skiing, kayaking, sailing and snorkeling. *Spanish Dancer* (670-0332 is an 11-m (36-ft) catamaran that makes daily Catalina trips, which include swimming, snorkeling, and lunch.

Where to Stay

A unique place to stay in the Playa del Coco area is **Rancho Armadillo Estate** (670-0108 FAX 670-0441 E-MAIL info@ranchoarmadillo.com WEB SITE www.ranchoarmadillo.com (moderate). Built by Texan Jim Proctor in 1978, after he discovered Costa Rica on an around-the-world sail, Armadillo is an inland estate rather than a beach hotel. Surrounded by lush jungle, the hacienda-style lodge features bungalows with hardwood floors and ceilings, as well as spacious bathrooms, hot water, and either air-conditioning or fan. The pool area offers a sweeping view of the Golfo de Papagayo. Armadillo also has a restaurant and bar with satellite wide-screen television.

Another United States expatriate, Don McCandless, left his home in Florida and opened the **Hotel Coco Verde** (670-0494 FAX 670-0555 E-MAIL cocoverd@racsa.co.cr WEB SITE www.coco verde.com two blocks from the beach (moderate). The two-story white building with bright green roof houses 33 rooms with air-conditioning; amenities include a large swimming pool, bar with satellite television, and restaurant (great ribs and steaks). The on-site PADI dive center runs dive trips in a custom-made boat, and anglers have two sport-fishing boats to choose from. Coco Verde is a good base for water sports fanatics; several different packages include diving and fishing with meals and accommodations.

A bit closer to the beach in the same price range is **Villa del Sol** (/FAX 670-0085 E-MAIL villasol@sol .racsa.co.cr WEB SITE www.villadelsol.com. Owned and operated by expatriate Canadians, this modest bed and breakfast features five rooms with private baths (hot water), fans and balconies, a pleasant garden and a small pool with hot tub.

A favorite with sport fishermen is the funky **Flor de Itabo** (670-0292 FAX 670-0003 WEB SITE www.flordeitabo.com on Playa del Coco, which has a range of poolside rooms and two-story bungalows to choose from, all with private bath and air-conditioning at moderate rates. The hotel features its own small casino and a tasty Italian restaurant. The only drawback is its remoteness

from the beach (a kilometer, or just over half a mile away).

A favorite backpacker haven is the cozy **Luna Tica** (670-0127 FAX 670-0459. Owner Emilia Barahona doesn't speak much English, but she keeps things neat and tidy. And it's only steps from the beach (inexpensive).

Where to Eat

There are many choices but nothing truly outstanding. All the following are in the moderate price category. **Restaurant Bar Café Latino** (670-0525 (formerly called San Francisco Treats) offers typical Italian eats such as pizza, lasagna, and pastas. **Le Bistro Oasis** (670-0463 tenders French food with a *tico* slant, including fish, chicken and steak

ABOVE: Sandy trails lead through forests to hidden beaches and bays. OVERLEAF: Playa del Coco is a favorite for *tico* teens on spring break.

dishes. **Papagayo** (670-0882 on the main road has probably the best seafood in town. **Da Beppe** at the **Hotel Flor de Itabo** is the hot Italian spot.

How to Get There

Playa del Coco is 255 km (158 miles) from San José and 35 km (22 miles) from Liberia. The turnoff is opposite the El Tamarindo gas station in the town of Comunidad on the Liberia–Santa Cruz highway. Coco is 15 km (nine miles) west of this junction, on a meandering country road that leads past shrimp farms, sugarcane fields and cattle ranches. Just before the coast, the road forks. The north (right) fork heads for Playa Hermosa. The south (left) fork leads to Coco.

There are daily express buses from San José and regular buses from Liberia. Taxis running from Liberia town and airport, or other nearby beaches, serve Coco.

PLAYA OCOTAL

Only three kilometers (two miles) west of Coco, Playa Ocotal has become something of an international buzzword for great diving and sport fishing. And for good reason: the offshore waters here are rich in marine life and local hotels tend to cater to scuba AND fishing aficionados. But that's not to say that landlubbers won't enjoy the place.

Bahía Ocotal is rather small, but it's a lovely stretch of gray and black sand framed by rugged cliffs. Punta Gorda, the headland west of Ocotal, is surrounded by reefs and excellent dive spots such as Las Corridas.

Where to Stay

Poised on a bluff above the bay is the ever-expanding **El Ocotal Beach Resort and Marina** (670-0321 FAX 670-0083 E-MAIL elocotal@solracsa.co.cr WEB SITE www.ocotalresort.com (moderate). The place is flush with sport-fishing enthusiasts. Tennis courts, three pools and a gym offer other distractions. The rooms are spacious and well-equipped including satellite television, air-conditioning, refrigerator and queen-sized beds. Both suites and bungalows are available. The newer rooms have Jacuzzi and sun decks. **Villa Casa Blanca** (670-0518 FAX 670-0448 E-MAIL vcblanca@sol.racsa.co.cr is one of Costa Rica's top bed-and-breakfast establishments (moderate). Nestled on a tropical

cove with sweeping views of the Golfo de Papagayo, this pleasant Spanish-style ranch is run by Canadians Jim and Jane Seip. Lush tropical gardens surround the swimming pool, which also has a swim-up bar. The rooms here feature private bath, hot water and either air-conditioning or fans. On the hillside behind are a honeymoon suite and condominiums.

Where to Eat

El Ocotal Restaurant offers excellent seafood and other international dishes with stunning views of the coast. **Father Rooster Bar**, in a turn-of-the-century ranch house on the beach, serves tacos, nachos and other typical fare on a breezy verandah.

How to Get There

Playa Ocotal is three kilometers (two miles) west of Playa del Coco. Bus service from San José and

Liberia terminates in El Coco, where you can easily pick up a taxi or walk to Ocotal.

PLAYA HERMOSA

Hermosa is a beautiful U-shaped bay protected by a pair of coral-fringed headlands covered in typical Guanacaste scrub. The atmosphere is much more cultivated than at nearby Playa del Coco and the region's relaxed ambiance makes Hermosa an excellent place to seek quiet and solitude. A couple of kilometers offshore are the Islas Pelonas, which offer good snorkeling and scuba diving.

Aqua Sport (672-0020 offers a good number of marine activities including snorkeling,

windsurfing, surfing, kayaking and sailing. **Bill Beard's Diving Safaris** (672-0012 FAX 672-0231 E-MAIL diving@sol.racsa.co.cr offers matchless instruction and expeditions to some of the best diving spots to be found in the area, including the Catalinas, Punta Gorda, Los Meros and Escorpiones.

Where to Stay

Dominating the hillside above the bay is **Sol Playa Hermosa** (672-0001 FAX 672-0212 E-MAIL hermosol@sol.racsa.co.cr, an expensive resort hotel that provides everything you need for a family vacation, including two swimming pools, tennis courts, a playground, a volleyball court, a discotheque and five restaurants. The 54 rooms in the main block all have fabulous views over the beach and there are 24 spacious villas with their own pools.

The best on the beach is a romantic little place called the **Hotel el Velero** (672-0036 FAX 672-0016 (moderate). Thirteen clean and spacious rooms each have private bath, hot water, and either fans or air-conditioning. Velero has a very good restaurant and a sailboat for coastal excursions. Special package rates (including full breakfast) are available for stays of three days or more. The proprietor is a former Royal Canadian Mountie who entertains guests with his tales of crime-fighting exploits in the frozen north.

The **Playa Hermosa Inn** (672-0063 FAX 672-0060 is a friendly bed and breakfast in an old house with large, airy rooms converted into guest accommodations (moderate). Each of the nine

rooms includes air-conditioning or fans, as well as private bath. There's a pool that overlooks the beach and you can count on a hearty breakfast. **Villa del Sueño** (/FAX 672-0026 is a *tico*-style villa set around a garden and swimming pool with clean spacious rooms with tiled floors, high hardwood ceilings and private baths (moderate). Just five minutes walk from the beach is **Villa Huétares** (672-0052 FAX 672-0051. Not much character, but the place is tidy, the management friendly and the price inexpensive. The *cabinas*, which feature private baths and kitchens, sleep six people.

OPPOSITE LEFT: Horses come in handy for traveling along the peninsula's dusty roads. RIGHT: Weekends bring youngsters from throughout the country to Playa Hermosa. ABOVE LEFT: Playa Hermosa bungalows decorate the hillsides. Catching the last rays at Playa del Coco ABOVE RIGHT.

Where to Eat

Nearly everyone who comes to Playa Hermosa eventually finds their way to the ever-popular **Popeye and Daddy-O's** (670-0245, a blue and yellow restaurant one block up from the beach which serves hot pizza, ice-cold beer and more (inexpensive). Popeye's also delivers. **El Velero** has great seafood and pasta in an outdoor seaside setting (moderate). Sol Playa Hermosa offers five restaurants ranging from the international cuisine of the upscale **El Roble** (expensive) to an inexpensive poolside snack bar called **Las Gaviotas**.

How to Get There

Follow essentially the same directions for Playa del Coco (above). Hermosa is about six kilometers (four miles) north of Coco along the coast road. Express buses from San José and regular buses from Liberia stop daily in Hermosa. Taxis run from Liberia, Aeropuerto Daniel Obudar, and other nearby beaches.

BAHÍA CULEBRA AND PLAYA PANAMA

There is nothing even faintly serpentine about Bahía Culebra (Snake Bay), a massive U-shaped bay on the Golfo de Papagayo that marks the northern frontier of the Guanacaste beach resort belt. The wild and rugged **Llano de la Palma** (Plain of the Palms) and Parque Nacional Santa Rosa are just north of the bay; Hermosa and Coco beaches are due south. So Culebra is ideally situated to take advantage of increased tourism in the region — which is either its fortune and misfortune, depending on which side of the ecological fence you favor.

Almost the entire shore of Bahía Culebra has been slated for development as part of a massive scheme called the Papagayo Project, the largest and most controversial real estate venture in Costa Rican history. Spread over 2,000 ha (4,940 acres) and primarily financed by foreign developers, the project is projected to result in more than 15,000 hotel rooms and condominiums spread across at least 22 properties. The master plan also calls for a large marina, several country clubs, and a major road (now only partially built) that would connect the resorts directly with Liberia's airport.

Proponents of the Papagayo Project say it will boost Costa Rica into the tourism big leagues, along with the likes of Mexico and Jamaica. They scoff at notions that most of the rooms will never be filled, espousing a "build it and they will come" attitude borrowed from an American baseball movie. Those who oppose the project say there isn't enough "sun and sea" tourism in Costa Rica to justify such a massive undertaking and that construction will cause permanent damage to the fragile shoreline, mangrove swamps and nearby pre-Columbian archaeological sites.

A few hotels are already up and running (see below), but fortunately they are mostly around Playa Panama. For the time being, most of Bahía Culebra remains pristine and secluded. It's still a wonder why the Spanish never turned this inlet into a major seaport because it's one of the finest natural harbors on Central America's Pacific coast. **Resort Divers** (/FAX 672-0106 at Costa Smerelda offers scuba diving instruction and organizes trips to the Islas Santa Catalina and Murciélago; they also organize sailing, sport fishing and horseback riding trips.

Where to Stay and Eat

At the end of the road that winds up from Playa Hermosa is an all-inclusive resort called **Blue Bay Village Papagayo** (670-0033 FAX 670-0300 WEB SITE www.bluebayresorts.com which sprawls across the hillsides above Bahía Culebra (very expensive). It has everything you would expect of a big resort: swimming pool with swim-up bar, gymnasium, massage, sauna and access to a secluded beach. A residential development is rising next door.

Another similarly-priced all-inclusive, **Hotel Occidental Costa Smerelda** (672-0191 FAX 672-0041 E-MAIL smerelda@sol.racsa.co.cr is operated by the Spanish Occidental hotel group, which has taken a very active role in the development of Papagayo. Everything is done on a grand scale from the immense lobby to the open-air dining room, the casino and the meandering free-form swimming pool. The 120 guest rooms dot the hillsides overlooking Bahía Culebra. The chain is also scheduled to open the 300-room Hotel Occidental Papagayo in 2001. Prices at these resorts are high because all meals and most activities are included.

Best value for money in the Playa Panama area is **Costa Smerelda Beach Club** (/FAX 672-0070, formerly the Sulu Sulu Beach Resort (expensive). Set beneath cool beachside trees, this friendly hotel has *cabinas* with private bath, hot water and air-conditioning. The beach club offers numerous activities including horseback riding, jet skiing, beach volleyball, mountain biking and a children's playground. The hotel has two restaurants.

How to Get There

Playa Panama is three kilometers (two miles) north of Playa Hermosa along a road that eventually deteriorates into rough flagstone. Costa Smerelda is at the northern end of this road. A daily express bus from San José and regular buses from Liberia serve the area. Taxis run from Aeropuerto Daniel Obudar and Liberia or other nearby beaches.

Sailing near Playa Hermosa.

The isolated beaches on the northern and western sides of Bahía Culebra are not accessible from Playa Panama except by boat. However, there is a paved road that runs from Guardia (on the Liberia–Santa Cruz highway) to this area. Look for the "Monte del Barca" sign and follow the road about 14 km (nine miles) through sugarcane fields and cattle pastures. Along the way is a turnoff to Playa Cabuyal. Eventually the road peters out into three dirt tracks. The left-hand-most fork leads to empty beaches at Nacascolo, Pochata, Prieta, Vierador, Blanco, Palmares and Zapatillal. A four-wheel-drive vehicle is recommended for reaching the more secluded strands.

PLAYA BRASILITO

Brasilito is basic when compared with neighboring Flamingo and Conchal (see below). The sand here is dull gray rather than pearly white; the accommodation is no-frills rather than flawless. But the people who run the *cabinas* and beachfront bars along Playa Brasilito are, for the most part, friendly and down to earth.

Where to Stay and Eat

Inexpensive **Hotel Brasilito** (654-4237 FAX 654-4247 E-MAIL compes@sol.racsa.co.cr, is a longtime favorite with sun-lovers searching for good value and friendly ambiance. Right off the main square in Brasilito and within meters of the tree-shaded beach, the hotel offers tidy rooms with private bath (cold water only). The young German owners have also created a fairly good restaurant. A big rancho covers **Restaurante Estrella del Mar** (654-4046 at the entrance to Brasilito. Fresh fish and shrimp are the standouts.

How to Get There

Playa Brasilito is 285 km (177 miles) from San José and 65 km (40 miles) from Liberia. The turnoff is at the town of Belén on the Liberia–Santa Cruz highway. Brasilito is 28 km (17 miles) west of this junction via Santa Ana and Huacas. There are daily express bus from San José, regular buses from Liberia and taxis from Liberia, Aeropuerto Daniel Obudar and other nearby beaches.

PLAYA FLAMINGO

Flamingo is more upscale than its neighbors, but less developed than Tamarindo to the south or Coco to the north. Many Europeans and North Americans — as well as wealthy Costa Ricans — have chosen Flamingo as their retirement spot, living in isolated villas on the rocky peninsula. Flamingo's main claim to fame is its marina, the only one on the Pacific coast of Nicoya (at least until Papagayo develops). Sport fishing is the area's biggest draw; the marina's captains hold several fishing records, and it's not uncommon for anglers to catch (and release) over 1,000 billfish during a four-day tournament. The best fishing occurs from May to October, when wahoo, dorado, roosterfish, tuna, marlin and sailfish feed around the nearby Catalina islands. Fierce winds blow through from November to March, and some of the captains take their boats south to Manuel Antonio.

What to See and Do

Several sport-fishing outfitters operate out of the **Marina Flamingo** (654-4203 FAX 654-4536 E-MAIL marflam@Marflam.com WEB SITE www.marflam .com. **Flamingo Bay Pacific Fishing Charters**

(253-6713 FAX 234-0906 E-MAIL billfish@sol.racsa .co.cr has several boats in the marina and runs packages including one night in San José and transfers from the city to Flamingo.

There's usually a boat available, but if your whole reason for visiting Flamingo is the fishing you should reserve a boat in advance. Several fishing tournaments are held in June and July, including an international billfish tournament in July.

Flamingo is also a prime scuba diving area; some dive publications call it one of the top 10 dive spots in the world. This isn't the place to go for coral reefs and pretty tropical fish. Instead, divers are entertained by manta rays, eagle rays, white-tipped sharks and other large pelagics. **Costa Rica Diving** (/FAX 654-4148 has an office at the entrance to town and another at the Flamingo Marina Resort (see below) and offers tailor-made excursions and

PADI instruction. **Tio Sports** (654-4349 at the Flamingo Bay Resort offers scuba and snorkeling trips and sports gear rentals. **Papagayo** (/FAX 654-4063, at the Mariner Inn, specializes in sailing charters on a yacht of the same name as well as sport fishing and scuba diving trips. **Ecotrans** (544-4141 or 654-4852 E-MAIL ecotrans@sol.racsa.co.cr offers transportation from the Liberia airport and tours to other beach areas.

There isn't much else to do in Flamingo except sunbathe on the virtually unmarred curve of light sand along the clear bay, or swim in the calm water. Flamingo is in a state of transition these days. Real estate signs abound, and several small hotels have either closed or gone on the market.

The **Flamingo Beach Resort** (654-4011 FAX 654-4060 is the only hotel right on Flamingo's main beach (expensive). Unfortunately, it has gone through several stages of management (most recently as the Aurola Playa Flamingo Resort) and was up for sale when I last visited. The property has become rundown and service is spotty. What this place needs is an infusion of enthusiasm and cash. The hotel has 88 rooms and suites (if you're not happy with the first one you're shown, ask to see others), three pools, a restaurant and bar, and a small gym.

Up the hill from the marina resort is the smaller, moderately-priced **Flamingo Bay Resort** (/FAX 654-4349 E-MAIL fun@flamingobayresort

Where to Stay

Perched on a bluff above the marina is the **Flamingo Marina Resort** (654-4141 TOLL FREE IN THE US (800) 276-7501 FAX 654-4035 E-MAIL tickledpink @flamingomarina.com WEB SITE www.flamingo marina.com (expensive). The largest property in the area, the resort sprawls along the hillside on both sides of the curving road. the resort's guests choose from hotel rooms, apartments, suites and condos, settling in for a few nights or several weeks. The hotel has a small beach, though most of the action takes place around the four swimming pools. A number of diving, fishing and tour operators have desks in the lobby, and rental cars are available. Kayak, jet skis and mountain bikes are available for rent. The hotel's Monkey Bar is a popular night spot, and its Sunrise Café and Laguna Snack Bar draw diners from other hotels.

.com WEB SITE www.flamingobayresort.com (also called Flamingo Fantasia) with 45 harbor-view rooms. Popular with *tico* tourists, the hotel has a restaurant, pool and casino (make sure your room is away from the noise). Set right beside the marina, the aptly named **Mariner Inn** (654-4081 FAX 654-4024 E-MAIL mariner@costarica.net is the least expensive option in the area (moderate). The rooms are small but adequate, and have air-conditioning and cable television. The pool, bar, and restaurant are popular gathering spots for boastful anglers.

Where to Eat

The hotels all have good restaurants, and guests without cars tend to stick with what they are offered. **Marie's** (654-4136 on the road between

Parque Nacional Santa Rosa extends along the Santa Elena Peninsula, north of Bahía Culebra.

the marina and the beach serves wonderful french toast, papaya pancakes, and yogurt with fruit and granola at breakfast, and fresh fish for lunch and dinner. Bookshelves near the counter are stocked with novels; trade in your castoffs for free. **Ambers** (654-4001 on the hill overlooking the marina is a seafood restaurant, casino, and disco — the hottest nightspot in town.

How to Get There

Playa Flamingo is three kilometers (two miles) north of Brasilito on the coast road. A daily express bus runs from San José and regular buses from Liberia. Taxis make the journey from Liberia, Aeropuerto Daniel Obudar and nearby beaches.

Where to Stay

Hotel Sugar Beach (654-4242 FAX 654-4239 WEB SITE www.sugar-beach.com is something special, one of Costa Rica's better small hotels and one of its most beautiful beaches all in the same package (very expensive). You can't beat the location: a secluded bay north of Flamingo. It's not easy to top the rooms either: all are spacious, well-decorated (native hardwood ceilings). The free-form pool, shaded by huge jungle trees, overlooks the beach.

Marked by casual elegance, the American-run **Bahía Potrero Beach Resort** (654-4183 FAX 654-4093, is set in a grove of giant shade trees (expensive). The hotel has a fabulous garden (with children's playground) and the best restaurant in

PLAYA POTRERO

Potrero lounges on a wide turquoise bay south of the Golfo de Papagayo. The sand here is pearly white and Potrero is much less touristy than some of its cousins to the south. Better still, a number of largely undeveloped beaches are within striking distance, including Playa la Penca, Playa Danta and Playa Azúcar (Sugar Beach), a remarkable coral beach that many people consider the most beautiful in all of Costa Rica.

Numerous tiny islands lie off Potrero's shores including Santa Catalina, Brumel, Plata and Chocoyas, all of which offer good scuba diving and snorkeling with the aid of a charter boat. Closer to shore, there are small reefs around Punta Salinas and Punta Guachipelines at either end of the bay.

these parts. Most rooms face the beach, which is just steps away. Private baths, hot water and air-conditioning complete the package.

The inexpensive **Cabinas Cristina** (654-4006 FAX 654-4128, with its nice garden and small pool, is tucked between cattle pastures about a five-minute walk from the beach. **Cabinas Isolina** (654-4375 FAX 654-4313 nestles in a grove of huge shade trees next to the beach (inexpensive).

Where to Eat

Richard's American Restaurant, at the Potrero Beach Resort, offers the best eats on the strand, serving everything from salads to seafood. Nearby is **Harden's Garden** (654-4271 with homemade pizza, bread, pastries and other baked goods. **Perla's BBQ** is a favorite *tico* hangout with a wide range of beach treats, including burgers, hot dogs, steaks, chicken, ribs, chili and ice-cold beer.

How to Get There

Playa Potrero is three kilometers (two miles) north of Flamingo and six kilometers (four miles) from Brasilito on the coast route (flagstone beyond Flamingo). Playa Azúcar is another five kilometers (three miles) north along the bay. Daily express bus service from San José and regular buses from Liberia terminate in Potrero village. You must walk, catch a taxi or hitch a ride to Playa Azúcar.

PLAYA CONCHAL

Conchal can give Playa Azúcar a run for its money as the most beautiful beach in Guanacaste. This tides) and sea kayaking. Offshore you can see the jagged outline of Isla Santa Catalina, a popular diving spot. Snorkelers should head for reef-fringed Punta Sábana.

There's a tiny village called Puerto Viejo perched on the south side of Bahía Conchal where the budget hotels and restaurants are situated.

Where to Stay

A touch of the Spanish Riviera comes to Costa Rica in the form of the **Meliá Playa Conchal** (654-4123 TOLL-FREE (800) 336-3542 FAX 654-4181 E-MAIL mconchal@solracsa.co.cr WEB SITE www .solmelia.es, which dominates Playa Conchal (very expensive). The 310-room Meliá bills itself

curl of fine white sand and turquoise water lies between Brasilito and a jungle-shrouded headland called Punta Sábana. The name derives from the fact that Conchal is comprised of billions of tiny shells and shell fragments. You can feel them crunch beneath your toes as you walk along the surf.

The valley behind Playa Conchal was a working cattle ranch until very recently, but most of the former hacienda now falls within the bounds of the giant Meliá resort which includes an 18-hole golf course. You can walk to Brasilito along a dirt road that hugs the coast, or you can trek in the other direction to an isolated fishing village called Playa Real (Royal Beach) on the western flank of Punta Sábana.

Conchal's bay is protected from the open ocean, so it doesn't offer much wave action, but it's placid waters are perfect for swimming (be careful of rip as the "largest and most opulent resort" in Costa Rica, a claim that worked for a while, but is now being challenged by Los Sueños in the Central Pacific. Thus far, I prefer the Meliá, especially for families. The hotel has about everything you need for a beach vacation: an 18-hole golf course designed by Robert Trent Jones, a huge free-form swimming pool, spa, gym, Vegas-style casino and adjacent disco, live stage shows every night, five different restaurants (the seafood is superb), a full range of water sports, and a gorgeous long beach. The resort is spread about the edges of a dry coastal forest that howler monkeys still call home. It's a long walk from some of the rooms to the lobby and beach.

OPPOSITE: Found on Isla de Caño, stone spheres weighing several thousand pounds are Costa Rica's archaeological wonders. ABOVE: Rocky islets rise above the water in the Golfo de Papagayo.

The El Condor Lodge and Beach Resort (654-4050 FAX 654-4044 WEB SITE www.condorlodge.com at Playa Real is a modest alternative to the splashy Meliá. For moderate prices the rooms have everything you need: king-sized or twin beds, private bath with hot water and air-conditioning or fan. The Condor's watersports center can arrange scuba diving, snorkeling, windsurfing, fishing and other aquatic expeditions.

Where to Eat

The El Condor Lodge has good food at great value. Cabinas la Paz specializes in homemade pizza. Under the umbrella of the Meliá Conchal are five restaurants including very good Italian and sumptuous seafood.

How to Get There

Follow essentially the same directions as for Playa Brasilito (above). Take the Liberia–Nicoya highway south to Belén, turn west on the coast resort access road and follow it 24 km (15 miles) to Huacas. From Huacas, a rough flagstone road leads west to Matapalo four kilometers (two and a half miles) and then further north to Puerto Viejo eight kilometers (five miles).

A daily express bus runs from San José to Brasilito or Matapalo, where you can catch a cab or walk to Playa Conchal. Taxis connect Conchal with Liberia, Aeropuerto Daniel Obudar and other nearby beaches.

PARQUE NACIONAL LAS BAULAS AND PLAYA GRANDE

Spectacular coastal scenery aside, Parque Nacional las Baulas exists for one reason: preservation of giant leatherback turtles that lay their eggs in the warm sands of Playa Grande each evening.

Mother turtles visit the beach throughout the year, but the best time to see them is between October and April, the prime nesting season on the Pacific coast. Better still, make an effort to visit during high tide on a full-moon evening when as many as 100 leatherbacks are jostling for space along the beach. Other species, including greens and Olive Ridleys, also use Playa Grande as a nesting site.

Egg poaching was rampant in the past, but in recent years local villagers have been employed as government rangers to guide visitors to nesting sites along the beach. In fact, it's now strictly forbidden to stroll the strand unless you are accompanied by a ranger. Turtle-watching groups are limited in size so as not to disturb these matronly reptiles. Other points to remember: no flashlights, no flash cameras, and be sure to wear sandals or shoes because it's difficult to see what you might be treading on in the dark. The park entrance is adjacent to the Hotel las Tortugas.

Check for information on turtle tours at the small museum El Mundo de la Tortuga (653-0471. The park also protects rich mangroves of the Estero Tamarindo. Bird life is abundant, but anyone who explores the swamp by boat (rented in nearby Tamarindo town) has a chance of seeing deer, monkeys and crocodiles, too. By daylight, Playa Grande is a sparkling white curve of sand. The offshore waters (also part of the national park) constitute one of the best surfing spots on the Central America's Pacific coast.

Beyond the mangroves is the gargantuan Royal Pacific Golf and Country Club (654-4089 FAX 293-4644, which includes vacation condominiums and an 18-hole championship golf course. Another 18-hole course is under construction.

Where to Stay and Eat

Anyone with an avid interest in turtle watching should stay at Hotel las Tortugas (653-0423 FAX 653-0458 E-MAIL nela@cool.co.cr WEB SITE www.tamarindo.com (moderate). Proprietors Louis Wilson and Marianela Paston led a successful 15-year struggle to have Playa Grande designated as a national park and their hotel is situated just outside the park boundary. They don't have any rooms facing the beach because the lights might disturb the nesting turtles. But each room does come with private hot-water bath and either air-conditioning or ceiling fans. The hotel restaurant looks out over the beach. Las Tortugas also rents out apartments and houses in the Playa Grande area by the week or month.

Also at Playa Grande is the moderately-priced Hotel Cantarana (653-0486 FAX 653-0491. Situated at the south end of the peninsula between the estuary and the beach, this German-owned and Mediterranean-flavored inn offers spacious rooms with air-conditioning, private bath and hot water. There's a small pool and an open-air restaurant. Room rates include breakfast.

Rancho Diablo (653-0490 is surfer dude central, with inexpensive dormitory rooms with shared bath, and a few moderately-priced private rooms. A surf shop stocks all the necessities, and the restaurant serves barbecued beef, seafood and burgers.

The Restaurante Playa Grande, opposite the national park information kiosk, offers affordable cabinas and camping under a big shade tree out front. There's also a swimming pool.

How to Get There

Playa Grande is eight kilometers (five miles) west of Huacas and 69 km (43 miles) from Liberia. Beyond Huacas the route is unpaved all the way through sleepy Matapalo village where you make a sharp left after the town square–soccer field.

No public transportation goes all the way to Playa Grande; however, there are buses from San

José and Liberia that serve Matapalo, where you can catch a cab or walk to Playa Grande.

PLAYA TAMARINDO

The friendliest town on this stretch of coast, Playa Tamarindo is a broad strand between Punta San Francisco and the Estuario Tamarindo, the bay protected by a rocky outcrop called Isla Capitán. Hotels, restaurants, and shops abound, most run by Europeans and North Americans. Surfers were once the backbone of Tamarindo's tourism activity, but the increase in boutique hotels and gourmet restaurants has made this small town one of the most popular destinations on the coast.

turtles at night. Langosta is at the end of the road past Capitán Suizo; look for the Cala Luna signs. Avellana can be reached by boat, but the quickest way is by road, 15 km (nine miles) via two sleepy inland towns called Villarreal and Hernández.

General Information

Tamarindo has more services than most beach towns, including a bank, several ATM machines, a row of public phones at the end of the beach and a post office. @ **Internet** in the small shopping center at the turnoff from the main road offers Internet access in its blissfully air-conditioned office. Lines form in early evening; they're open daily from 9 AM until 9 PM.

You're more likely to hear a California twang or Aussie drawl than native Spanish. Blond hair and blue eyes abound along the main drag, especially during the high season between November and April, when every day brings abundant sunshine, blue skies, and some of the gnarliest waves this side of Malibu.

But don't think "hang ten" is the only byword at Tamarindo. The resort area offers plenty of other activities including sport fishing, windsurfing, scuba diving, golf (at Royal Pacific Golf and Country Club) and jungle boat tours through the nearby Estuario Tamarindo. Dining and shopping are better here than anywhere else in the area, and there's also a good deal of nightlife ranging from merengue-flavored beach bars to surfer nightclubs.

More secluded beaches nearby include Playa Langosta and Playa Avellana. The beaches are dominated by surfers in the daytime, by nesting

What to See and Do

It's easy to while away several days just strolling the beach, swimming, grazing through the wide range of restaurants, or simply lying by your hotel pool. But Tamarindo also has several options for more active types. **Iguana Surf** (/FAX 653-0148 E-MAIL iguanasurf@aol.com WEB SITE www .tamarindo.com/iguana has an activities center in town near the end of the main road and another on the road to Playa Langosta. The largest activities center in the area, Iguana offers surf tours, surf lessons, transportation to out-of-the-way beaches, rental equipment (including surfboards, boogie boards, kayaks, bikes and snorkeling gear), kayak tours in the estuary, snorkeling tours in an inflatable boat, and motorized tours of the area

LEFT: Sea kayaks, high and dry on Playa Conchal. RIGHT: The Meliá Playa Conchal is a luxury resort on one of the most beautiful beaches in Costa Rica.

on four-wheel-drive all-terrain vehicles. Their enormous adventure center on the Playa Langosta road has a restaurant complete with splashing waterfall, a second-story rental shop packed with gear, and a store selling everything from surfboards to souvenirs. They even rent VCRs and movies. Stop here at the beginning of your stay and you'll never wonder what to do next.

Though it lacks the elaborate trappings at Iguana, **Papagayo Excursions** (653-0254 FAX 653-0227 E-MAIL papagayo@solracsa.co.cr has long been a leading operator in the area, offering horseback riding, boat trips through the estuaries, and tours to other nearby attractions. Contact them through hotel tour desks.

Several independent boat captains offer sportfishing trips; ask at your hotel desk for information. **Tamarindo Sportfishing** (/FAX 653-0090 E-MAIL tamspf@solracsa.co.cr, offers two vessels (seven and 11 m, or 22 and 38 ft) under Captain Randy Wilson, who has been fishing these waters since 1974. **Capullo Sportfishing** (653-0048 FAX 653-0112 E-MAIL info@capullo.com also comes highly recommended, as does Agua Rica Dive (653-0094. Sailing trips are arranged by **Samonique II** (653-0241 FAX 653-0243 E-MAIL samonique@sol.racsa.co.cr.

Where to Stay

Exclusive and elegant, **Cala Luna Hotel & Villas** (653-0214 FAX 653-0213 E-MAIL reservations@calaluna.come WEBSITE www.calaluna.com sits on a hill above Playa Langosta (very expensive). Private villas the color of ripe mangoes seem to glow in the sunlight; each has its own pool, full kitchen (with private chefs available for an additional fee), private garden, and several bedrooms and bathrooms with stenciled paintings on the walls and tropical hardwood furnishings. The 20 hotel rooms are just as grand (though hardly as spacious) and are located close to the beach. A free-form pool surrounded by silver palms and red hibiscus sits at the center of the rambling property, and the restaurant Cala Moresca serves international cuisine. It really helps to have a car if you're staying here, as cab drivers charge at least US$5 for a trip to town.

Hotel Capitán Suizo (653-0075 FAX 653-0292 E-MAIL capitansuizo@ticonet.co.cr is a longtime favorite with Tamarindo habitués (expensive). Buck for buck, this might well be the best beach hotel in all of Costa Rica. Owners Ruedi and Ursula Schmid have certainly created a picturesque setting that feels delightfully comfortable. Just steps from the beach, the Suizo features eight thatched-roof bungalows and 22 rooms in a two-story block (ground floor rooms have air-conditioning, upper floor rooms catch the sea breeze and have fans). The free-form pool is surrounded by lush tropical gardens. Suizo has its own stables — 14 horses waiting to take you splashing through the surf — and excellent bilingual workers at the tour desk who can arrange just about any excursion you can imagine. Many of the guests are returnees; some seem to have made the hotel their second home. Town is a short walk down the beach.

One local hotel that sits head and shoulders above all the others, literally, is **El Jardín del Edén** (653-0137 FAX 653-0111 E-MAIL hotel@jardin-eden.com WEBSITE www.jardin-eden.com (expensive). This small luxury hotel, run by an Italian couple, commands a hilltop overlooking Bahía Tamarindo. Each of the 20 rooms come with air-conditioning, private bath, hot water, minibar and safe-deposit box, as well as a balcony or terrace with sea view. Another reason to stay here is the superb Continental restaurant which serves some of the best food on the Guanacaste Coast. Eden does indeed have tropical gardens, as well as two pools and a 120-m-long (400-ft) private walkway to the beach.

Home never looked this good, though Suzye and Barry Lawson make their guests feel like family at **Villa Alegre** (653-0270 FAX 653-0287 E-MAIL vialegre@racsa.co.cr WEB SITE www.tamarindo.com/alegre. Their seven guest rooms and villas are as individualistic as the owners, who decorated each room with treasures gathered during their travels. The Guatemala suite is filled with vivid tapestries; the pale blue-and-white California room has a patio with ocean view. Some villas are large enough for families, rooms with shared bath are perfect for solo travelers, and some rooms are fully equipped for disabled travelers (an unusual and thoughtful touch). Guests gather in the living room and select books and games from the extensive library, lounge on the lawns beside the pool, or stroll over the beach, where hermit crabs and starfish hide in tide pools. Breakfast (included in the expensive rate) is a lavish affair, and guests are encouraged to help themselves to cool drinks from the 'fridge in the main kitchen. The Lawsons keep a huge notebook filled with restaurant menus, tour brochures and other information on the area, and are eager and enthusiastic activity directors.

Tamarindo Diriá (653-0031 FAX 653-0208 E-MAIL tnodiria@sol.racsa.co.cr WEB SITE www .tamarindodiria.co.cr sits right on the main beach

the beach or town. The staff is so amiable, the food and drinks so good, and the set up so comfortable, it seems a shame to waste time wandering about aimlessly. Better to swing in the hammock or rock in the chair beside the front door of your delightful room decorated with murals of birds, fish and mammals. Comfy lounge chairs surround the pool, and the gift shop has just the right balance of necessities (including a book exchange) and tasteful souvenirs. Book your room early in for high season; rates are moderate.

Another excellent choice in the moderate price range is **Hotel el Milagro** (653-0042 FAX 653-0043 E-MAIL flokiro@sol.racsa.co.cr across the main street from the beach. The 32 rooms are scattered about

in the center of town, blocking the sea view for most other businesses. It's wildly popular, of course, and underwent a major renovation in 2000. A new building increased the number of rooms to 120, making it the largest property in the area. Twelve new apartments offer all the comforts of home; the kitchen facilities make them a good base for families or groups of touring surfers. The best rooms with ocean views climb into the very expensive range in high season, but garden view rooms with air-conditioning and fans, minibar, cable television, and safe-deposit box stay in the expensive range. The beach is just a step away, as are the Diriá's two swimming pools (one for adults, one for kids).

Guests have a tendency to stay put at **Hotel Pasatiempo** (653-0096 FAX 653-0275 E-MAIL passtime@sol.racsa.co.cr WEB SITE www.hotel pasatiempo.com, except for occasional forays to

in bungalows up a slight hillside and have showers outside the front doors for sandy feet. The rooms have air-conditioning or fans (those with fans are cheaper) and comfy beds. Other amenities include a restaurant and bar, a swimming pool, and a shady garden. There's usually someone around who speaks English, Dutch, German or French.

Local hotelier Maria de los Angeles Molina has fashioned a pleasant budget value in the **Cabinas Marielos** (/FAX 653-0141. Set around a quiet garden with towering coconut palms, the *cabinas* offer a family atmosphere and great rooms for low rates. *Cabinas* sleep as many as four people and all have private cold-water bath. **Frutas Tropicales**

OPPOSITE: Boats of many sizes dodge into sheltered bays for an anchor and a swim. ABOVE: Commercial fishing boats cruise the Pacific in search of tuna, dorado and marlin.

(653-0041 has a few clean rooms at rock-bottom prices, and they even have television.

Where to Eat

Tamarindo has more eateries than any other beach in Guanacaste. It would probably take a month to feast your way through every single establishment. Several of the finest restaurants are in the hotels, though there are plenty of places to choose from in town and on the back streets.

You can dine at reasonable prices at the restaurants described here, or splurge on cocktails, imported wines, and several courses including dessert. **Capitán Suizo** stands out among the hotel restaurants for its excellent American, Swiss

and closed Sundays. In the same neighborhood, **La Meridiana** (653-0230 might well be the finest Northern Italian restaurant in the country. Using imported olive oil, cheeses and spices, chef Vittoria prepares absolutely divine lobster mousse ravioli, tender carpaccio, vegetable and pasta strudel, and the deeply satisfying brasato delle laghe, a hearty stew. The wine list includes several Italian imports and a wide selection of liqueurs. Though it looks like a cowboy bar, **El Vaquero** (653-0239 on the main road actually serves delicate crêpes filled with shrimp, cheese, or tropical fruits.

For an inexpensive meal, *casados* and other rice-based dishes are reasonably priced at **El Milagro's**

and Italian cuisine served by candlelight at its poolside restaurant. The salad bar is a meal in itself, especially when followed by the creamy chocolate mousse. Try the beef with roesti and the avocado and hearts of palm salad. Locals say the best lobster around is served at **Jardín del Edén**, and you can't beat the sunset view. Every night is a culinary adventure at **Pancho's Bar and Restaurant** at Pasatiempo, where the daily specials roam the globe from Greece to Jamaica. The regular menu has an Asian–Latin flair, with selections including Cuban chicken sandwiches, oriental salads, creamy guacamole and chips and Caribbean pork tenderloin with plantain stuffing.

The Swiss chef at **Stella's** (653-0127, on the hill above Pasatiempo, prepares shrimp flambé in brandy, chicken with orange sauce and savory wiener schnitzel. Stella's is open only for dinner

thatch-roofed restaurant on the main road into town. Fishnets hang about the ceiling and the open-air dining room, and seafood lovers can suit their tastes by combining shrimp, lobster and fresh fish in one entrée. As you might expect, **Frutas Tropicales** whips up a mean papaya smoothie. Homesick Americans can soothe their woes with an all-American grilled cheese sandwich or fried chicken. The aroma of fresh croissants and baguettes wafting from **Panadería de Paris** (653-0255, formerly called Johan's Bakery, is irresistible. The bakery displays all sorts of cookies, muffins, and cakes, and the backyard restaurant serves tasty breakfasts.

How to Get There

Tamarindo is 12 km (7.5 miles) south from Huacas (via Villarreal) and 73 km (45 miles) from Liberia. The drive down from Liberia takes about one hour and the entire route is paved until the last four kilometers (two and a half miles).

Daily express buses run from San José (five and a half hours) and local buses from Liberia and Santa Cruz. Both SANSA and TravelAir have daily flights from San José to Tamarindo's airstrip.

PLAYA NOSARA

Nosara is the sort of place where you can either drop in for a couple of days or drop out for the rest of your life. A multitude of foreigners have come to Nosara for a vacation and never left. Many of them own retirement homes in the area, and control most of the hotels and restaurants.

Although everyone refers to the area as Playa Nosara, the actual beach of that name is just one part of a broad coastal valley fed by two rivers, the ríos Nosara and Montaña. The estuary where the streams flow into the sea is a world-famous surf spot. Playa Nosara lies to the north of the estuary; Playa Pelada and Playa Guiones are to the south. All three beaches are popular with sun-seekers and surfers. Nosara village is about five kilometers (three miles) inland at the end of a serpentine road that winds down from Nicoya (34 km or 21 miles).

The entire Nosara coast — from Punta India in the north to Punta Guiones in the south — is incorporated into the **Refugio Nacional de Fauna Silvestre Ostional** (686-6760. The park features lush tide pools, coastal jungle, offshore reefs and patches of sand that serve as nesting sites for the Olive Ridley turtle. The Ridleys are famous for their *arribada*, or mass arrival, when as many as 100,000 turtles lay their eggs on several consecutive nights after the quarter moon. Peak season is August and September, but you may find at least a few turtles on the beach up to November.

Where to Stay

Big Sur comes to Costa Rica in the form of the **Nosara Yoga Retreat** (233-8057 FAX 255-3351 E-MAIL aroldan@sol.racsa.co.cr WEB SITE www .nosara.com/yogaretreat (very expensive). A superb spot for a beach holiday in its own right, the retreat offers all sorts of mind–body activities, including full body massage, daily Hatha yoga classes, breathing and meditation instruction, nutritional counseling, supervised fasting and detoxification. Retreat directors Amba Camp and Don Stapleton have more than 40 years of yoga experience between them.

Set on a leafy ridge with a view looking out over the bay, the moderately-priced **Almost Paradise** (/FAX 685-5004 is run with tender loving care by Gerlinde, a former German television producer. The six rooms here are spick and span, each with private bath and balcony. The hotel restaurant has some of Nosara's more savory cuisine.

There's some more Germanic ambiance at the **Rancho Suizo Lodge** (222-2900 or 223-4371 FAX 222-5173 E-MAIL aratur@sol.racsa.co.cr WEB SITE www.nosara.com/ranchosuizo, managed by Swiss expats Rene Spinnler and Rush Luscher. This pleasant little hotel located near Playa Pelada has bungalows each with their own hot-water baths. Amenities here include two bars, as well as and mountain bike and watersports equipment.

Where to Eat

With so many expatriate residents, Nosara offers more dining choice than most Costa Rican beaches. **Bambu Bar & Restaurant** claims the "best char-grilled burgers" in Costa Rica, as well as Sunday brunch with eggs Benedict and Bloody Marys. **La Dolce Vita** features pasta and pizza, while both **Rancho Suizo** and **Almost Perfect** have cafés with a variety of tasty cuisine. Other good bets include **Monkey Business** and **La Lechuza**.

How to Get There

Nosara village is 33 km (20.5 miles) southwest of Nicoya; the beach is five kilometers (three miles) further west. You can also drive the coast road from Playa Sámara 29 km (18 miles) or take a long scenic journey from Santa Cruz, 63 km (39 miles).

A daily express bus runs from San José and there's a local bus from Nicoya. TravelAir offers daily flights from San José; SANSA flies three times a week.

PLAYA SÁMARA

Sámara is a relatively secluded beach about 26 km (16 miles) south of Nosara on the coast road. Its tiny business district sits in the curve of Samara Bay; vacation houses and small resorts line the gray sand beach and dot the surrounding hillsides. There are several hotels spread far around the area; a vehicle is essential unless you plan to stay put at a resort.

Several good beaches can be found on either side of Bahía Sámara. Playa Garza to the north offers white sand and sweeping views of the Pacific. Playa Carrillo to the south is framed by palm trees and coral reef. Playa Camaronal is a world-famous surfing spot. Locals pull their cars right up to the sand and set up housekeeping for the day. On busy weekends, vendors sell cold drinks and fast food from the back of pickup trucks or carts on wheels.

Where to Stay

Guanamar Beach and Sportfishing Resort (656-0054 or 293-2000 FAX 656-0001 or 239-2405 WEB SITE www.guanamar.com, has long been considered one of the top sport-fishing resorts on the Nicoya

OPPOSITE: Dry hills curve beside beaches and bays on the Nicoya Peninsula.

coast (very expensive). The 41 *cabinas* cling to the hillside above Playa Carrillo, each unit equipped with air-conditioning, private bath with hot water, satellite television and safe. The swimming pool and restaurant sit atop steep peaks with views of the ocean below. Guanamar has its own small fishing fleet — a 7.5-m (25-ft) Boston whaler and an 11-m (36-ft) Hatteras — for expeditions to snag marlin, yellowfin, sailfish, wahoo and other tropical whoppers.

A few tiny signs point the way to **Punta Islita** (231-6122 (in San José) TOLL FREE IN THE US AND CANADA (800) 525-4800 FAX 231-0715 (in San José) E-MAIL ptaisl@sol.racsa.co.cr WEB SITE www .puntaislita.co.cr (very expensive), though most

guests fly in on private planes. Exclusive and elegant, the small hotel sits all alone amid lowland forest on a hill above a secluded bay. Pampered guests luxuriate in Islita's upscale version of "rustic" suites; complete with silky-smooth sheets, fresh floral arrangements and private hot tubs. The French chef manages to hold the guests' interest with innovative specials — there's nowhere else for them to eat. Horseback riding, fishing, hiking and tennis provide a break from lounging in padded chairs by the infinity pool, which seems to flow into the horizon. If you've got the money, Punta Islita is the ultimate romantic escape.

Villas Playa Sámara (656-0100 FAX 656-0109 is a less over-the-top escape, with 57 air-conditioned villas (one, two or three bedrooms) decorated with rattan furniture and mosaic tiles, at expensive rates. The Villa features a restaurant

and bar, swimming pool and Jacuzzi, and a small casino. Sports here include mountain biking, horseback riding, fishing, windsurfing, jet skiing and water skiing.

Situated on a forested hill overlooking the coast, moderately-priced **Hotel Mirador de Sámara** (656-0044 FAX 656-0046 indeed offers splendid views from most of the rooms and an unusual three-story observation tower. Owner Max Mahlich runs a tight ship that includes six large guest rooms with fully-equipped kitchens and private baths. The beach is a five-minute walk away. Be forewarned — it's a steep climb to some of the rooms. The largest establishment in Sámara is the **Isla Chora Inn** (656-0174 or 656-0175 FAX 656-0173 (moderate). Deluxe rooms include air-conditioning, satellite television and safe-deposit boxes and private baths with hot water. There's a swimming pool and the inn's restaurant serves Italian food.

The rates might nudge a bit over the inexpensive range in high season, but **Casa del Mar** (656-0264 FAX 656-0129, just one block in from the beach, is a good choice for those arriving by bus. The two-story building frames a small hot tub; the simple rooms have ceilings or fans. There's a restaurant on site, and management will help set up tours and transportation. I like the friendly feeling at **Hotel Belvedere** (/FAX 656-0213 E-MAIL belvedere @samarabeach.com up a slight hill a short walk from the beach. The owners were busily constructing several new rooms and a pool when I last visited, but I'm sure a few more rooms won't destroy the ambiance. Mosquito nets covering the beds are a nice touch, since the roar of the surf keeps you company when your door is open. Breakfast is served on a second-story terrace with ocean views, and the large hot tub is tucked in a pleasant garden.

Hotel Playa Sámara (686-6922 or 656-0190 is occasionally on the noisy side, but it offers modest rooms with fans and private cold-water baths.

Where to Eat

Isla Chora Inn's restaurant serves pizza and pasta dishes, as well as homemade Italian ice cream. **Villas Playa Sámara** has a good international restaurant. Try **Colocho's** for seafood or **Flor de Giruelo** for Costa Rican-style Chinese dining.

How to Get There

Playa Sámara is 38 km (23.5 miles) south of Nicoya along a road that's only partially paved at present. It can also be reached from Playa Nosara along a very rough coastal road.

A daily express bus runs from San José and a local bus from the town of Nicoya which continues on to Playa Carrillo. Both of Costa Rica's domestic airlines offer daily service from San José to Sámara's tiny airport.

EXCURSIONS INLAND

SANTA CRUZ

The crossroads town of Santa Cruz, with a population of 17,000, is a bustling metropolis by local standards, but it's a far cry from the big city. Founded in 1760, Santa Cruz is one of Guanacaste's oldest towns and the official Folklore City of Costa Rica. Traditional folk dancing, country music and (bloodless) bullfighting linger on here, and can be experienced at their flamboyant best during annual town fiestas such as the festival of **Cristo Negro de Esquipulas**, held on January 15,

and the celebration of **Guanacaste's annexation**, held on July 25.

During the remainder of the year there isn't much reason for travelers to pause in Santa Cruz, except to fill up their gas tank or change buses. But if you find yourself with spare time, have a look around the leafy town square with its mango trees and the ruined bell tower of an old church that was destroyed in an earthquake a half-century ago.

Twelve kilometers (seven and a half miles) east of Santa Cruz is sleepy **Guaitíl**, where the ancient tradition of Chorotega Indian pottery has been revived in recent years. The handmade ceramics come in various earthen shades and prices are very reasonable. Members of the village art cooperative are happy to demonstrate the process for visitors, from fashioning with local clay to firing in kilns behind their workshops.

Where to Stay and Eat

La Estancia Cabinas (680-0476 or 255-2981 FAX 680-0348 offers simple but clean rooms with private bath, cold water and fan. The **Hotel Diria** (680-0080 FAX 680-0442 has similar rooms and facilities but with the added advantage of a garden and swimming pool. Both charge inexpensive rates.

Unless you're into rice and beans, Santa Cruz doesn't offer too many choices. The **Bamboo** restaurant inside the Hotel Diria has a few international dishes on their menu. The best local cuisine is at the **Coope Tortillas** (no phone), with *tico* dishes and fresh tortillas cooked in wood-fired ovens.

How to Get There

Santa Cruz is 55 km (34 miles) south of Liberia and 20 km (12.5 miles) north of Nicoya on Highway 21 and can be used as a base for excursions to Playa Tamarindo, 34 km (21 miles) away, and other beaches on the central Guanacaste Coast.

There are daily express buses from San José, as well as local buses from Liberia, Tamarindo and Nicoya town. Taxis run to and from Nicoya.

NICOYA

One of Costa Rica's oldest towns, Nicoya (population 11,000) was founded in the mid-sixteenth century as a market town and religious center for the surrounding haciendas, which then relied heavily on Chorotega Indian slave labor. The fulcrum of local culture in Spanish colonial days was the **Iglesia San Blas**, a gorgeous whitewashed church which today simmers like a mirage in the Guanacaste heat. San Blas is still the town's most impressive structure and includes a small museum with modest pre-Columbian treasures.

The town's biggest celebration each year comes on December 12, feast day of the Virgin of Guadalupe. Like most Guanacaste festivals, this one includes local music and dance, bullfights and livestock shows and ample portions of food.

Nicoya is located on the banks of the Río Grande, half an hour's drive south of Santa Cruz and a good three hours north of Playa Naranjo and the ferry terminal on the Golfo de Nicoya. The town is a convenient jumping off point for excursions to Parque Nacional Barra Honda as well as for the beaches of the northern Península de Nicoya, including Playa Nosara, 39 km (24 miles) away, and Playa Sámara, 38 km (23.5 miles) distant.

OPPOSITE: Most beach towns have one or two small, palm-bedecked hotels perfect for romantic getaways. ABOVE: Guanacaste's colonial churches mark some of the earliest settlements in the country. OVERLEAF: An Easter procession winds its way through a Nicoya Peninsula village.

Where to Stay and Eat

Nicoya doesn't offer much choice when it comes to accommodation. Probably the most comfortable place in town (and certainly the most efficient) is the **Complejo Turistico Curime (** 685-5238 FAX 685-5530. Inexpensive *cabinas* and rooms include air-conditioning, hot water, television and a refrigerator.

Hotel Rancho Humo (255-2463 FAX 255-3573, 27 km (17 miles) north of Nicoya, is a secluded lodge on the banks of the Río Tempisque. The prices here are rather high for what you get, but the ranch has a swimming pool and all rooms have air-conditioning. The front desk can arrange boat trips into nearby Parque Nacional Palo Verde.

Café Daniela has the best pizza in town as well as tasty *tico* cuisine. **Papatan's Soda & Restaurant** serves up savory Costa Rican dishes.

How to Get There

Nicoya is 20 km (12.5 miles) south of Santa Cruz, 28 km (17 miles) west of Tempisque ferry and 72 km (44.5 miles) northwest of Playa Naranjo. The turnoff for the Río Tempisque ferry is located just north of the entrance to Nicoya.

Daily express buses run from San José, as well as local buses from Liberia, Santa Cruz, Nosara and Sámara. Taxis travel to and from Santa Cruz.

PARQUE NACIONAL BARRA HONDA

Barra Honda stands apart from other Costa Rican parks because the main attraction here is below the ground: the country's largest limestone cav-

ern system. More than three dozen labyrinths and caves have been discovered here over the past 20 years, with the deepest (Santa Ana Cave) gaping more than 200 m (660 ft) below the surface.

The caverns are marvelous, filled with stalactites and stalagmites of a thousand different shapes and sizes. Among the more remarkable caves are Terciopelo, La Trampa, Pozo Hedionda and Nicoa (where prehistoric man once lived). Millions of bats also call these caverns home, as do fish and salamanders which have adapted to life in total darkness.

Visitors must have reservations and a ranger guide to enter the caves, which can be arranged through the **park office (** 257-0922 FAX 223-6963 in San José. Another alternative is to join an organized spelunking expedition offered by a private tour company such as **Ríos Tropicales (** 233-6455 FAX 255-4354.

Above ground, Barra Honda offers more special attractions. The dry tropical forest here is home to numerous indigenous species including puma (who have been known to attack humans), deer, monkeys, peccaries, anteaters and myriad bird species. Las Cascades is an above-ground limestone formation that resembles a frozen waterfall. Cerro Barra Honda is a short 442-m (1,450-ft) rocky peak. Be aware that trails are not well marked. Lost hikers have died in this park.

Other than camping, no accommodation is available in the park. The nearest hotel is the Rancho Humo, north of Nicoya town (see above).

How to Get There

The entrance to Parque Nacional Barra Honda is 14 km (nine miles) east of Nicoya via the villages of Piave and Santa Ana. If you are coming directly from San José, the entrance is about 20 km (12.5 miles) west of the Tempisque ferry via a roundabout route that takes you through Tres Esquinas, Quebrada Honda, Nacaome, Pueblo Viejo and Santa Ana.

Buses depart daily at noon from Nicoya stopping at Santa Ana; it is then a two-kilometer (one-and-a-quarter-mile) walk to the park entrance.

GOLFO DE NICOYA BEACH RESORTS AND WILDLIFE RESERVES

PLAYA NARANJO

Naranjo is the western terminus of the vehicle-passenger ferries that ply the Golfo de Nicoya from Puntarenas, which makes it the jumping off point for excursions to the beach resorts (Tambor and Montezuma) and wildlife parks (Curu, Tortuga and Cabo Blanco) of the southern Península de Nicoya. The town of Naranjo is not particularly interesting in itself, but it is a good place to fill up your gas tank and stock up on food supplies before heading west to the wilder parts of Nicoya. Naranjo can also be used as a gateway to central Nicoya, but the road north to Quebrada Honda and Nicoya town is one of the worst highways in northwest Costa Rica.

Where to Stay and Eat

Inexpensive **Hotel Oasis del Pacifico** (661-1555 is the best place to stay in Naranjo. Rooms have private bath with hot water but no air-conditioning. Rates include breakfast. The Oasis has a restaurant and two pools. There are a variety of *sodas* near the ferry terminal.

every day from Puntarenas, and bus service is available to Naranjo, 22 km (13.5 miles), Tambor, 19 km (12 miles), and Montezuma, 37 km (23 miles).

REFUGIO DE FAUNA SILVESTRE CURU

This small reserve of 84 ha (207 acres) near Paquera is privately owned but open to the public. Seven distinct ecosystems thrive here, including pristine black-sand beaches, mangrove swamp, and several types of coastal forest. Birds are abundant, and among the mammals on the reserve are ocelots, white-tailed deer, sloths, anteaters, and capuchin and howler monkeys.

How to Get There

If you're coming south from Guanacaste, Playa Naranjo is 69 km (43 miles) south of Quebrada Honda and 72 km (45 miles) from Nicoya town. Heading west from Naranjo along the coast road are Paquera 22 km (14 miles), Playa Tambor 41 km (25.5 miles) and Montezuma 59 km (36.5 miles) via Cóbano.

There are at least five daily passenger-vehicle ferries from Puntarenas. The crossing takes around 90 minutes. Regular buses from Tambor, Paquera and Montezuma arrive near the Naranjo ferry pier.

PAQUERA

The little seaside town of Paquera has become an alternative ferry harbor for southern Nicoya in the last few years. There are three services

The owners are trying to reintroduce spider monkeys.

Bahía Curu with its lovely black-sand beach has good snorkeling, but you'll need to bring your own equipment. Permission from the owners is required and must be obtained before visiting the reserve (661-2392 or 223-1739. They live in an old house near the beach and will gladly give you a private tour of the reserve.

ISLA DE TORTUGA

Tortuga is an exquisitely handsome island off the southern Nicoya Coast, about two kilometers (one and a quarter miles) from Curu and within easy reach of Puntarenas. Its wonderful

OPPOSITE: A guide displays the skull of a man-eating crocodile at Hotel Rancho Humo near Barra Honda. ABOVE: A rancher on the Nicoya Peninsula.

white sand beach is framed by towering coconut palms and warm turquoise waters, perfect for swimming.

For the last 20 years, Tortuga has been operated as a private nature reserve by the Cubero family of San José. The Cuberos have replanted and reintroduced plant species that had disappeared from the island. They've developed a self-guided nature trail looping around the island that includes a climb to the island's highest point at 172 m (570 ft) and a canopy tour ride in leather harnesses attached to a cable.

Tortuga harbors many species of rare and endangered plants including orchids, bromeliads, and tropical hardwoods such as the indio desnudo tree and the madrono with its striking white flowers. The island also hosts several animal species including the agouti, as well as providing nesting sights for frigate birds and pelicans.

Although the beach can be enjoyed free of charge, there's a US$5 fee for the nature trail. Tortuga is 90 minutes from the port of Puntarenas by boat. Excursions can be arranged through **Calypso Cruises (** 256-2727 FAX 256-6767 in San José E-MAIL info@calypsotours.com WEB SITE www.calypsotours.com.

PLAYA TAMBOR

A well-kept secret among budget travelers until a few years ago, Tambor is now being discovered by more upscale travelers drawn by a couple of luxury resorts. Tambor village is a cluster of wooden shacks and fishing boats on Bahía Ballena (Whale Bay). The black-sand beach here is handsome and clean. Around the bay are several picture perfect strands, such as Tango Mar, which many consider one of the most beautiful beaches in Central America.

Bahía Ballena Yacht Club is a small marina that caters to visiting yachts. It offers scuba diving, fishing and sightseeing boat trips, as well as renting out snorkeling and windsurfing equipment and sailboats.

Where to Stay and Eat

Perched on rugged cliffs overlooking a splendid white-sand beach, **Tango Mar (** 683-0001 FAX 683-0003 E-MAIL tangomar@sol.racsa.co.cr WEB SITE www.tangomar.com is one of Costa Rica's prime seaside retreats (very expensive). It's difficult to pick the most delightful thing about this marvelous hotel: the thatched *cabinas*, the expansive 51-ha (125-acre) tropical gardens, the various sports activities (from a nine-hole golf course to beach volleyball), or the gourmet cuisine at Tango Mar's restaurant. If you want to pamper yourself, this is the place. **Tambor Tropical (** 683-0011/0012 FAX 683-0013 WEB SITE www.tambortropical.com may have only 10 rooms, but they're among the

best rooms in Costa Rica, each with kitchen, private hot-water bath and coastal panoramas (very expensive). This splendid little resort also has a swimming pool and access to multiple recreation activities.

Southern Nicoya's first Spanish-style mega resort is **Barceló Playa Tambor (** 683-0303 FAX 661-2069 WEB SITE www.barcelo.com (expensive). With 402 units, it has more rooms than all the other hotels on this coast combined. Rates include all meals and drinks; watersports activities are extra. Rooms feature private hot-water baths and air-conditioning. The adjacent **Barceló Los Delfines Country Club (** 683-0303 has a nine-hole course open to the public.

Inexpensive **Hotel Dos Lagartos (**/FAX 683-0236 is located right across from the beach. Carlos and Rita Entwes run this simple but pleasant little lodge that's a hit with young American and European travelers. Rooms are with shared or private cold-water baths.

How to Get There

Tambor lies between Paquera, 19 km (12 miles) away, and Montezuma, 18 km (11 miles) distant. Buses from Paquera ferry pier depart three times daily. Taxis also run to Paquera. Tambor's tiny airfield has three daily services from San José. The larger hotels can arrange boat service from Puntarenas.

OPPOSITE: Palms flourish in the island nature reserve at Tortuga. ABOVE: Isla de Tortuga is one of the last great escapes in the Golfo de Nicoya.

MONTEZUMA

If Tambor's chic resorts don't match your expectations of a Costa Rican beach holiday (or your budget), amble down the coast to Montezuma, a sleepy seaside retreat that has attractive beaches and reasonably-priced accommodations.

Much like Playa Nosara in northern Nicoya, Montezuma is something of a throwback to the 1960s. Plenty of surfers and long-haired kids, cold beer and cheap eats, fair-haired maidens on the beach by day, guitar music in the bodegas at night. It would be hard to find a more mellow place in all of Costa Rica. It's the kind of place you either love

Where to Stay and Eat

Downright fancy by local standards, **Nature Lodge Finca Los Caballos** (/FAX 642-0124 E-MAIL naturelc@sol.racsa.co.cr combines a horse ranch with a moderately-priced guest lodge. The rooms here are decorated with a Southwestern theme and have fans and private hot-water baths. There's a swimming pool on the property, and guests can mount the horses and ride nature trails. Montezuma's funky attitude is well displayed at **El Saño Banano** (642-0068 WEB SITE www .elsanobanano.com, the town's venerable vegetarian restaurant. The restaurant is just one part of the operation, which includes a cluster of beach bungalows north of town (moderate). Some have

or hate. Some visitors find it buggy, humid, and a bit squalid; others call it tropical and laid back.

Montezuma has its share of expatriate residents, many of them youngish Europeans and North Americans who consider southern Nicoya their little slice of paradise. Some of them manage the lodges and *cabinas* along the beach, while others keep a tight watch on development, heading off attempts to turn their tranquil community into a southern version of Papagayo or Flamingo. The struggle to improve the community's image without overselling it to potential developers continues, as hordes of backpackers claim the beaches as their personal turf. Reaching these beaches can be a challenge. Playa Grande and other beaches situated west of town are easily reached by road. But Quizales, Cocalito, Cocal and other beaches to the east can be reached only on foot, by horseback, or by boat.

domed roofs, some have kitchens, some have private baths.

The best on the beach is the inexpensive **Hotel los Mangos** (642-0076 FAX 642-0050, which has a choice of bungalows with private hot-water baths, rooms with private cold-water baths, or rooms with shared baths. Los Mangos doesn't have air-conditioning, but there's almost always a cool sea breeze. Amenities include an Italian restaurant, pool and lots of ocean. **Hotel Montezuma Pacífica** (642-0204 has basic rooms with private fans; some have air-conditioning. **Hotel Amor del Mar** (/FAX 642-0262 is on the beach and has moderately-priced rooms with private baths and inexpensive rooms with shared baths.

How to Get There

Montezuma is 18 km (11 miles) from Tambor and 37 km (23 miles) from Paquera along the coast road. Beyond Cóbano, the route is unpaved and may require a four-wheel-drive vehicle. Buses from Paquera ferry pier depart three times daily. Taxis are few and far between in this area.

RESERVA NATURAL ABSOLUTA CABO BLANCO

The "absolute" in Reserva Natural Absoluta Cabo Blanco (233-5284 refers to the fact that it's protected against all intrusion and possible future defilement. Cabo Blanco (White Cape) was the cornerstone of Costa Rica's national park system, founded in 1963 on a dazzling parcel of pristine land at the tip of the Península de Nicoya.

Blanco, harbor tide pools and small coral reefs. Cabo Blanco itself is Costa Rica's version of land's end, a windswept promontory that projects into the Pacific. Offshore is Isla Cabo Blanco, nesting sight of myriad sea birds including brown boobies. You'll need a boat to reach it.

Cabo Blanco's ranger station, at the park entrance, has trail maps and other information. **Sendero Sueco** leads from the station to the cape and both beaches. **Sendero Central** winds inland, through thick forest, reaching a terminus at Playa Balsita. **Sendero el Barco** leads along the wild bluffs west of Play Balsita.

There is no overnight accommodation inside the reserve and camping is not permitted.

The reserve was the brainchild of Olaf and Karen Wessberg, Swedish farmers who settled in Cabo Blanco in the mid-1950s. When logging and cattle ranching threatened to destroy the cape's wilderness, the Wessbergs launched an international campaign to save the area and create a national park system that would benefit the entire country. Their dream was realized, but not without a dark side: Olaf Wessberg was murdered in 1975 while carrying out an environmental survey of the reserve.

Three decades after its birth, Cabo Blanco remains a special place. It is not difficult to see why the Wessbergs and many others wanted this place preserved for all time. The lush coastal forest protects numerous bird and mammal species, including the puma, peccary, ocelot, white-tailed deer, kinkajou, and three different types of monkey. The park's two beaches, Playa Balsita and Playa Cabo

The closest place to stay is Cabuya village, a few kilometers beyond the park entrance, which has a handful of simple *cabinas* and guest houses.

How to Get There

Cabo Blanco reserve is 11 km (seven miles) west of Montezuma along a rough dirt road, which is often impassable during the rainy season. There is no public transportation to the reserve. Taxis are sometimes available in Montezuma. You can ride horses to the park entrance, but cannot take them into the reserve.

ABOVE: The sun shines more frequently along northern Pacific beaches than it does in the damp south. Small craft powered by pedals are an ecologically sensitive alternative to jet skis.

The
Central
Pacific
Coast

COSTA RICA'S MOST POPULAR BEACHES curve into tropical jungles west of the Cordillera Talamanca along the central Pacific coast. Close to San José and more urbane than the beach towns of the Península de Nicoya or the Caribbean coast, the Pacific communities of Jacó, Quepos, Manuel Antonio, and Dominical thrive on tourism.

One could say the central Pacific towns were created for tourism, though there were Indian settlements here long before the European conquest. More recently, the area was the second front of the United Fruit Company, deforested and cleared for banana plantations in the 1930s. The company, already firmly entrenched on the Caribbean coast, was responsible for the first transport link from the coast to the capital. Once a train line and a road were cleared in the 1960s and 1970s, word of these picturesque beaches spread through the country. By the 1980s, Manuel Antonio was one of the most popular destinations in the country; by the 1990s its national park was swarming with visitors.

Though Manuel Antonio in particular is firmly ensconced in the tourist circuit, the central Pacific still feels remote and wild. Spider and capuchin monkeys swing through the trees in parks and settlements all along the humid, lush coastline and in mountain foothills. The Costanera Sur, a semi-paved road that aims to be a coastal highway, runs south from the port city of Puntarenas, where cruise ships, freighters and ferries anchor in the Golfo de Nicoya. The road is paved all the way to the Reserva Biológica Carara, a popular day-trip destination from San José and Puntarenas. The coastal road continues to Jacó, known for its powerful surf, its party-town attitude, and its proximity to the park's primary tropical forest.

Potholes, ruts and knee-deep mud in the rainy season greet travelers headed farther south to Quepos and Manuel Antonio. The road gets so bad in places that signs warn drivers they are traveling at their own risk — an ironic twist when en route to one of the most densely populated beach towns in the country. Quepos, the nearest major town to Parque Nacional Manuel Antonio, has grown over the past two decades from a settlement of fewer than a dozen families into a hodge-podge of businesses and homes for nearly 15,000 residents. The Quepos–Manuel Antonio area has the country's largest selection of one-of-a-kind hotels and restaurants outside San José, all set amidst forest beside the most beautiful beaches in the country.

The rampant development tapers off as you pass outside Quepos, following along the Costanera Sur as it carves its way south through the coastline, past African palm plantations and identical workers' settlements made up of pink, yellow, green and blue houses built around soccer fields. Hotels, nature lodges, and private villas appear again as you arrive at Dominical, a popular surfing spot that's becoming much more upscale than Jacó. Electricity and telephones are scarce in this region, just 42 km (26 miles) south of Quepos. Yet plenty of speculators are betting on its emergence as both a tourist destination and expatriate settlement, and land prices along the wave-beaten shoreline here have skyrocketed. From here south the road passes the remote Parque Nacional Marino Ballena and a few hidden surf spots then cuts inland to Palmar Sur and the Carretera Interamericana to Panama.

Fishing, swimming and surf spots are the central Pacific's great strengths; there are few cultural attributes here. Travelers short on time

or money find relatively easy access to great beaches, abundant nature and sufficient options to meet their needs for excitement, shelter and food. To escape the crowds, schedule your visit at the beginning or end of rainy season; room rates will also be lower then.

PUNTARENAS

The largest city in this region, Puntarenas was a bustling, charming city a century ago when coffee barons shipped their crops to Europe from the port and wealthy *ticos* vacationed at nearby beaches. Today, Puntarenas is faded, shabby, and sultry, with a few vestiges of charm beneath its hoary exterior. Fishing boats, small cruise ships, and the occasional yacht bob in the gentle waters along the downtown waterfront, where seagulls and pelicans are as predominant as people. Larger cruise and container ships dock at Puerto Caldera,

PRECEEDING PAGES: Isla de Caño LEFT is one of the best places for divers to spot sea fan coral. A dinosaur lizard in Parque Nacional Manuel Antonio RIGHT emerges from its hiding place. OPPOSITE: A rare solitary moment on Manuel Antonio's popular main beach. ABOVE: Quepos has about 15,000 residents, many of whom work in the overabundance of hotels, restaurants and tour companies around Manuel Antonio.

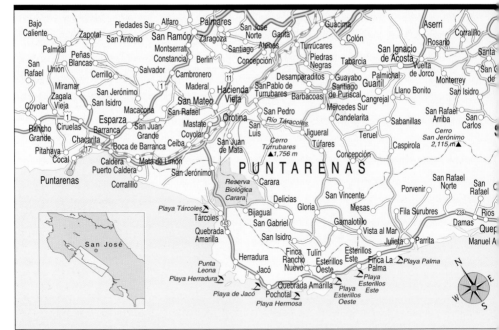

which the government constructed about 19 km (12 miles) south of the original port in Puntarenas.

The loss of status as the main Pacific port and the rise of far more scenic resorts tolled the death knell for Puntarenas, but the city is now battling to regain its status. Sewage plants, paved streets, and a projected convention center have sparked revitalization. The Paseo de los Turistas pedestrian path along 10 blocks of beachfront north of the city is now lined with *sodas*, souvenir shops, and ice cream stands, though it's still far from scenic.

Few travelers choose Puntarenas as a destination, though it is the closest beach to San José. Good highways run the 130 km (81 miles) from the capital, and cars and buses make the trip in under two hours. The city is used more as a day-trip destination, with visits to the beach combined with boat trips to uninhabited islands in the Golfo de Nicoya. The best of these trips are run by **Calypso Cruises (** 256-2727 FAX 256-6767 (in San José) E-MAIL info@calypsotours.com WEB SITE www.calypsotours.com.

WHERE TO STAY

Travelers heading out on cruises who must spend a night in Puntarenas typically pick the **Caribbean Village Fiesta Inn (** 663-0808 FAX 663-0856, a sprawling complex with 240 rooms, three pools, a casino and several restaurants (expensive). The price has risen considerably since the Allegro resort took over management and established an all-inclusive rate. It's a 10-minute cab ride south of town, close to Puerto Caldera.

The moderately-priced **Tioga Inn (** 661-0271 FAX 661-0127 E-MAIL tiogacr@sol.racsa.co.cr, across the street from the beach at the far side of town, is the traditional hangout in this neighborhood. It has 46 air-conditioned rooms and a swimming pool.

HOW TO GET THERE

Puntarenas is 130 km (81 miles) west of San José off the Carretera Interamericana; the drive takes about two hours. Buses run regularly throughout the day from San José to Puntarenas. The **Tambor Ferry (** 661-2084 to the southern Península de Nicoya departs from Puntarenas three times daily, as does the **Ferry Peninsular (** 661-3674 car ferry to Paquera.

JACÓ AND ENVIRONS

The road south of Puntarenas to Jacó is now smoothly paved, and several attractions beckon travelers to stop and stay a while. Reserva Biológica Carara and the Río Tárcoles north of Jacó both offer excellent wildlife experiences, while the new development of Los Sueños has consumed one of this area's loveliest bays.

Jacó, 60 km (37 miles) south of Puntarenas, has exploded into a major urban area and enormously popular surf destination in the past few years. The long beach is immensely popular with *ticos* on weekend getaways, and there are a few hotels that cater to Canadian groups on chartered, all-inclusive holidays. The town (population: 6,000) is

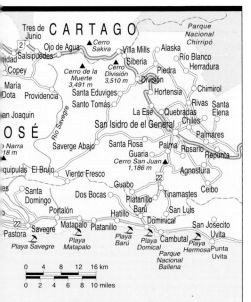

THE CENTRAL PACIFIC

surprisingly organized, with major businesses (grocery stores, gas stations) lining a paved road running parallel to the beach on block inland. Several hotels face the water; the roads to some are simple sand tracks.

GENERAL INFORMATION

Jacó does not have an official tourist information office. It does, however, have two banks, several gas stations, markets and pharmacies, and it is a good place to stock up on supplies when heading south. The **Costa Rica Connection Real Estate Office** (643-3510 serves as an informal information source, and distributes copies of *The Jacó News*, a monthly publication. The largest tour operator in the area is **Fantasy Tours** (643-3231 FAX 643-3383 E-MAIL fantasy@sol.racsa.co.cr. Car rentals are available through **Elegante** (643-3224, **Economy** 643-1719.

WHAT TO SEE AND DO

Crocodiles are the big attraction at the **Río Tárcoles** just north of Carara. Those driving by often pull off the road at the bridge straddling the river and peer down to the banks to spot the crocs. Good luck to them. First, the bridge is notorious for automobile break-ins. Secondly, no self-respecting crocodile is going to pose in the sun for tourists' enjoyment. Those serious about spotting one of these endangered creatures should schedule a boat ride up the river, with **Jungle Crocodile Safari** (661-0455, in Tárcoles, or through one of the Jacó

hotels. Grupo Mawamba operates a **Tropical Mangrove River Adventure** (223-2421 FAX 222-5463 E-MAIL tropicalmangrove@grupomawamba .com WEB SITE www.grupomawamba.com along the river to the Guacalillos Estuary. The trip involves hiking and a boat trip; both provide excellent bird watching opportunities. **Iguana Park** (249-6712 FAX 235-2007 is home to a forest canopy tour run by **Original Canopy Tours** (257-5149. Hikes into the jungle near the river are offered by **Aguas Viva Waterfall** (235-1787; the hike leads to a 183-m (600-ft) waterfall that splashes into several pools where you can stop and cool off after searching the trees for monkeys and macaws.

One of Costa Rica's most accessible and rewarding natural reserves is **Reserva Biológica Carara** (383-9953 on the south side of the Río Tárcoles. Until a few years back Carara was relatively unknown. I remember wandering down trails in the early 1990s with a small group and guide and encountering no other humans. Instead, we came upon a family of white-faced capuchin monkeys lounging in the forest canopy. We humans behaved in a most undignified manner, pointing binoculars and telephoto lenses at the babies clinging to their mothers, who stared back stoically, as if we were a barely tolerable intrusion. Your chances of stumbling upon such a scene are much less likely these days, since Carara has become a favorite tour for day-trippers from San José and cruise ship passengers from Puerto Caldera. The rangers attempt to keep the crowds down by allowing no more than 150 people into the park at one time.

The 4,700-ha (11,614-acre) reserve contains a large section of primary forest with a tree canopy spreading over a base of vines and ferns. Lemurs, anteaters, armadillos, iguanas and 850 species of birds live in the preserve, and though you can spot lots of wildlife on your own I strongly recommend hiring a guide for your trek. Carara is also the base for a long-term ecological study of scarlet macaws, which are becoming endangered due to poaching and loss of habitat. More than 200 macaw pairs (who mate for life) have been spotted in the region. The park opens at 7 AM in high season, 8 AM from May to October—be there when the rangers and guides arrive for the best wildlife viewing. Late afternoon is also good. The park closes at 5 PM; entry is US$6.

The biggest transformation on the central coast has taken place at Playa Herradura, where bulldozers continue to carve the hills into lots for exclusive villas. The **Los Sueños Resort and Marina** (see WHERE TO STAY, below) is the largest development on the coast, with an 18-hole golf course, a Marriott hotel, a large marina and private homes.

Surfing and partying are Jacó's two biggest attractions. The town is jam-packed on holidays, summer weekends, and during surfing competitions, but quiets down considerably in the green season. With all that young energy contained in one place, Jacó reverberates with music, laughter, and a fair amount of drunken revelry. The beach is long enough (three miles) for you to escape the crowds, however, and drop into town only when you feel like joining in the action. In addition to tours to Tárcoles and Carara, visitors can go horseback riding with **Mountain Top Tours (** 643-1126 or **Jacó Beach Equestrian Center (** 643-1569. **Maravillas Naturales (** 643-1113 rents mountain bikes and beach cruisers. Kayak tours and rentals are available at **Kayak Jacó (** 643-1233. **J.D.'s Watersports** at the Punta Leona Hotel **(** 257-3857

FAX 256-6391 WEB SITE www.jdwatersports.com, offers sport fishing, jungle river cruises, scuba diving, and water sports equipment rentals; you needn't stay at the hotel to use their facilities.

Surfers have a wide range of surf shops and tour companies to handle their needs. Several shops are located on the main street through town. **Surf Shop Jacó Center** (also called **Jazz Surf Shop**) **(** 643-3549 rents and sells gear and offers updates on surf conditions over the phone, as does **Chosita del Surf (**/FAX 643-3328. **Alacrán Surf Tours (** 777-1867 can arrange your accommodations and offer advice on surf spots.

The waves don't stop rolling at the end of town; there are several good breaks farther south at Playa Hermosa and Playa Esterillos. Part of the forest around playa Hermosa was declared a national wildlife refuge in 1998, protecting it from further development.

WHERE TO STAY

Jacó has a good range of accommodation, with inexpensive *cabinas* clustered in town and resort hotels sprinkled along the coast and forest north and south. I find it much nicer to stay outside town and buzz through on errands and for meals. Since Jacó is an immensely popular getaway for young

ticos, the hotels tend to fill up on weekends and general revelry takes over the pools and beaches. Try to visit during the week, if possible.

Very Expensive

A long, winding road leads uphill to **Villa Caletas (** 257-3653 FAX 222-2059 E-MAIL caletas@ticonet.co.cr, a Victorian-style mansion high above the sea. The ambiance is quite elegant and proper, with glossy black wicker chairs, black ceiling fans, gray and white tile floors, and dark antique armoires in a British colonial-empire scene. The main house has eight very formal guest rooms; white *cabinas* tucked under a forest of trees house 20 suites. The pool faces a staggeringly lovely view of the jungle and an aquamarine bay. Weddings take place frequently in the classy Greek amphitheater set in the mountainside, and honeymooners think they've landed in heaven. Caletas is relentlessly romantic. You might feel a bit out of place if you visit alone. The restaurants are excellent, serving a mix of classical French and tropical Costa Rican meals. The entrance is two and a half kilometers (one and a half miles) south of Punta Leona.

A far different experience awaits those checking into **Los Sueños Resort and Marina (** 630-9000 TOLL-FREE IN THE US 800-228-9290 FAX 630-9090 WEB SITE www.marriottHotels.com/SJOLS. The massive, hacienda-style Marriott hotel would fit in nicely in Cancún. In Costa Rica it's a bit startling. The enormous lobby glistens with waxed marble and shining crystal, and the pool area, complete with waterfalls, fountains, restaurants and a volleyball net, looks like it was imported from Hawaii. The large rooms have all the amenities you might expect, including ironing boards and irons, safe-deposit boxes, coffeemakers, robes, hair dryers — you name it, they've got it. Yachts and small cruise ships docked in the marina carry guests on sunset sails and tours to Isla Tortuga, and guests have use of the golf course, tennis courts, gym, and spa. The Marriott is wildly successful, especially for meetings and conventions. Holiday stays are booked up to a year in advance.

Expensive

I would be delighted to return repeatedly to **Villa Lapas (** 293-4821 FAX 293-4104 E-MAIL hvlapas @sol.racsa.co.cr WEB SITE www.villalapas.com, north of town adjacent to Reserva Biológica Carara. The Río Taracolitos runs through the 220-ha (543-acre) private reserve where pathways lead through plush lawns to several widely spaced one-story buildings with red-tiled roofs covered in blossoming vines during the rainy season. The 47 rooms have peaked wood ceilings and fans or air-conditioning, tiled floors, big desks and powerful, hot showers. Most have front terraces and lounge chairs on the lawns, and hammocks hang between trees throughout the property. The small pool is a gathering spot for guests cooling off after hikes on trails paralleling those in Carara. In early morning, tiger herons swoop down to the river, parrots and scarlet macaws screech overhead and bird watchers bearing binoculars flock to the river's edge. The hotel is sometimes filled with tour groups from Carara, who stop by to visit the butterfly garden filled with blossoming plants and fluttering mariposas extracting fruit nectars from hummingbird feeders and hanging gourds. The large restaurant and bar sometimes fills with tour groups, too, but is peaceful when left to the hotel guests at night. Tours to the Río Tárcoles and a nearby waterfall are available. The management adopted an all-inclusive policy in 2000, which jacked the rates higher than necessary. They may wisely abandon the idea.

The **Best Western Jacó Beach Resort** (643-1000 TOLL-FREE IN THE US (800) 528-1234 FAX 643-3246, sits right at the middle of the beach on the north side of downtown Jacó, and is the largest establishment in the neighborhood. The 98 rooms are a bit rundown, but have air-conditioning, satellite television and safes. Larger rooms sleep up to five persons and have kitchenettes. The restaurant and disco are packed in high season, when the hotel kicks into high gear and offers everything from horseback riding to crab races. It's much calmer in low season. The hotel's lifeguard is a savvy surfer who will keep an eye on novice surfers.

Moderate

A good choice for those who prefer to be surrounded by nature is **Punta Leona Hotel and Club** (661-1444 or 231-3131 (in San José) FAX 232-0791 E-MAIL puntaleo@sol.racsa.co.cr, north of Jacó and south of Villa Lapas. Some find the high-security in this gated community a bit disconcerting, but no one can fault the 300-ha (740-acre) forest, beach and grassy lawns. Part of the property is a private wildlife refuge; the rest is dotted with 123 rooms, bungalows and condominiums. This self-contained resort has three pools, six and a half kilometers (four miles) of beach, two restaurants and all the activities you could desire.

On the beach in Jacó, **Hotel and Chalets Tangeri** (643-3001 FAX 643-3636 has 14 moderately-priced rooms and 10 bungalows (expensive) that sleep five to eight people and have kitchenettes. The pools, restaurant, and bar look a bit rundown, but the price is good for what you get. The pleasant **Villas Estrellamar** (643-3102 FAX 643-3453 has apartments and bungalows with separate bedrooms and kitchenettes and hotel rooms in a two-story building facing the pool and hot tub. Mellow adults find a peaceful refuge at **Canciones del Mar** (643-3273 FAX 643-3290 WEB SITE www.cancionesdelmar.com, a Dutch and Canadian-owned condo complex on the beach.

Children are not permitted to stay in the one and two bedroom suites surrounding the gardens and pool. Rates are reduced for long-term stays.

On the south side of Jacó, **Terraza del Pacifico** (643-3222 FAX 643-3424 E-MAIL terraza@sol.racsa .co.cr WEB SITE www.terraza-del-pacifico.com is surf central at Playa Hermosa. The casual, comfortable two-story buildings frame the pool and its thatch-covered swim-up bar. The best rooms face the beach at the end of each wing; all 43 rooms have a double and single bed, satellite television and safe-deposit boxes. Beach towels and wet suits hang from the railings on many balconies, and sandy surfboards lean against all available wall space. Dinged boards can be repaired on site, and

the large surf shop sells boards, wax, and every piece of surfer paraphernalia you might require. Loaner bikes are available for free, and guests can access the Internet on the hotel's computers. Terraza is the headquarters for the annual International Surf Championship tournament held in July. The open-air restaurant is right by the sea, and a small casino operates during high season.

Also at Playa Hermosa, **Hotel Fuego del Sol** (643-3737 FAX 643-3736 WEB SITE www.fuego delsol.com is tucked in among tropical gardens atop a hill. The hotel boasts the largest gym in the area (in case the surfers don't get enough of a workout in the water). The rooms are among the nicest around, with murals painted on the walls and hammocks hanging on the balconies.

OPPOSITE: Jacó, population: 6,000. ABOVE: Locals beat the heat on a shady sidewalk in the port city of Puntarenas.

Inexpensive

You can't beat the location of **Balcón del Mar** (643-3251 or 283-2283 (in San José) FAX 283-2223 E-MAIL balcon@sol.racsa.co.cr WEB SITE WWW .balcon delmar.com. A strip of sand road is all that separates the small hotel from Jacó's main beach, and the crashing surf is the perfect accompaniment to a good night's sleep. Nearly all the rooms in the two-story building face the sea — claim an upstairs room if possible. The decor is basic and functional, designed to withstand salt and sand. The small pool sits beside the extremely popular restaurant, and the guarded parking lot is a major plus. **La Cometa** (643-3515, on the main street, rents rooms with shared or

private baths at low rates. Guests can use the communal kitchen.

WHERE TO EAT

Restaurants come and go in ever-changing Jacó, and there's always something new to check out. There's not a lot of variety; gringo tastes prevail. Most restaurant prices are in the inexpensive to moderate range. **Ríoasis** (643-3354 has taken over the ever-popular Killer Munchies, an open-air restaurant on the main drag where locals and tourists chow down on burritos, burgers, pizzas and pastas. Music blares from this place at night, as surfers congregate to relive the day's action on the waves. **Monica Pastas** (643-1776 serves what one local calls "the best pasta in the world." **La Piraña** (643-3725, in town, has an unusual menu featuring spicy blackened fish and steaks, pastas and *casados*. **Restaurant Emily** (643-1056 is considered the best seafood restaurant; reservations are a must in high season. **Banana Café** (643-3206 is the best place for pancakes and eggs, or huge plates of stir-fried veggies with chicken or beef. **El Zarpe** (643-3473 in front of the Best Western is nightlife central, and also has an Internet café. **Pancho Villa** (643-3571 starts the night serving Mexican food and ends by playing dance music

in its disco. Dance music plays until the wee hours at **La Central Discotheque** (643-3076.

HOW TO GET THERE

Jacó is around 60 km (37 miles) south of Puntarenas on the Costanera Sur. If your flight comes in early enough to San José, you should be able to rent a car and drive out to Jacó in the same day. The most direct car route is the Carretera Interamericana from San José, which links up with the Costanera Sur south of Puntarenas. A little bit longer drive, but so much more scenic, follows Highway 11 west from San José through Atenas and Orotina, where the road is lined with produce stands packed with homegrown watermelons, cashews, pineapples and other tropical snacks. Portions of this roadway were used by Spanish settlers in the sixteenth century; yucca trees planted as live fences cordon off the ranches and farms. Keep an eye out for the yucca's white flowers in February and March. Called the *flor de itabo*, these waxy flowers are eaten alongside scrambled eggs. The highway ends at the Costanera Sur near the small town of San Jerónimo; follow the signs directing you south to Quepos.

Buses depart frequently from San José, Quepos, and Puntarenas; the Jacó bus station (643-3135 is at the north end of town.

QUEPOS AND PARQUE NACIONAL MANUEL ANTONIO

The half-moon curves of the pale yellow-brown sand against the emerald forest at Parque Nacional Manuel Antonio are some of the most beautiful beaches in Costa Rica. The aquamarine water shimmers in the sun and glows by the light of the moon. Sailboats, cruise ships and luxury yachts pose against the backdrop of Isla Mogote and Punta Catedral jutting upward from the sea, where whales, dolphins and flying fish frolic in calm waters.

The park sits at the south end of the Quepos-Manuel Antonio region. Quepos is the main town and site of budget hotels and residents. The curving hillside road (which I call the Corridor) south of town to the national park is lined with ever-more luxurious inns and lodges. The Corridor ends at the edge of the park in the small settlement of Manuel Antonio, where a free public beach, a few small hostelries, and large parking lots are located.

Quepos and Manuel Antonio have grown faster than any other region in Costa Rica in the past decade. A couple of years back, during a major construction boom, I was sure the place had been ruined. But things have settled down and you can enjoy the natural setting without the clamber of hammers and saws. The road between Quepos and Manuel Antonio was paved in 2000; the President actually showed up to join in the celebrations. Quepos is now a busy town with several dirt and paved streets, no street signs, and little sense of organization (though locals swear their town is orderly). The waterfront has been cleaned up a bit, and plans are underway for development of a new *malecón* (seaside walkway and seawall) and streetlights. Plans for a mega marina big enough to hold three cruise ships and 800 boats have been scrapped for the moment, though some powerful people see Quepos as the perfect Pacific port for pleasure craft. The twisting, tortuous Corridor road is dotted with one-of-a-kind hotels and restaurants, many overlooking the sea. Manuel Antonio and the park are suffering from unprecedented popularity. Tourists and *ticos* alike can't resist the region's natural beauty.

BACKGROUND

The original residents of Manuel Antonio were the Quepoa people, who are believed to have lived here up to 1,000 years before the conquest. The first Spanish mission in Costa Rica is said to have been established here in 1570, but it languished in isolation for centuries. Until the 1930s the lands of Quepos and Manuel Antonio were inhabited by a handful of families who subsisted on fishing and agriculture; most of these land were forested hills and mangrove swamps converging with the sea. Then in 1938 the United Fruit Company was granted the rights to develop banana plantations along the Pacific coast. The fruit company first had to clear the virgin forest by logging miles of coastline and mountains, destroying the natural habitats of ocelots, marguays, mountain lions, jaguars, howler monkeys and scarlet macaws. Acres of wetland were drained to make way for a train line, constructed from the settlement of Quepos.

The banana business boomed until the 1960s, when a flood washed out the train lines and the banana trees were hit by Panamanian disease which destroyed the crop. The company then switched production to African oil palms and the government began construction of a road linking Quepos to Puntarenas. When Parque Nacional Manuel Antonio was established in 1972, the area was still sparsely populated. In 1980 the government allotted funds to pave the road to Puntarenas. Once the road was partially paved and completely graded people began arriving in droves, buying property and speculating on future tourism.

Costa Rica's financial boom in the 1980s fueled intense real estate speculation and hotel construction around the park, which became renown throughout the international tourism grapevine

as one of the most beautiful preserves in Central America. As the demand for palm oil has decreased, tourism has become the economic foundation for the ever-increasing population, who have become dependent upon the whims of tourism. Locals who have witnessed the changes in the region over the past 15 years are justifiably concerned about the future. Manuel Antonio's reputation has been sullied as word of overbuilding, congestion, and even the possible pollution of the sea has reached travelers. Still, it remains a special, unique place well worth exploring (but preferably during low season).

GENERAL INFORMATION

Quepos has no official tourist office. *Quepolandia*, a free English-language monthly publication is packed with tips, ads and information. Check for it in hotel lobbies and shops.

Getting around the area without a car is difficult. Most of the hotels are located between Quepos and the beach at Manuel Antonio, and only a few are within walking distance of either location. Car rentals can be arranged through hotels or **Elegante Rent-a-Car** (777-0115. A public bus runs between Quepos and Manuel Antonio every half hour from dawn until around 10 PM; depending on traffic, the trip takes about 20 minutes. Accommodating drivers will stop near your hotel. Taxis ply the Corridor all hours of night and day. Internet service is spotty along the Corridor, though the Costa Verde Hotel (see WHERE TO STAY, below) does offer access and may lower their rates. You're better off in Quepos, where **Internet Tropical** (777-2460 in front of the Hotel Malinche has several computers, a book exchange, long distance phone and fax service, and a café serving fruit smoothies and sandwiches. The **Jungle Net Café** (777-2595 across from Dos Locos restaurant in Quepos also has Internet access.

Given the area's popularity, it's wise to keep a close guard on your possessions: Don't leave keys or money lying on the beach and remove your luggage from your rental car before parking in public places.

WHAT TO SEE AND DO

Parque Nacional Manuel Antonio (777-0644 FAX 777-0654 is seven kilometers (five miles) from Quepos. Though it's one of Costa Rica's smallest parks at 683 ha (1687 acres), it's also one of the most lively. The wildlife that seems so elusive elsewhere is easily viewed here. In fact, hikers are warned to hold their packs and gear tight, since the park's monkeys are so accustomed to humans that they may try to snatch your lunch.

A guide pulls in an 11-kg (25-lb) wahoo, the highpoint of an exhilirating day on the water.

The entrance to the park is just a short walk from Manuel Antonio's hotels and parking lots across a shallow estuary. The stream that feeds the estuary and runs into the ocean sometimes rises waist high in rainy season. When it does, boaters are quick on the spot to carry you across for a small fee. The ranger station is just on the other side of the water. The park is open Tuesday through Sunday from 8 AM to 4 PM, and is closed Monday. No more than 600 people are admitted daily, so you may be turned away during high season. The fee is US$6 per day.

Trails lead to the three main beaches: Puerto Escondido, Playa Espadilla Sur and Playa Manuel Antonio. The surf and crowds are biggest at

snakes, and bashful spider monkeys. Unfortunately, the animals and humans grew too familiar with each other, the beaches became too crowded and the trails overtrodden. The park is now closed on Mondays and camping is not permitted at any time. More than 50% of the park's territory is closed; some out-of-the-way trails are accessible if you hike with a guide. Refrain from feeding the monkeys and touching the giant iguanas that perch on fallen logs by the trails; though the wildlife may seem abundant and friendly at first glance, many species are threatened by human interference. Manuel Antonio is one of the few natural habitats for spider monkeys, which have become the area's mascot. Hotels and restaurants near the park used

Espadilla; I prefer Playa Manuel Antonio's soft sands and tame waves. A longer, more arduous hike will bring you to the rocky beach at Puerto Escondido, accessible only at low tide. This is an agreeable hike for nature lovers even if you can not get all the way to the beach; with luck you will spot white-faced capuchin monkeys, sloths and coatis. Another trail leads to Punta Catedral, which was once an island and ceremonial site for the Quepoa Indians. The point is now linked to the beach by a *tómbolo*, a land bridge created by the accumulation of sediment and sand. Those who sweat through the 100-m (300-ft) climb up a steep trail to the point's *mirador* (lookout) are rewarded with wondrous views of the sea and Isla Mogote, another ceremonial Indian site.

The park was established in 1972 and for years visitors could camp on the beaches and underneath the trees and spot sloths, trogons, coral

to advertise "monkey hours" in the late afternoon, when the creatures crashed through the trees to the buildings and were rewarded with bananas and other food. Luring wild animals into civilization for human enjoyment makes the monkeys dependent on handouts. A campaign by local naturalists has succeeded in discouraging the hoteliers from this practice, but the monkeys haven't yet learned that the free handouts are over.

You needn't pay the park fee to appreciate Manuel Antonio's beaches. **Playa Espadilla**, also called Playa Número Uno, is just north of the park entrance. This public beach is immensely popular, though the surf can be very rough. Be very careful when swimming here. Vendors rent beach umbrellas, chairs and boogie boards beside the beach. Anyone owning a patch of dirt by the park and beach can call it a parking lot and charge a fee. In essence, there is no place to park for free.

At least your car will be somewhat safe in a pay lot, but don't leave any valuables in sight.

If you prefer to sample nature in a controlled setting, you'll be delighted with **Rain Maker** (777-2640 WEB SITE www.rainmaker.co.cr. Located about 48 km (30 miles) from Quepos in the Fila Chonta mountains, this 540-ha (1,334-acre) reserve has become a popular tourist attraction. The developers managed to combine excitement and safety in their rainforest experience by carving out well-maintained trails leading to a waterfall where hikers splash in chilly water and massage their muscles in the pounding cascade. The centerpiece of Rain Maker is a series of suspension bridges spanning a river gorge. The bridges are obviously

(/FAX 777-1262 E-MAIL iguana@sol.racsa.co.cr WEB SITE www.iguanatours.com in Quepos. Horseback riding tours to rivers, waterfalls and natural pools are available through **Quepos Trail Rides** (777-0489 and **Rancho Marlboro Stables** (777-1108. Riders compliment the quality of horses and guides at **Equus Stables** (777-0001. Sunset cruises and other boat excursions can be arranged through **Sunset Sails** (777-1304. The rivers around Manuel Antonio don't compare with those in the Meseta Central, but the rafting is decent, especially in the rainy season. **Amigos del Río** (777-0082 offers half-and full-day rafting excursions on the rivers Savegre and Naranjo; they also have ocean kayaking trips. If the traffic weren't so bad, mountain

well constructed and have railings you can grab as you walk along, but those with even a touch of acrophobia feel shivers of fear as they walk 20 stories above the river. The tour includes a very good *tico* lunch and transportation. Children must be seven years old to join the hikes, and twelve to cross the bridges. A bit more challenging is **Canopy Safari** (777-0100 WEB SITE www.odesafaris.com with cables strung through the treetops. Several operators now offer kayaking, rafting and sightseeing boat tours around **Isla Damas**, a small reserve surrounded by mangrove lagoons.

Costa Rica Adventure Travel (/FAX 777-0850 E-MAIL iguana@sol.racsa.co.cr, next to Hotel Sí Como No in the Corridor, is a full-service travel agency that can arrange nature hikes, canoeing and sport fishing, sunset sailboat rides and sea kayaking, in addition to other kinds of tours. Similar services are available from **Iguana Tours**

bikes would be the perfect transport along the Corridor. The more enjoyable bike trip with **Latin Outdoors** (383-1708 or 643-3433 E-MAIL outdoors@latinmail.com travels along dirt trails to a waterfall; the sunset tour is particularly enticing. You can climb and rappel or simply hike through jungle trails with **Canyoning Tours** (777-1924 WEB SITE www.canyoningtours.com.

Quepos is one of the main **sport fishing** centers on the Pacific coast. Serious anglers should reserve a boat and a captain in advance of their travels through **Pacific Coast Charters** (/FAX 777-1382, or **Blue Fin Sportfishing Charters** (777-1676 or 777-0674 FAX 777-0674 E-MAIL bluefin@sol .racsa.co.cr. The 13-m (42-ft) *Pescador* (777-0872

OPPOSITE: A baby monkey clings to its mother's back as she travels from tree to tree. ABOVE: It is possible to see capuchin monkeys swinging about in the trees that meet the beach on Playa Blanca.

E-MAIL jibmar@sol.racsa.co.cr is available for day and overnight fishing trips. **Aventuras Poseidon** (/FAX 777-0935 operates a 9.5-m (31-ft) Bertram.

An early morning or evening walk through the town of Quepos has its rewards. Start at the blue and purple **church** at the foot of the Corridor road, across from the ever-busy soccer field. Several small supermarkets, produce stands and sportswear shops line the main (unnamed) street from the Corridor to the waterfront, where a pathway leads past small fishing boats resting on the sand.

SHOPPING

Artists and artisans are drawn to this area — perhaps the natural beauty and international populace affects their creativity. **Regaleme** (777-0777 beside Sí Como No in the Corridor displays original paintings by Costa Rican artists, along with gorgeous handcrafted gold jewelry (including replicas of pieces found in San José's Museo de Oro), wooden boxes by Barry Beisanz, and unusual pottery. There is a second location in Quepos.

I usually stop by **La Buena Nota** (777-1002, at the Manuel Antonio end of the Corridor road, several times when I'm in the neighborhood. Anita Myketuk, who has been around Manuel Antonio for over 20 years, owns this souvenir, clothing, map and book shop filled with high-quality merchandise. Anita is one of the area's biggest promoters and defenders. She and her partner Donald (who passed away in 1999) were instrumental in creating the Fundación de Salvavidas, a foundation that helps pay lifeguards to patrol the public beaches, where drowning has been all too common. Anita stocks the shop with irresistible beachwear and a bounty of new and used books, and can answer most questions about the area with good humor.

Visitors who fall in love with Manuel Antonio buy bags of coffee from **Café Milagro** (see WHERE TO EAT, below) to bring back fond memories. The two locations also display works by local artists as well as a colorful array of cups, mugs, and other coffee accoutrements. Stop by **La Botánica** (/FAX 777-1223 in Quepos for a cup of herbal tea and browse through the enlightening array of herbs and spices gathered by owners Tey and Milo Bekins.

WHERE TO STAY

Manuel Antonio has an excess of rooms, yet the room rates here are higher than anywhere else in the country. In high season, budget travelers are relegated to small hostelries in downtown Quepos and *cabinas* just outside the park. Rates drop enough in low season that several places in the moderate range drop into the inexpensive category, especially in September and October. The most luxurious inns are in the Corridor facing the

sea, and though most are truly lovely, they might not live up to your expectations. Niceties like room service, direct-dial phones, televisions, gyms and spas are virtually nonexistent. Instead, you're paying for the view. Despite the abundance of rooms, advance reservations are essential for the hotels mentioned below. Some do not accept credit cards, or may tack on a service charge for their use. Some add a 10% service charge and 13% tax to the rate; to avoid sticker shock, ask if they are included when you check in.

Very Expensive

Los Angeles meets the jungle at **Sí Como No** (777-0777 FAX 777-1093 E-MAIL sicomono@sol.racsa.co.cr

WEBSITE www.sicomono.com. Owner Jim Damalas escaped a high-pressure life in California to build his low-key jungle resort, taking the environment in account along the way. The property may well be the most ecologically responsible in the neighborhood, with solar-powered energy, recycled water systems, and farm-grown hardwood used in construction. Guests are instructed to refrain from using the air-conditioning to save energy; it's nicer to open the doors to your balcony and catch the sea breeze. VIPs and regular old guests hang out at the hot tub, waterslide and free-form swimming pool and in the private peaked-roof villas tucked in the jungle. Stained-glass windows give the roadside lobby the feeling of a Pentecostal church, while hill trails and ocean views reflect a harmony with nature. It's the only hotel

OPPOSITE and ABOVE: Relaxation is a 24-hour affair at Sí Como No resort hotel.

around with its own movie theater, complete with popcorn stand.

It's hard to beat the secluded luxury at **Makanda by the Sea** (777-0442 FAX 777-1032 E-MAIL makanda@sol.racsa.co.cr WEB SITE www .makanda.com, on a winding road off the Corridor. The hotel's nine deluxe villas and studios are hidden amid the jungle and Japanese gardens and have vaulted hardwood ceilings, open-air living rooms with hammocks and cushioned couches, and king-sized beds draped with mosquito-net canopies. The pool seems to flow into the blue horizon, and the silence is broken only by chattering spider monkeys and birds. Employees outnumber guests, and the service is just one reason

the hotel stands out above the competition (it's also the most expensive place around). The villas are often claimed by wedding parties; Makanda has been featured in every bridal magazine on the stands. Children are neither seen nor heard; this is an adults-only property. The restaurant is excellent and exclusive.

One of the area's first deluxe hotels is on the same side road. A complete renovation has restored the beauty of **Hotel la Mariposa** (777-0355 TOLL-FREE IN THE US (800) 416-2747 (reservations) FAX 777-0050 E-MAIL mariposa@solracsa.co.cr WEB SITE www.lamariposa.com. Terracotta tiled roofs and white archways give the buildings a colonial flair, and the restaurant commands a breathtaking sunset view. Rooms seven to ten have hot tubs on the private terraces above the ocean, while rooms one to four have atrium bathrooms surrounded by plants. The Mariposa feels cozy and secluded,

which explains its continued popularity in the face of stiff competition.

Expensive

I like the friendly feeling at **Costa Verde** (777-0584 FAX 777-0560 E-MAIL costaver@sol.racsa.co.cr WEB SITE www.costaverde.com on the inland side of the Corridor road near the park. The variety of rooms is amazing, especially when you consider that the sprawling property has fewer than 50 of them. One building and pool is reserved for families with children, while another building houses standard rooms and gorgeous studios all with panoramic forest and ocean views and a separate pool. The newest suites are decorated with tile reproductions of famous paintings and custom made teak furniture. The older rooms (in yet another area) have a more rustic feeling; at times you feel as if you are alone in the forest. The fragrance of flowers from ilan-ilan trees wafts through the air like jasmine. Private nature trails lead through the jungle to the beach, the various clusters of rooms, and the restaurant. The hotel's property abuts the national park, and sloths and monkeys abound.

Stark white villas rise above the green forest at The **Hotel Casitas Eclipse** (777-0408 FAX 777-1738 E-MAIL eclipseh@sol.racsa.co.cr midway along the Corridor. You can book an entire *casita* with two bedrooms and a full kitchen, a suite with kitchenette, or a large standard room with a terrace or balcony. The pools and buildings are spread apart for optimum privacy.

Moderate

Monkeys do not need any handouts to encourage them to crash through the trees in front of the 12 villa suites terraced down a forested hillside at **Villas Nicolas** (777-0481 FAX 777-0451 E-MAIL nicolas@sol.racsa.co.cr WEB SITE www.villasnicolas .com, next door to Sí Como No in the Corridor. There were only two buildings in the complex when I first stayed here many years ago, watching the monkeys and a stray scorpion from the hammock on my hardwood deck. Most of the villas now have kitchenettes, and there's a large pool at the top of the property and long stairways leading to the nearly hidden villas. The rates are extremely reasonable, and many guests settle in for a week or more.

As soon as I climbed the tiled staircase to the open-air lobby I knew I'd found the friendliest accommodation in the Corridor at the **Hotel las Tres Banderas** (777-1871 or 777-1284 FAX 777-1478 E-MAIL info@hotel-tres-banderas.com WEB SITE www.hotel-tres-banderas.com near Quepos. I'd been hearing about this little gem from travelers all over the country, and quickly got the scoop from the guests sipping gin and tonics by the front desk. One couple had returned three times in two months to their favorite room after finding other beach towns and hotels lacking. The compact building is tastefully designed with white arches and wooden railings on the balconies of each of the 14 rooms, all with air-conditioning. The hot tub and swimming pool are backed by the jungle behind the property, where the presence of sloths, monkeys and birds make up for the lack of a sea view. The chef whips up gourmet breakfasts and dinners for the guests, who find little reason to leave the property. Rates are just a tad above the inexpensive range.

The guests are a polyglot crew at the **Plinio Hotel (** 777-0055 FAX 777-0558 E-MAIL plinio@sol .racsa.co.cr WEB SITE www.pliniopark .com, near

Quepos on the Corridor road. A pool, restaurant and 12 rooms, suites and apartments are staggered up a hillside (lots of stairs here); the three-story suites with rooftop decks and room for four persons are a good deal. Nearly five kilometers (three miles) of trails lead uphill to clearings with great views of the forest and sea. The restaurant is one of the best around. Down by the national park, **Hotel Villabosque (** 777-0463 FAX 777-0401 is a great choice for those without cars. The 15 rooms are air-conditioned and have good screens (bugs are a bit of a problem since the hotel sits right above a stream). From time to time you can see monkeys from the small swimming pool on a second-story deck. The beach and park are within easy walking distance.

One of the few *tico*-owned hotels in the area, **Divisamar (** 777-0371 FAX 777-0525 E-MAIL divisa mar@sol.racsa.co.cr WEB SITE www .divisamar.com

is on the inland side of the Corridor road. Rates for air-conditioned rooms are less than at most hotels in this category, and the three-story buildings face a good-sized swimming pool. A bank is supposed to open in the small shopping center next to the hotel, bringing ATM service to the Corridor.

The standout among the modest (and overpriced) selections in downtown Quepos is the **Hotel Sirena (**/FAX 777-0528, one block from the bridge into Quepos. Anglers fill most of the 14 rooms, which have air-conditioning, small refrigerators and powerful showers but no televisions or telephones. The rooms face the swimming pool and restaurant, secluded from the street noise by exterior walls. An acceptable alternative is the **Hotel Kamuk (** 777-0811 FAX 777-0258, across the street from the Quepos waterfront. The best rooms, if you don't mind street noise, are those on the third floor with balconies overlooking the sea. There's a pool and restaurant.

Inexpensive

Budget-priced options are extremely limited during high season. The most desirable option in the Corridor is **El Mono Azul (** 777-1548 FAX 777-1954 E-MAIL monoazul@racsa.co.cr WEB SITE www .monoazul.com. A small hotel run by Jennifer Rice, an American woman with a generous spirit, Mono Azul keeps growing and getting even better. There are 20 rooms now, with more to come. Some have air-conditioning, some have bathtubs, some face the pool. Rice has devoted part of the hotel's shops to the Amazing Arts Gallery, where local children are involved in saving the rare titi monkeys who are found only in this region. The kids sell a children's book, *The legend of the Blue Monkey*, and crafts; proceeds go to building monkey bridges above the roads and to financing the purchase of a plot of rainforest. Rice also hosts weekly AA meetings. **La Colina B&B (** 777-0231 FAX 777-1553 E-MAIL lacolina@sol.racsa.co.cr WEB SITE www .lacolina.com in the Corridor is a classy inn with 11 nicely furnished rooms.

Other inexpensive places are closer to the beach and park entrance in Manuel Antonio. **Hotel Cabinas Vela-Bar (** 777-0413 FAX 777-1071 WEB SITE www.maqbeach.com is next to the park and has 11 rooms of varying prices and comfort with hammocks on the front porches. **Cabinas Pisces (** 777-0046, located on the beach side of the road, has small, basic rooms with shared baths.

The least expensive rooms are in downtown Quepos. Before settling in here, take into account the money you'll spend on buses and taxis to and from the beach and park. Backpackers have long relied on the clean, basic rooms at **Hotel Malinche**

OPPOSITE: The beach can be utterly mesmerizing. ABOVE: A fresh coconut is essential for a day on the sand.

(777-0093, near the entrance to Quepos. Consider paying the few extra bucks for air-conditioning or a fan so you can close your windows and block out street noise. **Hotel Quepos** (777-0274 is at the opposite end of town near the bus station and the road to the Corridor. The rooms have ceiling fans, and the management is very accommodating.

WHERE TO EAT

Manuel Antonio has the best selection of gringo-style restaurants outside San José, with comparably pricey pasta, seafood and steaks. Many of the best places are in the hotels. There are precious few budget restaurants in the Corridor and only

reviving. Don't splurge on the most expensive items just yet; instead, come by at sunset, order cocktails, and linger over a dinner of grilled fish.

Moderate

Locals craving something different for dinner can count on Isolde at **Plinio's** (777-0055. One day she'll make Hungarian goulash; the next day its Chinese pot stickers, spinach lasagna or German sausage with mashed potatoes. The spicy Thai curries and satays are a wonderful alternative to a steady diet of grilled fish and rice, though even fish tastes better when Isolde wraps it in banana leaves and herbs. I've enjoyed every part of every meal I've ever had here. Plinio's **Ranchito Bar** by

a few overpriced markets and delis. Stock up on snacks at the grocery stores in Quepos.

Expensive

Make reservations for lunch or dinner at **Sunspot** (777-0442, the casually elegant restaurant at Makanda by the Sea. The lunch menu focuses on crowd pleasers including gourmet pizzas, burgers and sandwiches on grilled focaccia. Dinner is more elaborate, and you're sure to be stumped by the options. Try the grilled asparagus, rack of lamb with jalapeño glaze, chicken breast stuffed with goat cheese, or go all out and order the lobster with saffron garlic sauce. Save for best sundress or aloha shirt for the occasion. The dining room at **La Mariposa** (777-0456 commands the best views on the Corridor, and the food is beginning to equal the ambiance. After several years of shaky service and dubious quality, the restaurant seems to be

the pool is overseen by Albert, "The Sausage King," who serves spicy grilled bratwurst with onions and sauerkraut. **Barba Roja** (777-0331, midway along the Corridor road, is a traditional standby serving bountiful sandwiches, salads and piles of french fries at lunch and more expensive grilled fish and steaks at dinner. The wooden deck dining area and outside terrace are gathering spots for locals and travelers, and you'll pick up some great travel tips from the crowd gathered at the bar.

Don't let the steep dirt drive beside Barba Roja put you off. Just turn at the sign and head down to **Karolas** (777-1557, one of the prettiest secluded restaurants in Manuel Antonio. Once an out-of-the-way discovery, Karola's has become so popular dinner reservations are a must in high season. Tables covered with pastel cloths are set amidst flowers and trees; stop here for lunch on a clear day and you'll see the ocean shimmering below the forest. Fruit daiquiris are served by the pitcher to accompany lunches and dinners of yellowfin tuna sashimi with wasabi, coconut-fried fish, black bean and avocado quesadillas, and barbecued baby back ribs. Monkeys gather in the trees around sunset outside **Anaconda** (777-0584 at the Hotel Costa Verde. Maybe they're drawn by the salsa music playing in the second-story dance hall, where salsa lessons take place at 4:30 PM every afternoon. The restaurant is open from breakfast till after dinner, and serves good-sized portions of fresh fish and marinated beef. The hotel's other restaurant, **La Cantina**, is located across the street behind a 1912 vintage rail car from Chile. You can't miss it — a huge fire burns by the front door, reminding diners to order grilled steaks and shrimp. The chef prepares the best barbecued pork ribs with baked potato around. Sports events are shown on the cable television at the bar, and a live band plays most evenings. You can access the Internet from the computers in the train car. **Pickles** (777-1597, right next door to Sí Como No in the Corridor, is a wonderful deli that serves an assortment of salads, sausage and pepper subs, seared ahi on foccacio, rosemary lemon chicken, pastrami and rueben sandwiches and sinful ice cream sundaes. Eat at the outside tables or take your lunch to the beach.

Inexpensive

Early risers sip espresso while reading the *International Herald Tribune* at the bright yellow and purple **Café Milagro** (/FAX 777-2272 WEB SITE www.cafemilagro.com. The original branch of this coffee shop is located in Quepos across from the waterfront, and is a great spot for thumbing through used magazines, playing chess, and meeting local expatriates; the second branch is in the Manuel Antonio across from Karola's. Both brew up great coffee drinks (try the mocha caramel cooler to beat the heat), whip up fresh fruit smoothies and ice cream shakes, and display a tempting array of muffins (try the lemon poppy seed variety), brownies, and bagels. Full breakfast is served at the Manuel Antonio location. Café Milagro roasts its own coffee beans. Stuff as many bags as you can in your suitcase. Your friends will love the gift (though you're sure to hoard several bags for your personal stash).

Vegetarians are thrilled with the piles of grilled veggies topping salads and pizzas at **El Mono Azul** (777-1954, in the Corridor near Quepos. Carnivores needn't feel left out — the ribs, steaks, and grilled chicken are great, as are the burgers on whole-wheat buns. Too burned out to dine out? Order a pepperoni or pineapple pizza and have it delivered to your hotel.

You haven't visited Manuel Antonio until you've sipped a cool drink at **Mar y Sombra** (777-0468 by the beach. This outdoor café and bar has

been a popular gathering spot for more years than I can remember. You don't hang out here for the food, though the grilled fish, sandwiches, and *casados* are decent. Instead, you take up residence at one of the cement tables near the sand and watch the crowd pass by.

Most inexpensive *sodas* are located in Quepos, where locals feast on huge breakfasts of gallo pinto and eggs at **El Almendro** (777-1806 in downtown Quepos. Open 24 hours, this simple café is the best place to try Costa Rican casados. Fishermen favor the United States-style **El Gran Escape** (777-0395, both for the inspirational photos of huge marlin and sailfish on the walls and the reliable menu of salsa and chips, fajitas, spicy chicken wings and burgers. You can count on getting fish straight from the sea. **Wacky Wanda's** (777-2245 may well be the most happening bar in town. Fortunately, Wanda serves nachos, tacos, fried chicken, and sandwiches along with the piña coladas and beer. The bartenders at **Dos Locos** (777-1526 make a mean margarita, the perfect accompaniment to nachos and tacos.

How to Get There

Both SANSA and TravelAir have daily flights to the Quepos airstrip (which just happens to be next door to the hospital), about a 15-minute drive from town. Taxis meet all flights.

Drivers from San José arrive via the Costanera Sur, which meets the Carretera Interamericana at Puntarenas; the drive takes about four hours. The road is paved through stretches north of Quepos, but it is still quite rough in other places. Watch out for the horrid bridges made of metal pipes welded together — they're narrow, slippery, and downright dangerous. Workers were constructing new bridges in 2000, but they didn't seem to be in any rush to get them done. This section of road is one of the scariest in the country because so many unwary tourists race along merrily, and then brake suddenly when they hit potholes. Take your time. From the south, the Costanera Sur travels through palm plantations from Dominical.

There is frequent bus service from San José and Puntarenas; the bus station is two blocks north of the Corridor road to Manuel Antonio, near the soccer field. Express buses travel to Puntarenas and San José, and are by far the most desirable option. Purchase your tickets way in advance of your travel dates in high season. Buses travel hourly from dawn until 10 PM from the Quepos bus station along the Corridor to Manuel Antonio. Ask the driver to let you off at your hotel. **Gray Line**, in operation with **Fantasy Tours** ((800) 326-8279 in Costa Rica, offers private transport to and from San José.

Terraces are favorite sunset hangouts.

DOMINICAL

The throb and pulse of Manuel Antonio has yet to infect Dominical, some 42 km (26 miles) south of Quepos. The 200 or so residents here all seem to know each other and have a vested interest in keeping their town small and sedate. Gentrification by foreign residents has brought about a modern mini-mall which features a small supermarket, a real estate office, and the Mercado del Mundo gift shop. One developer is handing out glossy brochures seeking investors for a beachfront hotel–condominium project.

But for now, the small town of Dominical is a tranquil place with one main street, or two if you count the sandy beach road. Small *cabina* hotels and informal restaurants in town and along outlying beaches cater to the surf and budget crowd. Others are clustered in Escaleras (Stair-steps), a steep hilltop overlooking the ocean. The road to Escaleras is rough and rutted, more suited to a four-wheel-drive vehicle than a sedan (which might suffice in dry season).

Dominical is so remote that most homes and businesses didn't have phone service until 1999. Most hotels are now on line, though a few remote lodges rely on radio communications. Electricity is sporadic; many hotels have generators or use solar power.

WHAT TO SEE AND DO

Dominical's waves have long been popular with surfers, but the current is too rough for casual swimmers. **Playa Hermosa** to the south is cleaner and prettier than the beaches right in town.

Escaleras is a great area for horseback riding. Bella Vista hotel and ranch has both spirited and gentle native *crillio* horses for long rides up and down hillsides and onto the beach where the horses gallop with utter abandon and riders whoop and scream with glee. Most riders stop by **Cascada Dominicalito** for a brisk splash in small natural pools before heading back to the ranch. Full-day rides take in the hilltops and **Cascadas Nauyaca** and **Pozo Azul**.

Few vistas can beat the treetop view from the forest canopy at Hacienda Barú (see WHERE TO STAY, below). The 336-ha (830-acre) private nature reserve encompasses beach, the Río Barú valley, forests and highland fields with pre-Columbian petroglyphs hidden in the rocks. Hikes, horseback rides and a 30-m-high (100-ft) observation platform in the trees keep day-trippers busy. Overnight guests can choose from tents in the forest or cabins by the beach. The Río Barú feeds a spectacular double waterfall called Las Cataratas Nauyaca. You can hike to the falls on your own, but I recommend you join a tour with Don

Lulo's Nauyaca Waterfalls (787-0198 FAX 771-2003. Guides lead guests on a horseback ride along Dominical beach, breakfast and a tour of Don Lulo's mini zoo (with tame macaws and toucans), then a ride to the waterfalls for a dip in the natural pools. Lunch is served at a rancho in the woods. Don Lulo's has a few campsites with restrooms and potable water.

There are more humpbacked whales than tourists at Parque Nacional Marino Ballena, 16 km (10 miles) south of Dominical. The whales migrate to the marine preserve from December to March, while dolphins, pelicans and frigate birds are visible year round. The park is not developed for tourism, but you can arrange boat tours through hotels in Dominical.

WHERE TO STAY

Dominical has a wide range of accommodation, including luxurious small inns, *cabinas* on the beach and nature preserves. Make advance reservations by faxing or e-mailing the properties themselves, or contact **Selva Mar** (771-4582 FAX 771-1903 E-MAIL selvamar@sol.racsa.co.cr, a tour company with an office in San Isidro de el General.

Expensive

Guests are asked to take off their shoes before walking across the gorgeous purple-heart wood floor in the main dining room and deck at Dominical's most elegant property, the **Escaleras Inn** (/FAX 771-5247 in Escaleras. Three villas are decked out with Guatemalan textiles, Boruca Indian masks, and tropical plants and have huge bathrooms with powerful showers. The inn's excellent restaurant has closed, unfortunately, and guests must prepare their meals in the villas' blue-and-white tiled kitchen stocked with hand-painted dishes.

Moderate

The largest resort in the area is the **Villas Río Mar** (787-0052 FAX 787-0054 E-MAIL hotel@villas riomar.com WEBSITE www.villasriomar.com, north of town on the Río Barú. Each of the 40 large rooms has an outdoor living area with a wet bar, small refrigerator and cushioned bamboo chairs; white gauze curtains can be pulled aside or draped around the terrace for privacy. Constructed with interior bamboo walls and thatched roofs, the buildings are set amidst mature landscaping backed by forest. A large pool sits in the center of the complex, which also includes a tennis court, a restaurant suitable for large groups, a hot tub and exercise equipment. The only drawback here is the 20-minute walk to the sea. As one local wag put it, "The owners came 10,000 km (6,000 miles) from Holland to build a hotel. You'd think they would have gone the extra mile to the beach."

South of town, a small road twists to the end of a rocky point to **Cabinas Punta Dominical** (/FAX 787-0016 or 787-0017. Four older hardwood cabins (each housing up to six people) are set under huge mango trees on a point with water on both sides of the buildings. Air filters in through screened and louvered walls; the hammocks hanging on each porch are perfect perches for watching the sea. The restaurant here serves good seafood. Also in the south, **Roca Verde** (787-0036 FAX 787-0013 E-MAIL rocaver@racsa.co.cr WEB SITE www.doshermanos.com has a gorgeous view and rooms to match. The small inn has 10 artistically decorated rooms set in the hillside above the popular restaurant and large pool.

Camping and *cabinas* with hot showers are both available at **Hacienda Barú** (787-0003 FAX 787-0004 E-MAIL sstroud@sol.racsa.co.cr WEB SITE www .haciendabaru.com, just north of Dominical en route to Quepos. Guests rave about their time here and appreciate the full immersion in nature that Barú offers. Few other places so close to the coast do as well.

Inexpensive

The fairly modest **Bella Vista Ranch and Guest Lodge** (771-1903 or 388-0155 (cell phone) WEB SITE www.bellavistalodge.com is surrounded by forest on a hilltop in Escaleras, and has three guest rooms in a converted farmhouse on a working cattle ranch. The deck along one side of the house overlooks the ocean; meals are available on request. The ranch also offers horseback riding lessons and excursions. Across the dirt road from Bella Vista is **Finca Brian y Milena** (/FAX 771-1903, a working tropical fruit and nut farm with day and overnight tours. Guests stay in rooms with shared baths. The unusual wood-fire heated hot tub is the perfect star gazing spot. Also in Escaleras is **Pacific Edge** (/FAX 787-0031 or 771-1903 which has four cabins on a forested hillside, each with an outdoor living area, a kitchenette and solar-heated water.

Cabinas Nayarit (787-0033 is my favorite budget restaurant and hotel right on the beach in town. The white buildings with blue trim are well maintained; the more expensive buildings have air-conditioning. Aromas from the restaurant keep guests in a constant state of hunger, easily sated with a big plate of crisp french fries and grilled fish. The tables under fans within the restaurant are the coolest place to eat, but I prefer the cement tables with umbrellas right on the sand.

WHERE TO EAT

The hotel restaurants mentioned above serve some of the best meals in the area. **Roca Verde** is the happening place on Saturday nights, when diners fueled by pasta and fresh fish move onto the dance floor to the beat of salsa and merengue music. **Thrusters** (787-0127 right in town is a wave riders hangout serving sandwiches, burgers, brownies, and espresso. The dart board, pool tables, television and Saturday night disco make it the entertainment center of Dominical. Thrusters now has a few inexpensive rooms for rent. The **San Clemente Bar and Grill** (787-0026, across from Playa Dominical, is a Mexican-American homestyle restaurant serving inexpensive breakfasts and full meals. **Restaurant Su Raza** (787-0105, by the soccer field, is the best place for *gallo pinto* and *casados*, and they also serve excellent french fries and fried chicken.

HOW TO GET THERE

Dominical is 42 km (26 miles) south of Quepos on the Costanera Sur. The road is an alternate to the Carretera Interamericana south of San José and is partially paved. The drive past palm plantations and small workers' villages takes at least 90 minutes. The alternate route, if coming from San José, is to take the Carretera Interamericana south from the city through Cerro de la Muerte to San Isidro de el General. An unnamed road leads west from the main intersection in San Isidro to Dominical; the drive takes about 60 minutes. There is frequent bus service from San José to Quepos or San Isidro de el General with connections in both towns for Dominical.

A colorful café sign beckons vacationers.

The Zona Sur

UNTOUCHED FOR CENTURIES, the Zona Sur is the last great Costa Rican wilderness for travelers to explore in relative isolation. The Cordillera Talamanca divides the two coasts of southern Costa Rica, providing a landscape of high peaks, rushing rivers, cloud forests and fertile valleys. At the far south, the Pacific coast curves along the wild Península de Osa and Península de Burica, where tiny settlements are bordered by seemingly endless rainforest. Few roads pass along the mountains into the southern zone; in fact, the best route is the rough and risky Carretera Interamericana. Buses, huge logging and tractor-trailer trucks, and puny sedans power along the highway's twists and turns, providing a thrilling, albeit frightening, rush.

The highway runs south from San José and the Meseta Central, then quickly climbs the mountain foothills to a series of peaks, called *cerros*, many bordered by national parks and reserves. The most famous, and most aptly named, is Cerro de la Muerte — the Hill of Death. Though the name precedes the highway, which was completed in the 1950s, most drivers agree that this is indeed a deadly stretch of potholes, rough pavement and steep cliffs often shrouded in rain and fog. Many of the potholes were patched and sections of the road resurfaced in 1999 and 2000, but no amount

PRECEEDING PAGES: An iguana LEFT poses in the trees in a coastal rainforest. Villagers, such as this girl RIGHT, in the Bahía Drake must travel by foot, boat or horseback to leave their idyllic settlements.
ABOVE: Keel-billed toucans are among the forest's more amusing characters, and can be spotted in lodges on the Osa and Burica peninsulas. OPPOSITE: Burros transport milk through the highlands.

of roadwork can improve the weather conditions (and the insanity of suicidal drivers). When the skies are clear the views are astonishing — some days it's possible to see both coasts and the snow-shrouded Cerro Chirripó, the highest peak in the country. Small lodges tucked in valleys and hills provide their guests with some of the best bird watching and hiking in the country. Comparable to the wildly popular Monteverde region in northern Guanacaste, this untrammeled area harbors hundreds of reclusive resplendent quetzals, the sacred bird of the ancient Maya.

The highway continues on south to San Isidro de el General, where a side road meanders to the central Pacific coast and Dominical. Farther south at Palmar Sur, another side road travels north along the coast, past tiny beach communities popular with diehard surfers. The land becomes more rugged and unpopulated from Palmar south, as rivers carve the coastline into lagoons and mangrove swamps framing the sea. Those who brave tiny byways to the Golfo Dulce and two southern peninsulas, the Osa and the Burica, are rewarded with sublime isolation and superb natural settings. The nature lodges here have been built at great physical and financial expense. Owners talk of arriving via dugout canoe, slogging through deep mud, hacking trails with machetes and laying gravel roads by shovel load after shovel load of rock. Guests are similarly awed by nature's grasp on the area, and become accustomed to wearing knee-high boots on mud trails, accepting red clay stains on their socks, dodging and ducking through thrashing branches and clinging vines. Having traveled both coasts extensively, I can say this outpost of civilization is my favorite coastal region, filled with the morning growls of howler monkeys, the evening screeches of scarlet macaws and an overall sense of true wilderness.

There are no sources for tourist information in the region outside the hotels; telephones are few and electricity is sparse. The Cámara de Comercio (Chamber of Commerce) for the region has put together an excellent WEB SITE www.ecotourism .co.cr that helps spread the word about remote lodges, area hotels, and activities.

CERRO DE LA MUERTE

Several small towns dot the highway around Cerro de la Muerte, some bordering the Parque Nacional Tapantí. The park is one of the more difficult ones to access; the best entry is from Orosí (see OROSÍ VALLEY, page 104 in THE MESETA CENTRAL). The region sits 2,100 to 2,500 m (7,000 to 8,000 ft) above sea level, and some peaks poke into the cloud forests while valleys are often shrouded in mist. Easily accessed from San José, which is only about 80 km (50 miles) north, the region has become a popular day tour from the city.

ZONA SUR

CARTAGO

LIMÓN

Cordillera Talamanca

PUNTARENAS

Cerro Matama
2,251 m

Río Estrella

Penhurst

Guaria
Pandora   Cahuita

Vesta

Cerro
Tsuitebeta
2,378 m

Cuen

Reserva Biológica
Hitoy-Cereré

Valle de Las Rosas

Hotel
Bibri

Cerro
Dichíbeta
1,420 m

Uatsi

Tres de Junio
Salsipuedes

Ojo de Agua

Cerro
de la
Muerte
3,491 m

Villa Mills

Parque Nacional Chirripó

Teliré

Shiroles

Suretka   Bratsi

Katsi

San José Cabécar

Amubri

Namucki

Br

Cerro
Punibeta
2,345 m

Cerro Nimaso
1,093 m

Cerro División
3,510 m

Siberia

Alaska

Cerro Urán
3,333 m

División

Piedra

Santo Tomás

Río Blanco

Santa
Eduviges

Hortensia
La Ese

San Gerardo de Rivas

Cerro el Chirripó
3,819m

Alto Lari

Coriña

San Ramón Norte

Quebradas

Perez Zeledón

Cerro Amí
3,295 m

Cerro Eli
3,097 m

Cerro Dúrika
3,280 m

Purisquí

Santa Rosa

Rivas

Chimirol

San Isidro de el General

San Rafael Norte

Cerro Ena
3,126 m

Cerro
Cabécar
3,030 m

Cerro Utyum
3,078 m

Guaria

Palma Chiles

General Viejo

Santa
Elena

Cedral

Esperanzas

Parque

Cerro
Kámuk
3,549 m

Guabo

Rosario

Palmares

Santa María

Guaria

Internacional

Tinamastes

Agnostura

Repunta

Cajón

San
Pedro

La Amistad

Barú

Juntas

Fortuna

Altamira

Cerro Nai
3,122 m

Cerro Aká
2,259 m

San Luis

Ceibo

Patio de Agua

Santa Ana

Angel Arriba

San Rafael

Ujarras

Dominical

San Rafael

Mesas

Cacao

Cordoncillo

Volcán

Las Cañas

Salitre

Cerro Bine
3,204 m

Playa Hermosa

Uvita

Pejibaye

San
Antonio

Pavones

Peje

Palma

Buenos Aires

Cabagra

Punta
Uvita

Piñuela

Tortuga Arriba

Moctezuma

Danta

Caracol

Pilas

Animas
Térraba

Platanares
Florida

El Brujo   Bolas

Mosca

Helechales

Cerro Echandi
3,16

Playa Uvita

Tortuga Abajo

San Rafael

Colinas

Bijagual

San Antonio

Guadalupe

Potrero
Grande

Finca Colorado

Playa Ballena

Punta Mala

San Buenaventura

Maíz de Boruoa

Boruca

Paso Real

Quijada

Naranjal

Agua Caliente

Playa Piñuela

Ojo de Agua

Palmar
Norte

Indian Reserve

Puerto Nuevo

Currè

Alto Cacao

Vueltas

Coto Brus

Santa Fé

Santa Elena   Palmira

Cortés

Olla Cero

Cajón

Chánguena

Guácimo

Bonanza

Flor del Roble

Playa Boca Brava

Palmar Sur

Paraíso

Alto Angeles

Santa Cecilia

Jabillo

San Miguel

Piedro Pintada

Río Negro

Valle
de
Diquís

Finca

Río Sierpe

Villa Colón

Santa Lucia

Pilón

Sabanillo

Aguas Claras

Bahía
de
Coronado

San Francisco

Fila

Paraíso

Bajo Reyes

Lourdes   Sabalito

Sierpe

Cerro Anguciana
1,707 m

Limoncito

Santa Clara

San Vito   Río Se

Playa Violín

Potreoro

Chacarito

Piedras Blancas

Las Cruces
Biological Station

Wilson Botanical
Gardens

Copal

Cañas Gorder

Playa Ganado

Navidad

Agua Buena
dos y Medio

Los Planes

Bahía
Drake

Mogos

Ríyito

Guarito

Refugio
Nacional
de Fauna
Silvestre Golfito

Kilometro

Campo
dos y Medio

Aguajitas

Rincón

Golfo Dulce

Parque Nacional
Corcovado

Río Claro

Caracol

Abrojo

Playa San Josecito

Punta San
Pedrillo

San Pedrillo

Los Patos

La Palma

Playa Cativo

Golfito

Esperanza

Cuidad Nevilly (Villa)

Coto 47   Coloradi

Parque Nacional Corcovado

Barrigones

Playa Josecito

Santa Rita

Gloria

Dariz

Punta Llorona

Playa Llorona

Sirena

Playa
Platanares

Zancudo

Pueblo Nuevo

Colorado

Can

Playa Corcovado

Sirena

Puerto Jiménez

Playa
Zapote

Sábalos

Playa
Zancudo

Jobo Civil

La Cue

Playa Sirena

Madrigal

Península de Osa

Agua Buena

Playa
Tamales

Conte

Laurel

Punta
Salsipedes

Carate

Finca Ojo de Agua

Puerto Pilón

Bella Luz

Playa
Sombrero

Nicaragua

Península
de Burica

N
W   E
S

San José

0   4   8   12   16 km
0   2   4   6   8 10 miles

This is an area for hiking, bird watching and for relaxing in isolated lodges. Some lodges offer trout fishing in the Río Savegre, and mountain bikers who bring their own gear delight in the maze of dirt trails running through the forest. If you have a four-wheel-drive vehicle you can explore the small villages of Santa María de Dota and Copey by turning west off the highway at Empalme. San Gerardo de Dota, several kilometers south, is set in a valley at the foot of a narrow, twisting road, and has a few lodging options.

WHERE TO STAY

Small family-run lodges are nestled in forest and valleys off the highway. Most offer hot water and some have fireplaces or wood stoves to ward off the evening chill, which can be penetrating, especially during rainy season. Bring a warm jacket or sweater, heavy socks and a durable rain poncho. It's best to make reservations in advance through fax or phone; mail service is almost nonexistent here.

Expensive

Don Efraín Chacón and his multigenerational family operate **Cabinas Chacón**, also called **Savegre Lodge** (771-1732 or 284-1444 FAX 551-0070, in San Gerardo de Dota, at the Km. 80 turn-off from the highway. Don Efraín's name has long been synonymous with quetzals, and his property is filled with laurel trees that keep the birds happy year round. Hummingbirds, trogons, toucanettes, and at least 100 other species keep bird watchers occupied, while anglers delight in fishing for trout in the Río Savegre, which runs through the property. The complex includes 20 basic cabins with a restaurant and private baths that serves overnight guests and day trippers. **Costa Rica Expeditions** (see TAKING A TOUR, page 46 in YOUR CHOICE) works closely with Don Efraín and his family, and offers bird-watching and trout-fishing tours in this area. They also have guided hikes on Cerro de la Muerte. Meals are included in the rate, which bumps the lodge into the expensive range.

Moderate

A rough road leads east from the church in Cañon (look for the sign hand-painted with birds and bromeliads) to **Genesis II** (/FAX 381-0739 E-MAIL cinfo@genesis-two.com WEB SITE www.genesis-two.com. Settled into the cloud forest almost 2,360 m (7,500 ft) above sea level, this private reserve and lodge are run by Steve and Paula Friedman with the help of a cadre of volunteers. At least 150 species of birds have been spotted in the 38-ha (95-acre) reserve, including quetzals and rare three-wattled bellbirds with their distinctive folds of skin hanging from their beaks

and throats. Genesis has four guestrooms in a central lodge with two shared hot-water baths. Meals are served family style. The preserve at Genesis is an official private wildlife refuge, and there is a charge to hike the trails. New to the property is the **Talamanca Treescape Tour**, a canopy tour with three platforms, two ziplines and a suspension bridge. Unlike other such tours, this one overlooks primary forest and the Parque Nacional Macizo de la Muerte. You needn't stay at the lodge to tackle the canopy, but the Friedman's do appreciate advance notice if you'd like to take the tour or stop by for a meal. Genesis also has a wooden platform where campers can set up their tents for a small fee. Meals are not included in the rate.

In San Gerardo, the **Trogon Lodge** (/FAX 771-1266 WEB SITE www.grupomawamba.com, is operated by the same folks that own the excellent Mawamba Lodge in Tortuguero. Cabins spread around the gardens house 10 rooms with private baths and wood stoves. The hot tub and sauna are a great touch on chilly evenings. Meals, not included in the rate, are excellent, and the guides are top notch. Quetzal seekers are delighted with **Finca de Serrano**, also called **Alburgue Mirador de Quetzales** (381-8456 (cell phone), at Km. 70 off the Carretera Interamericana, where Don Eddie Serrano and his family have lived for over three decades. Two hardwood cabins have separate toilet and shower rooms, bunks, queen beds and private porches. The main lodge has seven rooms with shared bath, and a dining room serving *tico* meals. Don Eddie is a master at spotting quetzals, who nest in the giant laurel trees throughout the property; they're easiest to see from November to May.

Inexpensive

Turn off the highway at Km. 107 in División to reach **Avalon Reserve & Lodge** (/FAX 771-7264 or 380-2107 (cell phone) E-MAIL glenmom@racsa.co.cr. Avalon has 150 ha (375 acres) of cloud, primary and secondary forest, with portions of land that were cleared in the past for pastures. The best lodgings are in a private hardwood cabin with two beds downstairs and an upper sleeping loft, powerful hot showers and a back porch nearly buried in the forest. A second cabin has private and communal rooms with shared baths; camping is also allowed. Though Avalon began as a tourism project, new owners are concentrating on creating a research station where scientists can study the fauna and flora of the area. Volunteers are encouraged to spend a week or more helping to build a lab or maintain trails, in exchange for greatly reduced room rates and a chance to become immersed in the cloud forest. You can stay here quite cheaply, and eat good inexpensive meals in the main lodge.

Cabinas del Quetzal (771-2077, San Gerardo de Dota, near the Cabinas Chacón, is operated by Rodolfo Chacón. It's a good option for those on a budget. Two communal cabins with baths are available.

HOW TO GET THERE

By car, exit San José through the southeastern suburb of San Pedro and follow signs to Cartago and San Isidro de el General. Turn off the main road at the signs for the various lodges. Though a short distance, the trip can take two hours or more. Buses run from San José to San Isidro, with stops along the way. Most lodges will arrange

transport from the bus stop if you call ahead. Don't expect to find phones or taxis along the road.

SAN ISIDRO DE EL GENERAL

The Cerro División, just south of Cerro de la Muerte, is the highest stretch of the Carretera Interamericana, at 3,510 m (11,500 ft). From here the road descends into the Valle de San Isidro, a rich agricultural area that has grown steadily since the 1950s. If traveling this stretch of the highway in February and March you'll see roadside stands selling huge white flowers called the *flor de itabo*, a delicacy when mixed with scrambled eggs. The flowers bloom on the yucca hedge, which is often used as a live fence because it is easy to reproduce from wood cuttings and protects the soil from erosion. The entire landscape changes quickly here with the decrease in altitude as the road slides down into the valley; watch for mud, rocks and trucks with bad brakes.

San Isidro de el General, with a population of 41,000, is the largest town in the Zona Sur. A relatively new town, San Isidro has become popular with *ticos* and foreign residents seeking clean air, a favorable climate and uncrowded surroundings. The town makes a good rest stop when en route to Dominical and the central Pacific, 29 km

(18 miles) southwest of San Isidro on Highway 22. It also serves as a base for visiting the Parque Nacional Chirripó and other nearby sights.

There are plenty of markets, pharmacies, gas stations and public phones along the highway through town.

WHERE TO STAY AND EAT

Several small hotels in San Isidro cater to truck drivers and business people; none are particularly noteworthy but it's good to know you can probably find a room if you're running late on your drive south or just need a break.

The inexpensive, resort-like **Hotel del Sur (** 771-3033 FAX 771-0527 is located four kilometers (two and a half miles) south of San Isidro. A popular weekend getaway for *josefinos*, the resort has 47 rooms and 10 cabins set in a grove of trees and gardens just off the highway. The large pool is a blissful place to work out driving kinks, and facilities include a restaurant, volleyball and tennis courts and transportation to nearby sights.

I've been tempted to go far out of my way when touring the Zona Sur just for another meal at **Mirador Vista del Valle (** 284-4685, located at Km. 119 on the Interamericana Sur, a 20-minute drive north of San Isidro (moderate). I first discovered the restaurant one early morning after a night in División, and devoured a huge breakfast that satisfied my hunger throughout the day. Owners Flor and Roger Calderón Vega have created such a delightful spot that weekend visitors from the capital linger for hours watching hummingbirds dip their beaks into feeders and flowers encircling the rustic wooden building. The best seats are along the counter that runs the length of a back deck with mesmerizing views over the treetops into the valley. My breakfast consisted of an enormous fruit plate with fresh pineapple, bananas and papaya, moist, flavorful *gallo pinto* with eggs, and fried plantains smothered in melted cheese. I longed to return for a lunch of trout fresh from the Río Chirripó, or *olla de carne*, a typical stew made with lean beef and fresh vegetables from nearby farms. The menu is translated into English and makes a great souvenir for anyone interested in Costa Rican cuisine. The family raises gorgeous orchids that brighten the dining room. Don't drive by without stopping.

CERRO CHIRRIPÓ

Hikers can't wait to climb Cerro Chirripó — its looming presence is nearly irresistible. Chirripó is the highest peak in Central America south of Guatemala, and stands 3,819 m (12,529 ft) above sea level in the Parque Nacional Chirripó. Glacial lakes shimmer at the highest points, and the hike up the peak passes through swamps, fern groves, the stunted trees of Andean-like páramos, oak and cloud forests and hawks gliding on whistling winds. Steady hikers can make the 14-km (eight-and-a-half-mile) ascent to the refuge huts below the summit in about 10 hours, though it helps to start out acclimated to the base altitude at 1,219 m (4,000 ft). In all, the ascent is 2,600 m (8,500 ft) to the peak. Most hikers make it as far as the refuges in one day, and crash on the foam mattresses, grimace in cold-water showers and recover next to wood-burning stoves. The next day is devoted to the relatively easy two-hour climb to the summit and a bit of exploring, with the third day spent climbing and sliding back down. To ensure entrance (only 40 hikers are allowed in the park per day), you must make advance reservations through the national parks authorities in San José (257-0922 FAX 223-6963 or the park office in San Isidro de Pérez Zeledón (771-4836 FAX 771-3297. During the rainy season it may be possible for you to get a reservation and permit after you arrive in San José, but during high season you should contact them well in advance of your visit. When climbing the peak, remember that temperatures can drop to 4°C (40°F); carry warm clothing, water, a flashlight and food. The San Gerardo de Rivas ranger station (/FAX 771-3155 and park entrance is 15 km (nine miles) northeast of San Isidro. Make reservations to stay at the lodge on the summit through this station or the San José office.

It's best to spend the first night near the ranger station. **Chirripó Pacifico Mountain Lodge** (771-6069 FAX 771 2003 in San Gerardo de Rivas has eight moderately-priced rooms in a well-situated lodge by the Río Chirripó, just a short walk from the ranger station.

SAN VITO

South of San Isidro the Interamericana runs through farms and pineapple plantations and the small town of Buenos Aires, then begins curving west to Palmar and several side roads to Golfito and the southern coast. Before Palmar, at Paso Real, an unnamed, but paved, road runs southeast to San Vito, a small ranching and farming settlement largely populated in the 1950s by Italian immigrants. This town is renowned for its Italian restaurants, fresh produce and cheese. A road leads from here to the edges of the **Parque Internacional La Amistad** (771-4836 FAX 771-3297 named for the *amistad* (friendship) between Costa Rica and Panama. The Costa Rica portion of the park is enormous, spread over 193,929 ha (479,199 acres) of rainforest, watershed and páramos along the Talamanca range. Large portions of the park have yet to be explored except by jaguars and puma, which thrive in these wild ranges. The park is most easily accessed through **La Amistad Lodge** (773-3193 or 290-3030 FAX 232-1913, within **Hacienda**

The Zona Sur

La Amistad private biological reserve. The large wooden lodge has 10 guestrooms, some with private bath, and is a Mecca for biologists and botanists specializing in arthropods, mammals and birds. The hacienda includes acres of spice, coffee, citrus, sugarcane fields and produces organic products for export. Tour packages, including transportation from San José, overnight stays, meals and guided hikes are available.

Equally fascinating for plant lovers are the **Wilson Botanical Gardens** inside the **Las Cruces Biological Station** (773-4004 or 240-6696 (in San José) FAX 773-3665 or 240-6783 (in San José) E-MAIL lcruces@hortus.ots.ac.cr WEB SITE www.ots.ac.cr, five and a half kilometers (three and a half miles)

south of San Vito, which is operated by the Organization for Tropical Studies. The 10-ha (25-acre) gardens were created by Robert and Catherine Wilson, former owners of a tropical nursery in Florida. The Wilsons, with the help of Brazilian landscape designer Roberto Burle-Marx, started creating their showplace in 1962; ever since, it's been a magnet for those who love heliconia, ferns, bromeliads, orchids, ginger, bamboo and idyllic landscaping. Over 7,000 species of tropical plants, including 700 species of palms, create a gorgeous setting in the mist that attracts hummingbirds, tanagers, toucans, trogons and a bounty of butterflies. A 235-ha (580-acre) forest surrounds the gardens. After a disastrous fire destroyed the former lodge, library and laboratories in 1994, a new lodge

OPPOSITE: A tiny rainforest fern clings to a tree trunk in the Parque Internacional La Amistad. ABOVE: Bamboo trunks clatter in the rain like wind chimes.

opened in 1996. It contains 12 high-ceilinged rooms with private baths and balconies overlooking the gardens. Day and overnight guests wander along paths with alluring names — Tree Fern Hill Trail, Heliconia Loop Trail, Bromeliad Walk, Orchid Walk, the Hummingbird Garden and Fern Gully — and hike farther into the forest preserve. Reservations for day visits and overnights must be arranged through the **Organization of Tropical Studies (** 240-6696 FAX 240-6783 E-MAIL oet@ns.ots .ac.cr. Rates on a per person basis including meals are in the moderate range.

PALMAR

The Carretera Interamericana twists in hairpin curves south from Paso Real to Palmar Norte and Palmar Sur, where some travelers, on the way to the south coast, arrive at the airstrip via SANSA or TravelAir. Gas stations, markets and public phones line the intersection of the Interamericana and Highway 18 leading west to the tiny town of Cortés and the central Pacific coast. Boats depart from near here to travel the Río Sierpe to Bahía Drake (see below). South of Palmar another side road leads to Golfito, while the Interamericana continues south to the Panamanian border at Paso Canoas.

BAHÍA DRAKE

Palmar is the usual entry point to the Río Sierpe region and Bahía Drake. Sir Francis Drake spotted the sheltered bay two kilometers (one and a quarter miles) wide on the northern Península de Osa in 1579; that bowl of warm, calm water now bears his name. Arched into the rainforest between the Río Sierpe and Parque Nacional Corcovado, Bahía Drake is the perfect destination for adventuresome travelers who don't mind a bit of discomfort in their travels. It is one of the most isolated places on the coast, yet five settlements of hardy Costa Ricans reside on the hillsides, river banks and beach, living quite happily on the gifts from the sea, small vegetable and cattle farms and, increasingly, on the benefits of tourism. A few nature lodges, *cabinas* and vacation houses offer luxurious wilderness experiences. Visitors to Bahía Drake have the advantage of being able to explore the sea, the river and traditional Costa Rican towns from a single base.

GENERAL INFORMATION

There is one public telephone run by solar power in Aguajitas at the **pulpería (** 771-2336. Thus far, Bahía Drake does not have power lines and locals rely on generators for electricity. The clinic in town is sporadically staffed by a nurse; she rides a circuit of the five local settlements on

horseback then returns to what some call "the capital of Drake Bay" at Aguajitas, which has about 200 residents. Everybody in town knows how to find the local supply of snake bite anti-venin, which is typically needed by farmers and cattle ranchers who disturb the resident snakes. The local lodges use solar power, generators and radios to provide creature comforts, and they count on phones and faxes in San José for contact with the outside world.

WHAT TO SEE AND DO

I once had the privilege of touring the largest town in the area, **Aguajitas**, with a resident

nature guide who was working on the *Temptress* cruise ship. Tony had lived in the town for 18 years, and evidenced a tremendous fondness and pride for his community. What's not to like? Resident scarlet macaws, oblivious to the blare of reggae from a nearby radio and to our camera-laden group, munched on fruits from an almond tree spreading its shade over the beach. People stopped by to chat and stare from their porch chairs; children posed proudly before their new school. As we reached the river the housing improved considerably, and signs for rental rooms and horseback rides began to appear. We crossed the freshly-painted red, blue and yellow hanging bridge swaying over the Río Aguajitas, and entered the tourist zone at the mouth of the river. If you stay in any of the lodges in the area be sure to make at least one trip to town, to buy a few essentials (or nonessentials) at the neighborhood *pulpería* and practice your Spanish with the locals.

Sport fishing, boat rides up the river (great for bird watching), trips to Isla del Caño, horseback riding, kayaking — the opportunities to eat up a week's time are abundant. Corcovado is just 13 km (eight miles) south. Some visitors walk the beach and mountain trails from the river to the park's San Pedrillo entrance. Dolphins and whales frolic in the waters off Bahía Drake, and hotels and tour operators now offer guided boat trips to see these exciting creatures. Naturally, you should allot a bit of time for lounging in a hammock at the edge of the river or sea or on a private deck in the trees.

area overlooks the river. Rooms sit at the end of winding pathways (some quite steep) and are built of lustrous hardwoods. Many have downstairs living rooms and sleeping lofts; some have sunken tubs and skylights. Electric lights, ceiling fans, hot water, and purified drinking water are all civilized touches one wouldn't expect in this out-of-the-way location, and the superb cuisine is a pleasant surprise. The hotel offers fishing, diving, hiking, and river trips accompanied by gourmet picnic lunches.

Nudging the boundaries of Parque Nacional Corcovado, **Casa Corcovado Jungle Lodge (** 256-3181 FAX 256-7409 E-MAIL corcovdo@sol.racsa.co.cr WEB SITE www.casacorcovado.com is a naturalist's

WHERE TO STAY

Most of the lodges in this area base their rates on packaged tours including meals and some activities. The flight to Palmar usually costs extra; some lodges charge for the boat trip down the Río Sierpe to the lodge. Ask about all these factors — meals, transportation, tours — when choosing your package. You can usually save a bit by purchasing everything in advance. It's not a good idea to show up unannounced, since these places fill up quickly, especially in high season, and your options are limited.

Very Expensive

Classy yet casual, **Aguila de Osa Inn (** 296-2190 FAX 232-7722 E-MAIL reserve@aguiladeosa.com WEB SITE www.aguiladeosa.com draws rave reviews from its fans. The hotel's restaurant, bar and lounge

paradise. Bungalows with private tiled baths and mosquito nets draped over the beds are set along perfect lawns at the edge of primary forest. The amenities within these little houses are exceptional, and include a desk, large bathroom with separate toilet and hot-water shower areas, good screens on three walls so you feel almost like you're sleeping outside, and electricity (though you might want to use the candles by the bedside for ambiance). The meals are excellent. The real reason to stay at this remote lodge, however, is it setting above a perfect beach complete with waterfalls. A few guides have told me they've seen a larger variety of animals and birds here than anywhere else in the country — the best recommendation a lodge can receive. The lodge is best accessed by boat from Sierpe.

A secluded beach at Bahía Drake on the remote southern Pacific coast.

Expensive

Tranquility is the hallmark of the **Drake Bay Wilderness Camp** (/FAX 771-2436 WEB SITE www .drakebay.com, on the river. Herbert and Marleny Michaud began the camp in the 1980s on a point of land between the river and the sea. Today they have 20 comfortable rooms in cabins separated by long stretches of lawn and palm groves. The rooms have white walls with stenciled flowers, firm mattresses, tiled bathrooms with solar- and gas-powered water heaters and reading lamps over the beds. Windows have good screens, though bugs are not a major problem. Guests gather for meals in a large peaked-roof dining room where the walls and shelves are covered with fine balsa-

wood masks and animal carvings made by local Boruca Indians. Meals here include homemade breads and biscuits, piles of tropical fruits, and fish caught daily in local waters. The best accommodations for nature lovers are five spacious tents on platforms in isolated spots along the water. The tents have cement floors, fans and lights; a table and chair sit outside, offering a perfect spot for reading, writing or gazing at the turquoise sea. Facilities and activities include sport fishing, a professional scuba diving operation, kayaking, canoeing, horseback riding, river rafting trips and mountain biking. The best bargains are the four- and seven-day packages, which include chartered air transport from San José.

HOW TO GET THERE

Most guests arrive on flights from San José, either on scheduled flights on SANSA or on charter planes. The lodge staff transfer guests by car or van to Sierpe, where they board small boats for the trip to Bahía Drake. The trip of 30 km (18 miles) takes about two hours. The surge and surf can be rough when the river meets the open sea; most captains know the tides and best times for the trip. Once the boats enter Bahía Drake, the water is usually placid, but be prepared for a wet landing

in the small waves lapping the beach. Some lodges have docks on the smaller Río Aguajitas for dry landings. If you're driving, turn off at the Palmar intersection on the Carretera and leave your car in Palmar. You can drive to Bahía Drake on a gravel road from Rincón on the east side of the Península de Osa, but you'll still have to travel by boat to reach the lodges. If you haven't arranged transport in advance, negotiate with the boat captains in Sierpe for your trip.

ISLA DEL CAÑO

Isla del Caño is one of the most important archaeological sites in Costa Rica — believed to be a burial ground for the Diquis peoples. The tiny island, only three kilometers (under two miles) long by two kilometers (one and a quarter miles) wide, is also a prime snorkeling and diving spot, where lobsters, octopus, sea urchins and sea turtles can be seen when the waters are calm. Isla del Caño is now part of the Parque Nacional Corcovado and both the land and water are protected, but this designation came too late to preserve the Diquis burial grounds. Many of the graves have been looted; however, visitors can still see bits of pottery that date back to the first century. More exciting to archaeologists is the abundance of lithic spheres — huge, perfectly round stone balls found throughout the Diquis region. Little is known of their origin and meaning, but the presence of the spheres on the island suggests that the Diquis transported them across the sea to the island, a considerable feat. The island is 20 km (12 miles) west of Bahía Drake and has a small ranger station. Only 20 visitors are allowed on the island trails at one time; tours can be arranged through hotels in Bahía Drake, the Península de Osa, Dominical and Quepos.

PENÍNSULA DE OSA

One of the last large stretches of protected rainforest in Costa Rica, the Península de Osa juts into the Pacific at the southern tip of the country. Much of the peninsula is protected within the **Parque Nacional Corcovado**, established in the 1970s. Several conservation groups and individuals have created private reserves around the park, thereby increasing the amount of protected land. Difficult to get to (and equally difficult to leave) the peninsula captivates wanderers with its isolation, beauty and abundance of wildlife. It's one of the few areas where scarlet macaws still thrive, giving bird watchers the once-in-a-lifetime thrill of spotting a screeching flock of macaws soaring above the seaside rainforest canopy. Howler monkeys growl their wakeup call much like roosters crowing in farm communities, and keel-billed toucans lay claim to the fruit of papaya and mango trees. Tourists have discovered this remote paradise, and are willing to pay the highest room rates in the country to appreciate such beauty in comfort. Daring entrepreneurs have created a few truly outstanding lodges; others have more modest approaches and provide the basics. Some fear Osa will suffer from its increasing popularity, but enough *ticos*, foreign residents, and travelers are aware of the region's fragility that plans for development would undergo severe scrutiny.

BACKGROUND

The first known residents of the Península de Osa were the Diquis, who discovered a plentiful supply of gold in the rivers and streams. In the early

GENERAL INFORMATION

There are few settlements, telephones or roads on the Península de Osa, and no central source of information. The largest town here is **Puerto Jiménez** (population: 7,000), where the airstrip is conveniently located next to the town cemetery. Located on the Golfo Dulce side of the peninsula, Puerto Jiménez has grown steadily with the rise of tourism in the area, and the services are improving. A few *pulperías* have public phones. There is a very small branch of the Banco Nacional, though it's better to bring all the colónes you might need. There is a national park office in town (735-5036

twentieth century the peninsula was home to escaped prisoners and criminals fleeing the law, and the area was known as a Wild West-style frontier with dangerous terrain and even more dangerous residents. A frenzied gold rush struck the region in the 1960s when word spread that gold could still be panned in the peninsula's rivers. Fortunes were built in those days by the *oreros* (miners), their suppliers and customers. Outcasts, prospectors and hermits claimed their territory as squatters; land titles, as such, have always been a matter of great dispute. In 1968 the government began the controversial task of clearing the land of squatters, and in the mid-1970s, claimed an enormous chunk of the Península de Osa as the Parque Nacional Corcovado. By 1986, *oreros* were banned from within the park's boundaries. But people still camp beside the peninsula's rivers and pan for gold.

The Zona Sur

or 735-5282, where you can arrange last-minute permits to camp in the park (though it's best to get permits in San José or from abroad before your travels). Even if you have a permit check in at the office and get a tide table — you have to time your hikes in some areas to coincide with low tide.

The town nearest to the park is **Carate**, 43 km (27 miles) southwest of Puerto Jiménez. Charter planes fly the short hop between the two towns. There is a road connecting the towns, but you do need a four-wheel-drive vehicle to travel it most times of the year.

If you want to fly to Carate, Tiskita, or Bahía Drake from Puerto Jiménez contact **Alfa Romeo Aero Taxi** (775-1515 or 296-5596.

OPPOSITE: Dining companions provide much entertainment at remote lodges on the Osa Peninsula. ABOVE: Young *ticas* share a popular refreshment near Bahía Drake.

WHAT TO SEE AND DO

Much like the *oreros* of the past, birders and naturalists flock to the Península de Osa for its natural wealth. Though much of their attention is focused on the **Parque Nacional Corcovado (** 735-5282 FAX 735-5276, the surrounding areas are filled with the same abundance of wildlife — marguays, ocelots, keel- and chestnut-billed toucans, tapirs, peccaries and anteaters — to name just a few of the 360 species of birds and 100 or more species of mammals found in and around the park. The peninsula's land mass ranges through eight different habitats from coastal beaches to cloud

forests, and a coral reef attracts tropical fish off Punta Salsipuedes. Visitors to the park and nearby lodges fill their days with hikes, horseback rides and boat rides, and their nights with star gazing. The park includes over 54,000 ha (133,380 acres) of land and 2,000 ha (4,940 acres) of marine habitat, and it is controlled from ranger stations (called *puestos*) in Sirena, San Pedrillo, La Leona, El Tigre and Los Patos. Hiking the park is an undertaking. No roads lead to the entrances. Instead, you must walk along the beach during low tide, fording rivers and streams. Or, in some places, you can hike in through the hot, humid rainforest. As for wildlife encounters, La Sirena is your best option. To get there, you must get to Carate, then hike down the beach for about an hour to the La Leona entrance. Once you've paid your entry fee here, you hike on into the park 16 km (10 miles) to the La Sirena station, where you can camp so deep in the wilderness that you might even be able to see a puma (though sightings are rare). You can also reach La Sirena from the ranger station at El Tigre north of Puerto Jiménez. Those wishing to hike the park's trails must pay a US$6 entry fee. The

ABOVE: Tapirs snuffle and shuffle along the rainforest floor. OPPOSITE: Rewards such as this cascade await those who trudge through Corcovado's red mud.

fee is good for as long as you stay in the park, but if you leave and reenter you must pay again.

Most travelers set up their tours and hikes through the lodges. But if you're looking for something special, or you just want to check out your options, contact **Escondido Trex (**/FAX 735-5210 WEB SITE www.escondiotrex.com at Soda Carolina in Puerto Jiménez.

WHERE TO STAY AND EAT

Rooms are limited and best reserved far in advance, especially for visits during the dry season.

Very Expensive

John and Karen Lewis have created an extraordinary hotel in the middle of the wilderness and named it **Lapa Ríos (** 733-5130 FAX 735-5179 E-MAIL laparios@sol.racsa.co.cr WEB SITE www.laparios .com near Puerto Jiménez. Set in the midst of a 400-ha (988-acres) private preserve, the hotel sits atop of a hill overlooking a canopy of trees and a deserted beach. The 14 enchanting bungalows are scattered down the hillside (it's a bit of a climb down to the lower ones). When I first walked into my room, a haughty toucan gazed disapprovingly from the railing of my private deck, then withdrew only as far as the nearest tree. Gauzy white netting draped around the carved wood bed kept me protected from mosquitoes, as I slept with bamboo screens open to the breeze. Tropical hardwoods (from trees already felled) were used for the floors and furnishings. A 15-m-tall (50-ft) thatched palm A-frame roof covers the main lodge where guests sip tropical drinks, dine on fresh fish and fruits and sign up for forest trail, beach and night walks. Part of the hotel's proceeds go towards maintaining a small school for children in the area, and for reforestation of the region. Meals are included in the rates; transport from Puerto Jiménez and hikes are extra.

Lana Wedmore scaled new heights in creating her **Luna Lodge (** 735-5431 or 380-5036 (cell phone) WEB SITE www.lunalodge.com near Carate. I reached the lodge on horseback after a long uphill ride over streams and ruts. A couple of Jeeps passed me by, refuting my belief that you'd be best off dropping in via helicopter. Wedmore chose what must be the highest hill in the area for her lodge, then designed a soaring thatch roof for the main building. You could sit at the edge of the restaurant for hours watching hawks soar above the forest; on clear days you can see all the way to the sea. There's a telescope nearby if you care to identify birds and stars. The cabins scattered about the grounds define rustic luxury. Camp sites are also available, and if you happen to wander by, the restaurant is open to non guests. A generator provides electricity at the moment, though Wedmore plans to harness a bit of hydroelectric

power from a nearby waterfall. Once you have climbed the road you're pretty much stuck in the heavens, watching the forest from your terrace or hiking the trails. Not a bad take on Paradise.

Expensive

Michael Kaye, the founder of Costa Rica Expeditions and a leader in ecotourism, walked the Península de Osa for 12 days back in 1979 to find the right piece of land for his dream camp. It took until 1990 for him to purchase the land and construct the **Corcovado Lodge Tent Camp** (257-0766 FAX 257-1665 E-MAIL costaric@expeditions.co.cr WEB SITE www.costaricaexpeditions.com, the perfect base for wilderness explorers who like a bit of

when you're most likely to spot monkeys and birds. If you really love the view from above, schedule a night on the platform. The guides hoist a tent, sleeping bags, a picnic dinner and even chemical toilets to the platform. It's not all that romantic, however, as there's a guide with you at all times. Excellent trails lead through the 80-ha (198-acre) private reserve. On one hike I saw four types of monkeys gamboling about, many carrying their babies. Park hikes, both easy and difficult, are offered as well; you must pay the US$6 entry fee at the ranger station. Several packages including accommodations, meals, and tours are available.

Creature comforts in a rustic setting bring guests back many times to **Bosque del Cabo**

comfort. Guests arrive at Carate via plane or taxi, then hike for 45 minutes along the beach to reach the cluster of 20 tents sheltered by palms; their luggage is carried in a horse-drawn cart. The tents cover wooden platforms and two sturdy beds; the best sit on a slight rise above the pounding surf. Cold-water showers are located in two shared bathrooms. Electricity is provided a few hours a day by generator, and meals are served family style in a thatched-roof lodge. The food exceeds all expectations for such a remote region — so many fresh vegetables, piles of sautéed shrimp, pancakes at breakfast. The Hammock House holds several hammocks in a huge tree house, where amusements include a ping pong table, large lending library, and full bar.

One of the biggest attractions here is being hoisted atop a forest canopy platform on a 60-m-tall (200-ft) guapinol tree; try it early in the day

(735-5206 FAX 735-5043 E-MAIL boscado@sol.racsa .co.cr, hidden on a hilltop above **Playa Matapalo** at the southern tip of the peninsula. Mosquito netting over comfy beds, outdoor showers with a view of toucans in the trees, and solar-powered electric lighting provide the necessities to live amidst hummingbirds, howlers and sloths.

Inexpensive

There are a few small *cabina* hotels in Puerto Jiménez, and some more under construction. **Doña Leta's Bungalows** (/FAX 735-5180 E-MAIL letabell@sol.racsa.co.cr has several cabins by a small beach, along with a restaurant. **Agua Luna** (/FAX 735-5034 is located by the town dock and offers a few air-conditioned rooms and others with fans. Budget travelers gather information at **Soda Carolina** (735-5185, the main restaurant in town. Carolina's has a few very affordable, very basic rooms for rent. Some homeowners will take in travelers; ask the pilots and taxi drivers hanging around the airstrip.

Camping

Camping is allowed within the national park, but you must have reservations and a permit arranged through the national **parks authorities** ℂ 283-8004 FAX 283-7343 HOTLINE IN COSTA RICA ℂ 192. Facilities are beside the ranger stations, and you can dine with the rangers if you reserve and pay ahead of time. Otherwise, you'll need to pack your food along with a tent, bedding, mosquito netting, water, towels, first-aid supplies, and clothing. Hiking trails connect the stations, and dedicated

GOLFITO

Golfito, the main port on the Golfo Dulce between the mainland and Península de Osa, was a critical port for the United Fruit Company from the mid-1930s to the 1980s, when a Panamanian disease destroyed banana crops. Many of plantations were replanted with African oil palms, but the international market for palm oil has dwindled, as has Golfito's fortunes. Costa Ricans maintain a certain fondness for Golfito due to its status as a duty-free port, established in 1990. Most visitors to this city of 14,000 residents come in search of relatively inexpensive refrigerators, washers,

explorers can spend days and even weeks exploring the park. The terrain is difficult, however, and you must be vigilant about snakes, insects and trail accidents.

HOW TO GET THERE

TravelAir and SANSA have flights from San José to Puerto Jiménez. Buses run from San José via San Isidro de el General. A paved road runs from the Carretera Interamericana at Chacarita to Rincón; from there on you face ridges, ruts, bridges and mud en route to Jiménez. The road (actually barely a path) continues on from town paralleling the coastline to Carate; a four-wheel drive is essential for this stretch.

You can also reach the Península de Osa via boat from Golfito, where captains in Puerto Jiménez will ferry you to Carate.

The Zona Sur

dryers, and compact disc players (import taxes in the rest of the country are prohibitively high). There's little reason to pass through town unless you're headed to private reserves north of town or across the gulf on the Península de Osa.

WHAT TO SEE AND DO

Golfito is bordered by **Refugio Nacional de Fauna Silvestre Golfito**, a 2,300-ha (5,683-acre) refuge protecting virgin tropical hardwood trees (including the precious purple-heart wood), a community watershed and many species of birds, wild cats and monkeys. Some hotels in Golfito and lodges in the area offer tours to the refuge.

OPPOSITE: Hikers arrive by boat to access Parque Nacional Corcovado's remote trails. ABOVE: Spotting the plaintive white faces of capuchin monkeys can make or break a rainforest hike.

Tours from Golfito are also available to **Casa Orquideas**, where the McAllister family has lived on Playa San Josecito, north of town, for nearly two decades. Though not as spectacular as the Wilson Gardens, Orquideas has a lovely selection of 100 species of orchids, unusual tropicals and citrus, spices and vegetables — all grown organically. You can arrange a tour of Orquideas through an area hotel. The owners rely on radio communications only.

WHERE TO STAY

There are several small hotels in the town of Golfito, but most travelers head to the sport-fishing and nature lodges along the Golfo Dulce. Make reservations and transport arrangements in advance.

Delightfully secluded, **Rainbow Adventures** (775-0220 RESERVATIONS IN THE US ((503) 690-7750 TOLL-FREE IN THE US (800) 565-0722 FAX IN THE US (503) 690-7735 is a 45-minute boat ride north from Golfito to Playa Cativo (very expensive). On a beach rife with an abundance of wildlife, the lodge is an extraordinary three-story structure filled with antiques and handmade furnishings. The rooms are luxurious and the meals of gourmet quality. Fishing, hiking on well-marked trails through the rainforest, and swimming in the spring-fed pool or the Golfo Dulce are the main activities.

In Golfito the options include the moderately priced **Las Gaviotas Hotel** (775-0062 FAX 775-0544 WEB SITE www.adventuremarketing.com (also called the Yacht Club), between the highway and town. The waterfront location is ideal, and the 18 rooms face the sea across lawns, gardens, and pool. Boaters and anglers gravitate to the restaurant and bar; they don't have far to walk, since the hotel has its own pier. **Golfito Outfitters** operates out of the hotel and offers fishing trips and packages.

Samoa del Sur (775-0233 FAX 775-0573 in town also has a pier and dock, though its inexpensive rooms don't face the water. They are comfortable and fairly new. The large restaurant and bar is covered with a steep thatched roof; menu items include good steaks, barbecued chicken, and grilled fish.

SOUTH TO THE PENÍNSULA DE BURICA

Small pristine beaches dot the coast south of Golfito, past the marshlands around the Río Coto flowing into the Golfo Dulce. Be forewarned that traveling this far south has its disadvantages and a four-wheel-drive vehicle is essential year round. My instructions for driving to Tiskita Lodge near the Panamanian border were four pages long, and I've never been so traumatized behind the wheel in all my life. But the road (loosely speaking) led to what may be my favorite part of Costa Rica,

along the edge of the snaking Península de Burica, which is largely a part of Panama.

Costa Rica retains ownership of the peninsula's Pacific coast, a strip of white-sand beaches beloved by surfers and reclusive souls. Swimmers, anglers and sunbathers hang out at **Playa Zancudo**, where the waters of Golfo Dulce are protected by the southern tip of the Península de Osa. Surfers head further south to **Bahía Pavón** and **Playa Pavones**, where raging surf is juxtaposed with tranquil coves. Pavones is reputed to have the world's longest left break, a diagonally facing wave that seems to carry you forever — good luck getting back out to the break. Actually, you're better off walking back to the beginning before heading into the water. There's little to do in this region but play in the water, hike forest trails and mingle with the other tourists and the few locals who maintain permanent residence in outpost settlements.

Until recently, faxes, hot water, and electrical currents were nonexistent, but civilization has reached the Península de Burica. But settlements are few, and you certainly feel as though you have dropped off the map. Basic supplies can be purchased at *pulperías* in Pavones and Zancudo. Bring all the colónes you think you'll need; don't expect to be able to change money.

WHERE TO STAY

Very Expensive

As far as I'm concerned, **Tiskita Lodge** (296-8125 FAX 296-8133 E-MAIL tiskita@sol.racsa.co.cr WEB SITE www.tiskita-lodge.co.cr, just to the south of Playa Pavones on Punta Banco, is one of the top five lodges in the country. A note from 12-year-old Tim in the guest book sums it up well: "Chiggers, scorpions in my bathroom, scraped my back, stomach and chest, burnt my back, burnt my feet. I loved it! I got to see so many animals and ate so many different fruits. Thanks for a great time!" Helen from England wrote "On a cold winter's night in England I shall close my eyes and remember this place with a smile." I overheard and experienced similar lofty sentiments during my two-night stay. I stared out the screen by my bed the first morning listening for rustling leaves, then ran to the outdoor bathroom and shower to watch squirrel monkeys lope hand over hand through the trees, tails stretching and looping around branches. Chestnut-mandible toucans chattered nearly out of sight, while smaller tanagers, motmots and parakeets twittered. Keeping my eyes turned downward in fear of disturbing a boa, I walked from my cabin-on-stilts to the main lodge, grabbed a mug of coffee and settled on a lawn chair to watch for white hawks and glistening emerald-throated hummingbirds. Around 7 AM a group of diehard *pajareros* (bird watchers) emerged from the forest in search of sustenance.

Peter Aspinall, the fascinating and somewhat obsessed owner of Tiskita, led a group of us on a tour of his fruit orchards after breakfast. He clambered up trees, disappeared down slippery slopes and generally went far out if his way to make sure we sampled both bitter and sweet star fruit, wax jambu, custard apples, mangosteens, bitter arazau and sweet slimy cacao.

Trails range far and wide through the 100-ha (247-acre) private reserve and down a hill from the cabins, over the airstrip and onto the beach at Punta Banco. There's a safe swimming beach (with tide pools along a rocky reef) about a 10-minute walk from the lodge, and there are world-famous surfing beaches a few kilometers up the road.

FAX 776-0011 E-MAIL jruhlow@sol.racsa.co.cr. Anglers find just above everything they ever dreamed of here, since the lodge sits between the Pacific and the convergence of three rivers. Tuna, snapper, and sailfish ply the Pacific, while snook lie in wait in the rivers. Ray's has a fleet of 10 boats to accommodate the guests. While on land, visitors swim in the pool, soothe their muscles in a Jacuzzi, and sleep in air-conditioned comfort in buildings raised on stilts above the lawn.

Inexpensive

Locals gather at **Cabinas Sol y Mar** (776-0014 FAX 776-0015 E-MAIL solymar@zancudo.com WEB SITE www.zancudo.com at Playa Zancudo for

Horseback riding, bird watching and tours to Parque Nacional Corcovado and Wilson Botanical Gardens are available. Advance bookings are advised for these activities and to reserve one of the 14 cabins separated by secondary forest, fruit trees (of course) and giant heliconia and ferns. Aspinall recently built a small pool on the grounds and is installing hot water in the bathrooms. Basic, hearty meals are served buffet style in the main lodge and there is an honor-system bar; if you crave snacks, smokes and sodas, bring them with you or purchase them at the *pulpería* in Pavones. Many of Tiskita's guests arrive at Tiskita's airstrip via air charter from San José; transportation is included in some packages. The Tiskita Foundation works to reforest and protect land in the area and to support the local school and health clinic.

Playa Zancudo is home to **Roy's Zancudo Lodge** (776-0008 TOLL-FREE IN THE US (888) 308-3394

friendly conversation and hearty American-style meals. Guests fit right in, playing volleyball and badminton, swimming in the surf, and heading out to sea to catch billfish. Geodesic domes cover two of the rooms; the others are in more traditional buildings and there is also a house available for overnight or longer stays.

Small *cabinas*, bed and breakfasts, and rooms for rent dot the sandy road around Zancudo and Pavones to handle the surfer crowd. **Casa Impact** (775-0637 has a few rooms with private bath and rents surfboards. **Cantina de Pavones** (no phone) has a few rooms above the bar (forget about getting to bed early) and others in separate buildings. The Cantina is the central hangout for the area.

Macaws mate for life and depend on each other for beak-cleaning and other essential matters.

How to Get There

Wonderful challenges face the driver tackling the road to Pavones. First there's the ferry across the Río Coto, which runs from 6 AM to 7 PM. The restaurant next to the ferry is a great place to stop for a bracing cup of coffee or meal of fresh fish while studying the river.

Once you've driven onto the metal ferry platform and been guided via pulleys across the water, the fun begins. I counted at least 13 cement, dirt and rock bridges between the river and Tiskita, and I quickly developed an abiding respect for their deathtrap potential. I managed to hang my rental car off the edge of the first bridge we encountered, a skinny strip of cement which lacks guardrails at the top of a sandy rise in the rutted road. Onward I drove, past cows grazing beside bridges, kids snorkeling under them and even an occasional paved stretch of road. People have died trying to do this drive during the rainy season; unless you've got loads of time and temerity I suggest flying in over the astonishingly beautiful coastline and vast marshlands.

The nearest airport is in Golfito, and there are frequent flights in from San José. Tiskita has its own airstrip. Buses travel from Golfito to Zancudo in the dry season, but shut down when it rains. Boatmen in Golfito will shuttle you to the settlements at Zancudo and Pavones; from there you must rely on foot power and the kindness of strangers to get you to your destination.

PARQUE NACIONAL ISLA DEL COCO

Remember the scene in *Jurassic Park* when a helicopter hovers over a solitary mountainous island surrounded by rough seas? That fantastic landscape is Isla del Coco, a 22-sq-km (14-sq-mile) volcanic island, part of the Cocos chain of underwater volcanoes that runs almost to the Galápagos Islands off Ecuador. Only five kilometers (three miles) wide, the island rises to Cerro Iglesias at 634 m (2,080 ft). Waterfalls cascade down mossgreen hillsides; caves and underground passageways dot the coast; and forests of healthy coral are visible through the turquoise sea. Dedicated scuba divers dream of the hammerhead sharks, manta rays and huge pelagic fish in the waters around Isla del Coco, about 480 km (300 miles) off the southern coast of Costa Rica. Natural scientists delight in spotting the endemic animal, bird and plant species that have been discovered on scientific expeditions over the past century. Isla del Coco was included in the national park system in 1978, and access to the fragile ecosystem has been greatly limited since then. Only members of scientific research teams and those with permits arranged in advance through the national parks authorities are allowed on the island, where a ranger station keeps contact with the mainland via radio.

BACKGROUND

Pirates and buccaneers have been stashing their treasures on Isla del Coco since the late 1600s, when the English pirate Captain Edward Davis made the island his base camp for looting expeditions along the coast of New Spain from Baja California to Guayaquil. Wilson and his companions, William Dampier and Lionel Wafer, buried their treasures on the island and wrote journals of their expeditions that were best sellers in England. Davis eventually left much of his booty on the island and retired to Virginia. He made one last trip to retrieve his treasures, but stopped off along the Caribbean coast of Central America for a bit more looting and was never seen again. For a fascinating rendition of Davis' expeditions, read *Cocos Island — Old Pirate's Haven* by J. Christopher Weston Knight (San José: Imprenta y Litografía).

Naturally, the rumored buried gold has entranced treasure hunters ever since, and several expeditions have been launched over the centuries. Fishing boats have also found a wealth of billfish in the waters off the island. United States President Franklin Delano Roosevelt stopped by in 1935 on a fishing excursion; one of the endemic palms on the island is named after him. Jean-Michael Cousteau led an expedition in 1987 for an oceanographic survey of hammerheads and is now involved in an international consortium of nature organizations attempting to protect the island and nearby waters.

How to Get There

Visiting Isla del Coco is an expensive proposition, usually limited to serious scuba divers who arrive via live-aboard dive boats. **Aggressor Fleet (** (504) 385-2628 TOLL-FREE IN THE US (800) 348-2628 FAX IN THE US (504) 384-0817 WEB SITE www.aggressor .com operates the *Okeanos Aggressor*. The 36.5-m (120-ft) live-aboard dive boat travels from Coco Puntarenas to on nine- and ten-night cruises throughout the year. The boat trip takes 36 hours each way; in between, divers spend six or seven days amidst hammerheads, white-tipped sharks, whale sharks, rays and over 200 species of fish. **Undersea Hunter** TOLL-FREE IN THE US (800) 203-2120 E-MAIL cocos@underseahunter .com WEB SITE www .undersea hunter.com was one of the first companies to take divers to Coco. They have two live-aboard boats.

Childhood in a rural coastal settlement has its advantages.

The Caribbean Coast

THOUGH NOT SPECIFICALLY PART OF THE LEGENDARY Moskito Coast, the province of Limón has all its steamy mystique. Jungles and mangrove swamps border the sandy strip between Nicaragua and Panama, creeping into the turbulent sea, which doesn't seem Caribbean with its gray waves and log-strewn shores. Long separated from the rest of the country by rainforests and tall mountains, the Caribbean coast is bordered by the Cordillera Central to the west and the formidable Cordillera Talamanca in the south. Only two roads make their winding way from the capital to the coast; boats and planes are, thus far, the only transport north.

Such isolation has preserved the Caribbean's cultural attributes. Most of the population is Afro-

Caribeño, and the food, music and language all have a spicy Caribbean flare. English is more common than Spanish among the residents, while a few Indians still speak only the indigenous Bribrí and Cabécar tongues. Long stretches of the land mass and adjacent waters are protected in nature preserves, and explorers seeking the wilder side of the country find much to enjoy.

To the north, murky canals form a maze of waterways leading to the settlements of Parismina, Tortuguero and Barra del Colorado, where sea

PRECEEDING PAGES: Fine sand, clear waters and trails of seashells LEFT are among the southern Caribbean's natural attributes. An egret RIGHT balances above the marsh in the Refugio Silvestre Gandoca-Manzanillo. ABOVE: The jungle grows dense and fetid near Caribbean shores. OPPOSITE: Gandoca-Manzanillo, at the south end of the coastal road — where travelers find the Almonds and Corals Tent Camp hidden among the trees.

turtles nest in the sand and anglers ply the waters for tarpon and snook. Paul Theroux described Puerto Limón, at the center of the province, in *The Old Patagonian Express* as "…a beachhead of steaming trees and sea stinks." Much has improved since Theroux made his crabby way through Latin America by train, but similar impressions stick. Limón has little of the beauty of the towns to the south. Manzanillo, Puerto Viejo de Limón and Cahuita — all popular destinations for surfers, bird watchers and naturalists — are friendlier, cleaner and far more accommodating than their capital city.

PUERTO LIMÓN

Though disparagement is common, those who linger in Limón are quick to defend the city's character. Judy Arroyo zips up to Limón at least three times a week from Aviarios del Caribe (see below), near Cahuita. She points out the improvements, saying, "The pavement's better. We've got curbs and good sewage."

Arroyo, who is constantly fixing meals for her guests, justifiably praises Limón's central market, a cornucopia of tropical fruits from the land and sea. She swears she's never been accosted, robbed or hassled in the street. But then Arroyo, though obviously a gringo, doesn't stick out like a tourist with a camera and suitcase. Rumors abound when it comes to issues of safety in Limón, and I would never leave a packed rental car parked on the street. Like other backwater Caribbean ports, the city attracts drug dealers, scammers, schemers and desperate souls. Displays of wealth and abundance are targets for trouble. It's not wise to wander alone after dark; always practice your street smarts.

I prefer Limón in the morning, when *limónenses* escape the heat along shaded streets, visiting neighbors, running errands and following their languorous daily routines. If possible, treat Limón as a day trip from your hotel on the beach outside of the city unless you're looking for a bit of debauchery. If so, don't miss Carnival (see FESTIVE FLINGS, page 41 in YOUR CHOICE), which is celebrated on Día de las Culturas (Columbus Day) in October.

BACKGROUND

Christopher Columbus first discovered Costa Rica when he landed at Isla Uvita just off present-day Limón city in 1502. But the region was inhabited by only a few sparsely populated indigenous groups scattered along the coast and in the Cordillera Talamanca, and the Spaniards looked elsewhere for their booty and slaves. In the 1800s English-speaking African Caribbean workers were imported from Jamaica and other

islands to work on cacao plantations along the coast. English pirates stopped by occasionally to raid the plantations and take refuge in sheltered bays.

Coffee put Puerto Limón on the global shipping map. In 1871, coffee barons from the central region sought an eastern port for shipping the *grano de oro* (grain of gold) to Europe. They chose a small fishing village called El Limón as their port and began constructing a railway through uncharted mountains and jungles from San José to the coast. Workers from China, Italy and Caribbean islands provided the manpower. At least 4,000 lost their lives to the rail line, which took over 20 years to construct. Minor Keith, an American who over-

saw the construction, gained possession of some 324,000 ha (800,000 acres) of land along the railway and coast and began planting bananas as a second export crop. Eventually Keith joined with the Boston Fruit Company to create the United Fruit Company, which ruled the economy, coastal lands and labor force of much of Central America, well into the twentieth century.

Coffee, bananas and shipping shaped the fortunes of the Caribbean coast through booms and busts. The black residents, who these days make up 30% of the population of Limón province, were virtually cut off from the rest of Costa Rica. They were denied citizenship and prohibited from traveling into the highlands until 1949. Even today many *ticos* look down on the Caribbean and its residents being as inferior and dangerous.

The Jungle Train was the main form of transportation to the capital (and a tourism highlight) for nearly a century. Then the amazingly engineered Carretera Guápiles (Highway 32) through Parque Nacional Braulio Carrillo was completed in 1987. Suddenly the coast was open to explorers and a new wave of settlers seeking inexpensive

Banana plantations form the economic foundation of east coast villages, where descendants of Afro-Caribeño settlers live a tropical, laid-back lifestyle.

property and business opportunities by the sea. The earthquake of 1991 brought everything to a halt, blocking the highway and completely destroying the rail line.

The earthquake shaped the future of the Caribbean coast, bringing both devastation and restoration. It struck during the international celebrations of Earth Day on April 22, 1991 at 3:57 PM. Registering 7.4 on the Richter scale, it was centered just south of Limón.

More than 3,000 buildings were destroyed in Limón province. The Las Olas Hotel — a longtime favorite of mine with rooms built over the waves — dropped into the sea. Limón's streets rose one and a half meters (five feet); oil refinery tanks burst into flames. Over 400 people were injured; at least 25 died. Coral reefs rose above water level and dried into calcified skeletons. More than 40 km (25 miles) of roads were destroyed; trees torn from the Talamanca foothills tumbled in mud slides and floods to the sea. Canals leading to Tortuguero were left high and dry.

Years later you can still see the results of the quake's destructive force, along with its mixed blessings. Limón city is much more pleasant looking than it was in the late 1980s, and a modern suspension bridge now straddles the Río Estrella north of Cahuita. Many houses and businesses have recently been rebuilt, and foreigners are moving in to open upscale hotels and restaurants. The area's largely black population has been augmented by immigrants from Nicaragua, El Salvador, Honduras and Panama seeking peace and prosperity. The Indians who used to live in the lowlands have been driven into reserves in the hills, and are most evident in the southern Talamanca area.

All of the indigenous peoples of Costa Rica were finally granted full citizenship rights in 1992. Despite lingering prejudice on the part of Costa Rican and foreign inlanders against the region, tourism and local activism are both booming along the Caribbean coast. These days, the greatest threat to the region's prosperity is drugs. Costa Rica's coast is a convenient stop off or drug runners carrying shipment of cocaine between Colombia, Mexico, and the United States, and the drug lords actively seek support and assistance from poor families living in remote areas. Drugs are common in the north and south, and have changed the attitudes and temperament of the young. The region's environment is also threatened by the looming specter of oil drilling. Companies have begun to set up rigs in the north and south; though drilling was halted in mid-2000 it could very possibly start up again. Environmental groups throughout the Caribbean are soliciting support and assistance from individuals and agencies around the world in preventing the exploitation of their region.

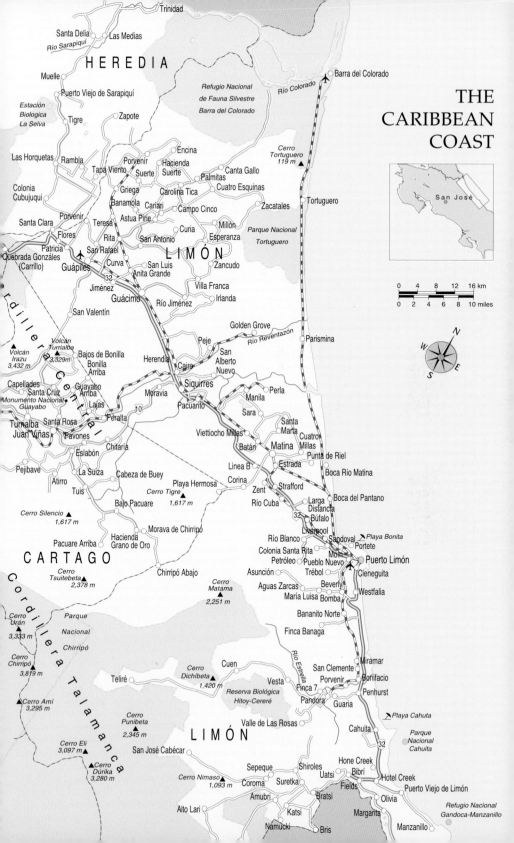

THE
CARIBBEAN
COAST

San José

| 0 | 4 | 8 | 12 | 16 km |
| 0 | 2 | 4 | 6 | 8 | 10 miles |

N
W   E
S

HEREDIA

Trinidad
Santa Delia   Las Medias
Río Sarapiquí

Muelle   Barra del Colorado
Puerto Viejo de Sarapiquí   Refugio Nacional   Río Colorado
Estación   de Fauna Silvestre
Biológica   Tigre   Barra del Colorado
La Selva   Zapote
                                              Cerro
Las Horquetas   Rambla   Porvenir   Encina   Tortuguero
                          Tapa Viento   Hacienda   119 m
Colonia   Suerte   Suerte   Canta Gallo
Cubujuqui   Griega   Palmitas
                          Banamola   Carolina Tica   Cuatro Esquinas
Santa Clara   Porvenir   Cariari   Campo Cinco   Zacatales   Tortuguero
Flores   Teresa   Astua Piñe   Curia   Millón
Patricia   Rita   San Antonio   Esperanza   Parque Nacional
Quebrada Gonzáles   San Rafael   Tortuguero
(Carrillo)   Guápiles   Curva   San Luis   Zancudo
             32   Anita Grande
          Jiménez   Villa Franca
          Guácimo   Irlanda
       San Valentín   Río Jiménez

LIMÓN

Golden Grove
Peje   Río Reventazón   Parismina
Volcán   San
Turrialba   Bajos de Bonilla   Herendia   Alberto
Volcán   3,329m   Bonilla   Cairo   Nuevo
Irazú   Arriba
3,432 m   Siquirres   Perla
Capellades   Guayabo   Moravia   Manila
Santa Cruz   Arriba   Lajas   Pacuarito   Sara
Monumento Nacional   Peralta   Santa
Guayabo   10   Marta   Cuatro
Turrialba   Santa Rosa   Viettiocho Millas   Matina   Millas
Juan Viñas   Pavones   Batán   Punta de Riel
            Chitaría   Estrada   Boca Río Matina
Pejibave   Eslabón   Linea B
         La Suiza   Cabeza de Buey   Corina   Zent   Strafford   Boca del Pantano
Atirro   Playa Hermosa   Río Cuba   Larga
Tuis   Cerro Tigre   Distancia
Cerro Silencio   1,617 m   32   Búfalo
1,617 m   Bajo Pacuare   Liverpool
            Morava de Chirripó   Río Blanco   Sandoval   Playa Bonita
Pacuare Arriba   Hacienda   Colonia Santa Rita   Portete
            Grano de Oro   Petróleo   Moín
CARTAGO   Pueblo Nuevo   Puerto Limón
         Cerro   Chirripó Abajo   Asunción   Trébol   Cieneguita
         Tsuitebeta   Cerro   Aguas Zarcas   Beverly
         2,378 m   Matama   María Luisa   Bomba   Westfalia
Cerro   2,251 m   Bananito Norte
Urán
3,333 m   Parque   Finca Banaga
         Nacional
Cerro   Chirripó   Miramar
Chirripó   Cuen   San Clemente   Bonifacio
3,819 m   Cerro   Vesta   Porvenir
Cerro Amí   Teliré   Dichibeta   Finca 7   Penhurst
3,295 m   1,420 m   Reserva Biológica
            Cerro   Hitoy-Cereré   Pandora   Guaria
            Punibeta   Playa Cahuita
Cerro Eli   2,345 m   Valle de Las Rosas   Cahuita
3,097 m   Parque
Cerro Dúrika   San José Cabécar   **LIMÓN**   32   Nacional
3,280 m   Cahuita
Cerro Nimaso   Sepeque   Shiroles   Hone Creek
1,093 m   Coroma   Suretka   Uatsi   Bibrí   Hotel Creek
Alto Lari   Amubri   Fields   Puerto Viejo de Limón
         Katsi   Bratsi   Olivia
Namucki   Bris   Margarita   Manzanillo
                              Refugio Nacional
                              Gandoca-Manzanillo

WHAT TO SEE AND DO

Limon's waterfront sidewalk, the *malecón*, is worth a stroll in the daylight; but, don't walk it alone at night. **Parque Vargas**, the main square, sits at the waterfront end of Avenida 2, the main drag through town. A sidewalk runs along the waterfront from here, past some restored classic Caribbean residences alongside those still in ruins from the quake. Sloths sometimes mimic lethargic humans as they slumber in the park's banyan trees and royal palms. Artist Guadalupe Alvarea's mural of Limón's peoples and history covers a wall sheltering the park, which faces town hall and the justice building.

The **Mercado Central** at the north side of Parque Vargas is one of Costa Rica's finest, with a grand array of regional produce. Purple and blue cacao fruit, bananas, plantains, pejibaye, mangoes and herbs compete in the stands with bundles of drab yucca, cabbage and chayote; naturally, fish is a staple of the market's aromas.

Surfers, hikers and history buffs hire captains with small skiffs to ferry them over to **Isla Uvita**, a national landmark one kilometer (just over half a mile) offshore. Hikers enjoy the small island's sandy trails and caves, while surfers come for the waves in December and January and during hurricane season (roughly August to November).

WHERE TO STAY

Limón's inner-city hotels are a sorry lot — I've never found one fit for vacationing. *Ticos* seeking a weekend getaway head for the more scenic establishments a few kilometers north of town at Playa Bonita (a misnomer, since it's not all that pretty) and Portete, a bay favored by surfers. Reservations are essential during Carnival week and on national holidays.

Although it's not right on the coast, **Selva Bananito Lodge** (/FAX 253-8118 E-MAIL conselva @sol.racsa.co.cr WEBSITE www.selvabananito.com, 20 km (just over 12 miles) southeast and 15 km (nine miles) inland from Puerto Limón, is one of the best places to experience the Talamanca region (expensive). The lodge sits beside Parque Internacional La Amistad on a 850-ha (2,100-acre) private reserve, part primary forest and part a family-owned farm. Tucked between the Río Bananito and the Matama mountains, the lodge feels rustic and remote. Guests shower in water heated by solar panels, dine by candlelight (as there's no electricity), and sleep in cabins on stilts surrounded by forest. Activities include hikes in the rainforest to waterfalls, horseback riding, mountain biking, and swimming in cool rivers and natural pools.

An old-time survivor of the quake, the moderately priced **Hotel Maribu Caribe** (758-4543 FAX 758-3541 has 52 rooms in thatched-roof bungalows, a good restaurant, a pool and transportation from San José for an additional fee. **Hotel Jardín Tropical Azul** (798-1244 FAX 798-1259, Playa Bonita, Limón, is more upscale, with 32 air-conditioned rooms in white buildings across the street from Playa Bonita (moderate).

The budget traveler's favorite in downtown Limón is the 39-room **Hotel Acón** (758-1010 FAX 758-2924, which also has one of the town's most popular discotheques. Choose your room accordingly, and be thankful for the air-conditioning, which will allow you to close your windows and escape the noise.

WHERE TO EAT

All of Limón's restaurants are inexpensive, but only a few give you the opportunity to sample the region's best cuisine. The best Creole-Caribe restaurant in town is **Springfield's** (no phone) at the north end of the *malecón*. **Brisas del Caribe** (758-0138 is the traditional favorite for Caribbean and gringo food. **Mares** (no phone) on Avenida 2 between Calles 3 and 4, is where expats head for burgers, sandwiches and clean surroundings. There is an abundance of cheap, mediocre Chinese cafés thanks to the descendants of the Chinese laborers who helped build the Jungle Train. Try the cleanest of them all: **Restaurant Sien Kong** (no phone) or **Restaurant Chon Kong** (no phone) by the market.

HOW TO GET THERE

Buses depart from San José for Limón (about a three-hour trip) from 5 AM to 7 PM; try to arrive during daylight as the city can be intimidating and threatening at night.

Drivers usually take the Guápiles Highway, a 148-km (92-mile) drive from San José. This drive takes about two and a half hours, and cuts through Parque Nacional Braulio Carrillo. Modern and relatively smooth as the highway is, it is also one of the most dangerous in the country. Its steep hills are often shrouded in mist and fog; rock and mud slides are common. Passing lanes are usually provided on the uphill stretches; drivers going both ways use them recklessly. Speed traps are often set on the flat stretch from Siquirres to Limón, where truck drivers gleefully pass each other without regard for tiny rental cars.

An alternate route from San José through Cartago and Turrialba takes about four hours and joins the main highway at Siquirres.

Those headed north to Tortuguero will likely avoid the city altogether by departing by boat from Moín just northwest of Limón, where cruise ships on day stops put in. Those headed south who wish to avoid Limón should look for the small road sign for a bypass route headed for Cahuita.

THE NORTHERN CARIBBEAN

About as isolated as any place can be, the northern Caribbean coast is made up of a sweltering maze of canals (both natural and manmade), swamps and beaches, all havens for nature. Canoes, small engine-driven skiffs and ferries are still the main modes of transportation in the region, bordered by the Mar Caribe and the Cordillera Central. Nicaragua's border undulates through the northern Río San Juan just above Costa

Parismina Lodge TOLL-FREE IN THE US (800) 338-5688 FAX (210) 824-0151 (expensive), 1800 NE, Loop 410, Suite 310, San Antonio, Texas 78217, is five kilometers (a bit more than three miles) south of Parque Nacional Tortuguero, the rooms and dining room are housed in red-roofed, white stucco buildings raised above the lawns. Both river and deep-sea fishing are available, along with a hot tub, swimming pool and nature tours; closed in July.

TORTUGUERO

As its name implies, Tortuguero is devoted to turtles. Archie Carr, of near-godlike status to turtle-watchers, began documenting the annual green

Rica's Río Colorado and the natural seaport at Barra del Colorado. This region has long been studied as an alternative to the Panama Canal, since the Río San Juan flows nicely west into Lago de Nicaragua and on to the Pacific coast.

Travelers, naturalists and pregnant sea turtles are drawn to the settlements of Tortuguero, Parismina and Barra del Colorado — all classically reminiscent of the Moskito Coast. Fishing, bird watching, culture and escape are the region's biggest draws year round. From May through September, turtle-watchers pack the lodges and research camps.

PARISMINA

Just south of Tortuguero on the Caribbean coast, Parismina is a tiny village that devotees prefer to keep secret. A favorite spot for anglers, the **Río**

turtle migration to Tortuguero's strip of coastline in the 1950s. Conservation groups from all over the world are now involved in research and preservation of the turtle's nesting grounds. The largest settlement in the northern Caribbean, Tortuguero village has some 500 residents, double the number who lived here in the early 1980s. When all guest rooms, dorms and camp sites are full, the population swells to over 1,000.

Tourism is a catalyst for both the rise in population and for concerns over Tortuguero's future. Some hotel owners would like their customers and supplies to arrive via a road; the only opposition to such "progress" are local protests and the boundaries of Parque Nacional Tortuguero. Spread over 18,600 ha (46,000 acres) of land and 52,000 ha (129,000 acres) of marine habitat, the park shelters

Green turtles migrate to the beaches of Tortuguero every spring to lay their eggs.

The Caribbean Coast

West Indian manatees, crocodiles, howler monkeys, and over 450 species of birds. Endangered mammals, including jaguars and cougars, are relatively safe in the mystifying melange of water and land; most of the guides I've talked to have yet to spot the cats.

Rain drips and pours out of the heavy air almost 365 days a year. They say an Englishman visiting the region years back grew overwhelmed with the incessant downpours. One day, he asked a boy in the village "When does it stop raining here?" — "*No se, señor*," the boy replied, "I don't know. I'm only 12."

With all the moisture, steam and tumescent air, Tortuguero feels surrealistic, like something

adventurous, keep in mind that the rural doctor pays visits to the town only every few weeks, and anyone in need of major medical care will have to be airlifted to San José. Naturalist Rafael Robles González has published a small *Field Guide to Plants of the Caribbean Coast of Costa Rica*, which helps amateurs understand what they're looking at. You can find it at hotels and *pulperías*. Bring all the cash you think you'll need while in the region; small shops and restaurants cannot change large bills or travelers' checks.

What to See and Do

One of the most popular destinations in the national park system, **Parque Nacional Tortuguero**

from a Gabriel Garcia Márquez dream. Everything moves slower than the speed of a hand-paddled canoe — at least it seems that way sometimes. Flights are unpredictable and you can get damned uncomfortable sitting by the airstrip as the afternoon sun melts the asphalt. And the region is buggy, to say the least. All those frogs hanging about have quite a lot to eat. But these drawbacks only increase the region's mystique — if you're in the proper mood. For me, Tortuguero is absolutely captivating.

General Information

Telephones, electricity and other modern creature comforts are sparse in these parts. The best places to gather information on the area are at the lodges, the park's ranger station and the Caribbean Conservation Corporation turtle museum (see WHAT TO SEE AND DO, below). When you are feeling

(710-2929 FAX 710-7673 is worth exploring for days on end. After three successive early morning boat rides through the park's canals, I still craved more — more howler monkeys, more skinny-legged, yellow-beaked northern jacanas perched on blue water hyacinths, Jesus Christ lizards walking on water, giant iguanas (nicknamed *gallina de palo* or "chicken of the tree"), chestnut-bellied herons, kingfishers, blue anhinga snake birds. Accompanied by three guides well-versed in local lore, we floated down the spooky blackwater canals, which mirror palms on the shore. I became utterly mesmerized by the sensations, not caring about bug bites, sunburn and a soaking wet T-shirt. I was oblivious to all but the boat's chugging engine, the flash of wings as birds stalked bugs like cats chasing mice and the sudden splashes in turgid waters. Since that time, several of the lodges have started using electric motors on the boats to reduce the noise and polluting emissions, and the park is even more peaceful. The daily fee to enter the park is US$6, payable at the ranger station south of the village.

Tortuguero's lodges, for the most part, line the Río Tortuguero between the Caribbean and the jungle. To term the strip along the sea a Caribbean beach is stretching the point — though some enjoy sunbathing and rain showers amidst driftwood, sea grapes and sargassum seaweed on mudbrown sand. Ghost crabs skitter about, dodging hook-billed brown whimbrels feeding upon crustacea, and butterflies and moths of all stripes hover about wild ginger and morning glories. The best beach lies between the lodges and the village; wear a hat and sweat-proof sunblock. Swimming in the sea is discouraged because of rip tides, high surf and occasional shark sightings.

It's a pleasure to take a leisurely walk around **Tortuguero Village**. Men of all ages loiter about the **Super Morpho Pulpería** (710-6716, where people line up before the public phone. The *pulpería* sells basic consumables, insect repellent, piñatas and blond dolls. The women prefer the front porch of Miss Rosie's and other informal home businesses selling clothing and basic necessities ferried up from Limón. The bright pink and green **Paraíso Tropical**, by the waterfront sells books, T-shirts, postcards, handcrafts and color print film. The **Jungle Shop** (391-3483 (cell phone) E-MAIL jungle@sol.racsa.co.cr is similarly well equipped, and also operates the **Vine Coffee House** (same phone) with a delightful selection of home-baked goodies.

The center of village social life is the playground and park on the sea side of town. The well-maintained kiosk at the plaza contains information on turtles; nightly tours depart from here during nesting season. When you spend time visiting the village, it seems as if everyone is related. The *union libre* (free marriage) concept is widespread here; some men boast of numerous children mothered by many local women and girls. More Nicaraguan and Honduran immigrants have settled here amidst the longtime Afro-Caribeño families; some say the population of Tortuguero is now 60% Nicaraguan. Many of them find the area's agriculture, fishing and tourism businesses far more prosperous than those in their homelands.

Tortuguero Natural History Visitor Center, just north of the village, is headquarters for the oldest sea turtle conservation organization in the world: the **Caribbean Conservation Corporation** (CCC) ((352) 373-6441 TOLL-FREE (800) 678-7853 E-MAIL ccc@cccturtle.org WEB SITE www.cccturtle .org, PO Box 2866, Gainesville, Florida 32602. The visitor center is a remarkable establishment, with displays on the region's history and the interwoven story of sea turtle preservation, highlighted with a film. Carr's classic books on turtles, along with

other informational materials, postcards and T-shirts are sold here. Donations are requested, and the center is open daily during daylight hours; closed for lunch.

Green, loggerhead and hawksbill turtles nest on the 35-km-long (22-mile) beach between Tortuguero and Parismina. **Turtle tours** are available through the lodges, the CCC and the independent guides operating from the kiosk in town. Only 200 people are allowed on the beach at any given time when the turtles are nesting, and everyone must be accompanied by a guide (10 people per guide). If you are seriously interested, arrange your tour through the CCC or your lodge; the merely curious might be satisfied with the kiosk

guides. The CCC enlists paying students volunteers, and researchers to assist with tagging sea turtles and other conservation efforts.

The only decent hike in the area is to the top of **Cerro de Tortuguero**, 119 m (390 ft) above sea level, where, on a clear day, you can see the outlying areas of the park.

Fishing for snook and tarpon is also a big draw at Tortuguero, though the dedicated tend to favor the fishing lodges at Barra del Colorado and Parismina.

Guests at the lodges usually rely on the guides and boats provided there. If you're staying in town, contact Daryl Loth at **Tortuguero Safaris** (392-3201 E-MAIL safari@sol.racsa.co.cr for guides and tours.

OPPOSITE: Surf-watching Caribbean style in Tortuguero. ABOVE: A Tortuguero nature guide describes the local flora.

Where to Stay and Eat

Tortuguero's lodges are surprisingly well outfitted and comfortable, and are becoming increasingly fancy. Nearly all have pools — a significant change that's occurred since 1998. Purists find such amenities pretentious, but the growth of comfort-based tourism seems inevitable. The pools are delightful, especially in Tortuguero's muggy heat, and some are fed from natural springs and use minimal chemicals.

Consider location when choosing a lodge — those on the sea side of the river have the advantage of proximity to the beach and may be within walking distance of the village. Those on the jungle side have more wildlife and will ferry you over to

the village by boat. Most places offer morning and night canal tours and transport from San José; rates are typically based on packages including transport, a two- or three-night stay, meals and tours. These extras mean that most rates are in the very expensive to expensive range. Meals are usually served family or buffet style and have set menus; if notified in advance, some lodges will accommodate vegetarians and those with special dietary needs. Reservations are essential during turtle nesting; most can be arranged through offices in San José. Budget travelers are best off at the small *cabinas* in town.

I'm partial to both the staff and the ambiance at the **Tortuga Lodge** (257-0766 FAX 257-1665 E-MAIL costaric@expeditions.co.cr WEB SITE www.expeditions.co.cr. Set amidst 20 ha (50 acres) of private property on the outskirts of civilization, the lodge has wood and leather rocking chairs outside the front and back doors of the 24 rooms, beckoning guests to wildlife watching. Flocks of white egrets skim across the river, spider monkeys swing in the trees, crickets and red poison-arrow frogs provide background chirping. The lodge has undergone a major expansion in the past few years, and now has a large screened in restaurant with an outer deck by the river, along with a pool designed with green and brown textured

finishes to resemble a lagoon. The rooms have screened French doors which open onto a back verandah; all have ceiling fans and hot water provided by solar panels. Excellent meals are served family style in the main lodge. Rubber boots, ponchos, and umbrellas are available. The orchid, croton, and heliconia gardens are filled with uncommon species, and frogs croak from the riverside behind the lodge. A Costa Rica Expeditions property, Tortuga Lodge manages to be both tourist-friendly and kind to nature; the management always attempts to reduce the lodge's impact on the environment.

A three-hectare (seven-acre) private reserve adjoins the ocean side's most pleasant accommodations, at the **Mawamba Lodge** (/FAX 771-1266 or 223-2421 (in San José) FAX 222-5463 E-MAIL mawamba@racsa.co.cr WEB SITE www.grupomawamba.com. Pathways lead past ginger plants to several bungalows on stilts housing 54 wood-paneled rooms with private baths and minimal furnishings. Hammocks and rocking chairs abound on porches, under shady ranchos, beside the docks. I like Mawamba's pool, with its oasis of palms and arcing bridge leading between the lobby and classrooms and the restaurant. The *tico*-style buffet meals are very good, especially the marinated grilled lomito, buttery mashed potatoes, and dinner salad bar. The guides are all top notch, as are the tours. You can easily walk along the beach to town from here.

Across the river is the aptly named **Jungle Lodge** (233-0155 FAX 233-0778 E-MAIL cotour@sol.racsa.co.cr WEB SITE www.tortuguero.com, marked by a blue and white tire-like sign visible above the trees. The lodge has a laid-back Caribbean look, with white and green buildings and green wicker furnishings set amid trees. It attracts a young, clientele who enjoy the rasta music in the "disco bar" and the reduced rates on tours. Hammocks hang around the rooms and pool. Somewhat worn down, the lodge has 45 rooms with ceiling fans and hot water; meals are served family style.

Architecturally distinct, the **Pachira Lodge** (256-7080 FAX 223-1119 E-MAIL paccira@sol.racsa.co.cr is set back from the river amidst palms and heliconia. The 28 rooms are in wooden cabins spread about the grounds and interconnected with thatch-roof plank pathways. A floor-to-ceiling window offers unobstructed vistas of the jungle from the enormous bar and restaurant area. Meals are served buffet style, and include vegetarian selections. The large pool has a tiled turtle on the bottom, and chairs on the dock are the perfect perch for watching the boats go by. Pachira has a newer section called the **Evergreen Lodge** on a back canal far from civilization. The 10 cabins are built on high stilts and have electricity and huge windows with screens, and there is a small pool and restaurant on property. Guests also have use of the facilities at Pachira. I like the remote feeling at Evergreen, and the rooms feel like private tree-houses tucked in the rainforest.

The friendly staff and management make the **Laguna Lodge** (225-3740 (in San José) FAX 283-8031 E-MAIL laguna@sol.racsa.co.cr WEB SITE WWW .lagunalodgetortuguero.com one of the best choices on the sea side of the river. The lodge keeps growing, and now has 42 rooms in wood cabins on stilts with thatched roofs with fans, private bathrooms, and few frills. The Laguna's gardens are its best feature; hibiscus, heliconia, orchid and ginger plants attract butterflies and tree frogs. The frogs also gather on the little island of palms in the swimming pool. A new restaurant sits right over the river; meals are served buffet style. A long trail leads to the village — a steamy 45-minute walk.

Fernando and Lilia Figuls have a passion for manatees; thus the name of their simple, inexpensive **Manati Lodge** (/FAX 383-0330 out on the northern outreaches of the river. Establishing a foundation for manatee research is but one of the their projects. Providing inexpensive rooms for travelers who favor nature over frills is another. The eight guest cabins are simple but comfortable, and have private baths with hot water. Tourists either arrive with an inexpensive tour company such as Ecole (see BACKPACKING, page 33 in YOUR CHOICE) or on their own by boat from Moín. The Figuls have kayaks for rent and can arrange all tours with local guides. In town, **Miss Junie** (710-0523 has several rooms for rent in a two-story building beside her restaurant. The rooms have good screens and private bathrooms with showers. A few small *cabina* operations offer rooms on the sea side of town, none have phones but you may be able to make reservations through the **Super Morpho Pulpería** (710-6716. Try **Cabinas Sabrina** or **Cabinas Merry Scar**. **Camping** is permitted by the park entrance south of town; at most times of the year you'll need a tent to protect you from the rain.

Bar la Culebra, the biggest night spot in town, hangs over the water at the southern end of the village; unfortunately, its canned music echoes in the canals here. **Miss Junie** (710-0523 is said to be the best cook in town. Diners stop by her small restaurant in the morning to say they'll be by for dinner so she knows how much fresh fish to purchase. **Restaurante Pacana** and **Restaurante Sabina** are also good choices for seafood and Caribbean fare.

BARRA DEL COLORADO

Reserva Biológica Barra del Colorado sits at the far northeastern corner of the country. The 98,000-ha (242,000-acre) refuge is a top sport-

fishing destination, and it also serves as a hide-away for nesting sea turtles. Birds abound; even the scarce, endangered green macaws can be spotted above the treetops. Small settlements and farms lie within the park's boundaries, connected by a web of waterways.

Where to Stay

The most famous building in the area is the **Río Colorado Lodge** (232-4063 TOLL-FREE IN THE US (800) 243-9777 FAX 231-5987 or (813) 933-3280 (in the US) E-MAIL tarpon@sol.racsa.co.cr WEB SITE www.sportsmansweb.com/riocolorado (very expensive). Built by the legendary Archie Carr in 1974, the lodge sits at the mouth of the Río

Colorado and the Caribbean Sea, prime fishing grounds for tarpon and snook. The entire complex is roofed and built on stilts above the muddy ground; the 18 wood-paneled rooms have hot showers and ceiling fans. Meals with generous portions are served family style. Air transfers from San José are available. Better yet are the boat transfers down the Río Sarapiquí to the Río San Juan and the Colorado.

Luxurious by fishing outpost standards, the **Silver King Lodge** (/FAX 381-0849 or 381-1403 TOLL-FREE IN THE US (800) 847-3474 FAX (813) 943-8783 (in the US) E-MAIL slvrkng@sol.racsa.co.cr WEB SITE www.silverkinglodge.com has large rooms with hardwood floors, bamboo ceilings, in-room coffee makers, firm mattresses, and ceiling fans (very expensive). The gourmet meals are downright amazing for such a remote area. Nature tours, fishing, air transfers and boat transport are available, and there is a large hot tub to soothe muscles strained by fighting the big ones.

Fishing isn't the only focus at **Samay Lagoon Lodge** (384-7047 FAX 383-6370 or (707) 202-3644

OPPOSITE: Caimans slither up river banks in search of unwary birds. ABOVE: Dugout canoes glide peacefully through lagoons at Cahuita without disturbing herons, kingfishers and other birds feeding on shore.

(reservations in the US) E-MAIL info@samay.com WEB SITE www.samay.com. The setting, between a lagoon and the Caribbean, makes for excellent bird watching both from the lodge and on boat tours. The rooms are simple but sufficient; were it not for biting bugs, I'd be content to sleep in one of the hammocks strung about the property. There's no better way to really experience the river than in an old-fashioned paddle-driven canoe, and Samay has several for rent. If the river life haunts your imagination, consider boarding a houseboat for a few days. The *Rain Goddess* (231-4299 FAX 231-3816 E-MAIL bluewing@sol.racsa.co.cr cruises the northern regions for days. Riverboat *Francesca* (/FAX 226-0986 E-MAIL fwatson@sol

and some of the wildest land in Costa Rica. Most lodges in the three areas can arrange air transportation. Passengers are restricted to 11 kg (25 lbs) of luggage.

Day trippers, and travelers with time, cruise the northern passage in boats, spotting howler monkeys, herons and crocodiles en route. Tour, ferry and private boats depart from Moín (close to Limón) for the three- to four-hour ride to Tortuguero; go in early morning or evening when the canals and wildlife appear much as they would from the village's lodges. Most tour companies in San José and the lodges in Tortuguero offer bus or van transfers to Moín and scheduled boat transport.

.racsa.co.cr is run by Francesca and Modesto Watson, well known and respected residents of the region who've been guiding naturalists and tourists for years. The operate several boat trips and turtle-nesting tours.

HOW TO GET THERE

Small airlines and boat tour companies compete for the tourist traffic through the region. TravelAir, SANSA and several air charter companies fly small prop planes for two to 20 passengers into small airstrips at Parismina, Barra del Colorado and Tortuguero. You should fly at least once, in spite of the size of these airplanes and their undependable flying schedules. The 20- to 30-minute flight from San José heads northeast over the fog-shrouded peaks of the Cordillera Central, the outer regions of Parque Nacional Braulio Carrillo

CAHUITA

Marking the start of the southern Caribbean Talamanca coast (named for the Cordillera Talamanca), Cahuita didn't even have a road to Limón until 1979. The first major town 44 km (27 miles) south of Limón, Cahuita has fewer than 1,500 residents and one of only two protected coral reefs on the Caribbean at the Parque Nacional de Cahuita. It's an established community with several generations of family living side by side in faded green and pink wooden houses raised on stilts above sandy streets. Clusters of hand-painted signs point the way to small *cabina* hostelries in the village, and to more luxurious hotels and bed and breakfasts on side roads along the beach.

Bright orange, yellow, green and red stripes adorn the main businesses as if boasting their

Jamaican rasta roots; Bob Marley is practically a god in these parts. Long the province of dropouts, surfers and budget travelers, the village is relaxed and laid-back. The tourist crowd is young and parsimonious, willing to spend a few colónes to obtain the rasta look by hiring a local woman to plait their hair into dozens of tiny *trencitas* (braids).

Cahuita has its downside, largely due to drugs. Ganja has long been readily available here (some of the *pulperías* sell rolling papers). Lately cocaine and crack have added an ugly edge to the scene here. Reports of thefts are common. Two American women were murdered in Cahuita in 1999, and news agencies covered the incident worldwide. The tourism industry suffered an almost immediate drop in trade, and the ICT (Costa Rican Tourism Institute) quickly announced an increase in bilingual police for the area. Though the majority of residents and travelers are friendly and trustworthy, a few persistent thieves give this area a bad reputation. Keep a close eye on your possessions at all times, and don't leave cameras and keys lying on the beach. Lock your doors and windows at night.

The pickup scene between local rasta boys and young blonde tourists is intense, and the girls seem happy to supply their short-term Caribbean boyfriends with beer, food and companionship. As a result, some of the guys can be quite persistent. Women travelers should take sensible precautions. The pickup scene grows at the central park and bus stop in the evenings, when locals and tourists perched upon backpacks size up new arrivals.

Cahuita village has achieved a sense of order after years of haphazard building, and it's now relatively easy to navigate the two main roads and several side streets that make up the village proper. Street addresses are nonexistent and unnecessary; everything you need is either in the village or on the one road running north of town along Playa Negra (Black Beach). A few lodges and inns attract a more upscale clientele who stick to the hotel pools and beaches at Playa Negra and venture into town for a meal.

BACKGROUND

Until the road south from Limón was bulldozed through and a bridge built over the Río Estrella in the 1970s, Cahuita and other Caribbean settlements were virtually cut off from the rest of the country. A few families worked fishing and farming, enjoying the solitude of Cahuita's forest-sheltered bay. Most residents were Afro-Caribeño settlers brought in to work on the Jungle Train and banana plantations; today's population is comprised of their offspring, and of United States and European émigrés banking on the tourist trade.

The completion of the Guápiles Highway from San José to Limón in 1987 drastically changed Cahuita's peaceful scene, bringing *ticos* curious about this untrammeled part of their country. Tourism was steadily rising until the earthquake of 1991 tossed half the village, along with its bridges and roads, into the ocean. The quake's destruction is still evident. Bridges leading nowhere have been replaced but not removed, and piles of fallen trees litter the beaches.

GENERAL INFORMATION

Until December, 1995, the entire village of Cahuita had only one phone number (758-1515) and businesses and residences were accessed through extension lines. Now phones and faxes ring all over town, making it easier to arrange reservations and tours. **Cahuita Tours and Adventure Centre (** 755-0232 FAX 755-0082 E-MAIL exotica@sol.racsa.co.cr is headquarters for information, changing money, sending mail and faxes and making public phone calls. They also set up tours to jungles and Indian reserves, glass-bottom boat rides and rent gear. Several other tour companies have popped up along the main drag; ask other travelers about their experiences before forking over cash. I've had good reports about **Roberto Tours (**/FAX 755-0117.

Buses from Limón and points south stop at the park across from Salón Vaz; tour agencies and hotels post the latest schedules. If you're driving, be sure to unload and lock up your gear at your hotel before cruising the town. There are no banks in town; change money at tour agencies or hotels.

WHAT TO SEE AND DO

The biggest attraction and best beaches in the area are at the **Parque Nacional de Cahuita (** 755-0302 with 1,068 ha (2,639 acres) of beaches and jungle and 22,409 ha (55,350 acres) of ocean preserve. Though brochures make the park sound idyllic, the beaches are actually tan rather than white and the aquamarine sea is sometimes murky with sediment, depending on the season.

Several factors have endangered the reef and darkened the waters at Cahuita. Deforestation in the Cordillera Talamanca and the banana plantations creates sediment that runs down the foothills into the sea. The 1991 earthquake caused more problems when buildings close to the sea crumbled and debris floated in the currents. Several environmental groups are working to clean up the beaches; you can help by carrying along a plastic bag and picking up any trash and cigarette butts you see.

Nature trails wind through the tropical forest fringing the beach; early morning hikers may spot howler monkeys, sloths and green parrots in the trees. There are two entrances to the park; one at

Snorkelers find clear waters in the marine refuge off Cahuita.

the south end of Cahuita town, and another four kilometers (two and a half miles) farther south at Puerto Vargas, with camping facilities, picnic tables and toilets. Admission to the park is US$6. There are lockers and restrooms at the entrance by the town and showers and restrooms by the Puerto Vargas campground.

From December to May, when the coast's persistent rains are less torrential, snorkelers and divers have the best view of tropical fish around the **Punta Cahuita reef** and a sunken eighteenth-century slave ship. Parrotfish, lobsters, sea urchins and green turtles are protected in these waters and can be spotted in abundance. But this is not Cozumel or the Cayman Islands, and dedicated divers may be disappointed. Tour companies and hotels can arrange boat trips to the reef, 500 m (1,640 ft) from shore.

North of town is **Playa Negra**, a long stretch of black sand and blue waves. Strong surf and rip tides make swimming dangerous here, but it's a lovely spot for walk.

Local agencies offer tours to **Indian reserves** in the area, though if you're truly interested in the culture you're better off taking a tour from the ATEC office in Puerto Viejo (see below).

The seldom-visited **Reserva Biológica Hitoy-Cereré** (758-3996 in the hills of the Cordillera Talamanca, is 60 km (37 miles) southwest of Limón; a road to the park is located just north of Cahuita off the main coastal highway. Much of the 8,910-ha (22,000-acre) park is virtually unexplored. A few rugged trails run under the forest canopy along rivers and waterfalls, and wildlife is abundant. Guides are essential; arrange for one through hotels and tour agencies in Limón, Cahuita or Puerto Viejo.

Far more accessible and quite delightful is **Reserva Biológica Aviarios del Caribe**, on the Río Estrella, 10 km (six and a quarter miles) north of Cahuita. Though not directly on the ocean, the reserve has its own water attractions — a river island where caimans, river otters and herons have free range in a private wildlife refuge. Owners Luis and Judy Arroyo have a way with nature's injured creatures, who thrive under their care. Buttercup, the resident three-toed sloth whose mother was killed in an auto accident, has her own swinging chair and an album of photos sent by guests (she also stars on a greeting card from the Nature Conservancy). Three toucans thrive in large wire buildings beside the reserve's lodge. When I last visited, Judy was caring for two newborn sloths whose mother had been killed by a logger.

Day visitors are treated to languid canoe trips down the river through canals and lagoons, where guides easily spot herons, kingfishers, manakins, northern jacanas, warblers and sloths high above the canopy in cecropia trees. Rain

ponchos, binoculars and umbrellas are provided. Back at the lodge, a trail leads through tropical forest; watch out for hundreds of frogs hopping about in the rainy season.

Tours can be arranged through Cahuita and Limón hotels and travel agencies, or with the **Arroyos** (/FAX 382-1335. Day trippers typically envy those spending the night.

WHERE TO STAY

Small, rundown *cabinas* and hotels are the norm in Cahuita. If the hotels below are all full and you must stay elsewhere, be sure your room has a good lock on the door, and put your valuables in the hotel's safe. It can be hard to make reservations since few places have faxes or post office boxes. When writing for reservations, address your letter to the hotel's name, Cahuita, Limón, Costa Rica. Start the process a couple of months before your visit. Cahuita Tours and Adventure Centre (see GENERAL INFORMATION, above) acts as a booking agent for many of the area's hotels.

Moderate

I took up residence at **Aviarios del Caribe** (/FAX 382-1335, Apdo 569-7300, Limón, on a whim while traveling the coast, and ended up canceling other reservations in order to extend my stay. While my companion dozed in a womb-like waterbed, I woke up every morning with the howler monkeys and sipped coffee on the verandah, watching herons, kingfishers and egrets slowly swooping up from their sleeping perches along the lagoon. Aviarios has six comfortable guest rooms with private baths and hot showers (one room has a tub); all rooms and public spaces are decorated with imaginative wildlife paintings by Mindy Lighthip. Breakfast is served on the deck; guests drive into Cahuita for other meals. The huge enclosed lounge area is packed with books. Guests can catch the latest soccer games and satellite movies with Luis on the color television. Tours to the Reserva Hitoy-Cereré, Punta Uva and Bribrí are available, along with fresh and saltwater fishing and endless bird watching (the Arroyos have counted 312 species from their verandah, so far). Best of all is the night frog walk, where guests wear headlamps to spot these tiny, elusive creatures which proliferate during the rainy season.

I didn't expect to see tropical wood desks, wood and glass French doors, oriental rugs and clipper-ship prints in a six-room Cahuita hotel. But the **Magellan Inn** (/FAX 755-0035 E-MAIL borgato @sol.racsa.co.cr about two kilometers (about one and a third miles) north of Cahuita, has all that, plus a coral reef left exposed by the receding sea 10,000 years ago. A bougainvillea-covered path leads through the fossilized reef alongside a small swimming pool; some heliconia, hibiscus and citrus trees are artfully planted around the lawns. There's a distinct sense of refined comfort here. As owner Elizabeth Newton says, "We chose to build in Cahuita because there was no place we would have wanted to stay here." Now there is a place for those in search of luxury.

El Encanto (/FAX 755-0113, just south of the village at Playa Negra, is a pleasant bed and breakfast with three comfortable bungalows with hot showers. The Elcanto will also arrange tours. **Chalet and Cabinas Hibiscus** (755-0021 FAX 755-0015 has an ideal location beside the pounding waves at Playa Negra; swimming is not advised, but you can splash about in the small pool while listening to the sounds of the sea.

railings on the front porch. All rooms are unusually large, with two double beds, ceiling fans, wood tables and chairs and louvered windows looking out to sea. The adjacent restaurant serves Spanish and Caribbean dishes, with the seasonings influenced by the French and Spanish owners. Advance reservations are essential and must be made by phone.

WHERE TO EAT

Cahuita dining spots are limited but the menus are varied thanks to many Caribe and European restaurateurs. Some of the best places are open for dinner only and few accept credit cards.

Three bungalows and three houses are scattered about the lawns.

The principle attraction at the **Atlantida Lodge** (755-0115 FAX 755-0213 E-MAIL atlantis@sol .racsa.co.cr WEB SITE www.atlantida.co.cr, Playa Negra, Cahuita, Limón, is the freshwater swimming pool. The 30 rooms with ceiling fans and hot-water baths are in ochre-colored buildings. Facilities include a full-service restaurant, a gymnasium with free-weights, and a tour desk.

Inexpensive

An exception to the rundown accommodations in Cahuita village is **Kelly Creek Hotel** (755-0007 E-MAIL kellycr@sol.racsa.co.cr, right next to the national park between the jungle and the sea. The four rooms are in a varnished laurel-wood building reminiscent of a New England beach house, with high sloping roofs and wood

Moderate

After weeks of eating greasy eggs, dry *gallo pinto* and bland *casados*, I nearly fainted at the astonishing menu at **Casa Creole** (755-0104. Pâté, blue cheese, spicy fish *beignets*, lobster with vanilla oil and ginger *vinaigrette*, steak *au gingembre*. That pretty pink house with white gingerbread trim and the table set with white linens, crystal and candlelight had to be an hallucination, and the aromas drifting from the kitchen just a fantasy for undernourished senses. But no, Casa Creole is for real, thanks to Hervé and Terry Kerinec's ambitious dreams. Using the finest ingredients from local gardens (including their well-tended herb patch), meat markets and the sea, the couple proves that the ingredients for fine dining do exist in Costa Rica, even if you have to drive all the way

Lovable three-toed sloths get mildly curious between naps on their favorite limbs.

to Cahuita to find them. Don't miss dinner here — and save room for the astonishing profiteroles. The Casa is located on the road along Playa Negra; closed Sundays.

Inexpensive

The hours are erratic (it's open for breakfast and dinner), but locals rave about the home-baked breads, seafood and salads at **Margaritaville (** 755-0038 on Playa Negra.

Several small restaurants in Cahuita village offer typical fish and Caribe fare, heavy on the rice and beans. The best of the lot is **Restaurante Roberto (** 750-0117 other popular spots are **Restaurant National Park** and **Restaurant Vaz** (not

Drivers can make it from Limón to Cahuita in 45 minutes; look for road signs pointing the way into the village.

PUERTO VIEJO DE LIMÓN

The road bumps along south of Cahuita past wood-stilt houses to Hotel Creek (also called Home or Hone Creek) and the turnoff to Puerto Viejo de Limón. Less than a decade ago Puerto Viejo could barely be called a town. My enduring image of it, from a trip in 1990, is the sight of an old man sleeping on his folded arms in the glassless window of a faded green house. The town has changed considerably since, but the beaches are still free (no

to be confused with Salón Vaz down the street, which happens to be Cahuita's hottest dance spot). **Miss Edith's (** 755-0248 at the north end of the village has long been acclaimed for its Creole food, but the service can be slow; as one customer said, "You know it's bad when you have to bring along a deck of cards to keep you busy while you're waiting." For oily yet yummy pizza try **Cactus (** 755-0276.

How to Get There

The 43-km (27-mile) dirt road from Limón to Cahuita was completed in 1979 and destroyed in the quake of 1991. It took many months to repair the road, which is now paved in most places. Bus travelers can avoid changing buses in Limón by taking the Sixaola-bound (Panama border) line from San José; the ride takes about four hours.

park fees here), the surf can be downright awesome, and everyone appears to be in a state of tropical bliss, enjoying hammock culture in full swing.

The 1991 earthquake was, perversely enough, the catalyst for Puerto Viejo's growth. It devastated the area. As one witness wrote: "Call it exquisite timing. I'd been in the southern Atlantic town of Puerto Viejo a bare 25 minutes when my friend Ana's house began to shake... Ana, who is Salvadorian and something of a connoisseur of earthquakes, dove for the kitchen table and yelled at me to get under it with her. 'What are you waiting for, a bus? Get down here.'

"The reef was totally exposed. Stranded fish flopped in the sunlight. The obvious question, 'Where has the water gone?' immediately led to the scarier 'What if it comes back all at once?' A few people with knapsacks and bedding started heading for higher ground in the jungly hills west of the village." Andrew Wilson who wrote about the event for the *Tico Times* (May 10, 1991) described helicopters shuttling the injured to San José and the aftermath of crumbled buildings and shattered lives.

Then it seemed that all 1,500 residents of Puerto Viejo cried in unison, "If I'm gonna stay here, I'm gonna make money." The post-earthquake building boom has died down, and the sounds of wailing saws and jackhammers no longer compete with the salsa, reggae, and cumbia music blasting from radios. The scents of ganja, coconut oil, and frying fish fill the air. Vendors sell beaded jewelry, incense, candles and bongs along the road closest to the black sand beach, which starts at the entrance

extremely vociferous in its protests against oil drilling in the area. A few foreign companies have bought the rights to drill along the Caribbean coast, and work has begun in some regions. It was all brought to a screeching halt in mid-2000, but there is no guarantee it won't start up again. You'll likely be asked to sign brochures or contribute cash to the cause — it's definitely a worthy one.

Some nights it seems everyone in town is lined up on the benches by ATEC's public phone. They also have a fax service and sell stamps, postcards and printed information on the region. Notices of events and causes are posted on the bulletin board.

You can gather some information about Puerto Viejo by checking out the WEB SITE www.puerto

to town across from a rusted, waterlogged barge sprouting trees. Puerto Viejo is rapidly displacing Cahuita as the budget destination of choice.

GENERAL INFORMATION

The **Asociación Talamanqueña de Ecoturismo y Conservación** (750-0398 FAX 750-0191 E-MAIL atecmail@solracsa.co.cr (Talamanca Association for Ecotourism and Conservation, or ATEC) operates a general information and tour office in town. Pick up a copy of the *Coastal Talamanca Cultural and Ecological Guide* for background and touring possibilities.

The association does its best to promote ecologically sound tourism, encouraging local culture and business; their pro-environment stance is evidenced in the "Stumps Don't Lie" bumper sticker posted above the front door. ATEC has been

viejo.net. It's worth a look, if only for the steel drums in the background music — sure to get you in the mood.

Buses stop at the edge of the beachfront road past the entrance to town, across from the Taberna Popo where street vendors and tourists converge.

WHAT TO SEE AND DO

Puerto Viejo's windswept, log-cluttered, black-sand beaches are its biggest attraction. They don't invite lounging, *per se;* the combination of jungle fauna, skittering crabs, ruthless no-see-ums and sand flies discourage the uninitiated. The cleanest sands and prettiest vistas are at **Punta Uva** south

OPPOSITE: Poison dart frogs, barely the size of a child's fingernail, hide under jungle leaves and sing in the night. ABOVE: A white-tailed deer pauses in a lowland rainforest near Limón.

of the village; farther south, **Punta Uvita** has big waves, and the best surfing of all is at the notorious **Salsa Brava**, where massive waves break over a reef. The best surfing months are from December to May and in June and July; the Salsa Brava is a Mecca for surfers from South America, Australia and the United States who add their distinct character to the village when surf's up.

Tours to **Kéköldi Indigenous Reserve** (/FAX 750-0119, home to about 200 Bribrí and Cabécar peoples are a must for the culturally curious; both ATEC (see above) and Mauricio Salazar of Cabinas Chimuri (see below), offer culture and nature tours to the reserve. ATEC also offers educational tours to Indian towns, nature preserves, a banana plantation, and some turtle-nesting sites; with advance reservations you may be able to arrange a trip to the remote Cordillera Talamanca or to Panama.

Spend a few hours searching for poison dart frogs amid the bromeliads at the **Finca la Isla Botanical Gardens** (750-0046, north of El Pizote Lodge. The guided tour is a delight for those interested in medicinal plants, tropical fruits, and spices. Admission is charged.

Atlantico Tours (/FAX 750-0004 on the coastal road rents beach cruisers, boogie boards, and snorkel gear, and runs tours through the jungle. **Aquamor Adventures** (391-3417 (cell phone) E-MAIL aquamor@sol.racsa.co.cr specializes in kayaking and scuba diving, and offers trips to the reefs, lagoons and caves of Gandoca Manzanillo (see above).

Puerto Viejo has hosted a **Caribbean music festival** in March for the past couple of years. Plan ahead and make hotel reservations if you're traveling at that time, then enjoy the festivities.

WHERE TO STAY

Ever-increasing options now include every thing from rustic cabinas to a sprinkling of higher quality accommodations. Reservations for the best places are essential during surfing season and *tico* holidays, and they are a hassle to arrange. Start at least three months in advance faxing or writing to the properties at Puerto Viejo, Limón, Costa Rica and follow up frequently. Some properties use ATEC's e-mail address for reservations; others are signed up with puertoviejo.net. If you're web savvy, check with both sites.

Moderate

The most artistic lodgings on the coast are at **Shawandha Lodge** (750-0018 FAX 750-0037 near Playa Chiquita. The thatched-roof bungalows are meant to replicate the homes of local indigenous peoples, though these are far more luxurious. Hardwood floors, tiled showers, hand-painted wall murals, and balconies with hammocks tempt guests to linger in their rooms. But no one can resist

the nearby beach, flower-filled garden, and the aroma of tropical recipes simmering at the open-air restaurant. **El Pizote Lodge** (221-0986 (in town) or 750-0080 (at the lodge) FAX 255-1527, just north of the bridge leading into town, has several wood cabins set far apart on lawns interspersed with large trees. Rooms with shared baths are in a long building at the end of the grounds; the six private bungalows have cold showers and somewhat ineffectual ceiling fans (beware of termites in the old wooden bed frames). Parrots, oropendolas and other birds twitter about the grounds; monkeys and frogs stay hidden in the forest behind the property. Breakfast is available for an additional charge, and there is a full bar, complete with darts, billiards and a ping pong table. The prices are high for what you get (especially since some nearby properties have pools and hot water), but the place has a desirable wilderness feeling. Hire a guide to lead you into the adjoining jungle. Management has changed and the hotel is undergoing refurbishing. A pool is in the works, and Pizote should be even nicer by the time you get there.

A place of dreams for architect Julian Grae and his wife Marlena, a decorator, **La Perla Negra** (750-0111 FAX 750-0114 E-MAIL perlanegra@desafio costarica.com is crafted from tropical hardwoods and bordered by forest. The 24 spacious rooms have bathrooms with separate toilet areas and hot water, ceiling fans, and balconies or terraces. Guests mingle at the swimming pool, leaving only to explore Puerto Viejo's restaurants. Many rooms face the ocean, just a few yards away, and you can walk to Cahuita from here.

The gardens are exceptional at **Miraflores Lodge** (/FAX 750-0038 E-MAIL mirapam@sol .racsa.co.cr, four kilometers (two and a half miles) south of Puerto Viejo, thanks to owner Pamela Carpenter Novarro's green thumb. Carpenter is active in ATEC and takes a responsible attitude toward the community, and her guests benefit from her knowledge. The two-story lodge has rooms with shared kitchen facilities and rooms with kitchenettes, or you can rent the entire top floor with a full kitchen and separate bedrooms. You may not want to leave Puerto Viejo once you set up housekeeping at **Villas del Caribe** (750-0202 or 233-2200 FAX 750-0203 or 221-2801 WEB SITE www.villas caribe.net, at Playa Chiquita. The two-story villas are completely equipped with kitchenettes, terraces with barbecue grills, living rooms, separate bedrooms and balconies with hammocks. The villas sleep six (there is an additional charge for more than two people). The market stocks all necessities, and the management rents snorkeling equipment and can set up all tours. Other pluses include a volleyball court in the sand, a ping pong table, and a boat for fishing trips.

Caribbean Coast transportation ranges from light aircraft TOP to traditional dugout canoes BOTTOM.

If you must have air-conditioning and a swimming pool, your best choice is south of town at **Hotel Punta Cocles** (234-8055 FAX 234-8033. You will sacrifice character for comfort, however. The 60 rooms are in white cabins spread along lawns with play equipment for kids; the beach is across the street. Some rooms have kitchenettes.

Inexpensive

Casa Verde (750-0015 FAX 750-0047 is by a long shot the most pleasant budget hotel in town, with immaculate rooms set in gardens on a quiet residential street. The 14 rooms have hammocks in front and two single or one double bed; rooms with shared baths are the least expensive. It's the first in-town spot to fill up, so reserve well in advance. Cabins built in the Bribrí style (A-frame roofs covered in cane thatch) house guests at **Cabinas Chimuri** (/FAX 750-0119, set in a 20-ha (49-acre) private reserve near the sea. Shared baths and cooking facilities allow guests to mingle as if they are family, boasting together about sightings of boa, kingfishers, armadillos and bats. Owner Mauricio Salazar guides morning and night hikes through the reserve's trails and a full-day hiking tour (for the hardy) to an Indian reserve. **Playa Chiquita Lodge** (/FAX 750-0062 offers all the necessities in a gorgeous setting on the beach of the same name. Cabins have hot water, fans, beds, rocking chairs, and hammocks and are next to a trail to the beach. Meals are available with advance notice.

WHERE TO EAT

Moderate

Some say it's worth traveling the rutted road to Puerto Viejo to dine at the **Garden Restaurant** (750-0069, where the Trinidadian chef prepares Caribbean, Thai and Indian dishes served in a candlelit dining room. The menu is extraordinary — passionfruit salsa on grilled chicken, Jamaican jerked chicken, curries, ginger cake — though the daily offerings are determined by the chef's whims and the availability of ingredients. The restaurant is only open from December through March and June to September, and also closes whenever the help needs a day off. **Amimoda** (no phone) by Punta Uva gives the Garden some fierce competition with its homemade ravioli and gnocchi, grilled lobster, and smoked shark. Pizzas, pastas and *postres* (desserts) bring crowds to **Restaurant Coral** (750-0051 at dinner; breakfasts of wholewheat pancakes, Mexican omelets and baskets of muffins fuel surfers before they hit the waves.

Inexpensive

Gallo pinto prepared with coconut milk is the standard side dish at **Restaurant Tamara** (750-0148, though you can have french fries or *patacones*

(refried plantains) with your fish, chicken or beef. Across from the beach, **El Parquecito** (no phone) is a favorite for lobster and fish, while **Stanford's** (no phone) stokes a young crowd with rice and beans before they hit the reggae dance floor. Several sodas line Puerto Viejo's sandy streets. Follow your nose until something smells especially enticing. The women who run these little shacks make some mean Caribbean soups, stews and spicy seafood concoctions.

MANZANILLO

More a settlement than a town, Manzanillo sits within **Refugio Silvestre Gandoca-Manzanillo**, which extends south to the Panama border. This remote region with few roads comes the closest to fulfilling television-inspired images of white-sand beaches and swaying palms, and residents are committed to keeping it that way. The Federación de Organizaciones de Corridor Talamanca–Caribe is comprised of at least 13 groups creating a conservation corridor connecting the Refugio Gandoca–Manzanillo with Parque Internacional La Amistad. They hope to extend the corridor into Panama's Parque del Boca Verde.

GENERAL INFORMATION

The nearest telephones and tourist services are at Puerto Viejo. Buses are infrequent; buses to Sixaola at the Panamanian border drop passengers at the edge of Manzanillo. If you're driving, go slowly. The roads are rutted and sandy, with narrow bridges that appear suddenly.

WHAT TO SEE AND DO

Beaches and a small coral reef are Manzanillo's biggest draw. The **Refugio Silvestre Gandoca–Manzanillo** (754-2133 spreads along the coastline from Punta Uva south; a wooden sign near the Hotel Punta Cocles marks the beginning of the refuge. Classified as a mixed-management preserve, the park contains a few hotels and camps, which aim to stabilize the economic base of the area. Offshore, a coral reef spreads for about 200 m (650 ft); the best snorkeling is at Punta Uva and just south of the Almonds and Coral Tent Camp (see below). One of the park's biggest attractions are its dolphins. Atlantic spotted, bottlenose, and tucuxi dolphins all swim in the waters, surfing in the wake from tour boats. You may see the dolphins from shore; to get closer you need to go in a boat. Contact the **Talamanca Dolphin Foundation** (754-2133 for information and guides. Trails lead from the beach into forested foothills and along mangrove lagoons, where manatees, crocodiles and caimans are protected from human predators. There are several turtle nesting sites in the area, and howler monkeys, sloths and ocelots find shelter in the forest. Explorers can arrange boat trips along the shore and lagoons or hikes into the forest through hotels in the area.

WHERE TO STAY AND EAT

Moderate

My favorite accommodations are the net-covered tents on stilts at **Almonds and Corals Tent Camp** (750-0232 FAX 750-0231 E-MAIL almonds@so .racsa.co.cr WEB SITE www.geoexpediciones.com. Platforms built a few feet above the jungle undergrowth support waterproof green tents (you can close the flaps for privacy) with private bathrooms

Geo Expediciones (272-2024 FAX 272-2220, which specializes in out-of-the-way tours to the Caribbean and Sarapiquí regions.

ON TO PANAMA

Sixty kilometers (37 miles) south of Limón, the road to Manzanillo passes through **Bribrí**, a small village and management center for Indian reserves in the Cordillera Talamanca. The only bank in the region, a branch of the Banco Nacional, is located here. The village sits at the edge of **Parque Internacional La Amistad**, which spreads over 194,00 ha (479,200 acres) of mountains, cloud forests and watershed. Entrance to the park is at

with cold showers, single beds, and electric lamps and portable fans. Big white hammocks hang by the entrances. The 20 units are camouflaged under tall trees and thick foliage. At night it's easy to imagine you've struck out alone like a modern-day Robinson Crusoe. Raised wooden boardwalks connect the tents with the large dining room where fixed-menu meals are served to the beat of cumbia tunes. Howler monkeys greet the morning with rumbling roars; answer their call and walk along the lengthy beach to spot toucans, parrots and trogons in the trees. The best swimming is 100 m (110 yards) south of the camp near the solitary Maxi's restaurant, the only nearby option for meals. The camp is in a private reserve surrounded by the Refugio Silvestre Gandoca–Manzanillo. Tours include snorkeling, kayaking, and visits to a nearby Bribrí Indian village. Owner Aurora Gamaz handles reservations through her agency

the west side near San Vito (see SAN VITO, page 199 in THE ZONA SUR).

Indian reserves for the KéköLdi, Bribrí and Cabécar groups are located in the area. You must have prior permission to visit the settlements; contact the ATEC office in Puerto Viejo (see above) for information.

Many foreigners on long-term stays in Costa Rica use the Sixaola border crossing as a quick way to enter another country (Panama) to renew their Costa Rican visas. Buses run to the border from Limón and San José. Geo Expediciones (see above) offers tours farther into Panama, and there is talk of creating a circuit tour running down Costa Rica's Caribbean coast, along Panama's northern area and back into Costa Rica at the Pacific coast border crossing at Paso Canoas.

A four-wheel-drive vehicle maneuvers the rocky road to the Panama border.

The Caribbean Coast

Travelers'
Tips

GETTING TO COSTA RICA

BY AIR

Most flights come in to the **Aeropuerto Internacional Juan Santamaría** (443-2682, located 16 km (10 miles) northwest of downtown San José in Alajuela. The airport underwent a major overhaul in 1999–2000, and now has a more efficient terminal and parking lot. In high season some charters arrive at the **Aeropuerto Daniel Obudar** (667-0014 in the northwest province of Guanacaste.

Most airlines from Canada and Europe make connections through Miami, Dallas, Houston, Los

Angeles or Mexico City en route to San José. Airlines with daily flights include Continental, American, Delta, Air Canada, Aviateca, Iberia, Mexicana and United. European travelers usually pass through Miami or Houston; Virgin Atlantic and Iberia have direct flights. Martinair flies from Amsterdam via Miami. Condor stops in Tampa on its Frankfurt–San José route. British Airways offers a weekly flight from Gatwick. The Costa Rican Airline LACSA now flies under the Grupo TACA name; some of their flights from the United States stop in Mexico, Guatemala and/or

PRECEEDING PAGES: The rainforest canopy LEFT etches a lacy pattern on the sky. RIGHT: Butterflies provide flashes of color in the dense green rain forest. ABOVE: Most churches, such as this one in Quepos, are functional and simple. OPPOSITE: Sailors find shelter in several remote bays along the Pacific Coast.

Honduras. Grupo TACA has announced plans to offer flights from San José to South America. Fares are highest from December through April; some airlines now keep their high-season rates until mid-August, then drop them through October.

Several operators now offer charter flights to San José and Liberia, particularly in high season. The charters are usually booked by major tour operators (see below).

BY INTERNATIONAL BUS LINE

There is good bus service between Costa Rica and Panama, Nicaragua, Honduras and Guatemala, though the trip can be long and rough. Cost Rica's international bus company, **Ticabus** (221-8954 FAX 223-8158 has direct service from Guatemala, El Salvador, Honduras, Nicaragua and Panama. Since peace has settled in Central America, bus travel is far safer than in the past, and first-class long-distance buses have comfortable seats, air-conditioning and toilets.

BY SHIP

Several cruise lines stop in Costa Rica's Caribbean port at Moín near Limón and the Pacific port of Puerto Caldera near Puntarenas. You might be able to arrange to disembark at these points.

BY CAR

Inveterate travelers with plenty of time to spend driving on the Carretera Interamericana Highway through Central America can cross the border from Nicaragua into Costa Rica at Peñas Blancas, or from Panama at Paso Canoas. These border crossings are open only during daylight hours; check with the Costa Rican embassy regarding current red tape. Once you have entered Costa Rica, the Pan-American is called the Carretera Interamericana, or Highway 1.

TOUR OPERATORS

Fortunately, Costa Rica is represented by many excellent travel agencies, some with web sites and e-mail addresses. Most will work with individual travelers, as well as groups. Those specializing in special interest tours are also listed in YOUR CHOICE (see page 45). The following Costa Rican companies are particularly professional and knowledgeable.

Aguas Bravas (292-2072 FAX 229-4837 E-MAIL info@aguas-bravas.co.cr offers rafting trips on the Sarapiquí, Peñas Blancas, and Toro rivers, as well as horseback riding and mountain bike tours.

Alacrán Surf Tours (/FAX 777-1721 E-MAIL info @alacransurf.com WEB SITE www.alacransurf.com arranges customized surf trips.

Aventuras Naturales (225-3939 FAX 253-6934 E-MAIL avenat@racsa.co.cr, Boulevard la California between Calles 33 and 35, San José, is one of the oldest adventure tour operators in the country and specializes in river rafting and mountain biking trips.

Bi.Costa Rica (/FAX 446-7585 E-MAIL bicostarica @yellowweb.co.cr leads bicycle tours from one coast to the other.

Calypso Tours (256-2727 FAX 256-6767 E-MAIL info@calypsotours.com, Edificio Las Arcadas, Third Floor, San José, offers catamaran cruises off the Península de Nicoya.

Camino Travel (257-0107 or 234-2530 FAX 257-0243, Calle 1 at Avenida Central, is conveniently

located in downtown San José; its agents are quite adept at arranging on-the-spot itineraries for any budget, and they work well with undecided travelers. Your options are greater if you contact them well in advance.

Coast to Coast Adventures (280-8054 FAX 225-6055 or 225-7806 E-MAIL info@ctoadventures.com, operates river rafting, mountain biking, and trekking tours around the country.

Costa Rica Expeditions (257-0766 FAX 257-1665 E-MAIL costaric@expeditions.co.cr WEB SITE www.expeditions.co.cr, Apdo 6941, Calle Central at Avenida 3, San José, was one of the first to offer adventure travel arrangements in the country. It's still one of the best, with lodges in Tortuguero and Monteverde and an exciting tent camp in Corcovado. The company's nature guides are excellent, and their web site contains a wealth of information.

Costa Rica Sun Tours (296-7757 FAX 296-4307 WEB SITE www.crsuntours.com represents two excellent private nature reserves: Tiskita Jungle Lodge on the southwest coast, and Arenal Observatory Lodge next to the Volcán Arenal. Quite a lot of international tour operators use Sun Tours for their in-country services and guides, and the company offers several unusual itineraries.

Costa Rica's Temptations (220-4437 FAX 220-2792 E-MAIL tours@crinfo.com is a full-service company offering all levels of tours and bookings.

Destination Costa Rica (223-0744 or 233-4758 FAX 222-9747 TOLL-FREE (800) 835-1223 designs comprehensive adventure tours.

Ecole Travel (223-2240 FAX 392-7275 E-MAIL ecolecr@racsa.co.cr WEB SITE www.travel costa rica.net, Calle 7 between Avenidas Central and 1 inside 7th Street Books, is a good source for the budget traveler.

Geo Expediciones (272-2024 or 272-4175 FAX 272-2220 E-MAIL almonds@sol.racsa.co.cr WEB SITE www.geoexpediciones.com/geo.html operates two nature reserves in less-traveled parts of the country — Quinta Sarapiquí in the northeast and Almonds and Corals Tent Camp on the southern Caribbean coast. The company specializes in travel to remote regions, including trips into Panama.

Horizontes Nature Adventures (222-2022 FAX 255-4513 E-MAIL horizont@sol.racsa.co.cr WEB SITE www.horizontes.com, Paseo Colón 150, San José, is known for its superb multilingual guides and individualized itineraries.

Latii Express Travel (296-1146 FAX 231-7957 E-MAIL latiiexpress@costarica.com WEB SITE www .latiiexpress.com is a full-service company and also operates a marina in Puntarenas.

Otec International (256-0633 FAX 257-7849 E-MAIL otec@gotec.com WEB SITE www.gotec .sol.racsa.com, 275 m (300 yards) north of the Teatro Nacional, San José, specializes in student and budget travel and uses a travel voucher system to allow its clients to pick and choose transportation and accommodations.

Ríos Tropicales (233-6455 FAX 255-4354 E-MAIL info@riostropicales.com WEB SITE www.rios tropicales.com, was one of the first river-rafting expedition companies in the country and also specializes in kayaking and trekking.

Safaris Corobicí (/FAX 669-1091 E-MAIL safaris @sol.racsa.co.cr is the largest operator leading tours on the Río Corobicí, a perfect venue for bird watching.

Serendipity Adventures (556-2592 TOLL-FREE FROM THE US (877) 507-1358 FAX 556-2593 E-MAIL costarica@serendipityadventures.com WEB SITE www.serendipityadventures.com offers a unique balloon trip over Volcán Arenal.

Swiss Travel Service (668-1020 FAX 282-4890 E-MAIL swisstvl@sol.racsa.co.cr WEB SITE www .swisstravelcr.com is one of the largest agencies in the country and handles large groups as well as individuals.

TRAVEL AGENCIES ABROAD

Several United States companies specialize in travel to Costa Rica and work directly with in-country operators and guides. Most have arrangements with European and Canadian travel agents.

Backroads ((510) 527-1555 TOLL-FREE (800) 462-2848 FAX (510) 527-1444 WEB SITE www.backroads.com, 801 Cedar Street, Berkeley, California 94710, arranges bicycling, trekking and adventure tours. The office staff are particularly knowledgeable.

Costa Rica Connection ((805) 543-8823 TOLL-FREE (800) 345-7422 FAX (805) 543-3626 WEB SITE www.crconnect.com, 1124 Nipomo Street, Suite C, San Luis Obispo, California 93401, is linked by family and business ties to some of the country's best nature lodges. They do a great job with individual itineraries, suggesting unusual options.

Costa Rica Experts ((773) 935-1009 TOLL-FREE (800) 827-9046 FAX (773) 935-9252 E-MAIL crexpert@ais.net WEB SITE www.crexpert.com, 3166 North Lincoln Avenue, Suite 424, Chicago, Illinois 60657, is aptly named. Its agents are extremely knowledgeable and are always coming up with new places for their clients to sample.

Field Guides ((512) 327-4953 TOLL-FREE (800) 728-4953 E-MAIL fgileader@aol.com, PO Box 160723, Austin, Texas 78716, specializes in birdwatching tours in various parts of the country.

Golf Costa Rica Adventures ((970) 356-028 TOLL-FREE (800) 477-8971 FAX (970) 352-6324 E-MAIL golf@centralamerica.com WEB SITE www.crsite.com/golf, Interlink 854 PO Box 02-5635, Miami, Florida 33102, arranges golf tours.

Holbrook Travel ((352) 377-7111 TOLL-FREE (800) 451-7111 FAX (352) 371-3710 WEB SITE www.holbrooktravel.com, 3540 NW 13th Street, Gainesville, Florida 32609, is connected with the Selva Verde Lodge in Sarapiquí, and offers nature and adventure tours of the country.

Journey Latin America (0161-832-1441 FAX 0161-832-1551 WEB SITE www.journeylatinamerica.co.uk, Suites 28–30 Barton Arcade, Deansgate, Manchester M3 2BH, is a British agency with considerable experience in Latin America.

Ladatco Tours ((305) 854-8422 TOLL-FREE (800) 327-6162 FAX (305) 285-0504 E-MAIL info@ladatco.com WEB SITE www.ladatco.com 2220 Coral Way, Miami, Florida 33145, is a full-service agency with extensive expertise in the area.

Overseas Adventure Travel TOLL-FREE (800) 493-6824, One Broadway, Suite 600, Cambridge, Massachusetts 02142, offers off-the-beaten path itineraries for small groups (maximum, 16 people).

Remarkable Journeys ((713) 721-2517 TOLL-FREE (800) 856-1993 FAX (713) 728-8334 E-MAIL cooltrips@remjourneys.com WEB SITE www.remjourneys.com, PO Box 31855, Houston, Texas 77231, offers tours for independent travelers and groups, including a yoga tour and several adventure tours.

Tico Travel TOLL-FREE (800) 493-8426 E-MAIL tico@gate.net WEB SITE www.ticotravel.com,

161 East Commercial Boulevard, Fort Lauderdale, Florida 33334, can arrange surfing tours and provide information on surf areas.

Wildland Adventures ((206) 365-0686 TOLL-FREE (800) 345-4453 FAX (206) 363-6615 E-MAIL info@wildland.com WEB SITE www.wildland.com, 3516 NE 155th Street, Seattle, Washington 98155, emphasizes various levels of adventure travel, from family cruises to mountain climbing.

ARRIVING AND LEAVING

International travelers need a valid passport stamped at the airport immigration desk or border crossing. The stamp is good for 30 to 90 days;

in theory (though rarely in practice at the airport), you are required to possess a ticket out of the country and sufficient funds (around US$400) for the duration of your stay. Once your passport has been stamped, copy the photo and immigration stamp page. Keep it with you at all times. Traffic police and even museum guards can ask to see your passport whenever they wish. A photocopy usually suffices.

A departure tax of US$17 is due when you leave the country. Vendors selling tax coupons mob travelers outside the airport; it's perfectly OK to pay your tax there, or at the counter inside the office. Make sure you pay before getting in line at the airline counters; if you wait,

OPPOSITE: Bicycles are a preferred mode of transport throughout the country, despite the steep and rutted roads. ABOVE: A park sign points the way to one of Costa Rica's most popular destinations.

Travelers' Tips

you'll have to retrace your steps, pay the tax, and return to the counter for your boarding pass. Travelers must reconfirm their flights 24 hours before departure.

CONSULATES AND EMBASSIES

The following countries have embassies or consulates in San José.

Canada (296-4149 FAX 231-4783, Oficentro Ejecutivo la Sábana, Sábana Sur (Building 5, 3rd Floor).

France (225-0733 or 225-0933, Road to Curridabat, 200 m (585 ft) south and 25 m (24 yards) east of Indoor Club.

Germany (232-5533, Rohrmoser.

Great Britain (221-5816, Edificio Centro Colón, 11th Floor, Avenida Colón at Calle 38.

Holland (296-1490, Oficentro Ejecutivo, La Sábana Sur (Building 3, 3rd Floor).

Italy (224-6574 or 234-2326, Los Yoses, Avenida 10 between Calles 33 and 35.

Spain (222-1933, Calle 32 between Paseo Colón and Avenida 2.

Switzerland (221-4829, Centro Colón, 10th Floor, Paseo Colón at Calle 38.

United States (220-3939 FAX 220-2305, Calle 120, Avenida 0, Pavas.

COSTA RICAN EMBASSIES ABROAD

Costa Rica has embassies and consulates in the following countries:

Australia ((02) 9261-1177 FAX (02) 9261-2953 Level 11, 30 Clarence Street, Sydney 2000.

Canada ((613) 562-2855 FAX (613) 562-2582, 135 York Street, Suite 208, Ottawa, Ontario K1N 5T4.

France ((01) 4578-9696 FAX (01) 4578-9966, 78 Avenue Emile Zola, 75015 Paris.

Germany ((022) 854-0040 FAX (022) 854-9053, Langenbachstrasse 19, 53113 Bonn, Germany.

Great Britain ((020) 7706-8844 FAX (020) 7706-8655, Flat 1, 14 Lancaster Gate, London W2 3LH.

Holland ((070) 354-0780 FAX (070) 358-4754, Laan Copes Van Cattenbuch 46, 2585 G.B. Den Haag.

Italy ((06) 4425-1046 FAX (06) 4425-1048, Via Bartolomeo, Eustacho 22, Interno 6, Roma 00161.

Japan ((03) 3486-1812 FAX (03) 3486-1813, Kowo Building, No. 38 9 F. 901, 4-12-24 Nishi-Azabu, Minato-Ku, Tokyo 106-0031.

South Africa ((011) 705-3434 FAX (011) 705-1222, PO Box 68140, Bryanston 2021, South Africa.

Spain ((91) 345-9622 FAX (91) 353-3709, Paseo de la Castellana 164, 17A, 28046 Madrid.

Switzerland ((031) 372-7887 FAX (031) 372-7834, Schwarztorstrasse 11, 3007 Berne.

United States ((202) 234-2945 or (202) 328-6628 FAX (202) 265-4795, 2114 S Street, NW, Washington DC, 20008.

TOURIST INFORMATION

The main **Costa Rican Tourism Institute (ICT) office (** 223-1733 FAX 223-5452 WEB SITE www.tourism-costarica.com is in the Edificio Genaro Valverde, on Avenida 4 between Calles 5 and 7. This office operates a TOLL-FREE NUMBER FOR THE US AND CANADA (800) 343-6332; they'll send a color tourist brochure on the country's highlights with a little service information. Travel agencies and tour companies are much better sources for practical information. There is a **Tourist Information Office (** 223-1733, extension 2777, Calle 5 between Avenidas Central and 2 in the Plaza de la Cultura. The quality of assistance offered varies considerably, but the office does distribute maps, some brochures, and general information. They also have fairly up-to-date information on the location of bus terminals (which change frequently). The office is open Monday to Friday from 8 AM to 4 PM. There is also an information booth at the airport.

GETTING AROUND COSTA RICA

BY AIR

Two regional airlines serve the many small airstrips located in remote regions of the country. Weather conditions often hamper flight schedules; it's not unusual to sit around for hours waiting for the clouds to clear. Fares are reasonable when compared with the cost of rental cars. Passengers are usually limited to 11 kg (25 pounds) of luggage. **TravelAir (** 220-3054 FAX 220-0413 E-MAIL reservations@travelair-costarica.com is relatively reliable and has flights from San José's Tobias Bolano Airport (** 232-2820, seven kilometers (four and a third miles) west of downtown San José in the suburb of Pavas, to most airstrips. **SANSA (** 221-9494 FAX 255-2176, Calle 24 between Paseo Colón and Avenida 1, is the government-subsidized line. It flies nearly everywhere out of a terminal near San José's Aeropuerto Internacional Juan Santamaría.

Always book your flight far in advance and reserve your seat with a credit-card deposit. Be sure to confirm and reconfirm your reservation, know which airport you're flying from, and arrive at least one hour before the scheduled departure. Overbooking is common. Some hotels in outlying areas offer air transportation on private or charter flights.

BY BUS

Bus travel is cheap, easy and fairly comfortable. Buses travel to all parts of the country, though most use San José as their hub. Thus, those traveling by bus may be forced to overnight in the city as they travel from one part of the country to another. Most intercity buses currently depart from the area around the main bus station at Calle 16 between Avenidas 1 and 3. Commonly called the Coca-Cola Station (named for a long-gone bottling plant), the station is in a rough part of town. Travelers must keep a close eye on their belongings at all times. Urban buses, and those traveling to nearby cities, depart from *paradas* (bus stops) all over town. The government recently shuffled the stops around in an effort to avoid congestion; as a result, travelers are often directed to one stop when they should be at another. If you plan to travel extensively by bus, stop at the ICT information office or École Travel (see above) for the latest information.

By Rental Car

Many travelers prefer to see Costa Rica at their own pace in the comfort of a car. Sedans and four-wheel-drive vehicles are both available; air-conditioning is optional. If you plan to leave the few major highways, you're best off in a four-wheel-drive vehicle with high suspension and durable tires. Rental rates are very high, as is gas. Rates for a four-wheel-drive vehicle are nearly twice those for a standard car. You may get a better rate renting ahead with Budget, Hertz or National (Europe-Car) in your home country.

Car rental agencies barely meet the demand for cars in the dry season (November to March). Always reserve far in advance of your travels, and be specific about your requirements. Most foreign auto insurance policies do not cover rental cars in Costa Rica, and collision insurance is mandatory. I suggest you get insurance that covers any deductibles. Given the rough condition of the roads, you're bound to return the car with a few dings — I learned my lesson after a rock flew up and cracked the windshield.

Costa Rican agencies have competitive rates. You can rent in advance by faxing or calling the company; most have English-speaking clerks. In addition, most of the tour companies listed above can arrange for a car. You may be able to talk them into a bargain during low season. My favorite agency is **Adobe** (258-4242 or 442-2422 FAX 221-9286 E-MAIL adobecar@sol.racsa.co.cr. They provide complimentary drop off and pick up at your hotel or at any destination where SANSA airlines flies. They also give drivers a list of preferred gas stations around the country for repairs. I have found them to be prompt and helpful.

All the car rental companies have offices in San José, usually at the airport; drop-off offices are located near the airport in Alajuela. It's difficult to rent a car outside the city, though there are small agency branches in Quepos, Jacó, Liberia, and Limón. Some companies will deliver your car to Puntarenas, Heredia and other outlying areas for an additional fee.

Driving Tips

Conquering Costa Rica's roads is a rite of passage and certainly as exciting as spotting a two-toed sloth. Travelers tell stories, with surprising equanimity, of Volkswagen-sized potholes, flooded riverbeds, flat tires and busted suspensions. Range Rovers, Suzukis and Toyotas are vehicles of choice for those with unlimited budgets and time. But even a short cruise through the countryside in a Nissan sedan has its rewards.

Part of the adventure is the very real danger inherent in driving in Costa Rica. For all their

amiability, *ticos* are deadly on the road. Costa Rica has one of the highest auto fatality rates in the world (18 deaths per 100,000 km or 60,000 miles, compared to 2.7 per 100,000 km in the United States), due to horrendous weather, road conditions and the native pursuit of reckless driving. Don't drive in San José unless you've already conquered Buenos Aires, Quito or Mexico City. First-timers are best off renting cars at the airport or at their hotel.

Outside San José the few main highways quickly access the full spectrum of landscapes: forested ocean cliffs; barren, fog-shrouded volcano peaks; vast, rolling cattle ranges; banana, coconut, coffee and macadamia plantations; and all the irreplaceable snapshot scenes of village life. Most highways are two-lane affairs with few directional signs and plenty of holes, ruts and ridges. Rain runoff causes *derrumbes* (rock slides) in the mountains. Pavement dissolves into ruts in an instant.

Local drivers may try to intimidate you by riding your tail and flashing their headlights. All drivers pass with impunity, impervious to like-minded suicidal souls coming toward them. Drive slowly until you've grown accustomed to the roadways and your vehicle's limitations.

Four-wheel-drive vehicles come in handy in mountainous areas.

Speed Limits

Speed limits are 80 km/h (50 mph) on all primary roads and 60 km/h (37 mph) on secondary roads, dropping down to 40 km/h (25 mph) around towns and schools. Traffic police use radar, and speed limits are enforced by handing out moving violations (pay them through your rental company). Beware of the speed trap between Guápiles and Limón.

Road Rules

When undertaking to drive in Costa Rica, you should be aware of a few rules. First, a foreign driver's license is valid for the first three months you are in Costa Rica. Seat belts are mandatory and motorcyclists must wear helmets. It is illegal to make a right turn on a red light unless a white painted arrow on the road indicates otherwise. It is illegal to enter an intersection unless you can also leave it. At unmarked intersections, yield to the car on your right. Drive on the right side of the road; pass on the left.

HITCHHIKING

Hitching is relatively uncommon in Costa Rica, even among budget travelers. The frequency and range of public buses make it unnecessary. If you do hitch, make it an active, friendly affair. Smile and wave at passing drivers, dress neatly and try to look nonthreatening. *Ticos* consider many budget travelers to be an unruly lot, ill-mannered and shabbily dressed. Once you get a ride, practice your Spanish and converse with the drivers and passengers. Offer to pay for the ride by asking, *"¿Cuanto le debo?"* (How much do I owe you?).

Use discretion when accepting a ride; if possible, try to hitch with a companion at a store, gas station or restaurant. Avoid hitchhiking on major roadways or in urban areas and bear in mind that if a bus does not go to your destination, few cars will either.

One of the great pleasures in driving through rural areas is the opportunity to offer a ride to locals accustomed to walking for hours to work or school. It's a good way to learn more about the country, the people and the language.

ACCOMMODATION

Costa Rica is blessed with hundreds of one-of-a-kind small hotels sprinkled around the main tourist attractions. A continuing boom in construction has resulted in an astonishing number of properties in certain areas, especially along the coast. Many outlying lodges are set in private nature reserves or amidst macadamia, coffee and fruit plantations.

Large chain-operated resorts are mostly found in San José's suburbs and along the Pacific coast,

and are becoming grander in scale. Holiday Inn, Meliá and Marriott all own or manage San José properties, and Meliá and Marriott have luxury resorts on the Pacific coast.

The ICT (Costa Rican Tourism Institute) does not have an official star rating for hotels, and few hoteliers take their list of inspected and approved hotels seriously. Most hoteliers operate independently, working with national and international travel agencies and independent guests. The majority of hotels spread throughout the country have less than 100 rooms. Some have developed a fervid following. Advance reservations for all the hotels mentioned in this book are absolutely necessary in the high season, though you might

stumble upon an unclaimed room at the last minute. Make your reservation through the fax numbers or e-mail addresses listed. The postal system is notoriously unreliable; some hotels have postal drops in Miami, Florida, with courier air service to Costa Rica, which seems to be reliable.

HOTEL PRICES

Room rates in Costa Rica are higher than those in neighboring countries, and an expensive room does not mean you'll get telephones, television, air-conditioning—even hot water, in some cases. Within San José and the surrounding regions such amenities are common in most hotels. In remote areas, the expense of building, maintaining, and transporting supplies causes rates to rise.

Showers in some inexpensive places may have an electric unit in the shower head that heats the water. These "suicide showers" can be quite disconcerting at first. To get hot water, turn on the heating switch while the water is off (wear rubber-soled shoes), then turn the water on.

Nature lodges typically include meals in their rates and offer packages for several nights' stay. The rates quoted are set per person rather than per room. Some include transport from San José via small plane or van. In such cases the flat room rate may be deceptive, since the cost of setting up your own transport may be much higher than what the hotel offers.

Our categories for hotel room prices are calculated at the cost of a standard double room during high season (November through April

bed and breakfasts springing up around San José and small coastal towns, though the network is informal.

YOUTH HOSTELS AND CAMPING

There are a few official youth hostels, such as the Toruma in San José, that are affiliated with international organizations. For information contact **Red Costarricense de Alburgues Juveniles (RECAJ)** (/FAX 224-4085, Apdo 1355-1002, San José, Paseo de los Estudiantes, Avenida Central between Calles 29 and 31. For information about camping see BACKPACKING, page 33 in YOUR CHOICE.

and again in August). Many establishments drop their rates by about one-third in the low, or green, season. Most hotels post their rates in United States dollars. A 16.4% sales tax is added to the bill; often, there is a 10% service charge added as well.

Very Expensive	Over US$150 (45,000 colónes)
Expensive	US$100 to US$150 (30,000 to 45,000 colónes)
Moderate	US$50 to US$100 (15,000 to 30,000 colónes)
Inexpensive	under US$50 (under 15,000 colónes)

BED AND BREAKFASTS

Many small hotels offer breakfast with their room rates though they are not bed and breakfasts, per se. There are more officially-termed

EATING OUT

Costa Rica's dining scene has improved over the past few years, especially in the most popular tourist destinations. International dishes are available in many areas, and pizza, pastas and burgers are as prevalent as rice and beans. Vegetarians are in luck here, since meat is typically served as a side dish and most restaurants serve a few non-meat entrees. Dining hours are like those in the United States rather than other Latin American countries. Hearty breakfasts including eggs, tropical fruit salads and *gallo pinto* are commonly eaten before work. Lunch is a one-hour break at midday, and dinner is served around 7 PM.

Lavish resorts such as the Meliá Playa Conchal continue to rise in the northern Pacific.

PRICES

Our restaurant prices are based on the average cost of a meal per person, not including drinks. Restaurant bills include a 13% tax and often a 10% service charge.

Expensive	US$10 or more (3,000 colónes)
Moderate	US$5 to US$10 (1,500 to 3,000 colónes)
Inexpensive	US$5 or less (1,500 colónes)

TIPPING

Tips are generally not expected. Taxi drivers aren't tipped unless they provide an additional service like carrying luggage. A 10% service charge is added to most restaurant (and some hotel) bills and is supposed to be distributed among the servers. Unfortunately, this often is not the case, and waiters are beginning to realize that American tourists are accustomed to tipping. If the service is exceptional, leave a few extra colónes (about five percent of the bill). Tour guides and drivers do expect tips, about 10% of the tour's cost.

BANKING

Banks are generally open weekdays from 9 AM to 3 PM, and their service has become more efficient. Ask at your hotel for the best bank for travelers; some agree to exchange travelers' checks but aren't familiar with the process. Exchange rates offered by hotels are usually competitive with those at the bank. If you're traveling to outlying regions carry enough colónes for your entire stay, and make sure you have some small bills. Some lodges accept travelers' checks, but they may not have change for large amounts; very few take credit cards. Automated teller machines are becoming more common in San José and major tourist areas.

BASICS

TIME

Costa Rica time is six hours behind Greenwich Mean Time, one hour behind New York and two hours ahead of the United States' west coast. It is the equivalent of United States standard time, but changes to mountain time during daylight saving time in the United States.

ELECTRICITY

Costa Rica operates on 110 volts AC (60-cycle) nationwide. Some remote lodges are not connected to power lines and generate their own electricity. Check in advance to see if they run on direct current (DC) or a nonstandard voltage. Two types of United States plugs are used: flat, parallel two-prong plugs and rectangular three-prong pins. A two-prong adapter (found at most hardware stores or *ferreterias*) is useful.

WATER

I used to say it was safe to drink tap water throughout Costa Rica, but times have changed. San José's environment has been so severely affected by development and overpopulation that I hesitate to recommend drinking tap water in older hotels. The same goes for the overbuilt coastal regions such as Manuel Antonio and for the Caribbean coast. While I've never gotten sick from tap water

in Costa Rica, and I drink it everywhere, you don't want to ruin a short vacation with stomach problems. When in doubt, don't drink the water. Hotels usually do not provide bottled water, but you can buy it in small markets nearly everywhere.

WEIGHTS AND MEASURES

Costa Rica operates on the metric system. Liquids are sold in liters; vegetables and fruits by the kilogram.

Distance
1 km = 0.625 (5/8) mile, 1 meter = 3.28 feet

Weight
1 gram = 0.035 ounces, 1 kilogram (kilo) = 2.2 pounds

Volume
1 liter = 2.1 United States pints = 1.76 United Kingdom pints

Temperature

To convert Fahrenheit to centigrade, subtract 32 and multiply by ⁵⁄₉. To convert centigrade to Fahrenheit, multiply by 1.8 and add 32.

CLIMATE

Costa Rica lies eight to eleven degrees north of the equator, right in the middle of the tropics. Although it is a small country without a lot of variation in latitude, the climate varies greatly depending on the terrain (mountain, rainforest, beach). The temperature can drop over short distances because of the rugged mountain chains that affect weather patterns. Costa Rica has over a

dozen microclimates; temperatures are based more on elevation and location than on the season. They range from tropical on the coastal plains to temperate in the interior highlands. Mean temperatures on the central plateau are 22°C (72°F), and 27°C (82°F) on the Caribbean coast.

Most regions have a rainy season between May and October. The intense rains hamper road conditions and flight timetables, but they also provide rushing rivers and waterfalls; fresh, clean air — even in San José; and a pleasant dearth of large tourist groups. It's a good time to travel if you're flexible. Prices are generally lower for hotels and car rentals (though you'll definitely need a four-wheel drive for extensive exploring). There are drawbacks, however. If you happen to be there when a low tropical depression settles over the country for days, the rain can drive you mad. Dry season usually lasts from November through

April, and is called summer. The Caribbean coast tends to be drier than other areas during the rest of the country's wet season.

COMMUNICATION AND MEDIA

TELEPHONES

The country code Costa Rice is 506, which is followed by a seven-digit local number. Local numbers are listed throughout this book.

The Directory Assistance number is (113.

Dial only the local number from anywhere in the country. Calls within the country are fairly inexpensive.

Several international phone cards can be used in Costa Rica; contact your provider for the access code. To call collect from private or public phones dial 09 or 116. Prepaid phone cards are becoming more common. CHIP cards can be used for calls within the country in blue public phone booths (most often found in larger destinations). Two other prepaid cards can be used from any touchtone phone, and can be used for international calls.

Public phones accept 5-, 10- and 20-colónes coins. In remote areas, the public phone is typically located in the neighborhood market or *pulpería*. Give the operator the number; he or she will dial it and signal you to pick up the phone when the connection is made. When done, pay the operator. Ask in advance how much it will cost per minute to call your number. Long lines often form at these public phones, and the caller ahead of you may stay on the phone interminably.

Many businesses use the same number for phone and fax lines. If you're trying to send a fax and someone answers the phone say, *"Necesito enviar un fax, por favor,"* (I need to send a fax, please) and they'll turn on the machine. You can receive faxes through most hotels, for a fee.

You can make international calls and receive faxes at the main phone office in San José, Radiográfica Costarriccense (287-0087, Avenida 5 at Calle 1.

RADIO AND TELEVISION

Radio and television service is available at most tourist areas, except in the remote areas. The radio stations typically play a mix of Latin music, news and talk shows. There is one all-English station at 107.5. Many hotels and private homes have satellite dishes and receive several English-language stations; fewer offer movie and sports channels.

ABOVE: Bus stops advertise local products in the countryside. OPPOSITE: Many small towns have only one or two public phones where residents line up in the cool evenings to make calls.

THE INTERNET

Cybercafés are becoming more common in Costa Rica, especially in San José. Some hotels allow their guests computer access — some small hotels include it in the rate, while larger, business-oriented hotels charge a fee.

MAIL

Postal service in Costa Rica is abysmally poor, and many businesses prefer to not give postal addresses for reservations. Some hotels have postal drops in Miami with courier air service to Costa

Rica. Postal codes (zip codes) are not used outside San José. In many places the mailing address is simply the business name, town, province and country. Post offices (*correos*) are open weekdays from 8 AM to 5 PM, *más o menos* (more or less). In small towns the *correo* may be in a small market or private home.

NEWSPAPERS AND MAGAZINES

Costa Rica has a relatively free press, able to investigate scandals and corruption. *La Nación* is the leading daily newspaper; *La República* is a bit more lowbrow, while *Al Día* tends toward sensationalism. The English-language *Tico Times*, SJO 717, PO Box 025216, Miami, Florida 33102, comes Fridays and is greeted with much joy by foreigners craving news. Subscriptions are available for international readers. The paper does a good job of summarizing national news and has an informative entertainment section with articles on cultural events, new hotels and restaurants, and tourist destinations. The entertainment listings are invaluable and the letters section usually controversial. *Costa Rica Today* caters more to tourists and tends to reflect its advertising. International newspapers are available at several hotels and bookstores in San José. *Costa Rica Outdoors*

focuses on fishing, and does an excellent job of covering various regions in its bimonthly editions.

ETIQUETTE

Ticos are extraordinarily polite (except when driving), and they expect the same treatment from visitors. The Costa Rican character is based on peacemaking and negotiation rather than confrontation; *ticos* turn stubborn and cold when facing enraged, shouting tourists. Services may not be as efficient as you are accustomed to at home, but direct anger will rarely solve the problem.

HEALTH AND EMERGENCIES

EMERGENCY PHONE NUMBERS

Emergencies (911
Fire (118
Police (222-1365 or 221-5337
Transit Police (222-9330 or 222-9245
Red Cross Ambulance (128

HEALTH CONCERNS

There are few health risks for the tourist in Costa Rica. The water supply is relatively pure, though there have been reports of unsafe levels of bacteria in San José's water supply. It is no longer safe to drink water from mountain streams or springs; campers should carry their own. As a rule, food in restaurants and hotels is prepared hygienically. I've never gotten a case of "Montezuma's Revenge" here, just the occasional stomach upsets from too much fresh fruit, beer and sunshine. If you do get a case of diarrhea, try treating it first with over-the-counter products such as Pepto Bismol. Don't take more potent medications such as Lomotil for long; they can prevent the bacteria from leaving your system and make you far sicker.

Infectious diseases such as cholera, hepatitis, dengue fever and malaria are rare but do occur, particularly on the Caribbean coast. Inoculations are not required, though it's always a good idea to make sure your tetanus shot is current. Some travelers prefer to get hepatitis A and B vaccinations before visiting Latin America.

Social Security health care is available to all employed Costa Ricans and their families, and private health care is quite good. Travelers and foreign residents tend to rely on the excellent private Clínica Bíblica (257-0466, Main Street between Avenidas 14 and 16, San José, for medical treatment. Pharmacies (*farmacias*) sell antibiotics and other nonnarcotic drugs without prescriptions and pharmacists are usually able to help diagnose and care for minor ailments.

Most rural areas have medical clinics. Doctors and nurses travel a circuit within a region, seeing patients in each village one day a week or so. Most outlying lodges have access to doctors and are able to airlift emergency cases to San José.

Snake bites are a major risk to farmers and field workers, and nearly every small town has a readily available supply of antivenin. As for travelers, many never encounter a snake, try as they might. But take precautions, nevertheless. Always wear hiking boots and socks when walking through rainforest and high grass, and watch where you step. Don't grab trees and vines without looking at them closely first. If you are bitten try to study your attacker's features so that first-aid workers can give you the correct antivenin. Scorpions abound, but their sting is not deadly. Chiggers can

leave a nasty itch that lasts for days. If you're doing a lot of hiking in grassy areas such as Guanacaste, sprinkle sulfur powder on your legs and socks. Mosquitoes, no-see-ums and other irritating wildlife are common nearly everywhere. Nature guides suggest you carry bug repellent but not use it until necessary. Though Deet is the best repellent it can cause skin irritations. Always take along bug repellent on hikes and river trips. "Africanized" honey bees, also called "killer bees" are present and defend their hives with fierce attention. The bees typically attack in large swarms. If you encounter a swarm, run like mad for the nearest shelter or river.

Sexually transmitted diseases, including AIDS (SIDA), are a definite concern if you're sexually active during your travels. Bring condoms and use them; don't depend on the low-quality condoms sold in the country. Prostitution is rampant,

particularly in San José. Some prostitutes carry health cards and claim they are disease free. Don't believe it. Child prostitution is common. After years of looking the other way, the government is now clamping down on the sexual abuse of children. Police officers will arrest customers who hire children for sex.

Public toilets, even in gas stations, are usually fairly clean. Carry your own tissues or toilet paper, however.

SAFETY AND SECURITY

Sad to say, Costa Rica is no longer as free of crime as it once was. Thefts and muggings are common in parts of San José and some coastal towns. These crimes horrify peaceful Costa Ricans, who tend to exaggerate rumors of tragic occurrences. Travelers accustomed to the street crime scenes of Manhattan, Buenos Aires or Jakarta will not be fazed. Use the same precautions you would in any large city. Hold on tight to your cameras, wallets and purses; don't flash money or jewelry; don't wander down deserted streets late at night. Stash your passport, plane ticket and extra money in your hotel's safe; carry a photocopy of your passport in a money belt, since the police can ask you for identification at any time.

Rental cars are easy targets for thieves more interested in the contents than the vehicle itself. Resist the temptation to leave your packed car by the side of the road while exploring. There have been several reports of automobile break-ins at car lots by parks, reserves and beaches (including Braulio Carrillo, Carara and Jacó). Leave your gear at your hotel before parking in remote areas. Don't stroll too far along deserted beaches at night. And don't park on the street in San José, Limón, Puntarenas, or other big towns. Guarded parking lots are common and inexpensive. Use them.

The drug trade has grown quite intense, especially around the Caribbean towns of Limón, Cahuita and Puerto Viejo. The area is a favorite of young, budget travelers who are frequently accosted with offers of everything from marijuana to crack. Drugs are illegal, and anyone in possession of these substances can be arrested. As in most places, drug dealers are not the most reputable folks, and there have been occasions when buyers have been robbed.

Adventure travel is always accompanied by a few risks, and there are some major concerns when dealing with certain Costa Rican companies. At the moment there are no licensing requirements for businesses. Anyone can buy an inflatable boat

OPPOSITE: Dairy ranchers use many modes of transportation to get their product to town. ABOVE: San José attracts *ticos* from around the country.

and a few brochures and claim they have a rafting company, for example. In most cases, these individuals have their hearts in the right place and are trying to earn a few colónes from the tourist trade. But they may not be insured or safe. I suggest you deal with one of the tour companies listed above when planning your trip—most will recommend responsible operators and warn you away from shady deals. Be particularly cautious when taking part in anything that is inherently dangerous such as canopy tours or rafting. Follow your instincts. If the weather is bad, or if you just have a worrisome feeling about a particular situation, back away. You don't have to risk your life to have fun.

bad until you get on the road. You must rent a four-wheel-drive vehicle if heading toward dirt or sand roads, and you must take flooding, rock and mud slides and slippery surfaces seriously. I once hung my Suzuki Samurai off the side of a bridge with no guardrails en route to the far southern Pacific coast. Several strangers helped me push it back onto the road; only after we finished did they inform me that four German tourists had died in the same place when the river was high.

Air, car rental and hotel rates typically drop about 20 to 30% when tourism is at its lowest; ask about special "green season" rates. As Costa Rica becomes more popular, however, tourists are beginning to mob the most popular resort areas in

WHEN TO GO

The waves of tourism peak during Costa Rica's summer dry season (November to April), when prices soar and room availability is limited. Advance reservations for the best lodges and inns are essential during high season. Once the rains begin in May, the roads start disintegrating into muddy, impassable messes and tourism declines.

Costa Rica's tourism industry promotes the rainy winter season (May through October) as the "green season," definitely an appropriate moniker. The country becomes lush and wet and everything shimmers in the sporadic sunlight. The rains are not constant, except in the northern Caribbean; instead, there are afternoon showers timed nicely to coincide with siestas. The southern coastal areas, which can be unbearably hot in February, are cooler in the winter months. All in all, the rain isn't that

June and July, when children are out of school in the United States. The crowd tapers off by mid-August. Some hotels and lodges close in September and October, when tourism is lowest.

WHAT TO TAKE

Though travel gear, clothing and books are available in San José, you're best off bringing whatever you'll need with you. Prices for toiletries and all imported goods are elevated, and quality is often questionable. Bring lightweight, comfortable long pants, shorts, skirts, and shirts, and one warm jacket or sweater for the mountain climates. A waterproof, breathable poncho is essential at almost any time of year; rain and cloud forests have no dry season. A lightweight umbrella will come in handy as well. You will need at least two pairs of sturdy walking shoes. Pack twice as many pairs of socks as you think you'll need, and throw in one knee-high pair to wear under rubber boots. Knee-high rubber boots come in handy during the rainy season, but are a hassle to cart around. Most lodges have a few extra pairs around, and the boots are sold at general stores and hardware stores around the country.

Camera buffs should bring all the film and batteries they'll need, since supplies are expensive. Disposable waterproof cameras come in handy for boat trips. You'll be sorry if you don't bring binoculars for wildlife sightings.

Bug bites, scratches and bruises are a part of any Costa Rican adventure; your first-aid kit should include strong insect repellent, calamine lotion for itches and stings, an antiseptic such as Bactine and gauze or bandages for covering wounds.

Foreign language books are expensive; many hotels have book exchanges with selections in English, German, Italian and French (depending on the clientele). San José has a couple of shops devoted to selling used books, and other stores that carry a range of titles on Costa Rica. Guidebooks published outside the country are difficult to come by, but there are a few excellent English-language nature and history books published in the country.

WOMEN ALONE

Women operate businesses, hold political office, pay taxes and are generally respected — though a certain kind of Latin machismo still lingers. Women travelers are usually treated with courtesy and respect, though even women who might consider themselves immune to casual come-ons will find themselves dealing with *piropos* (flirtatious comments). Younger women, particularly those who dress scantily, will quickly become all too familiar with the snakelike hisses that follow them when they walk alone down the street or beach. Costa Rican men seem to believe that a woman traveling by herself is almost pitiful — a lost soul to be rescued, guided, coddled and fondled (if possible). Direct assault is not a common occurrence, however.

COSTA RICAN SPANISH FOR TRAVELERS

Costa Ricans speak a more formal version of Latin Spanish, as opposed to Castillian Spanish with its lisping c- and z-sounds. Unlike their neighbors in Honduras and Panama, Costa Ricans speak slowly and clearly as a rule, making it easier for beginners to follow a conversation. But they also have a wide range of regional expressions and words that can confuse travelers accustomed to the Spanish of Mexico or South America. Costa Ricans are extraordinarily patient with travelers who mangle

their language, and appreciate all attempts regardless of their content. Practice your Spanish everywhere, using basic phrases to show your respect for the country.

Ticos (as Costa Ricans are informally called) are quite fond of the diminutive, changing *un momento* (one moment) into *un momentito, mi amigo* (my friend) into *mi amigito, un café* (a coffee) into *un cafecito*. Terms of endearment are common and sometimes amusing; girlfriends are fond of calling each other *gordita* (little fatty) and all friends refer to each other as *mi amor* (my love).

Below are some common Costa Rican words and phrases, called *tiquismos*, followed by basic Spanish for travelers in Latin America.

TIQUISMOS

hello, good-bye, see you later   *¡Adios!*
Is anyone home? I'm here   *¡Upe!* (typically used when approaching someone's home.)
great, terrific, life is good   *¡Pura vida!*
cool, okay, great   *tuanis*
uncool, bad   *mala nota* or *furris*
That's wonderful!   *¡Qué bruto! ¡Qué bárbaro!*
That's horrible! *¡Qué horror! ¡Qué fatal! ¡Qué maje!*
buddy   *maje* (used by males among their peers)
Costa Rican   *tico*
San José resident   *josefino*
San José   *Chepe*
coffee shop   *soda*

OPPOSITE: Farmers haul their produce to busy roadsides where passersby pick up great deals. ABOVE: Travelers and guides alike delight in spotting birds at Monteverde.

small store *pulpería*
taxi meter *maría*
carbonated soda *gaseosa*

PLACES AND THINGS

bakery *panadería*
beach *playa*
boarding house *pensión*
book shop *librería*
bridge *puente*
bus station *estación de autobús*
bus stop *parada de autobús*
butcher *carnicería*
cake shop *pastelería*

tourist office *oficina de turismo*
viewpoint *mirador*

ON THE ROAD

accident *accidente*
brakes *frenos*
bus *autobús*
diesel *diesel*
fill it up *lleno*
lights *luces*
oil *aceite*
petrol station *gasolinera*
pothole *hueco*
regular gas *gasolina regular*

cathedral *catedral*
church *iglesia*
cigarette *cigarrillo*
cigar *puro*
city *ciudad*
dry cleaner *intorería*
grocer *pulpería*
supermarket *supermercado*
harbor *puerto*
lane or alley *callejón*
market *mercado*
mountain *montaña*
pharmacy *farmacia*
police station *delegación*
post office *oficina de correo*
restaurant *restaurante*
river *río*
street *calle*
square *manzana*

super gas *gasolina super*
tire *llanta*
water *agua*

ROAD SIGNS

detour *desvio*
rock slides *derrumbes*
slow down *despacio*
stop *alto*

KEY WORDS AND PHRASES

yes *sí*
no *no*
none *ningun(o)*
much, very, a lot (of) *mucho/a*
please *por favor*
thank you (very much) *(muchas) gracias*

you're welcome   *de nada*
okay, fine, I agree   *está bien*
hello   *hola*
good morning   *buenos días*
good afternoon   *buenas tardes*
good evening/night   *buenas noches*
good-bye   *adios*
welcome   *bienvendios*
excuse me   *con permiso, desculpe*
get in line   *haga fila*
I'm sorry   *desculpe, lo siento*
see you later   *hasta luego*
see you soon   *hasta pronto*
well, good   *bien, bueno*
beautiful   *bello(a), hermoso(a)*

this/this one   *éste(a)*
that   *ese(a)*
here   *aquí*
there   *allá*
right there   *allí*
near   *cerca*
far   *lejos*
left   *izquierda*
right   *derecha*
straight on, straight ahead   *derecho*
hot   *caliente*
cold   *frío(a)*
big   *grande*
small   *pequeño(a)*
open   *abierto(a)*

how?   *¿cómo?*
how are you?   *¿cómo está?*
how many?   *¿cuánto(a)s?*
what?   *¿qué?*
who?   *¿quién?*
why?   *¿por qué?*
where is?   *¿dónde está?*
how much is it?   *¿cuánto vale, ¿cuánto cuesta?*
I understand   *entiendo*
I don't understand   *no entiendo*
I don't know   *no sé*
can/may I…?   *¿puedo…?*
I would like   *quisiera*
do you have…?   *¿tiene…?*
do you sell…?   *¿hay…?*
I don't speak Spanish   *no hablo español*
do you speak English?   *¿Habla usted inglés?*
he/she/it is/you are   *está*
there is/are   *hay*

closed   *cerrado(a)*
new   *nuevo(a)*
old   *viejo(a)*
cheap   *barato(a)*
expensive   *caro(a)*
money   *dinero*

IN THE HOTEL

room   *habitación, cuarto*
single room   *habitación sencilla*
double room   *habitación doble*
with a double bed   *con cama matrimonial*
with a bathroom   *con baño*
without a bathroom   *sin baño*
shower   *ducha*

OPPOSITE: Outdoor markets display seasonal produce. ABOVE: Small towns with simple houses and shops dot the countryside.

soap   *jabón*
towel   *toalla*
toilet paper   *papel higénico*
laundry   *lavandería*
key   *llave*
registration form   *papel de inscripción*

AT THE POST OFFICE

stamp   *timbre*
letter   *carta*
postcard   *tarjeta postal*
parcel   *paquete*
air mail   *por avión*
general delivery, poste restante   *lista de correos*

IN EMERGENCIES

doctor   *médico*
nurse   *enfermera*
sick, ill   *enfermo*
pain, ache   *dolor*
fever   *fiebre*
I am allergic to   *tengo alergia a*
I have a toothache   *tengo dolor de muela*
help   *ayuda*
I am diabetic   *soy diabética*

IN RESTAURANTS

breakfast   *desayuno*
lunch   *almuerzo*
tea   *té*
dinner   *cena*
menu   *menú*
fixed-price menu   *plato el día*
wine list   *lista de vinos*
bill, check   *cuenta*
glass   *vaso*
pepper   *pimienta*
salt   *sal*
sugar   *azúcar*
bread   *pan*
butter   *mantequilla*
sandwich   *emparedado*
mineral water   *agua mineral*
carbonated water   *agua con gas*
still water   *agua natural*
fruit juice   *jugo de fruta*
milk   *leche*
ice   *hielo*
coffee with milk   *café con leche*
beer   *cerveza*
red wine   *vino tinto*
white wine   *vino blanco*
rosé wine   *vino rosa*
cheese   *queso*
olives   *aceitunas*
salad   *ensalada*
green salad   *ensalada verde*

meat   *carne*
beef   *carne de res*
goat   *cabra*
ham   *jamón*
beans   *frijoles*
rice   *arroz*
hot sauce   *salsa picante*
beefsteak   *bistek, lomito*
rare   *poco hecho*
medium   *tres cuartos*
well done   *bien cocido, entero*
boiled   *hervido*
baked   *al horno*
grilled   *a la plancha*
smoked   *ahumado*

fish   *pescado*
crayfish   *langostina*
shrimp   *camarones*
clams   *almejas*
tuna   *atún*
lobster   *langosta*
sea bass   *corvina*
red snapper   *pargo colorado*
mahi mahi   *dorado*
swordfish   *pez espada*
crab   *jaiba*
octopus   *pulpo*
squid   *calamar*
vegetables   *verdura, legumbre*
potatoes   *papas*
mushroom   *champiñón*
onion   *cebolla*
garlic   *ajo*
fruit   *fruta*

pineapple   *piña*
orange   *naranja*
watermelon   *sandía*
strawberry   *fresa*
blackberry   *mora*
dessert   *postre*
ice cream   *helado*
cake   *queque*
rice pudding   *arroz de leche*

ANIMALS

agouti   *tepezcuintle* (in Costa Rica), *guatusa*
armadillo   *cusuco*
bat   *murciélago*
bird   *ave, pájaro*
butterfly   *mariposa*
coati   *pizote*
cougar, mountain lion   *puma, león*
crocodile   *cocodrilo*
deer   *venado*
frog   *rana*
howler monkey   *mono congo*
jaguar   *jaguar, tigre*
jaguarundi   *león breñero*
kinkajou   *martilla*
lesser anteater   *oso hormiguero*
ocelot   *manigordo*
opossum   *zorro*
parrot   *loro*
peccary   *pecarí*
raccoon   *mapache*
river otter   *nutria*
scarlet macaw   *lapa*
sloth   *perezoso, perica*
snake   *culebra, serpiente*
spider monkey   *mono araña, mono colorado*
squirrel monkey   *mono ardilla, mono tití*
tapir   *danta*
toad   *sapo*
turtle   *tortuga*
white-faced capuchin monkey   *mono cara blanca*

NUMBERS

1   *uno*
2   *dos*
3   *tres*
4   *cuatro*
5   *cinco*
6   *seis*
7   *siete*
8   *ocho*
9   *nueve*
10   *diez*
11   *once*
12   *doce*
13   *trece*
14   *catorce*
15   *quince*
16   *diez y seis*
17   *diecisiete*
18   *dieciocho*
19   *diecinueve*
20   *veinte*
21   *veintiuno*
30   *treinta*
40   *cuarenta*
50   *cincuenta*
60   *sesenta*
70   *setenta*
80   *ochenta*
90   *noventa*
100   *cien*
200   *doscientos*
500   *quinientos*
1,000   *mil*
2,000   *dos mil*
100,000   *cien mil*
1,000,000   *millón*
2,000,000   *dos millones*

CALENDAR

Sunday   *domingo*
Monday   *lunes*
Tuesday   *martes*
Wednesday   *miércoles*
Thursday   *jueves*
Friday   *viernes*
Saturday   *sábado*
January   *enero*
February   *febrero*
March   *marzo*
April   *abril*
May   *mayo*
June   *junio*
July   *julio*
August   *agosto*
September   *septiembre*
October   *octubre*
November   *noviembre*
December   *diciembre*
spring   *primavera*
summer   *verano*
autumn   *otoño*
winter   *invierno*
day   *día*
week   *semana*
month   *mes*
year   *año*

TIME

morning   *mañana*
noon   *mediodía*
afternoon, evening   *tarde*
night   *noche*

The promise of tourists' colónes brings out the
entrepreneurs who offer tours led by local guides.

today *hoy*
yesterday *ayer*
tomorrow *mañana*
What time is it? *¿Qué hora es?*
now *ahora, ahorita*
later *más tarde*

WEB SITES

Costa Rica is well connected to the Internet through RACSA, the country's telecommunications company. Its main Internet web address is www .racsa.co.cr. Many businesses have e-mail and web sites which are included in listings throughout this book. Useful web sites for travelers include the following.

www.ticotimes.com is the site for the weekly English language newspaper. The paper's archives are available on the web for an additional fee.

www.nacion.co.cr is the site for the Spanish-language newspaper.

www.tourism-costarica.com is managed by the Costa Rican Tourism Institute (ICT) and covers most tourist attractions.

www.incostarica.net includes information on tourism, real estate and banking.

www.entretenimiento.com.co.cr is a Spanish language site loaded with ads (its restaurant site begins with ads for Taco Bell). But it's fun to browse through and read the movie and book reviews.

www.costarica.com is packed with factual information, and has good links to other sites.

www.cocori.com looks like a one-man operation that's loaded with information, interesting articles and a lively forum.

www.planeta.com is an award-winning site covering environmental issues throughout Latin America. You can spend hours browsing through postings on environmental issues, reading articles and checking out chat rooms.

Recommended Reading

AMERINGER, CHARLES D. *Democracy in Costa Rica.* New York: Praeger, 1982.

BAKER, BILL. *Essential Road Guide for Costa Rica.* San José: Editorial Incafo, 1992.

BIESANZ, RICHARD et al. *The Costa Ricans.* Englewood Cliffs. New Jersey: Prentice-Hall, 1987.

CAUFIELD, CATHERINE. *In the Rainforest.* Knopf, 1984.

COLE-CHRISTENSEN, DARRYL. *A Place in the Rainforest: Settling the Costa Rica Frontier.* University of Texas Press, 1997.

DEVRIES, PHILLIP J. *The Butterflies of Costa Rica and Their Natural History.* Princeton University Press, 1987.

DRESSLER, ROBERT L. *Field Guide to the Orchids of Costa Rica and Panama.* Ithaca, New York: Comstock Publishing, 1993.

EDELMAN, MARC AND JOANNE KENEN, eds. *The Costa Rican Reader.* New York: Grove Weidenfeld, 1988.

EMMONS, LOUISE H. *Neotropical Rainforest Mammals —A Field Guide.* University of Chicago Press, 1990.

FRANK, JOSEPH. *Costa Rica's National Parks and Preserves: A Visitor's Guide, Second Edition.* Mountaineering Books, 1999.

HALL, CAROLYN. *Costa Rica: A Geographical Interpretation in Historical Perspective.* Boulder, Colorado: Westview Press, 1985.

HERRERA, WILBERTH. *Costa Rica Nature Atlas Guidebook.* San José: Editorial Incafo, 1992.

HOWARD, CHRIS. *The Golden Door to Retirement and Living in Costa Rica* (8th ed.). San José: Costa Rica Books, 1997.

LARA, SILVIA AND TOM BARRY. *Inside Costa Rica.* Albuquerque, New Mexico: Resource Center Press, 1995.

LOBO, TATIANA. *Assault on Paradise: A Novel.* Curbstone Press, 1998.

MAYFIELD, MICHAEL W. AND RAFAEL E. GALLO. *The Rivers of Costa Rica: A Canoeing, Kayaking and Rafting Guide.* Birmingham, Alaska: Mensha Ridge Press, 1988.

PALMER, PAULA. *What Happen: A Folk History of the Talamanca Coast.* San José: Editorama, 1993.

PALMER, PAULA, JUANITA SANCHEZ AND GLORIA MAYORGA. *Taking Care of Sibos Gifts.* San José: Editorama, 1991.

PEREZ-BRIGNOLI, HECTOR. *A Brief History of Central America.* University of California Press, 1989.

PERRY, DONALD. *Life Above the Jungle Floor.* New York: Simon & Schuster, 1986.

PRITCHARD, AUDREY AND RAYMOND PRITCHARD. *Driving the Pan-Am Highway to Mexico and Central America.* Heredia: Costa Rica Books, 1997.

RAS, BARBRA, ed. *Costa Rica: A Traveler's Literary Companion.* San Francisco: Where-abouts Press, 1994.

STEPHEN, JOHN LLOYD. *Incidents of Travel in Central America, Chiapas & Yucatan.* Rutgers University Press, 1949.

SKUTCH, ALEXANDER. *Nature through Tropical Windows.* University of California Press, 1983.

STILES, F. GARY AND ALEXANDER SKUTCH. *A Guide to the Birds of Costa Rica.* Ithaca, New York: Cornell University Press, 1989.

THEROUX, PAUL. *The Old Patagonian Express: By Train Through the Americas.* U.S. Pocket Books.

WALLACE, DAVID R. *The Quetzal and the Macaw: The Story of Costa Rica's National Parks.* San Francisco: Sierra Club Books, 1992.

YOUNG, ALLEN M. *Sarapiqui Chronicle.* Washington DC: Smithsonian Books, 1991.

The scarlet macaw is a rare and beautiful member of the parrot family.

Travelers' Tips

Quick Reference A–Z Guide
to Places and Topics of Interest with Listed Accommodation, Restaurants and Useful Telephone Numbers

The symbols Ⓕ FAX, Ⓣ TOLL-FREE, Ⓔ E-MAIL, Ⓦ WEB-SITE refer to additional contact information found in the chapter listings.

The symbols (F) FAX, (T) TOLL-FREE, (E) E-MAIL, (W) WEB-SITE *refer to additional contact information found in the chapter listings.*

259

The symbols Ⓕ FAX, Ⓣ TOLL-FREE, Ⓔ E-MAIL, Ⓦ WEB-SITE refer to additional contact information found in the chapter listings.

The symbols Ⓕ FAX, Ⓣ TOLL-FREE, Ⓔ E-MAIL, Ⓦ WEB-SITE *refer to additional contact information found in the chapter listings.*

265

Photo Credits

All photographs were taken by **Nik Wheeler**, with the exception of the following:

Buddy Mays: pages 3, 4, 5 *left and right*, 6 *left and right*, 7 *right*, 11, 12, 14, 15, 16, 21, 22, 24, 29, 32, 39, 40, 42, 44, 57, 58, 59, 60, 64, 65, 67, 71, 75, 76, 83, 84, 85, 86, 91, 95, 97, 99, 106, 108, 109, 117, 163, 172, 174, 180, 186, 192, 193, 194, 195, 198, 199, 201, 202, 203, 204, 205, 206, 207, 209, 211, 212, 213, 214, 215, 216, 219, 220, 222, 223, 224, 227, 228, 229, 233, 235, 248, 249, and 255.

Joe Yogerst: pages 18, 23 *bottom*, 26, 33, 36, 92, 128, 131, 145, 157 *right*, 159, 168, 171, and 122–123.

Marybeth Mellin: pages 10, 13, 17, 33, 102, 103, 105, 221, and 237 *top and bottom*.